Natsume's BOOK of FRIENDS

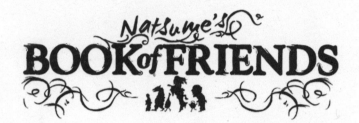

Shojo Beat

Natsume's BOOK of FRIENDS

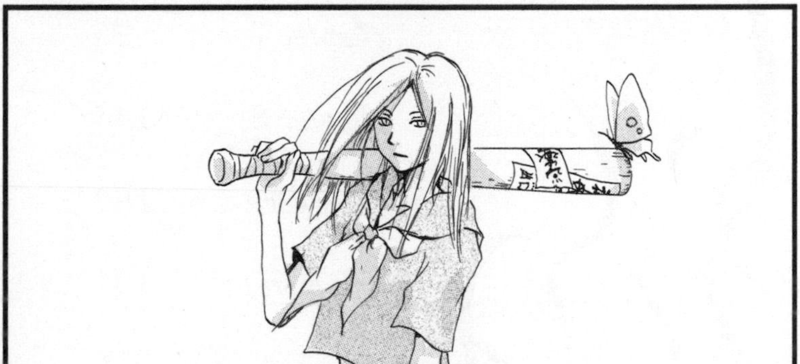

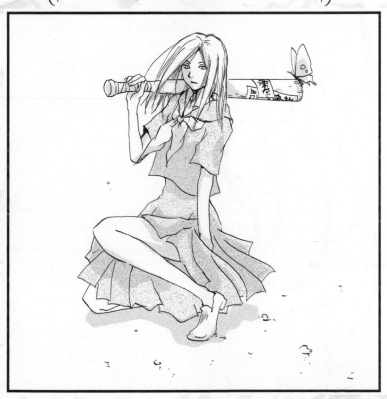

STORY and ART by
Yuki Midorikawa

VOLUME 2

Natsume's
BOOK of FRIENDS

VOLUME 2 CONTENTS

Chapter 5 ——— 5

Chapter 6 ——— 55

Chapter 7 ——— 95

Chapter 8 ——— 145

Afterword ——— 187

End Notes ——— 191

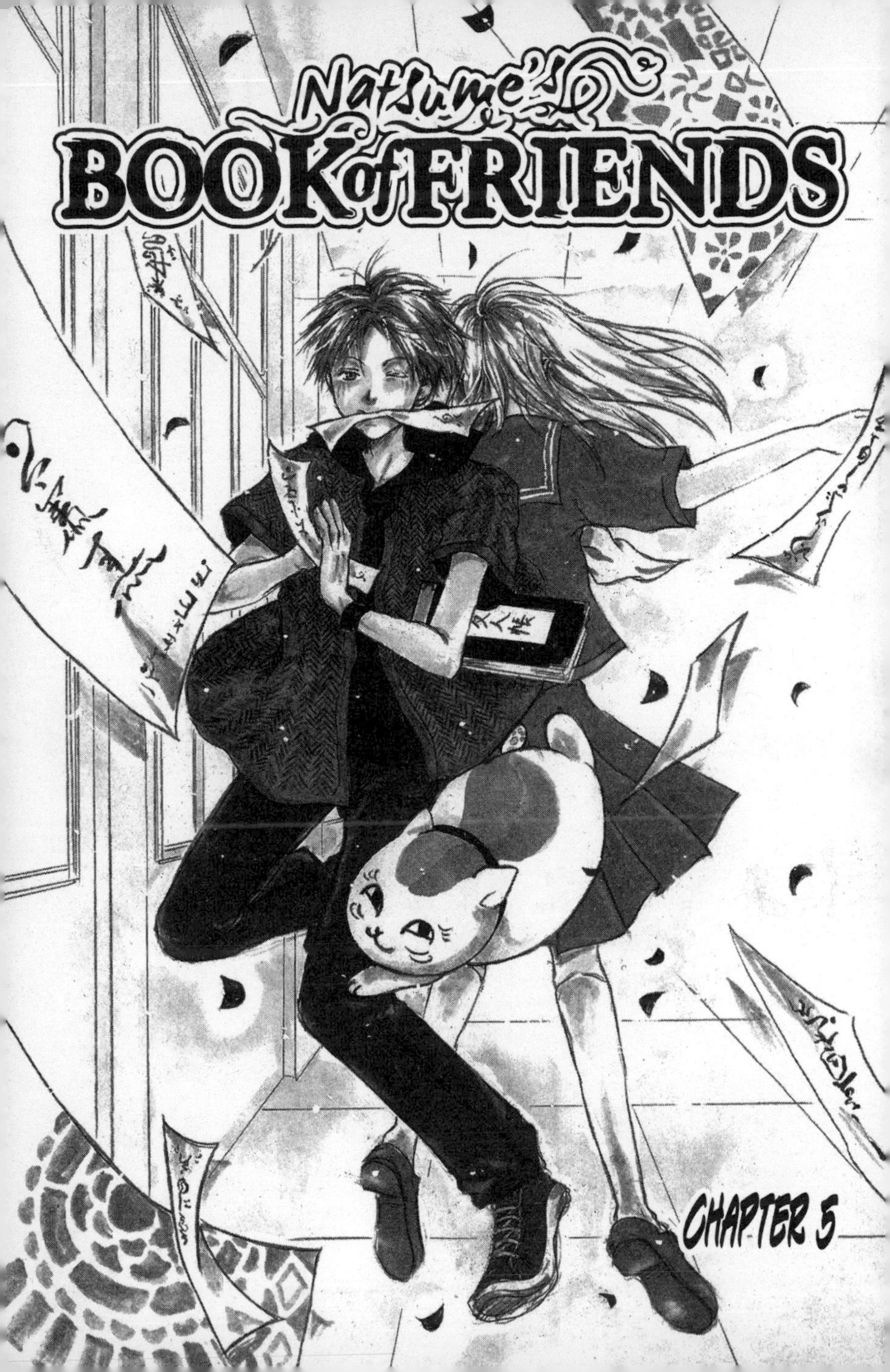
Natsume's
BOOK of FRIENDS
CHAPTER 5

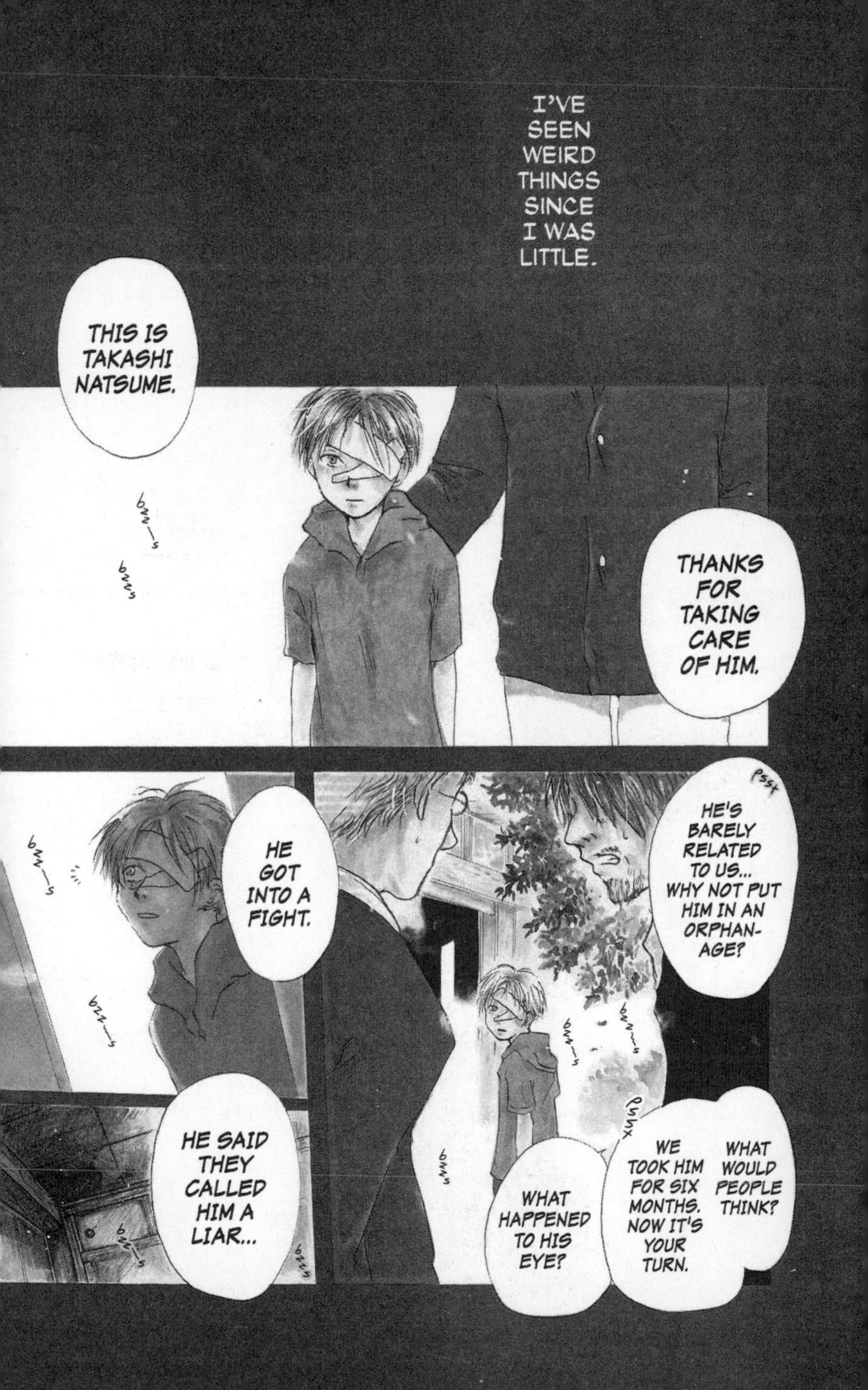
I'VE SEEN WEIRD THINGS SINCE I WAS LITTLE.
THIS IS TAKASHI NATSUME.
THANKS FOR TAKING CARE OF HIM.
Psst
HE'S BARELY RELATED TO US... WHY NOT PUT HIM IN AN ORPHAN-AGE?
Psst
WHAT WOULD PEOPLE THINK?
WE TOOK HIM FOR SIX MONTHS. NOW IT'S YOUR TURN.
WHAT HAPPENED TO HIS EYE?
HE GOT INTO A FIGHT.
HE SAID THEY CALLED HIM A LIAR...

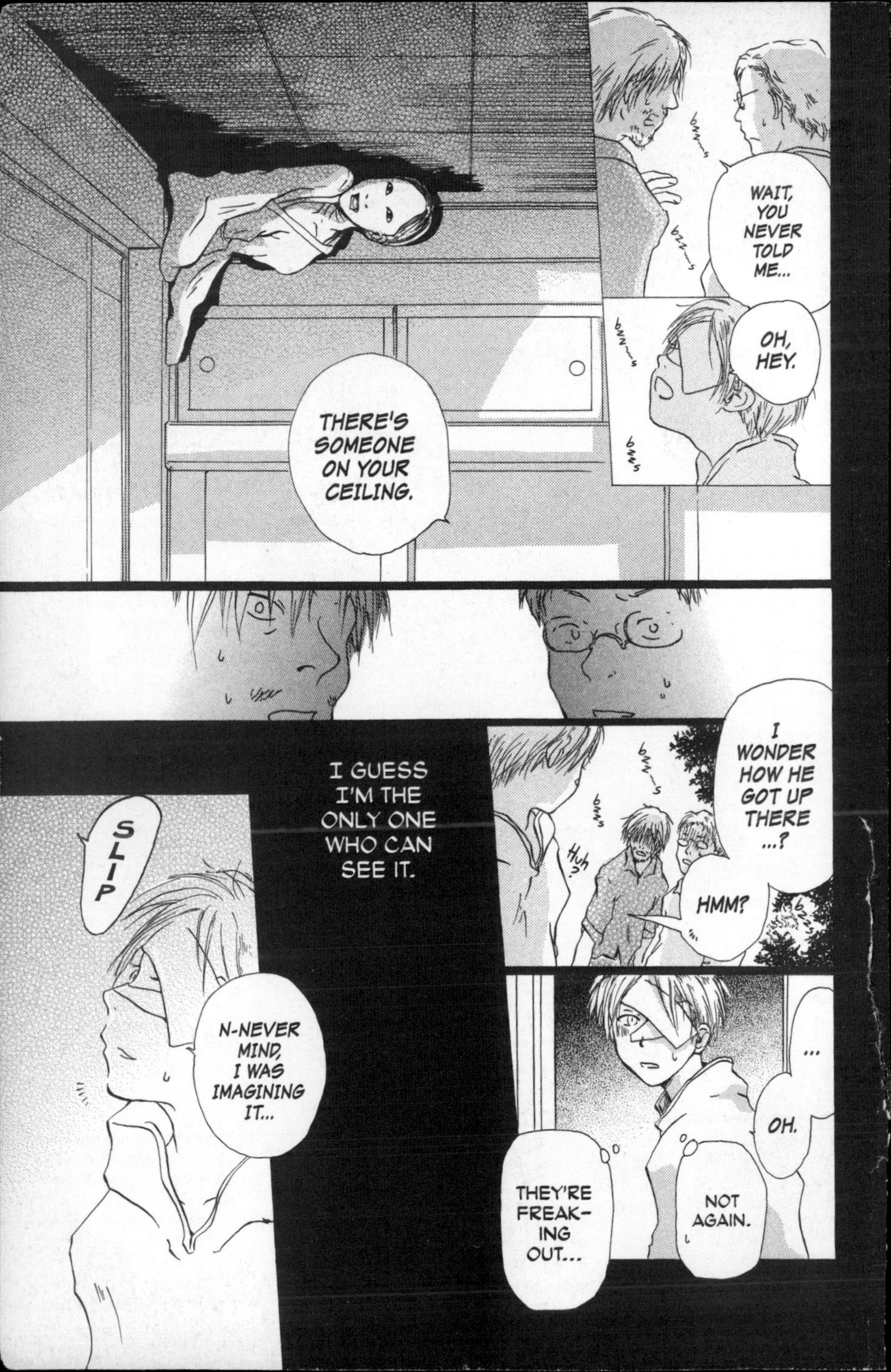
WAIT, YOU NEVER TOLD ME...
OH, HEY.
THERE'S SOMEONE ON YOUR CEILING.
I WONDER HOW HE GOT UP THERE ...?
Huh?
HMM?
...
OH.
NOT AGAIN.
THEY'RE FREAK-ING OUT...
I GUESS I'M THE ONLY ONE WHO CAN SEE IT.
SLIP
N-NEVER MIND, I WAS IMAGINING IT...

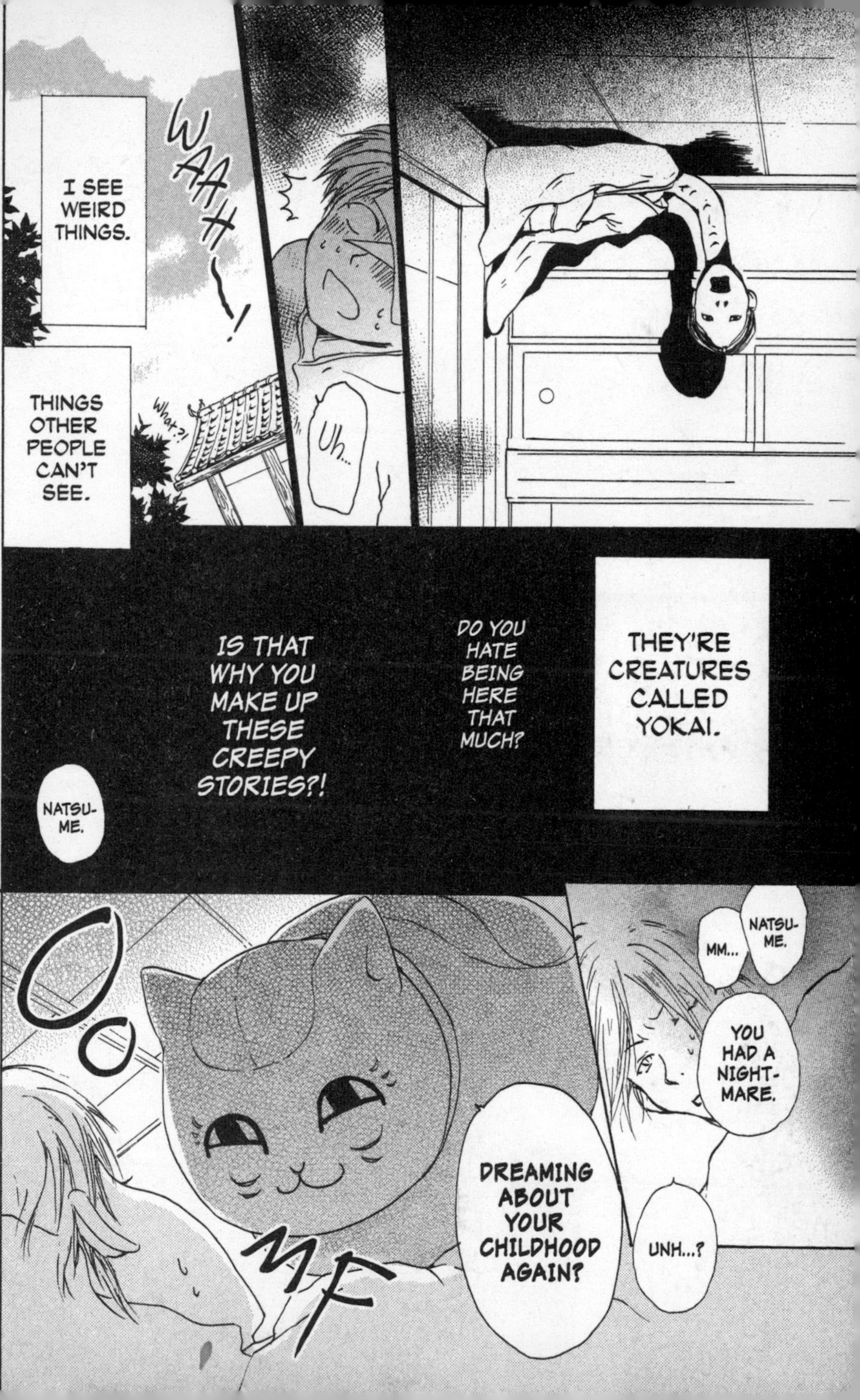
WAAAH--!
Uh...
I SEE WEIRD THINGS.
What?!
THINGS OTHER PEOPLE CAN'T SEE.
THEY'RE CREATURES CALLED YOKAI.
DO YOU HATE BEING HERE THAT MUCH?
IS THAT WHY YOU MAKE UP THESE CREEPY STORIES?!
NATSU-ME.
NATSU-ME.
MM...
YOU HAD A NIGHT-MARE.
UNH...?
DREAMING ABOUT YOUR CHILDHOOD AGAIN?
OOMF

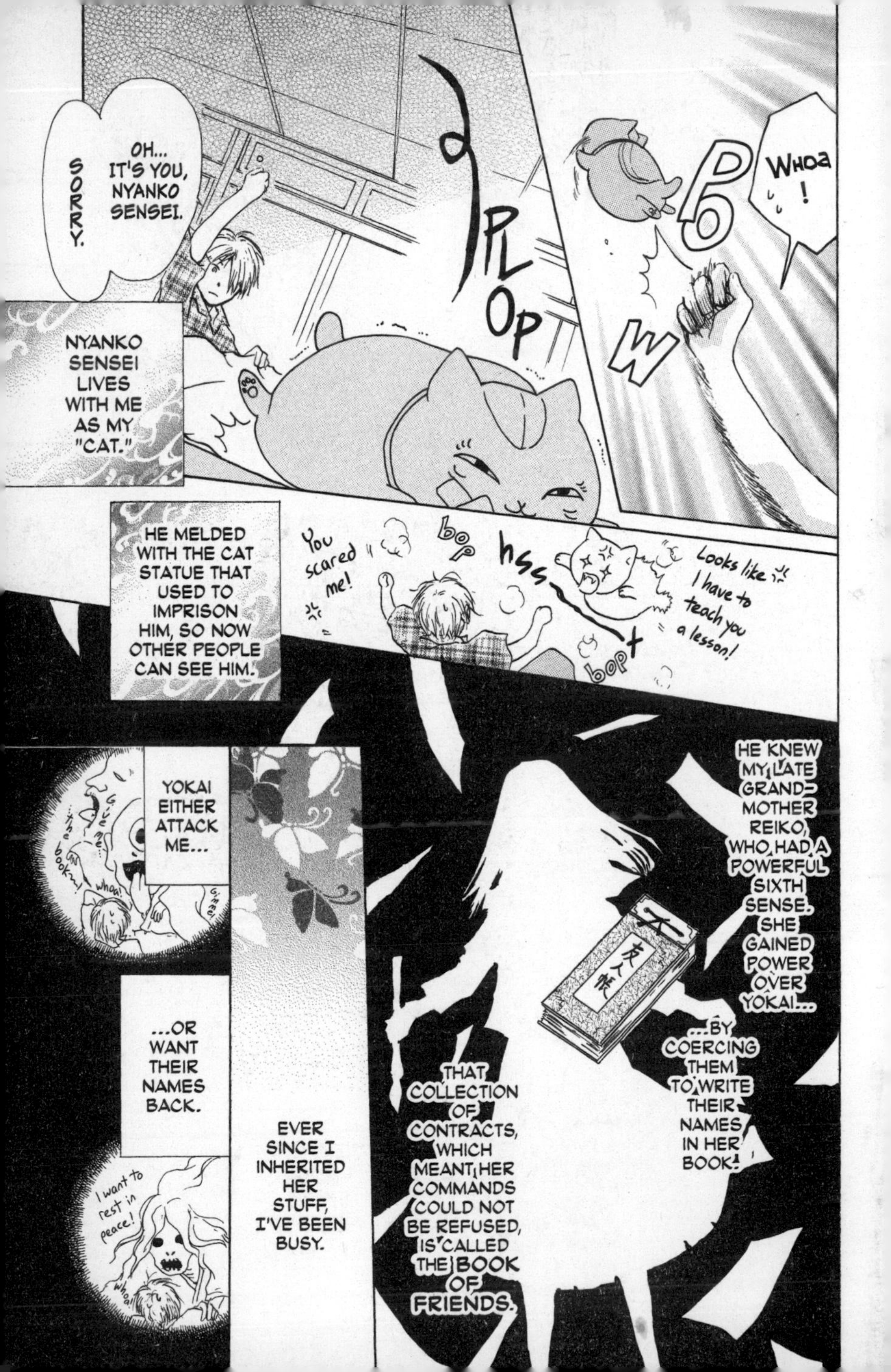
POW
WHOA!
PLOP
OH... IT'S YOU, NYANKO SENSEI.
SORRY.
NYANKO SENSEI LIVES WITH ME AS MY "CAT."
HE MELDED WITH THE CAT STATUE THAT USED TO IMPRISON HIM, SO NOW OTHER PEOPLE CAN SEE HIM.
Looks like I have to teach you a lesson!
hiss
bop
You scared me!
bop
HE KNEW MY LATE GRANDMOTHER REIKO, WHO HAD A POWERFUL SIXTH SENSE. SHE GAINED POWER OVER YOKAI...
...BY COERCING THEM TO WRITE THEIR NAMES IN HER BOOK!
友人帳
THAT COLLECTION OF CONTRACTS, WHICH MEANT HER COMMANDS COULD NOT BE REFUSED, IS CALLED THE BOOK OF FRIENDS.
YOKAI EITHER ATTACK ME...
Give me... the book~!
whoa!
Gimme
...OR WANT THEIR NAMES BACK.
I want to rest in peace!
whoa!
EVER SINCE I INHERITED HER STUFF, I'VE BEEN BUSY.

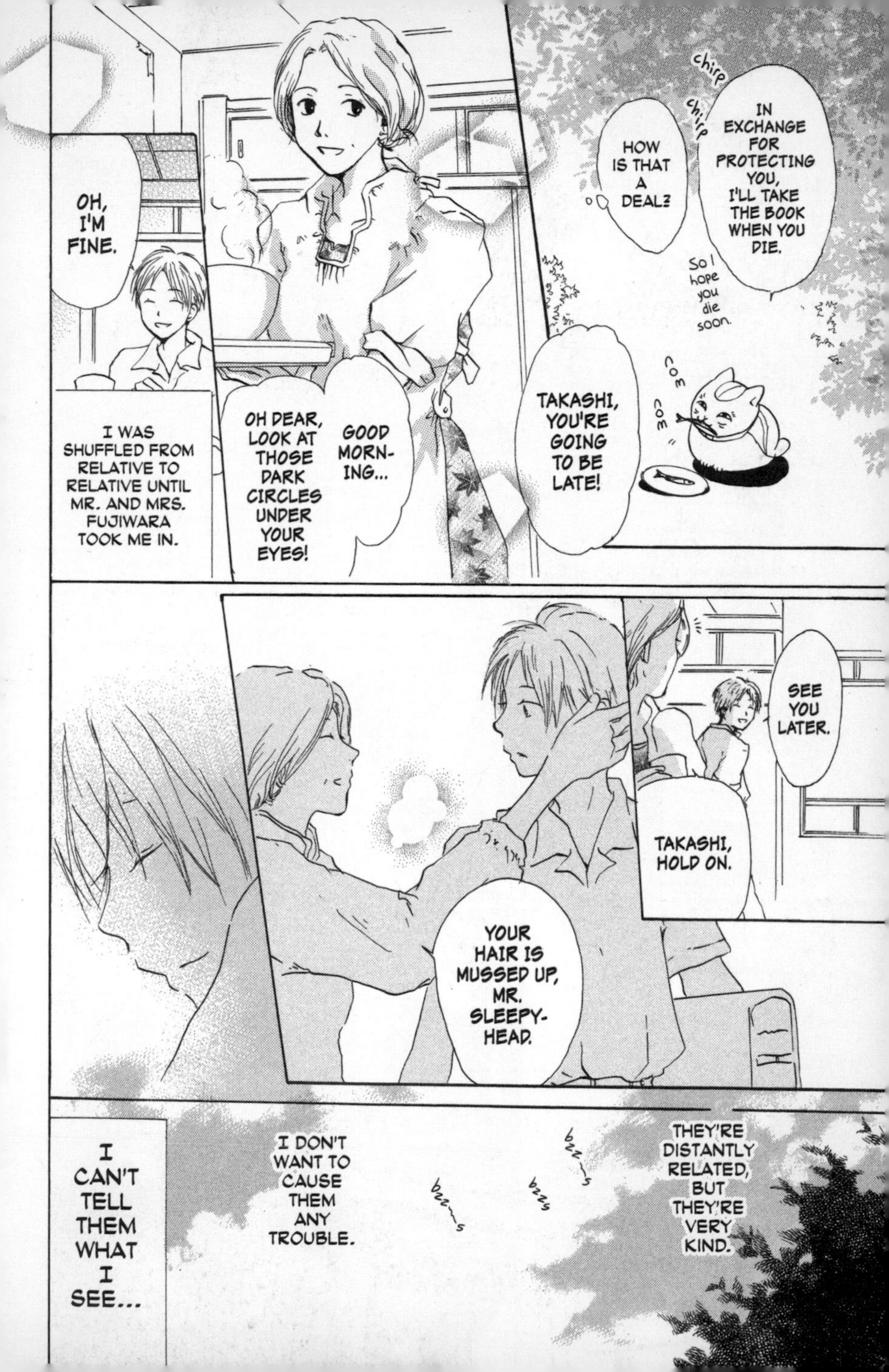

IN EXCHANGE FOR PROTECTING YOU, I'LL TAKE THE BOOK WHEN YOU DIE.
chirp
chirp
So I hope you die soon.
HOW IS THAT A DEAL?
TAKASHI, YOU'RE GOING TO BE LATE!
GOOD MORNING...
OH DEAR, LOOK AT THOSE DARK CIRCLES UNDER YOUR EYES!
OH, I'M FINE.
I WAS SHUFFLED FROM RELATIVE TO RELATIVE UNTIL MR. AND MRS. FUJIWARA TOOK ME IN.
SEE YOU LATER.
TAKASHI, HOLD ON.
YOUR HAIR IS MUSSED UP, MR. SLEEPY-HEAD.
THEY'RE DISTANTLY RELATED, BUT THEY'RE VERY KIND.
bzz~s
bzzs
bzz~s
I DON'T WANT TO CAUSE THEM ANY TROUBLE.
I CAN'T TELL THEM WHAT I SEE...

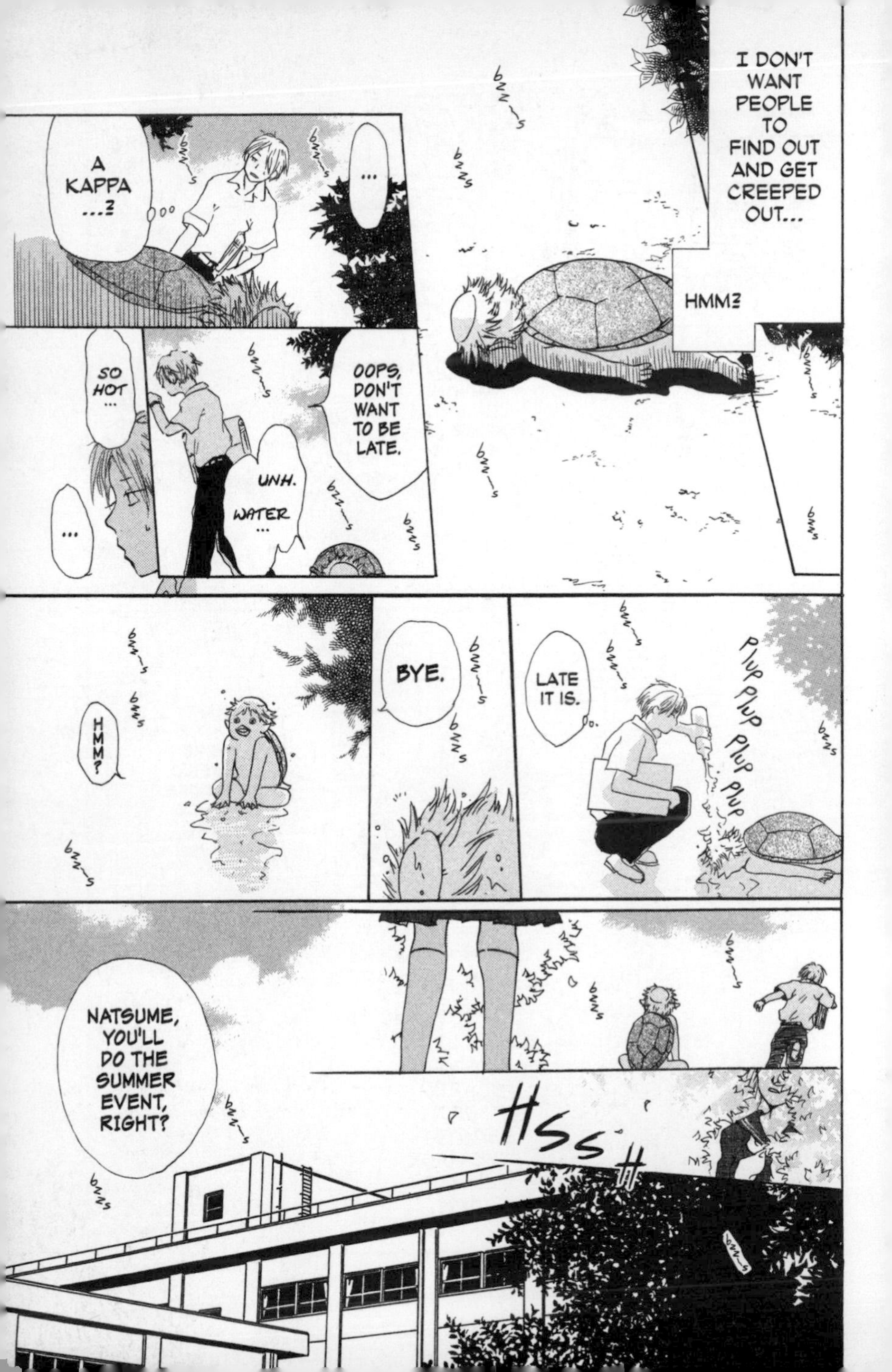
I DON'T WANT PEOPLE TO FIND OUT AND GET CREEPED OUT...
HMM?
...
A KAPPA ...?
OOPS, DON'T WANT TO BE LATE.
UNH. WATER ...
SO HOT ...
...
PLUP PLUP PLUP PLUP
LATE IT IS.
BYE.
HMM?
HSSH
NATSUME, YOU'LL DO THE SUMMER EVENT, RIGHT?

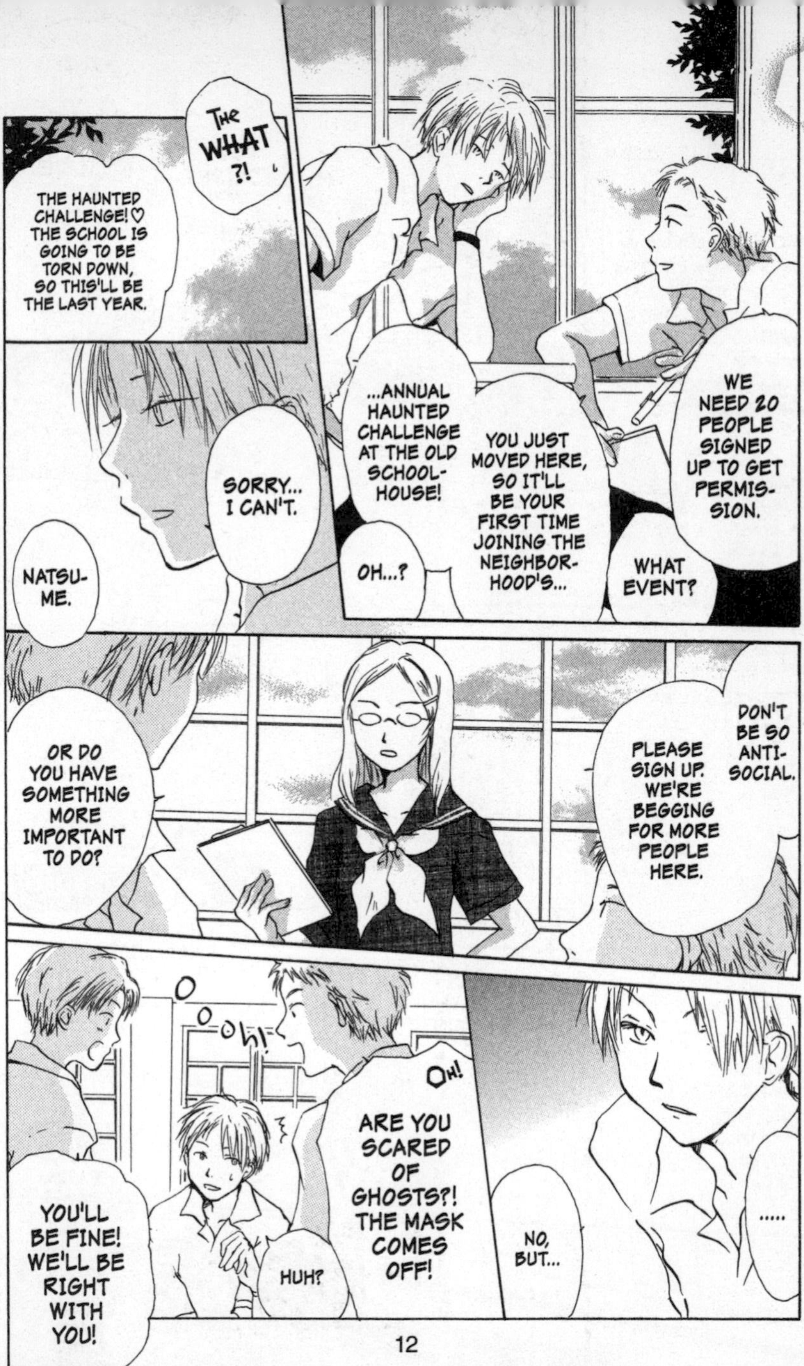
THE WHAT ?!
THE HAUNTED CHALLENGE! ♡ THE SCHOOL IS GOING TO BE TORN DOWN, SO THIS'LL BE THE LAST YEAR.
WE NEED 20 PEOPLE SIGNED UP TO GET PERMIS-SION.
WHAT EVENT?
YOU JUST MOVED HERE, SO IT'LL BE YOUR FIRST TIME JOINING THE NEIGHBOR-HOOD'S...
...ANNUAL HAUNTED CHALLENGE AT THE OLD SCHOOL-HOUSE!
OH...?
SORRY... I CAN'T.
NATSU-ME.
DON'T BE SO ANTI-SOCIAL.
PLEASE SIGN UP. WE'RE BEGGING FOR MORE PEOPLE HERE.
OR DO YOU HAVE SOMETHING MORE IMPORTANT TO DO?
.....
NO, BUT...
OH!
ARE YOU SCARED OF GHOSTS?! THE MASK COMES OFF!
OOOH!
YOU'LL BE FINE! WE'LL BE RIGHT WITH YOU!
HUH?

01

Hello, I'm Midorikawa. This is finally, at long last, my tenth graphic novel. I was pinching myself to see if it were really true and had to line the books up and count them.

I would like to say a huge thank-you to the readers who are picking this up for the first time, to those who have patiently stayed with me from the beginning and to everyone in the editorial department. I'll keep working hard to make manga enjoyable.

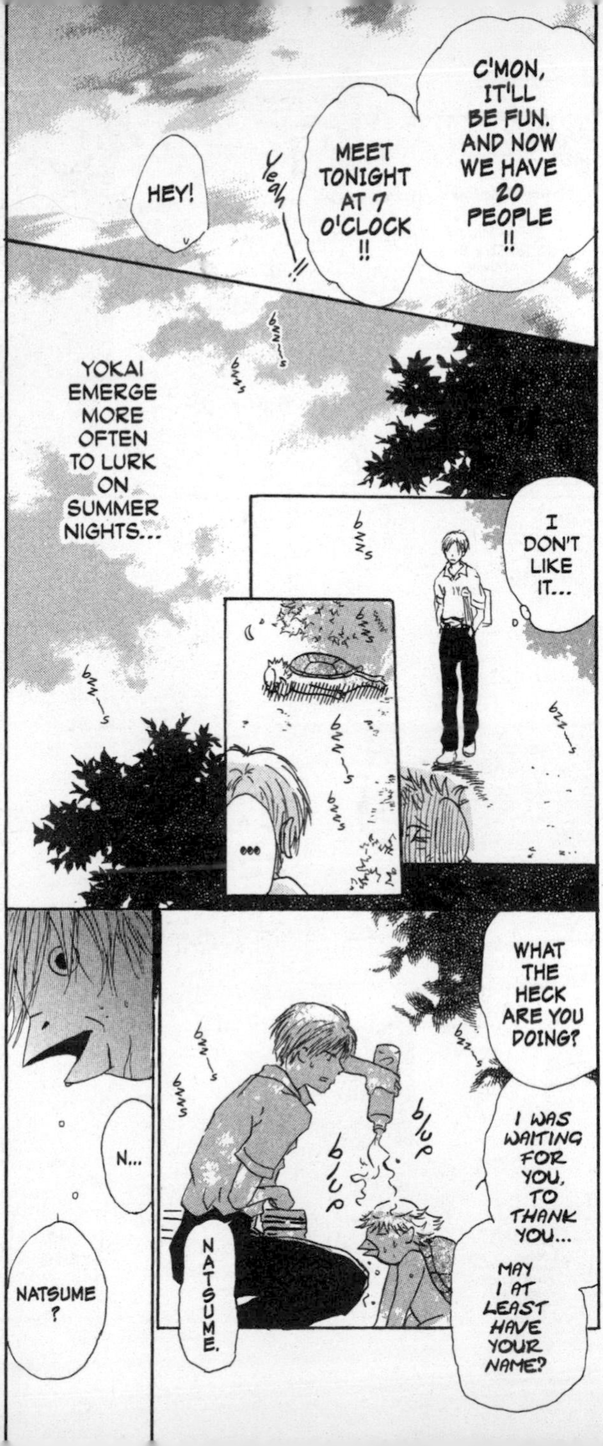
C'MON, IT'LL BE FUN. AND NOW WE HAVE 20 PEOPLE !!
MEET TONIGHT AT 7 O'CLOCK !!
Yeah!!
HEY!
bzzs
YOKAI EMERGE MORE OFTEN TO LURK ON SUMMER NIGHTS...
I DON'T LIKE IT...
bzzs
...
WHAT THE HECK ARE YOU DOING?
I WAS WAITING FOR YOU, TO THANK YOU...
MAY I AT LEAST HAVE YOUR NAME?
blup
blup
NATSUME.
N...
NATSUME ?

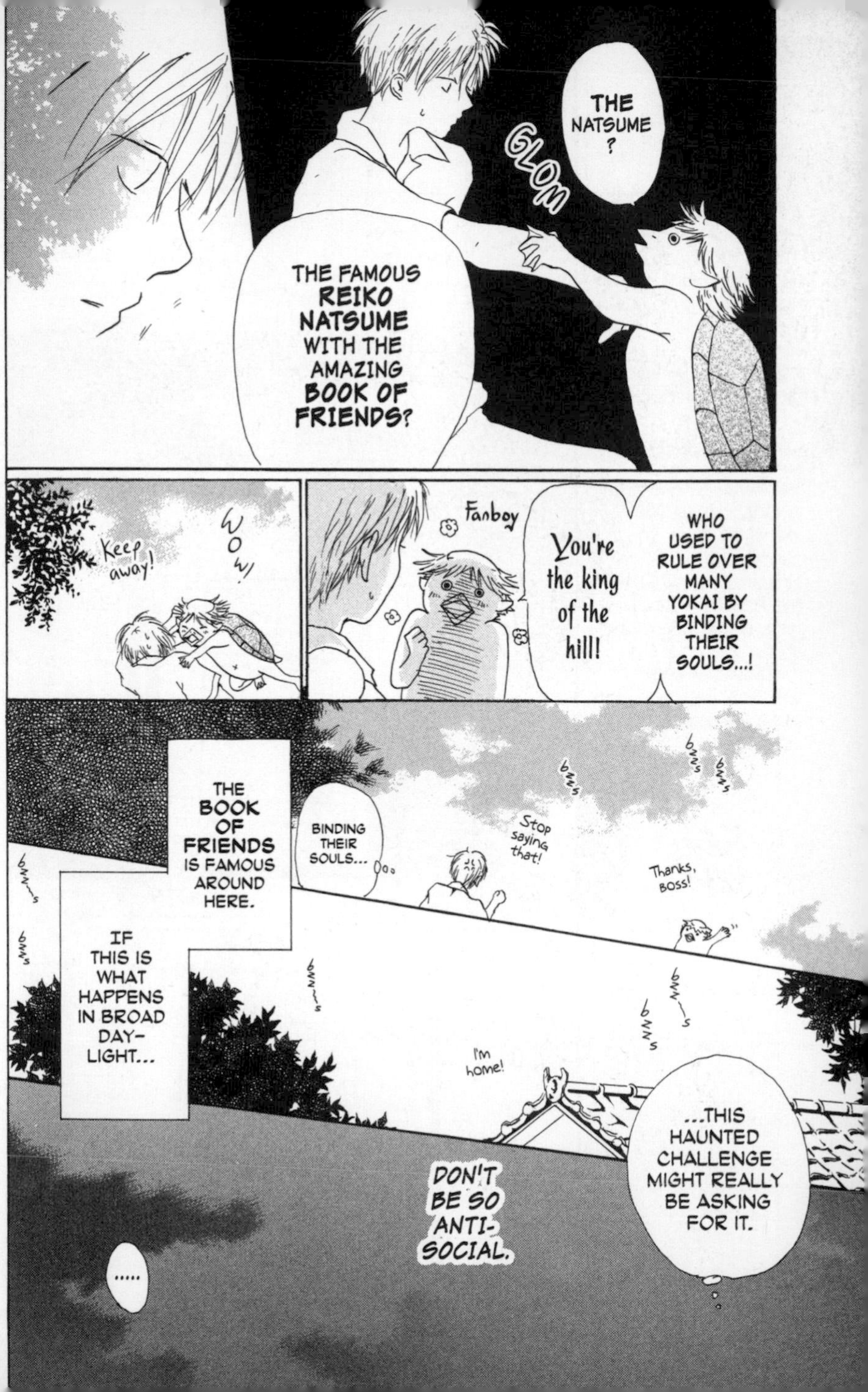
THE NATSUME?
GLOM
THE FAMOUS REIKO NATSUME WITH THE AMAZING BOOK OF FRIENDS?
Fanboy
WHO USED TO RULE OVER MANY YOKAI BY BINDING THEIR SOULS...!
You're the king of the hill!
WOW!
Keep away!
bzzs
bzzs
bzzs
Thanks, boss!
Stop saying that!
BINDING THEIR SOULS...
bzzs
bzzs
THE BOOK OF FRIENDS IS FAMOUS AROUND HERE.
IF THIS IS WHAT HAPPENS IN BROAD DAY-LIGHT...
bzzs
bzzs
bzzs
...THIS HAUNTED CHALLENGE MIGHT REALLY BE ASKING FOR IT.
I'm home!
DON'T BE SO ANTI-SOCIAL.
......

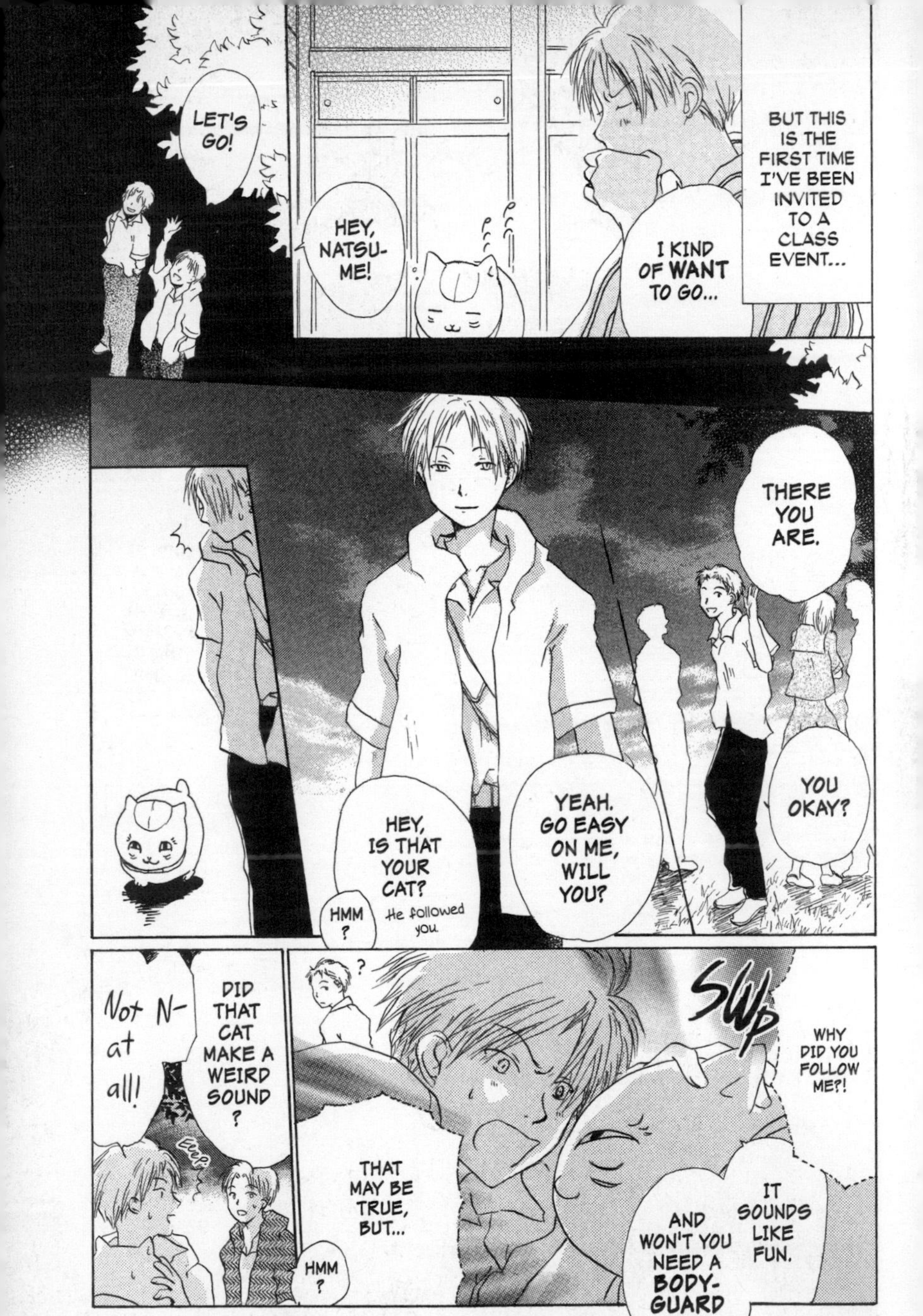
BUT THIS IS THE FIRST TIME I'VE BEEN INVITED TO A CLASS EVENT...
I KIND OF WANT TO GO...
HEY, NATSU-ME!
LET'S GO!
THERE YOU ARE.
YOU OKAY?
YEAH. GO EASY ON ME, WILL YOU?
HEY, IS THAT YOUR CAT?
He followed you.
HMM?
SWP
WHY DID YOU FOLLOW ME?!
IT SOUNDS LIKE FUN.
AND WON'T YOU NEED A BODY-GUARD?
THAT MAY BE TRUE, BUT...
HMM?
DID THAT CAT MAKE A WEIRD SOUND?
Not N-at all!
Eeep

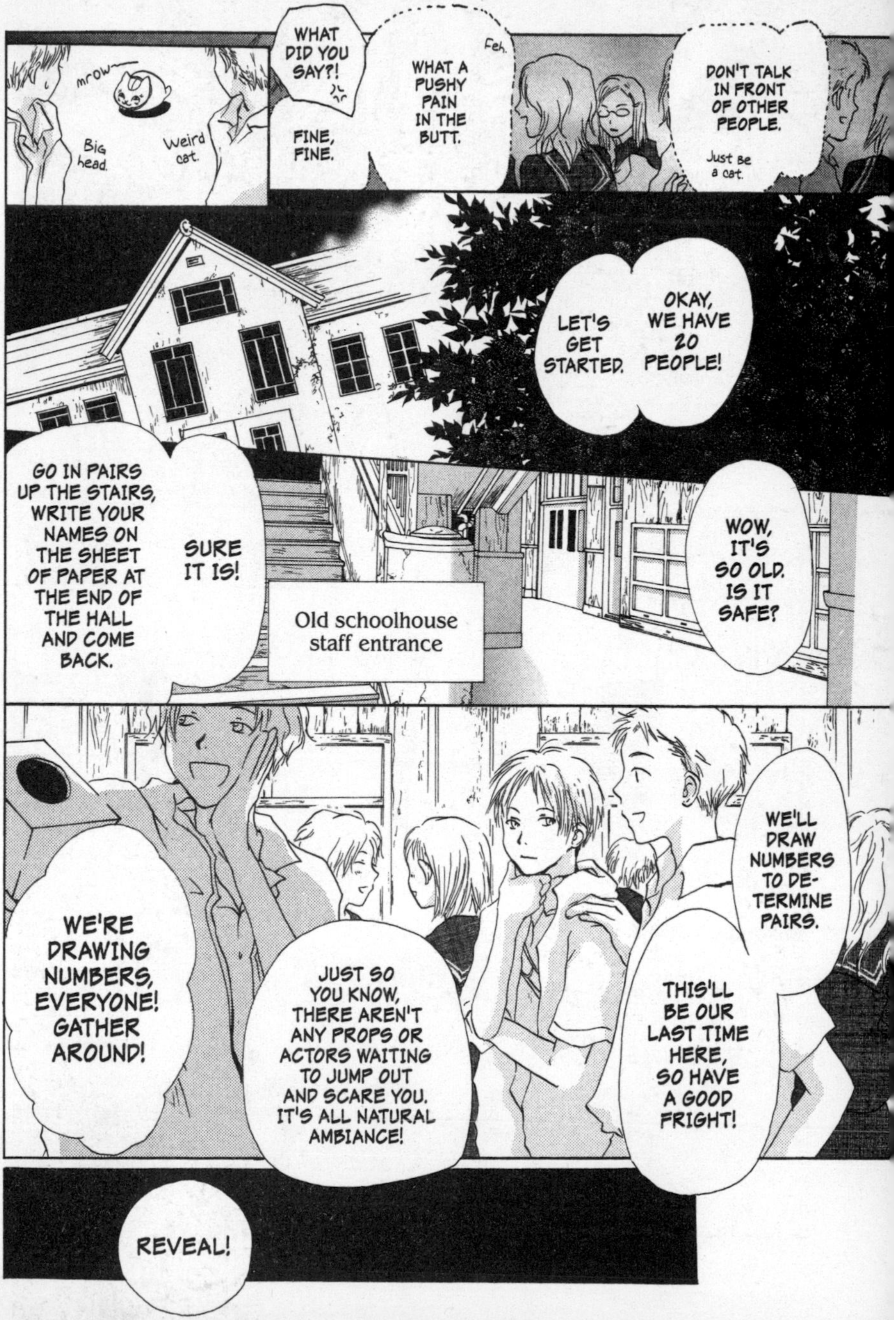
DON'T TALK IN FRONT OF OTHER PEOPLE.
Just be a cat.
Feh.
WHAT A PUSHY PAIN IN THE BUTT.
WHAT DID YOU SAY?!
FINE, FINE.
mrow~~
Weird cat.
Big head.
OKAY, WE HAVE 20 PEOPLE!
LET'S GET STARTED.
WOW, IT'S SO OLD. IS IT SAFE?
Old schoolhouse staff entrance
SURE IT IS!
GO IN PAIRS UP THE STAIRS, WRITE YOUR NAMES ON THE SHEET OF PAPER AT THE END OF THE HALL AND COME BACK.
WE'LL DRAW NUMBERS TO DE-TERMINE PAIRS.
THIS'LL BE OUR LAST TIME HERE, SO HAVE A GOOD FRIGHT!
JUST SO YOU KNOW, THERE AREN'T ANY PROPS OR ACTORS WAITING TO JUMP OUT AND SCARE YOU. IT'S ALL NATURAL AMBIANCE!
WE'RE DRAWING NUMBERS, EVERYONE! GATHER AROUND!
REVEAL!

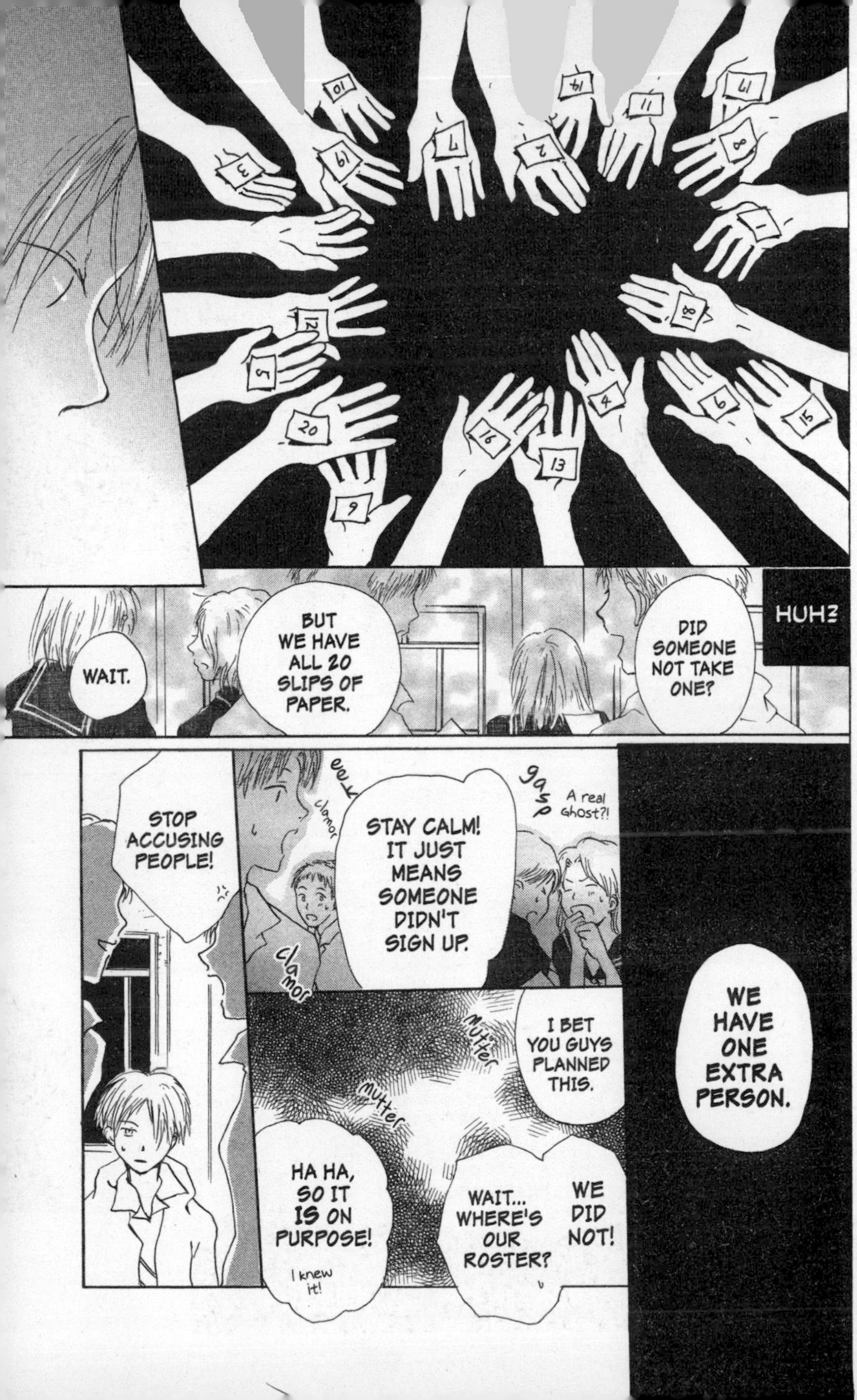

HUH?
DID SOMEONE NOT TAKE ONE?
BUT WE HAVE ALL 20 SLIPS OF PAPER.
WAIT.
WE HAVE ONE EXTRA PERSON.
gasp
A real Ghost?!
STAY CALM! IT JUST MEANS SOMEONE DIDN'T SIGN UP.
eek
clamor
clamor
I BET YOU GUYS PLANNED THIS.
mutter
mutter
WE DID NOT!
WAIT... WHERE'S OUR ROSTER?
HA HA, SO IT IS ON PURPOSE!
I knew it!
STOP ACCUSING PEOPLE!

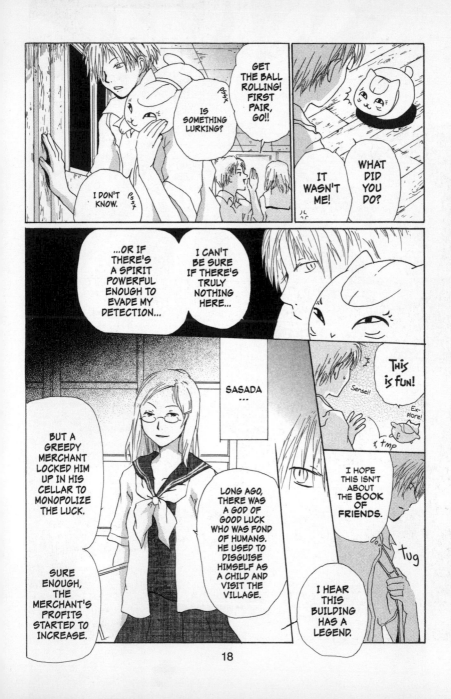

WHAT DID YOU DO?
IT WASN'T ME!
GET THE BALL ROLLING! FIRST PAIR, GO!!
IS SOMETHING LURKING?
PSSX
I DON'T KNOW.
PSSX
I CAN'T BE SURE IF THERE'S TRULY NOTHING HERE...
...OR IF THERE'S A SPIRIT POWERFUL ENOUGH TO EVADE MY DETECTION...
This is fun!
Sensei!
Ex-plore!
tmp
I HOPE THIS ISN'T ABOUT THE BOOK OF FRIENDS.
tug
I HEAR THIS BUILDING HAS A LEGEND.
SASADA ...
LONG AGO, THERE WAS A GOD OF GOOD LUCK WHO WAS FOND OF HUMANS. HE USED TO DISGUISE HIMSELF AS A CHILD AND VISIT THE VILLAGE.
BUT A GREEDY MERCHANT LOCKED HIM UP IN HIS CELLAR TO MONOPOLIZE THE LUCK.
SURE ENOUGH, THE MERCHANT'S PROFITS STARTED TO INCREASE.

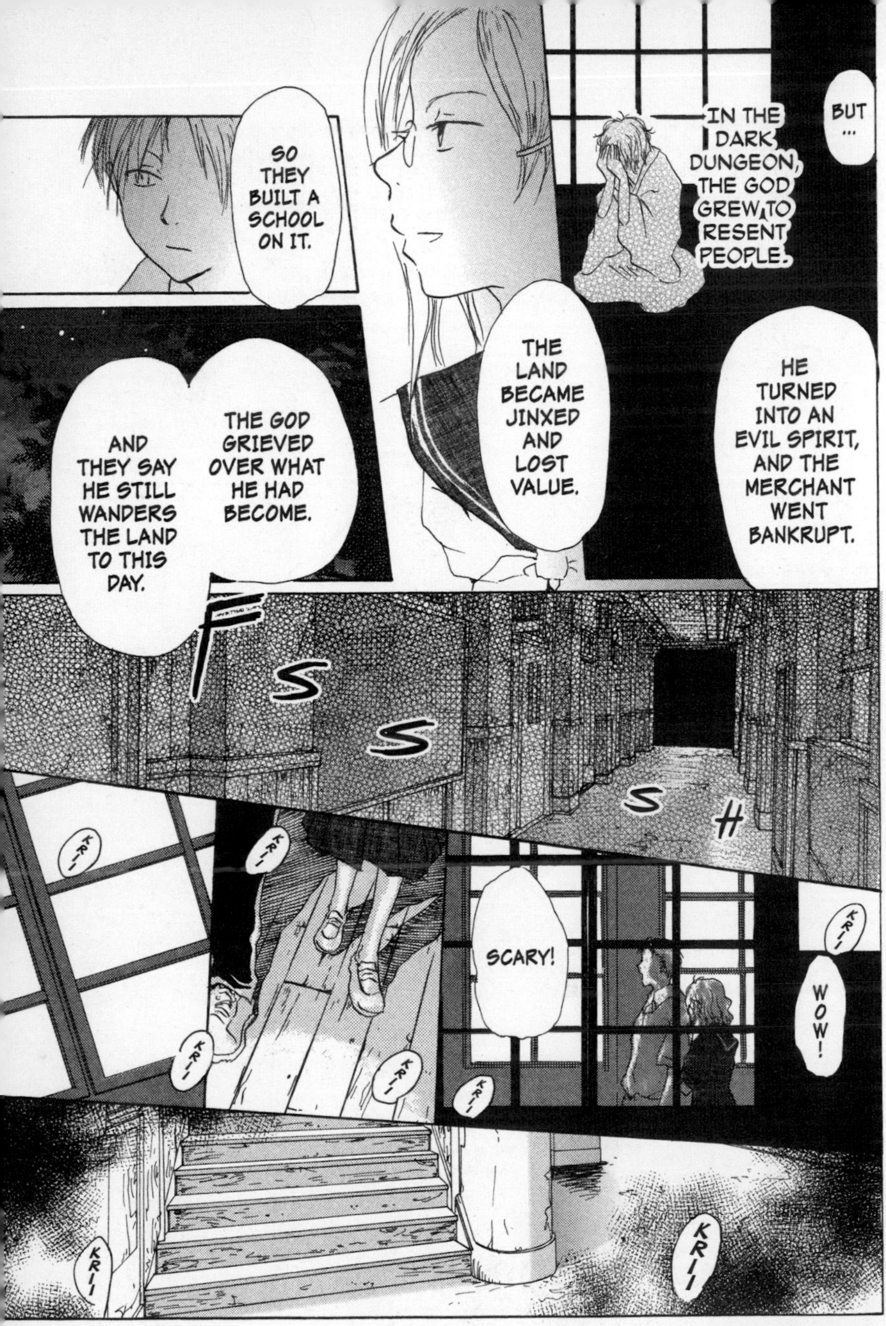

BUT ...
IN THE DARK DUNGEON, THE GOD GREW TO RESENT PEOPLE.
HE TURNED INTO AN EVIL SPIRIT, AND THE MERCHANT WENT BANKRUPT.
THE LAND BECAME JINXED AND LOST VALUE.
SO THEY BUILT A SCHOOL ON IT.
THE GOD GRIEVED OVER WHAT HE HAD BECOME.
AND THEY SAY HE STILL WANDERS THE LAND TO THIS DAY.
FSSSH
KRII
WOW!
SCARY!
KRII
KRII
KRII
KRII
KRII
KRII
KRII

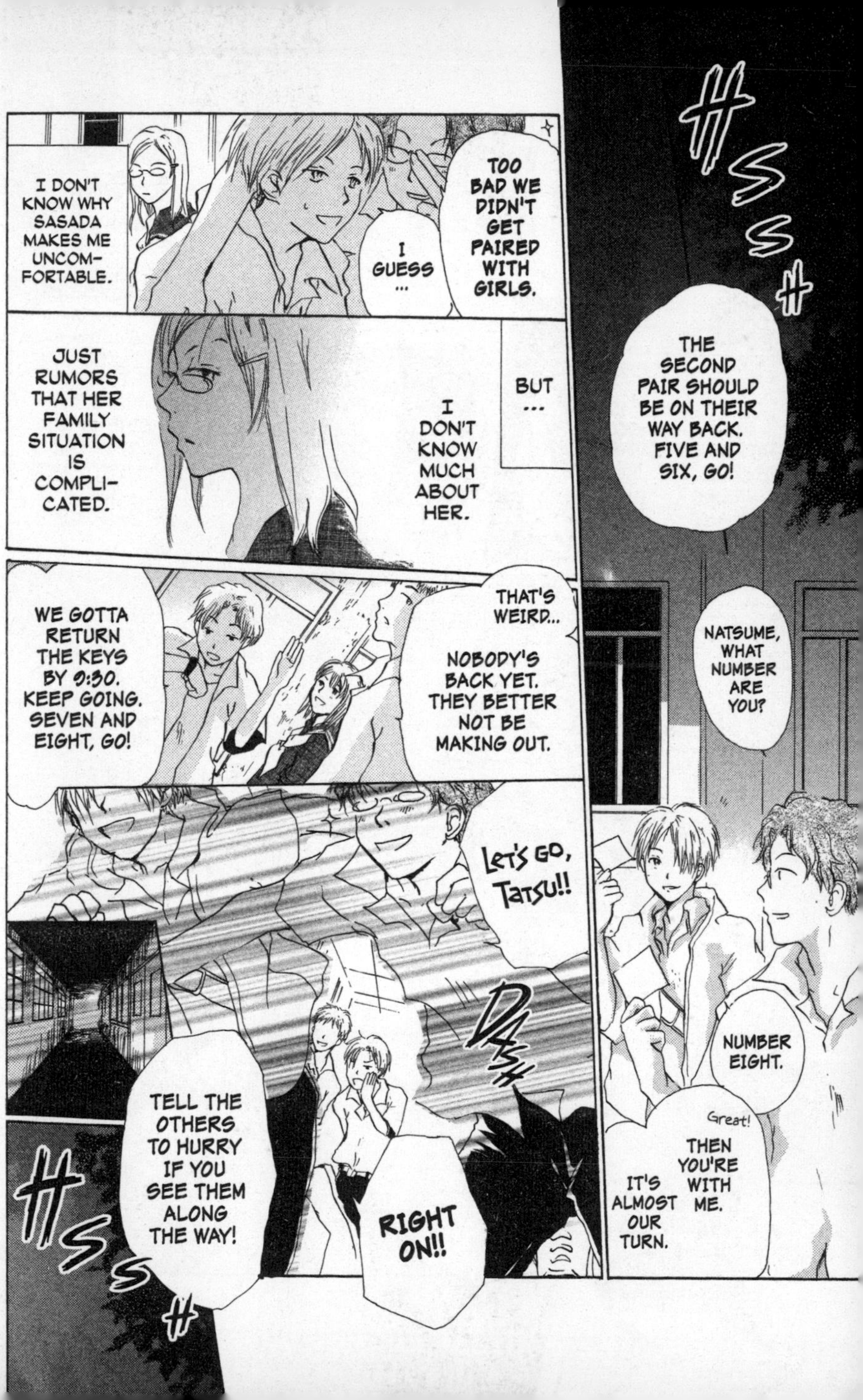
HSSH
THE SECOND PAIR SHOULD BE ON THEIR WAY BACK. FIVE AND SIX, GO!
NATSUME, WHAT NUMBER ARE YOU?
NUMBER EIGHT.
Great!
THEN YOU'RE WITH ME.
IT'S ALMOST OUR TURN.
TOO BAD WE DIDN'T GET PAIRED WITH GIRLS.
I GUESS ...
I DON'T KNOW WHY SASADA MAKES ME UNCOM-FORTABLE.
BUT ...
I DON'T KNOW MUCH ABOUT HER.
JUST RUMORS THAT HER FAMILY SITUATION IS COMPLI-CATED.
THAT'S WEIRD...
NOBODY'S BACK YET. THEY BETTER NOT BE MAKING OUT.
WE GOTTA RETURN THE KEYS BY 9:30. KEEP GOING. SEVEN AND EIGHT, GO!
LET'S GO, TATSU!!
DASH
TELL THE OTHERS TO HURRY IF YOU SEE THEM ALONG THE WAY!
RIGHT ON!!
HSSH

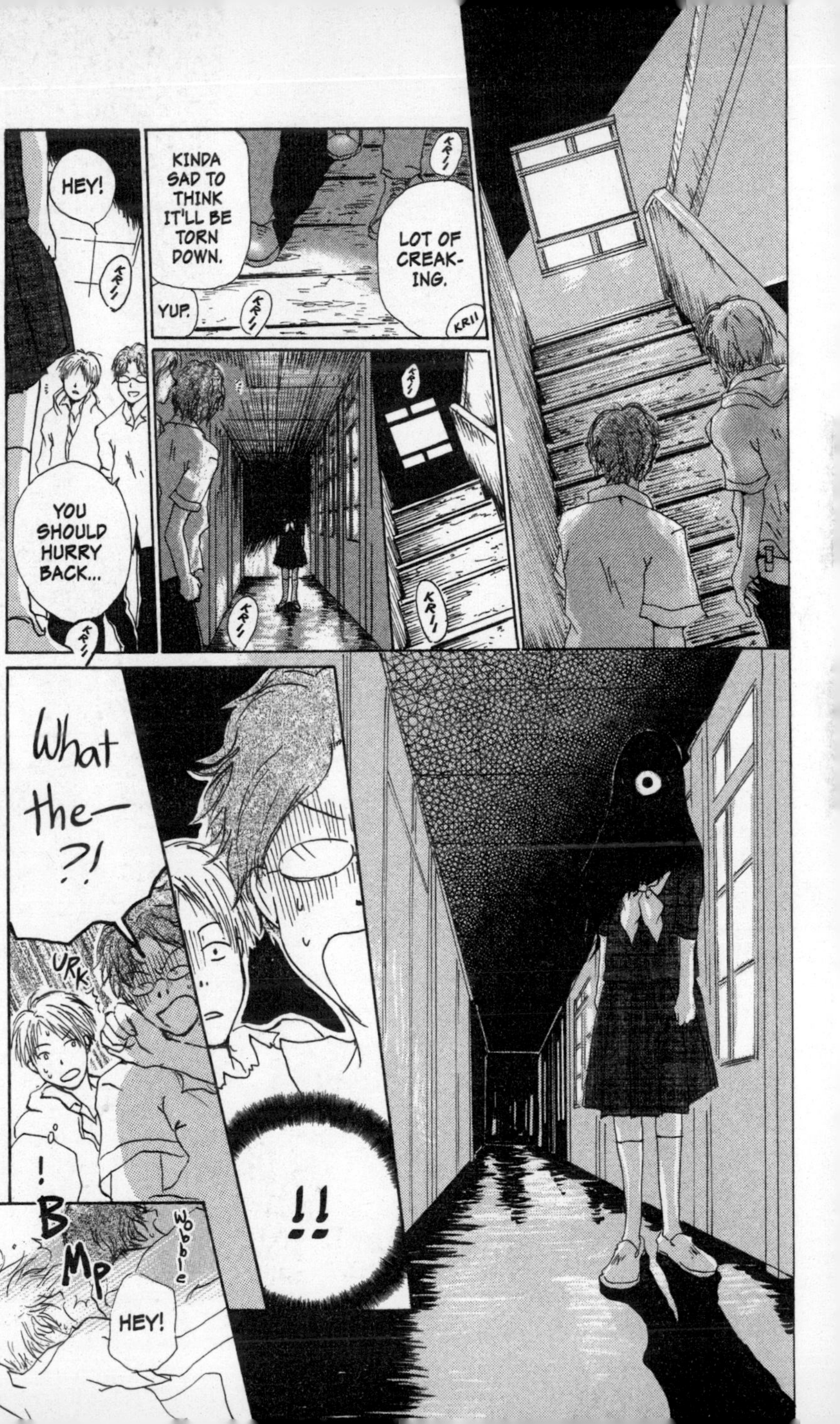
KRII
KRII
LOT OF CREAKING.
KINDA SAD TO THINK IT'LL BE TORN DOWN.
KRII
YUP.
KRII
KRII
KRII
KRII
KRII
HEY!
KRII
YOU SHOULD HURRY BACK...
KRII
!!
What the—?!
URK
!
BMP
Wobble
HEY!

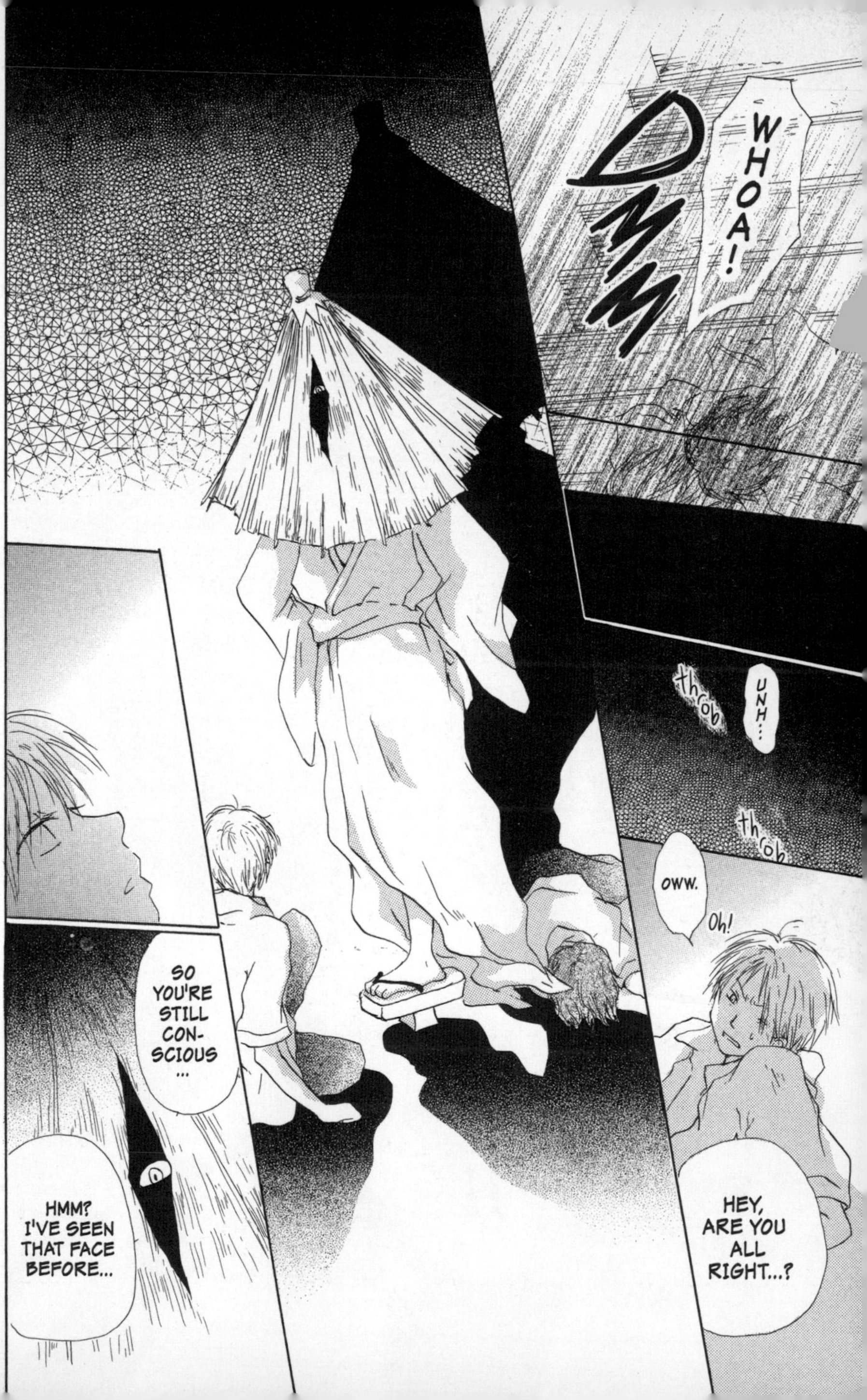

WHOA!
DMM
UNH...
throb
throb
OWW.
Oh!
HEY, ARE YOU ALL RIGHT...?
SO YOU'RE STILL CONSCIOUS...
HMM? I'VE SEEN THAT FACE BEFORE...

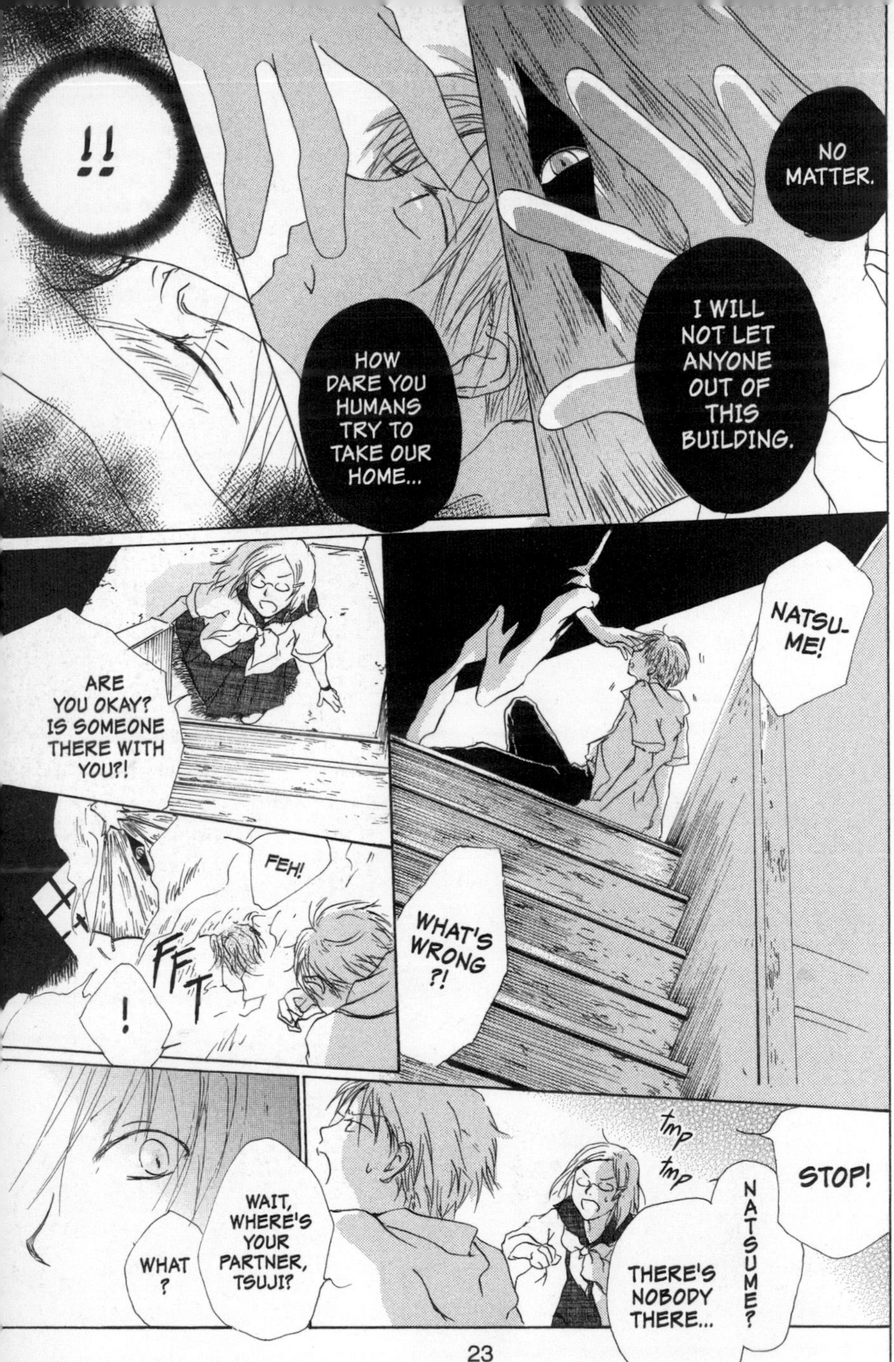
NO MATTER.
I WILL NOT LET ANYONE OUT OF THIS BUILDING.
HOW DARE YOU HUMANS TRY TO TAKE OUR HOME...
!!
NATSU-ME!
ARE YOU OKAY? IS SOMEONE THERE WITH YOU?!
WHAT'S WRONG ?!
FEH!
FFT
!
STOP!
tmp tmp
NATSUME?
THERE'S NOBODY THERE...
WAIT, WHERE'S YOUR PARTNER, TSUJI?
WHAT ?

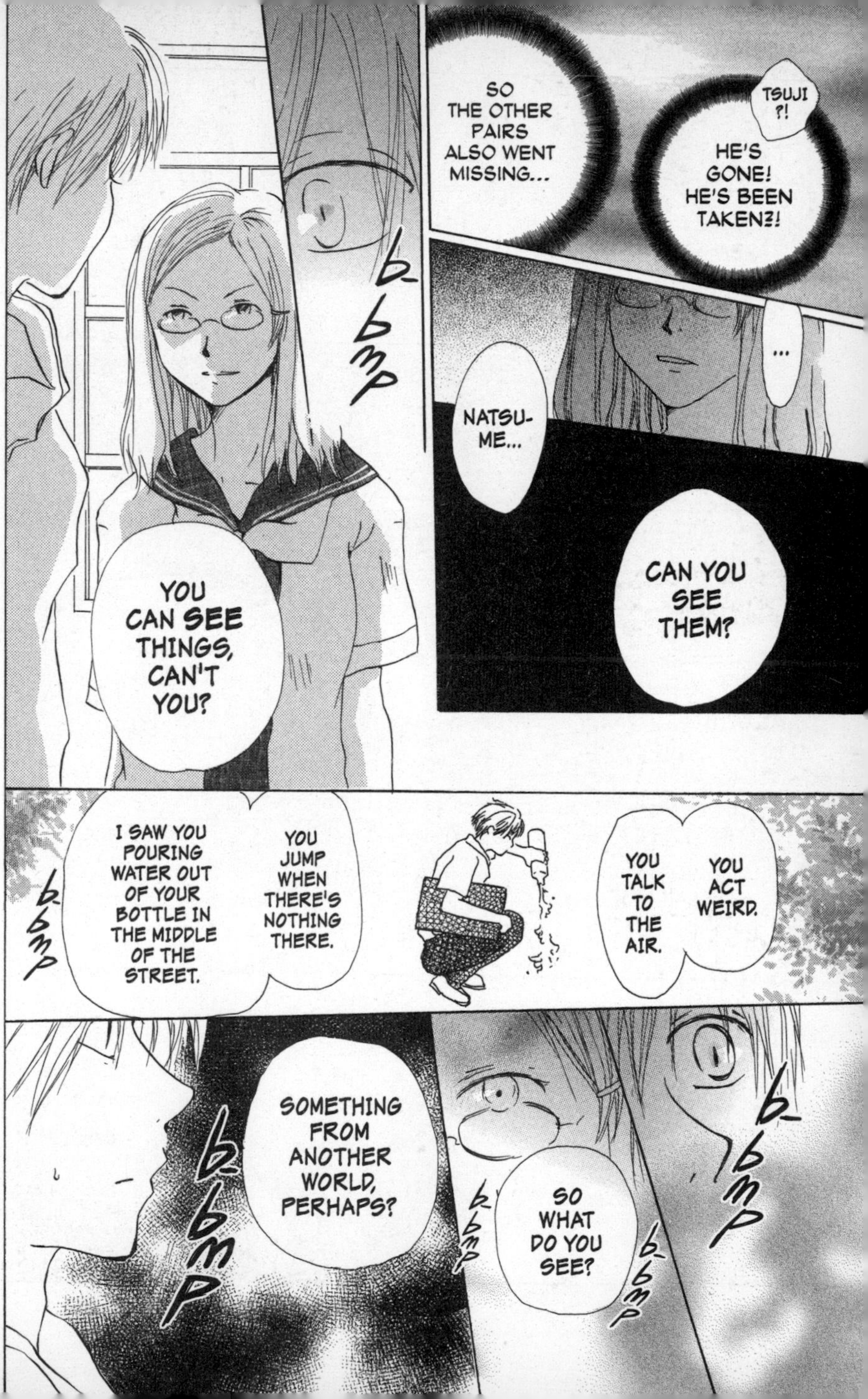

TSUJI?!
HE'S GONE! HE'S BEEN TAKEN?!
SO THE OTHER PAIRS ALSO WENT MISSING...
...
NATSUME...
CAN YOU SEE THEM?
b-bmp
YOU CAN SEE THINGS, CAN'T YOU?
YOU ACT WEIRD.
YOU TALK TO THE AIR.
YOU JUMP WHEN THERE'S NOTHING THERE.
I SAW YOU POURING WATER OUT OF YOUR BOTTLE IN THE MIDDLE OF THE STREET.
b-bmp
b-bmp
SO WHAT DO YOU SEE?
b-bmp
b-bmp
SOMETHING FROM ANOTHER WORLD, PERHAPS?
b-bmp

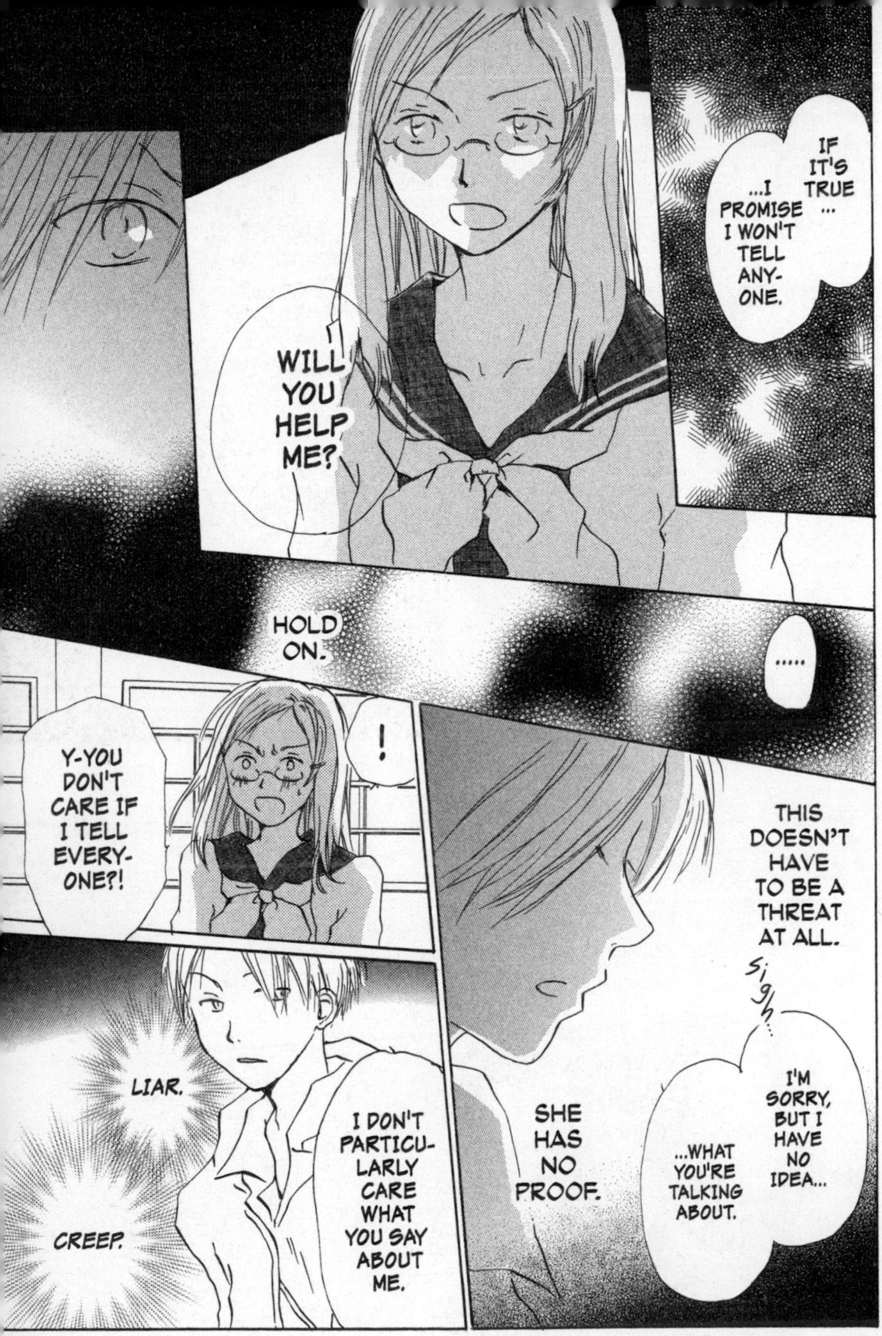

IF IT'S TRUE ...
...I PROMISE I WON'T TELL ANY-ONE.
WILL YOU HELP ME?
.....
HOLD ON.
THIS DOESN'T HAVE TO BE A THREAT AT ALL.
sigh...
I'M SORRY, BUT I HAVE NO IDEA...
...WHAT YOU'RE TALKING ABOUT.
SHE HAS NO PROOF.
!
Y-YOU DON'T CARE IF I TELL EVERY-ONE?!
I DON'T PARTICU-LARLY CARE WHAT YOU SAY ABOUT ME.
LIAR.
CREEP.

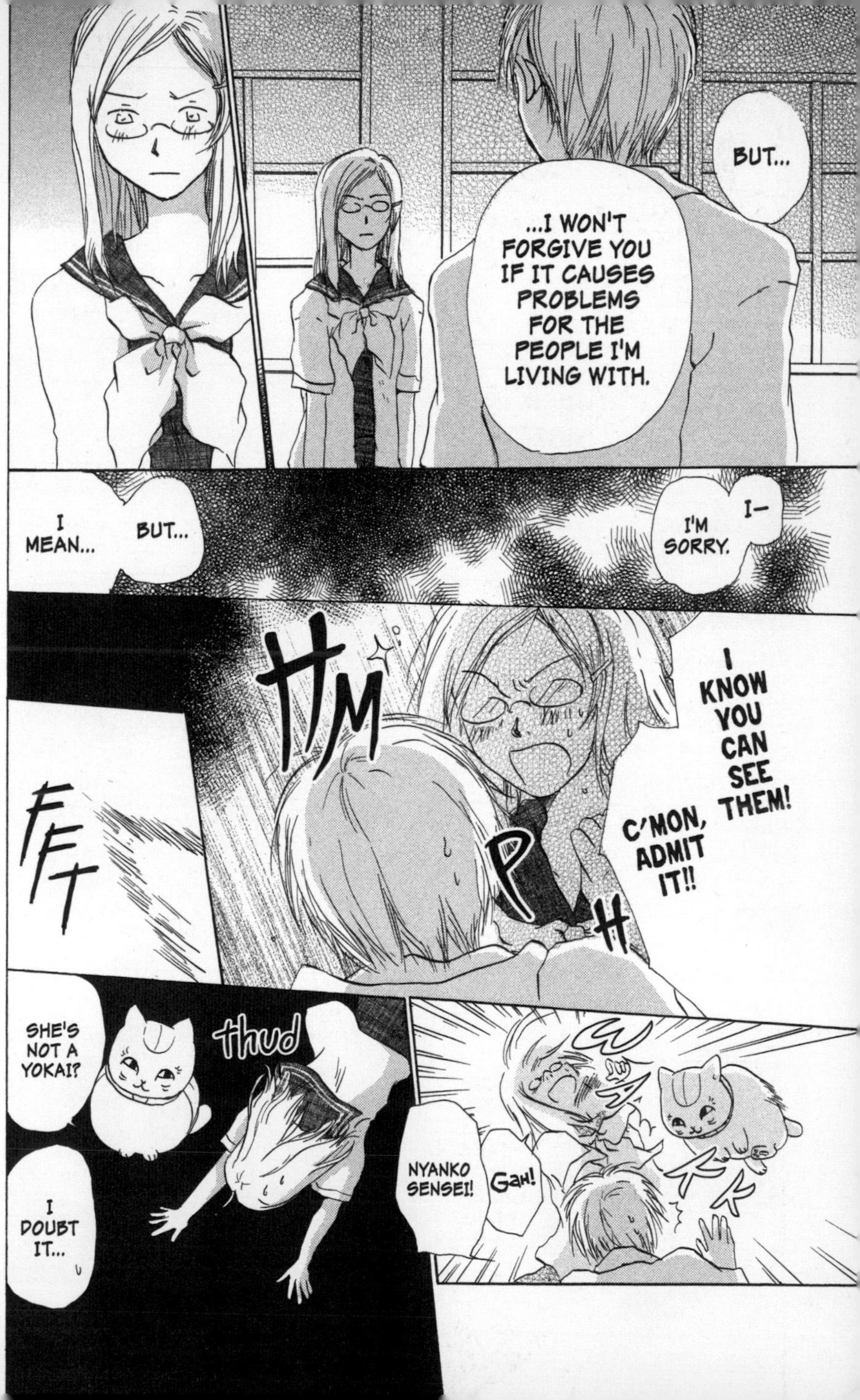
BUT...
...I WON'T FORGIVE YOU IF IT CAUSES PROBLEMS FOR THE PEOPLE I'M LIVING WITH.
I— I'M SORRY.
BUT... I MEAN...
HM
I KNOW YOU CAN SEE THEM!
C'MON, ADMIT IT!!
PH
FFT
Gah!
NYANKO SENSEI!
thud
SHE'S NOT A YOKAI?
I DOUBT IT...

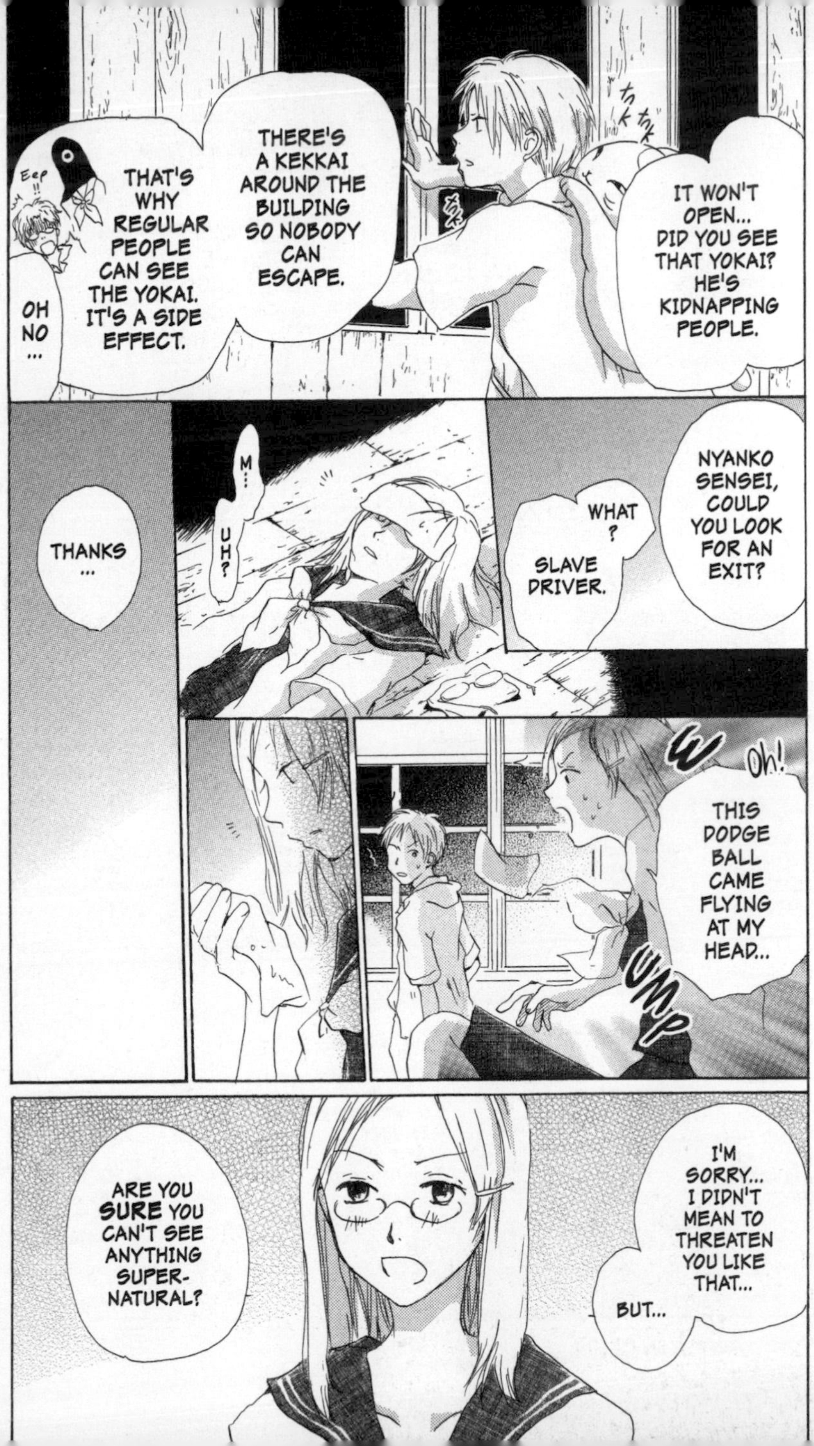
IT WON'T OPEN... DID YOU SEE THAT YOKAI? HE'S KIDNAPPING PEOPLE.
THERE'S A KEKKAI AROUND THE BUILDING SO NOBODY CAN ESCAPE.
THAT'S WHY REGULAR PEOPLE CAN SEE THE YOKAI. IT'S A SIDE EFFECT.
Eep!!
OH NO...
NYANKO SENSEI, COULD YOU LOOK FOR AN EXIT?
WHAT?
SLAVE DRIVER.
M...
UH?
Oh!
THIS DODGE BALL CAME FLYING AT MY HEAD...
WUMP
THANKS...
I'M SORRY... I DIDN'T MEAN TO THREATEN YOU LIKE THAT...
BUT...
ARE YOU **SURE** YOU CAN'T SEE ANYTHING SUPER-NATURAL?

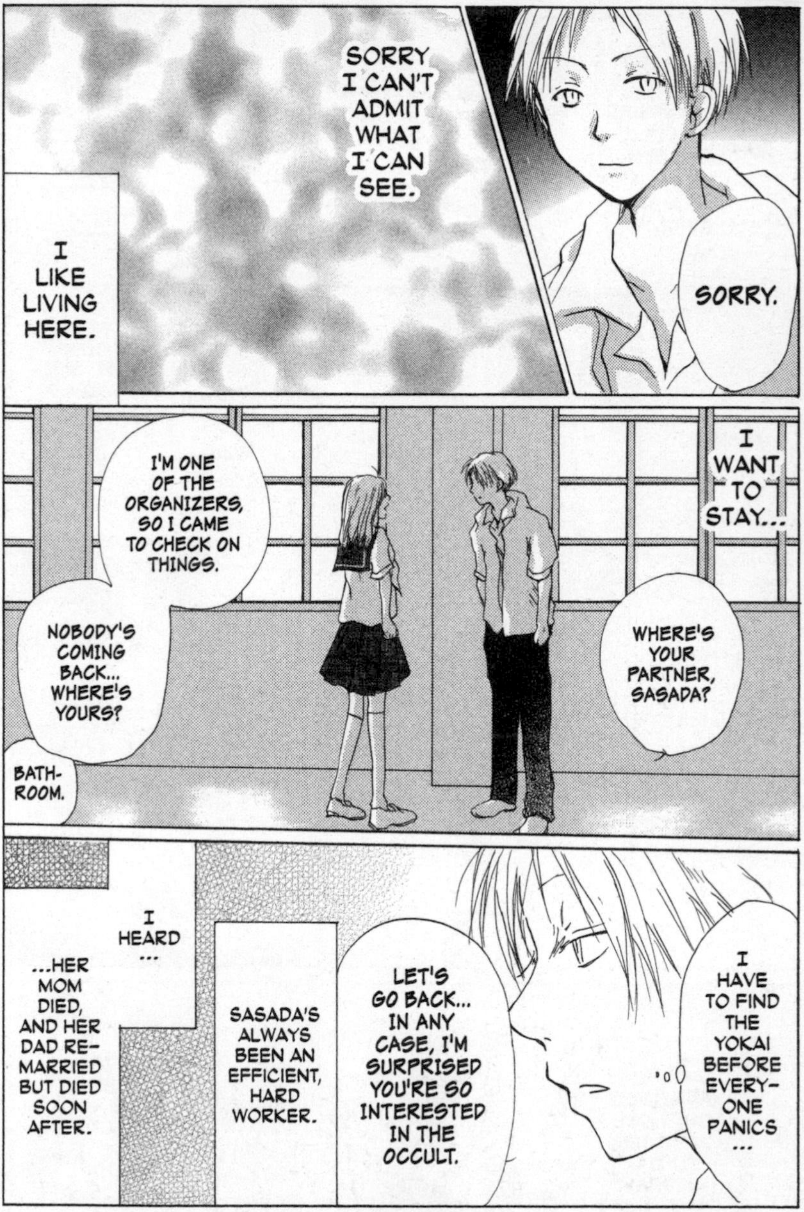
SORRY.
SORRY I CAN'T ADMIT WHAT I CAN SEE.
I LIKE LIVING HERE.
I WANT TO STAY...
WHERE'S YOUR PARTNER, SASADA?
I'M ONE OF THE ORGANIZERS, SO I CAME TO CHECK ON THINGS.
NOBODY'S COMING BACK... WHERE'S YOURS?
BATH-ROOM.
I HAVE TO FIND THE YOKAI BEFORE EVERY-ONE PANICS...
LET'S GO BACK... IN ANY CASE, I'M SURPRISED YOU'RE SO INTERESTED IN THE OCCULT.
SASADA'S ALWAYS BEEN AN EFFICIENT, HARD WORKER.
I HEARD...
...HER MOM DIED, AND HER DAD RE-MARRIED BUT DIED SOON AFTER.

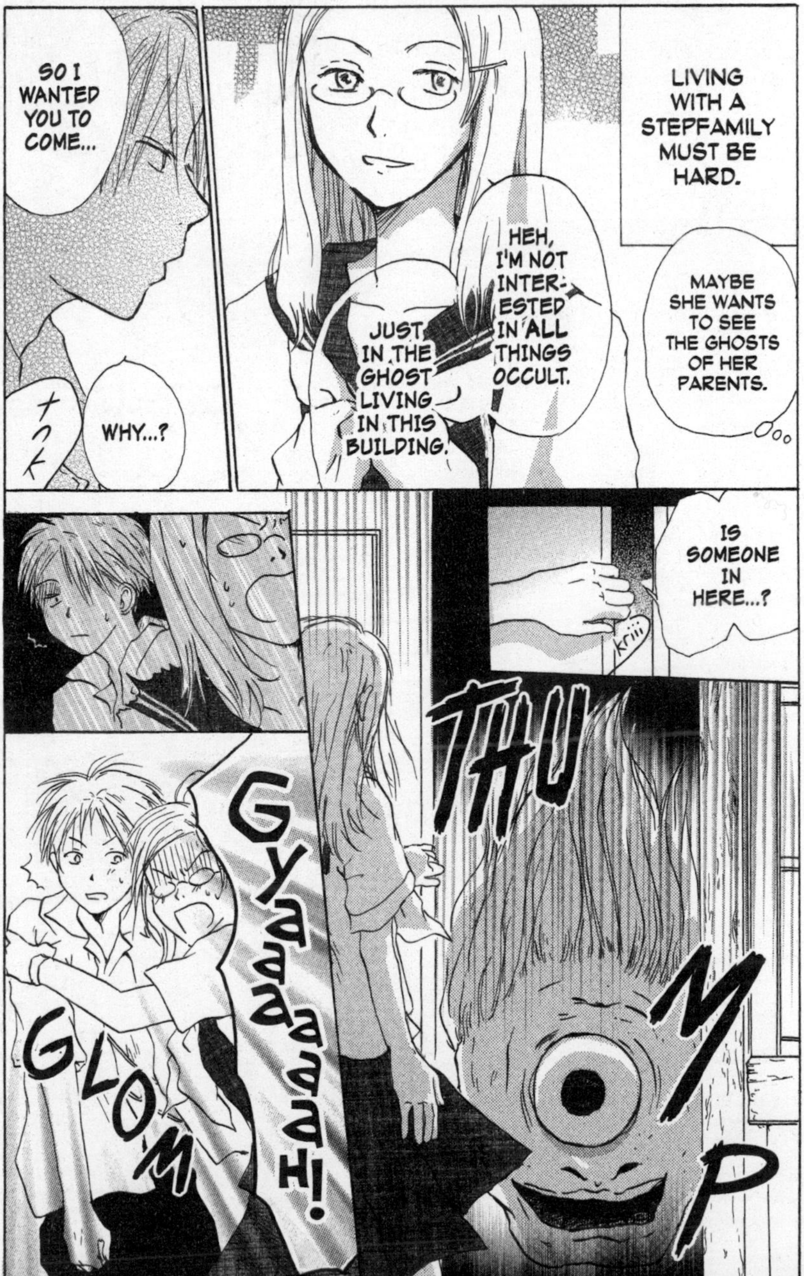
LIVING WITH A STEPFAMILY MUST BE HARD.
MAYBE SHE WANTS TO SEE THE GHOSTS OF HER PARENTS.
HEH, I'M NOT INTER-ESTED IN ALL THINGS OCCULT.
JUST IN THE GHOST LIVING IN THIS BUILDING.
SO I WANTED YOU TO COME...
WHY...?
IS SOMEONE IN HERE...?
kriii
THUMP
GYAAAAAAAH!
GLOM

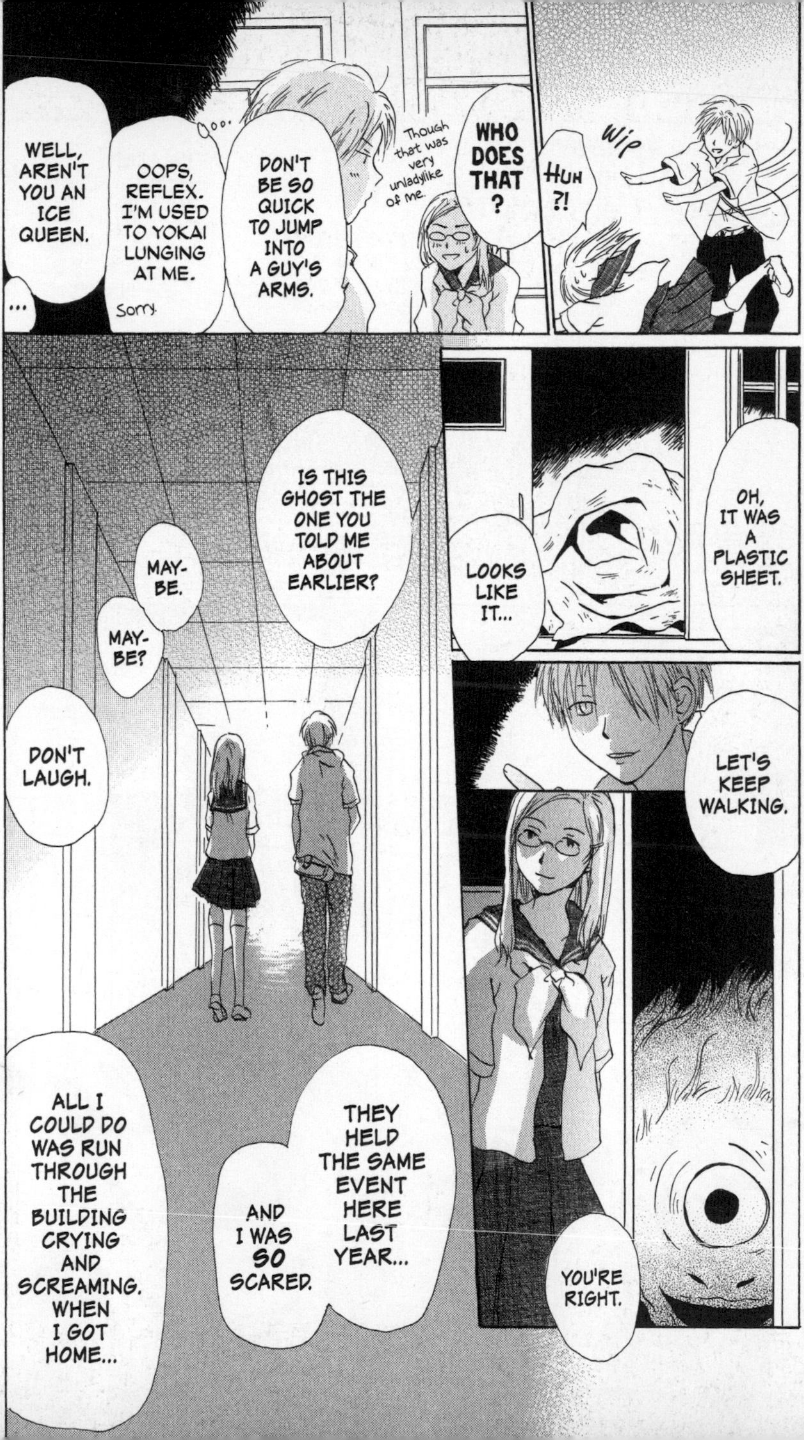
Wip
HUH ?!
WHO DOES THAT ?
Though that was very unladylike of me.
DON'T BE SO QUICK TO JUMP INTO A GUY'S ARMS.
OOPS, REFLEX. I'M USED TO YOKAI LUNGING AT ME.
Sorry.
WELL, AREN'T YOU AN ICE QUEEN.
...
OH, IT WAS A PLASTIC SHEET.
LOOKS LIKE IT...
LET'S KEEP WALKING.
YOU'RE RIGHT.
IS THIS GHOST THE ONE YOU TOLD ME ABOUT EARLIER?
MAY-BE.
MAY-BE?
DON'T LAUGH.
THEY HELD THE SAME EVENT HERE LAST YEAR...
AND I WAS SO SCARED.
ALL I COULD DO WAS RUN THROUGH THE BUILDING CRYING AND SCREAMING. WHEN I GOT HOME...

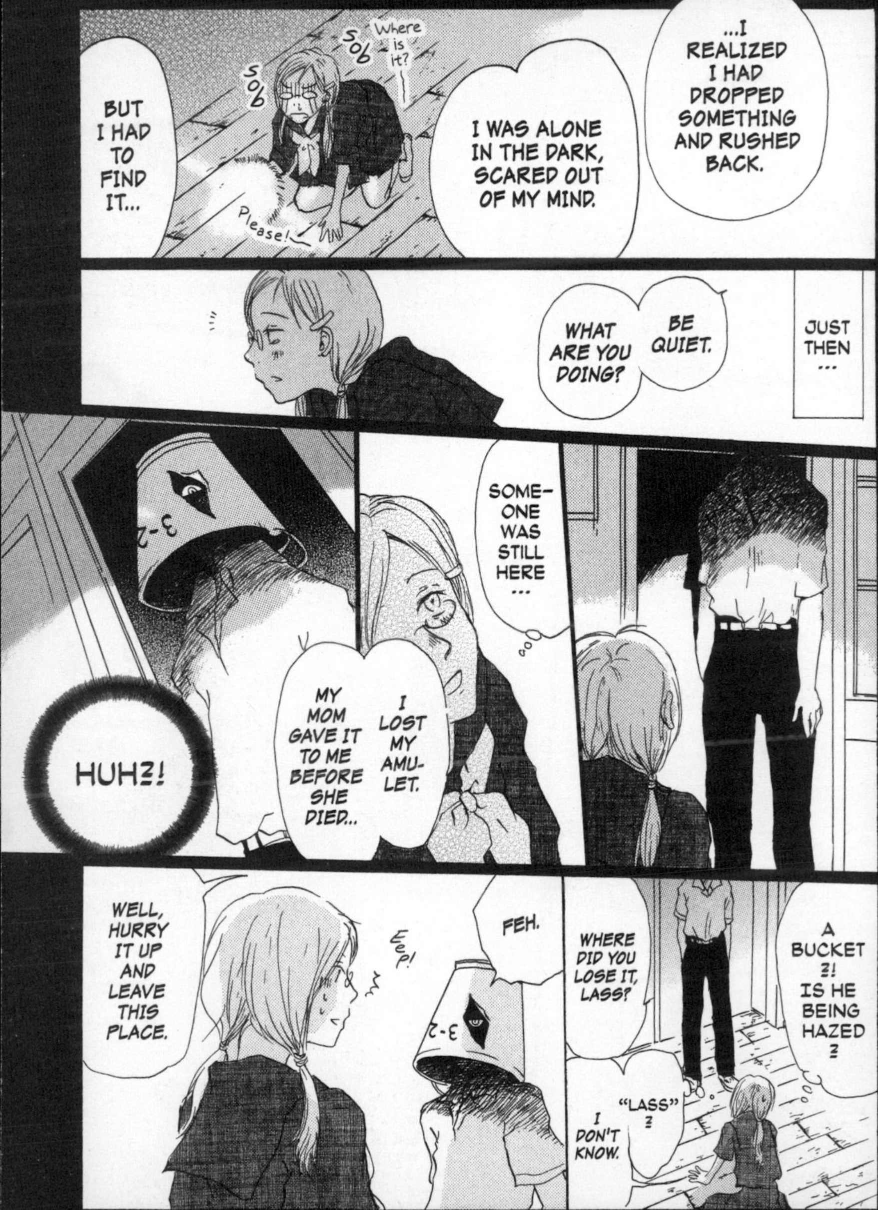
...I REALIZED I HAD DROPPED SOMETHING AND RUSHED BACK.
I WAS ALONE IN THE DARK, SCARED OUT OF MY MIND.
Where is it?
sob
sob
Please!
BUT I HAD TO FIND IT...
JUST THEN...
BE QUIET.
WHAT ARE YOU DOING?
SOME-ONE WAS STILL HERE...
I LOST MY AMU-LET.
MY MOM GAVE IT TO ME BEFORE SHE DIED...
3-2
HUH?!
A BUCKET?! IS HE BEING HAZED?
WHERE DID YOU LOSE IT, LASS?
"LASS"?
I DON'T KNOW.
FEH.
3-2
Eep!
WELL, HURRY IT UP AND LEAVE THIS PLACE.

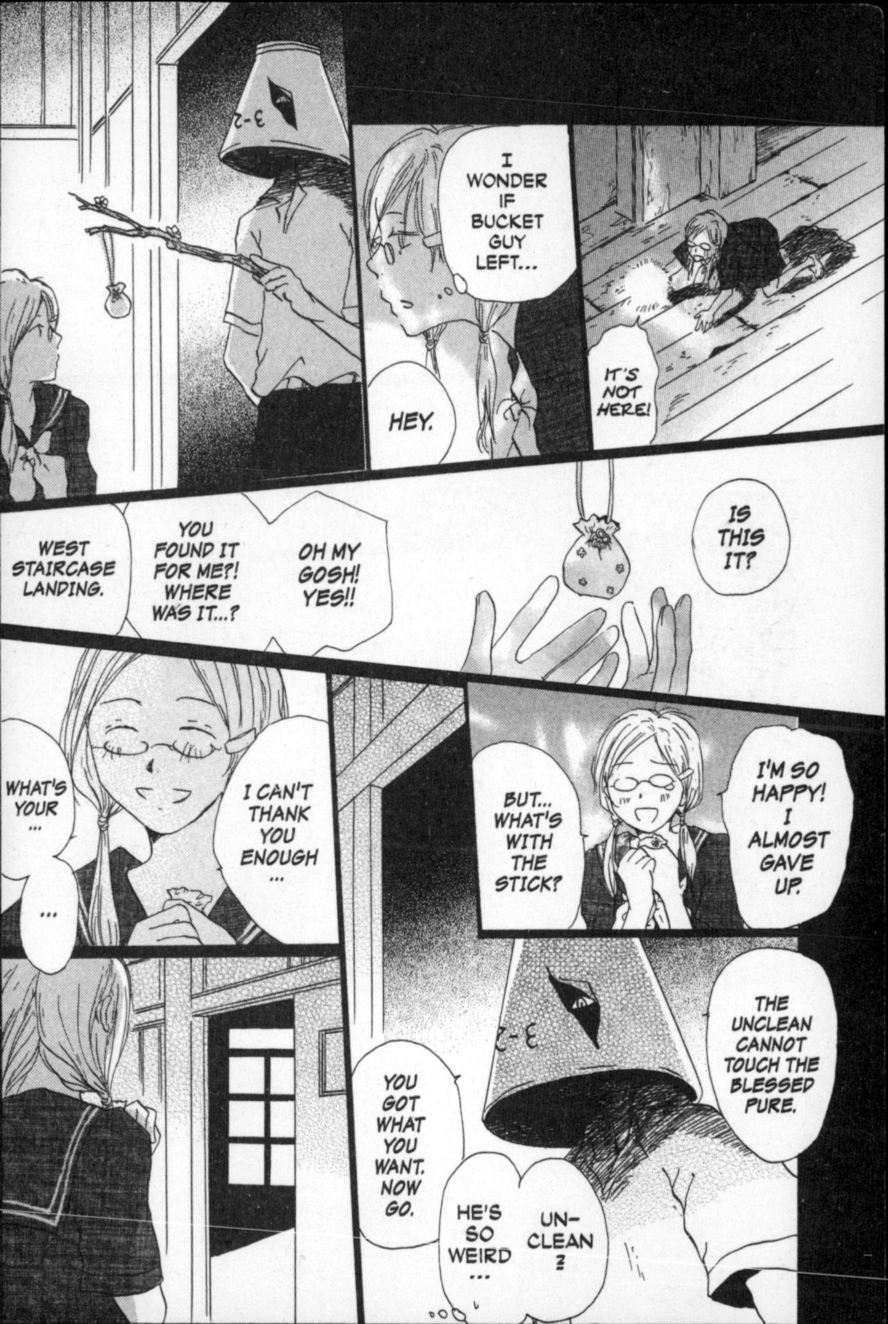
IT'S NOT HERE!
I WONDER IF BUCKET GUY LEFT...
HEY.
IS THIS IT?
OH MY GOSH! YES!!
YOU FOUND IT FOR ME?! WHERE WAS IT...?
WEST STAIRCASE LANDING.
I'M SO HAPPY! I ALMOST GAVE UP.
BUT... WHAT'S WITH THE STICK?
I CAN'T THANK YOU ENOUGH ...
WHAT'S YOUR ...
...
THE UNCLEAN CANNOT TOUCH THE BLESSED PURE.
YOU GOT WHAT YOU WANT. NOW GO.
UN-CLEAN?
HE'S SO WEIRD ...

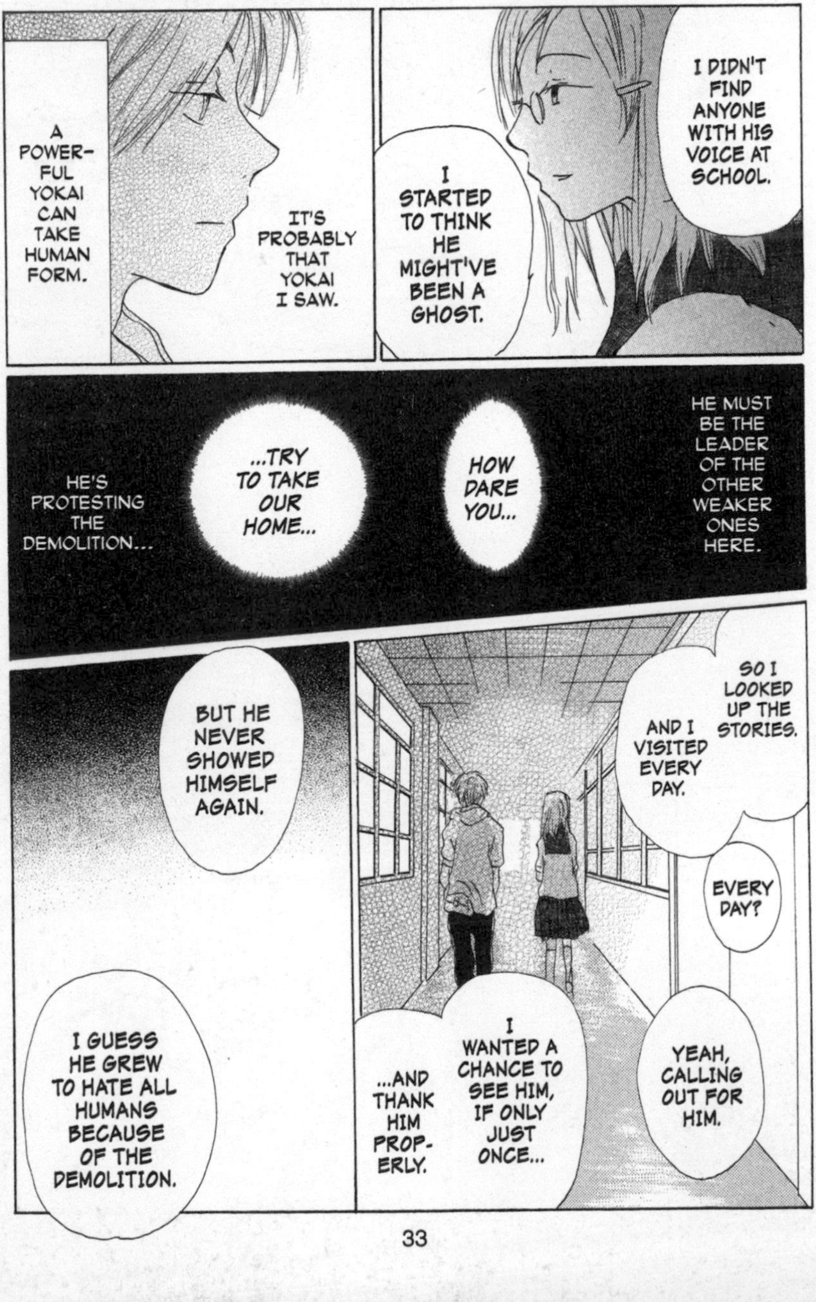
I DIDN'T FIND ANYONE WITH HIS VOICE AT SCHOOL.
I STARTED TO THINK HE MIGHT'VE BEEN A GHOST.
IT'S PROBABLY THAT YOKAI I SAW.
A POWER-FUL YOKAI CAN TAKE HUMAN FORM.
HE MUST BE THE LEADER OF THE OTHER WEAKER ONES HERE.
HOW DARE YOU...
...TRY TO TAKE OUR HOME...
HE'S PROTESTING THE DEMOLITION...
SO I LOOKED UP THE STORIES.
AND I VISITED EVERY DAY.
EVERY DAY?
YEAH, CALLING OUT FOR HIM.
I WANTED A CHANCE TO SEE HIM, IF ONLY JUST ONCE...
...AND THANK HIM PROP-ERLY.
BUT HE NEVER SHOWED HIMSELF AGAIN.
I GUESS HE GREW TO HATE ALL HUMANS BECAUSE OF THE DEMOLITION.

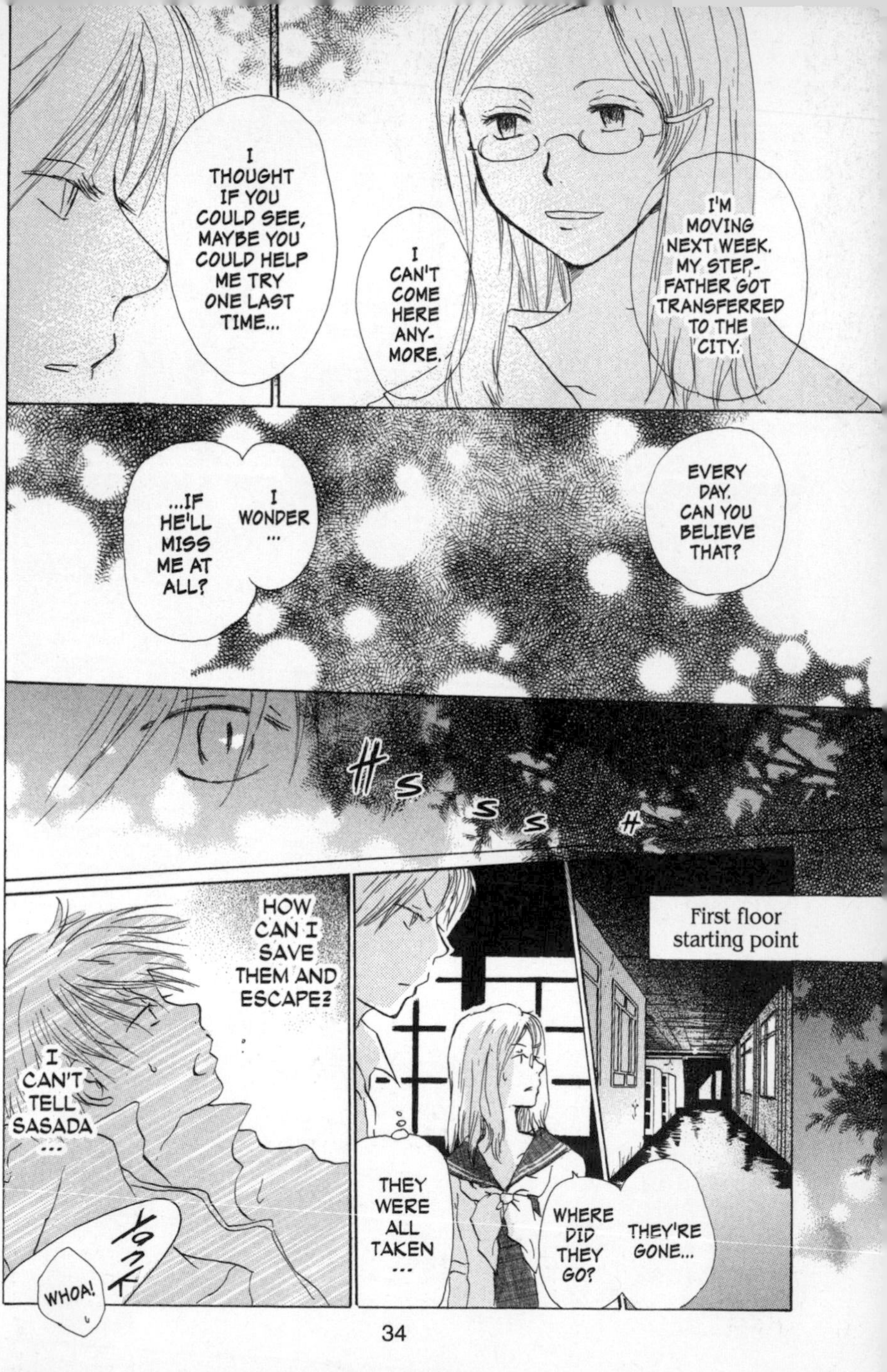
I'M MOVING NEXT WEEK. MY STEP-FATHER GOT TRANSFERRED TO THE CITY.
I CAN'T COME HERE ANYMORE.
I THOUGHT IF YOU COULD SEE, MAYBE YOU COULD HELP ME TRY ONE LAST TIME...
EVERY DAY. CAN YOU BELIEVE THAT?
I WONDER...
...IF HE'LL MISS ME AT ALL?
HSSSH
First floor starting point
THEY'RE GONE...
WHERE DID THEY GO?
THEY WERE ALL TAKEN...
HOW CAN I SAVE THEM AND ESCAPE?
I CAN'T TELL SASADA...
YANK
WHOA!

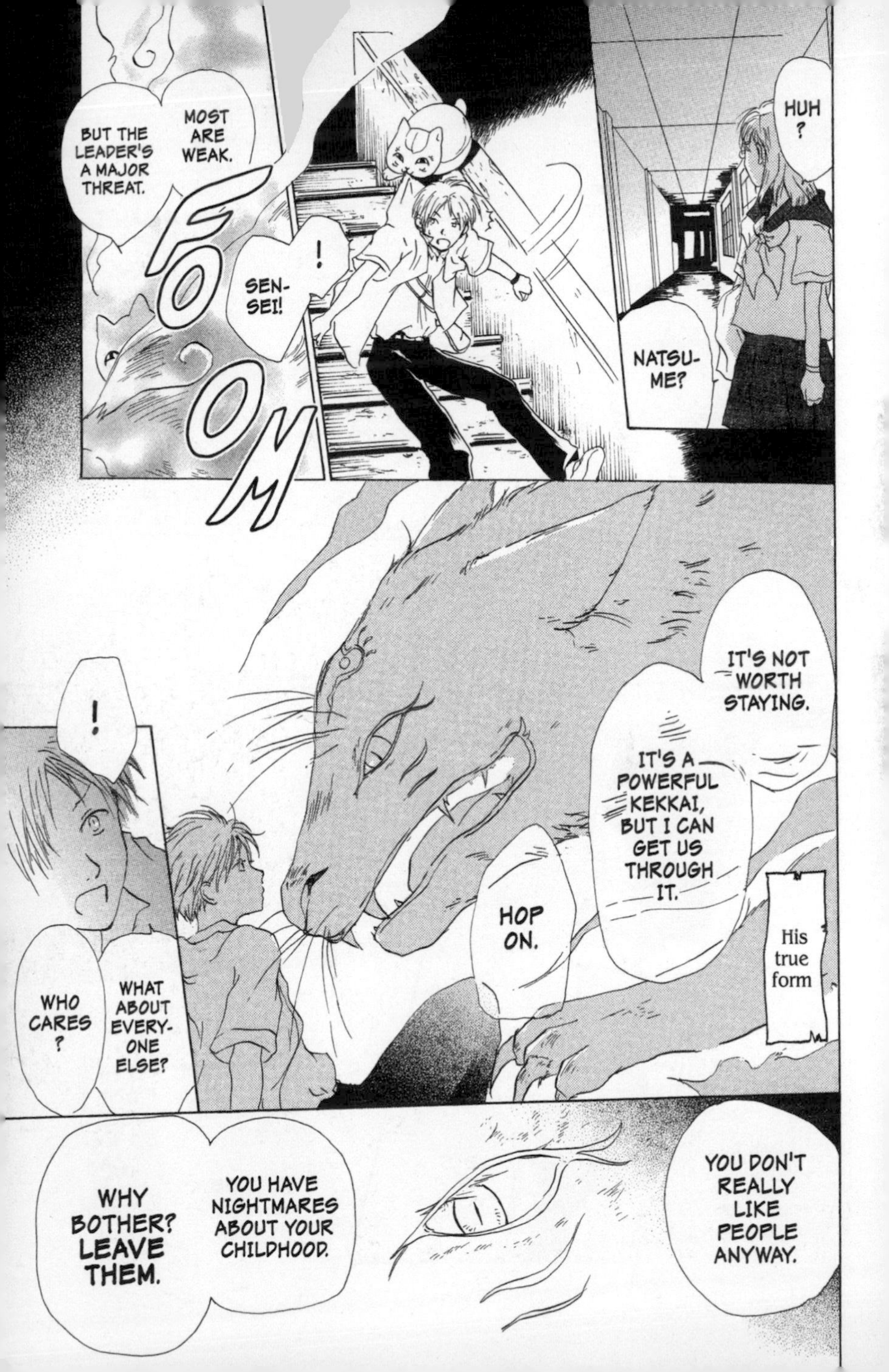
HUH ?
NATSU-ME?
!
SEN-SEI!
FOOM
MOST ARE WEAK.
BUT THE LEADER'S A MAJOR THREAT.
IT'S NOT WORTH STAYING.
IT'S A POWERFUL KEKKAI, BUT I CAN GET US THROUGH IT.
His true form
HOP ON.
!
WHAT ABOUT EVERY-ONE ELSE?
WHO CARES ?
YOU DON'T REALLY LIKE PEOPLE ANYWAY.
YOU HAVE NIGHTMARES ABOUT YOUR CHILDHOOD.
WHY BOTHER? LEAVE THEM.

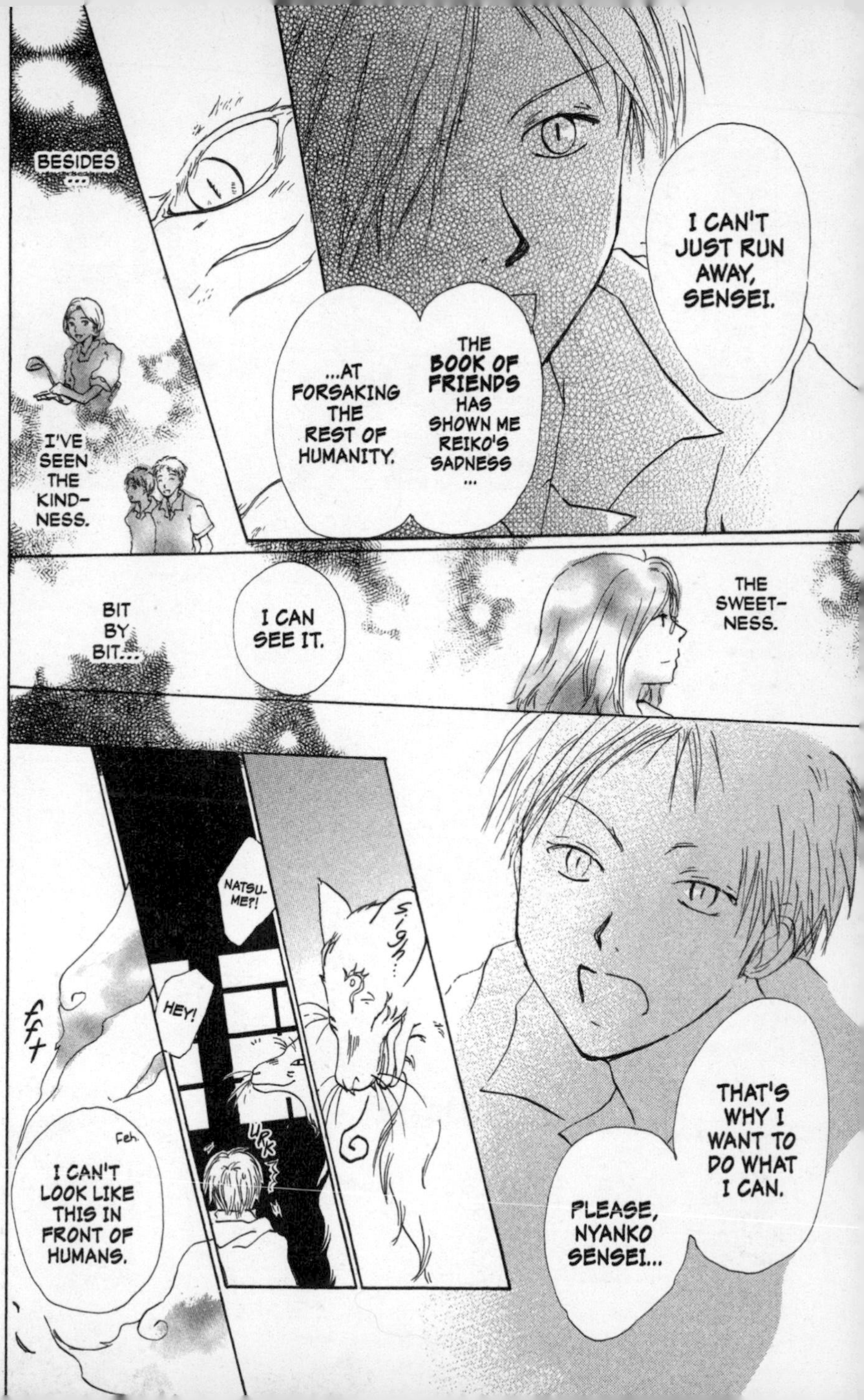
I CAN'T JUST RUN AWAY, SENSEI.
THE BOOK OF FRIENDS HAS SHOWN ME REIKO'S SADNESS...
...AT FORSAKING THE REST OF HUMANITY.
BESIDES...
I'VE SEEN THE KINDNESS.
THE SWEETNESS.
I CAN SEE IT.
BIT BY BIT...
THAT'S WHY I WANT TO DO WHAT I CAN.
PLEASE, NYANKO SENSEI...
sigh...
NATSU-ME?!
HEY!
URK
ffx
Feh.
I CAN'T LOOK LIKE THIS IN FRONT OF HUMANS.

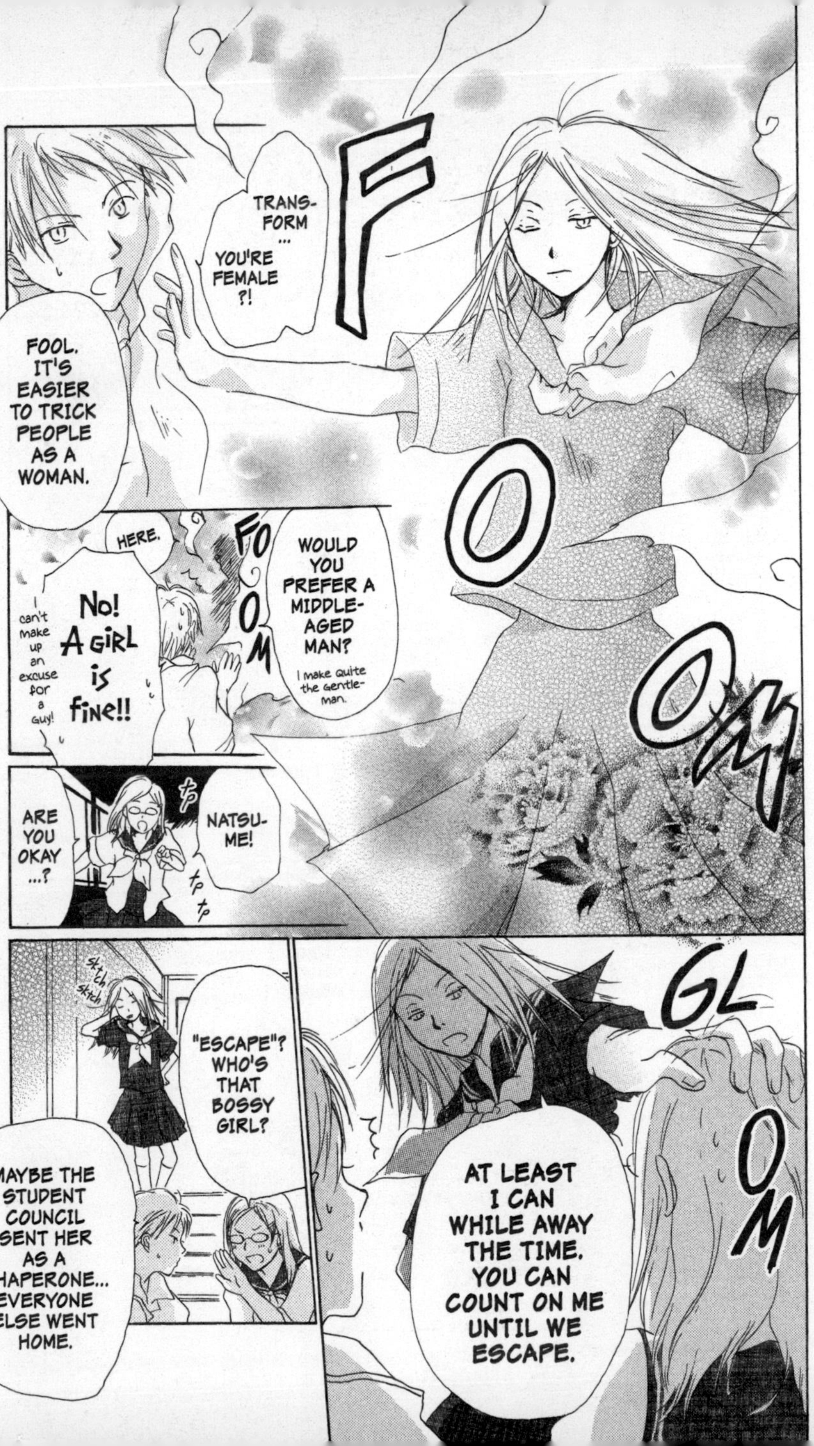
FOOOOM
TRANS-FORM... YOU'RE FEMALE?!
FOOL. IT'S EASIER TO TRICK PEOPLE AS A WOMAN.
FOOM
WOULD YOU PREFER A MIDDLE-AGED MAN?
I make quite the Gentle-man.
HERE.
No! A GIRL is fine!!
I can't make up an excuse for a Guy!
NATSU-ME!
tp
ARE YOU OKAY...?
tp tp
GLOOM
AT LEAST I CAN WHILE AWAY THE TIME. YOU CAN COUNT ON ME UNTIL WE ESCAPE.
"ESCAPE"? WHO'S THAT BOSSY GIRL?
sktch sktch
MAYBE THE STUDENT COUNCIL SENT HER AS A CHAPERONE... EVERYONE ELSE WENT HOME.

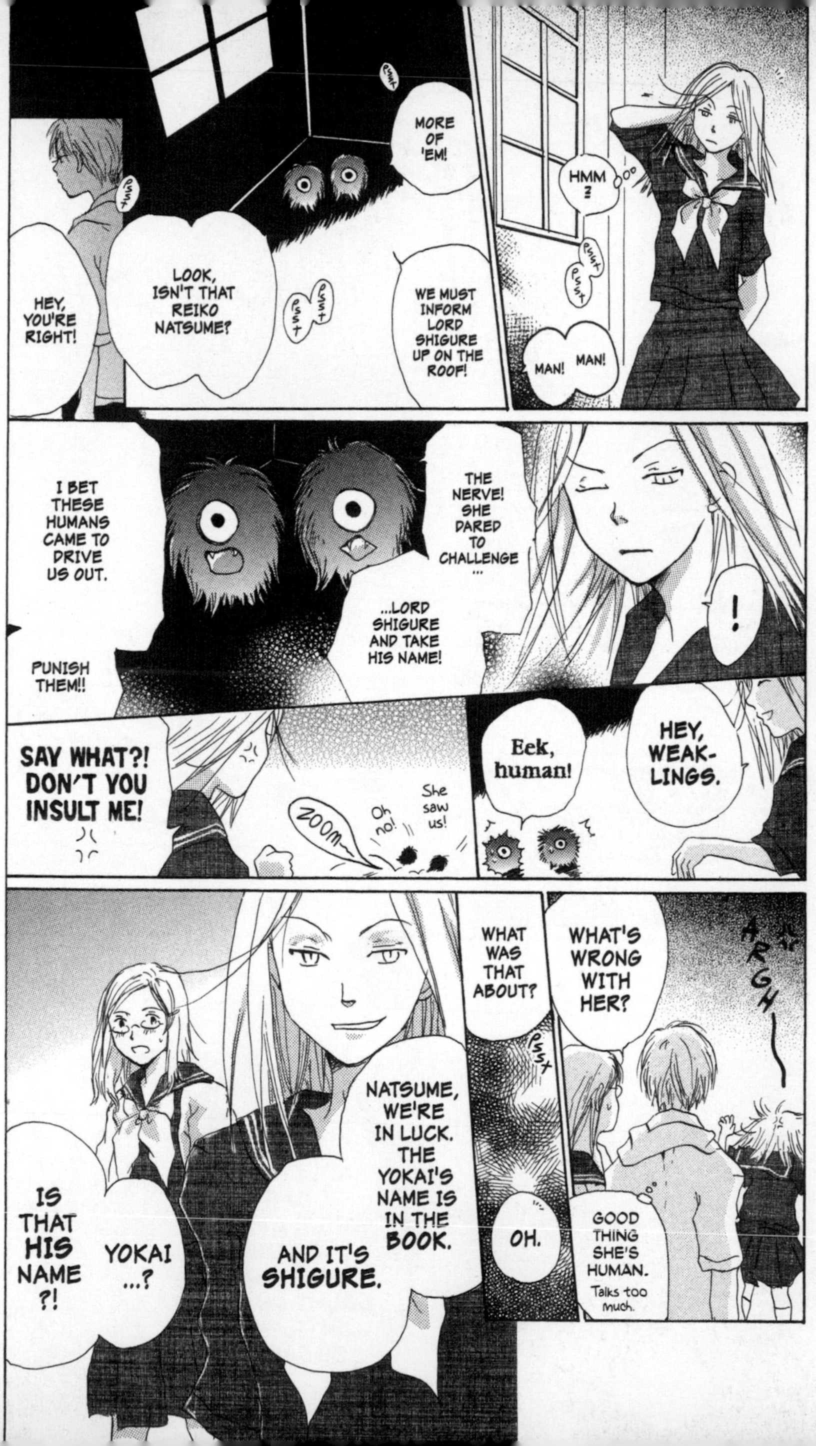
HMM
PSST
PSST
MAN!
MAN!
PSST
MORE OF 'EM!
WE MUST INFORM LORD SHIGURE UP ON THE ROOF!
PSST
PSST
LOOK, ISN'T THAT REIKO NATSUME?
PSST
HEY, YOU'RE RIGHT!
!
THE NERVE! SHE DARED TO CHALLENGE...
...LORD SHIGURE AND TAKE HIS NAME!
I BET THESE HUMANS CAME TO DRIVE US OUT.
PUNISH THEM!!
HEY, WEAK-LINGS.
Eek, human!
She saw us!
Oh no!
ZOOM
SAY WHAT?! DON'T YOU INSULT ME!
ARGH
WHAT'S WRONG WITH HER?
WHAT WAS THAT ABOUT?
PSST
GOOD THING SHE'S HUMAN. Talks too much.
OH.
NATSUME, WE'RE IN LUCK. THE YOKAI'S NAME IS IN THE BOOK.
AND IT'S SHIGURE.
YOKAI ...?
IS THAT HIS NAME?!

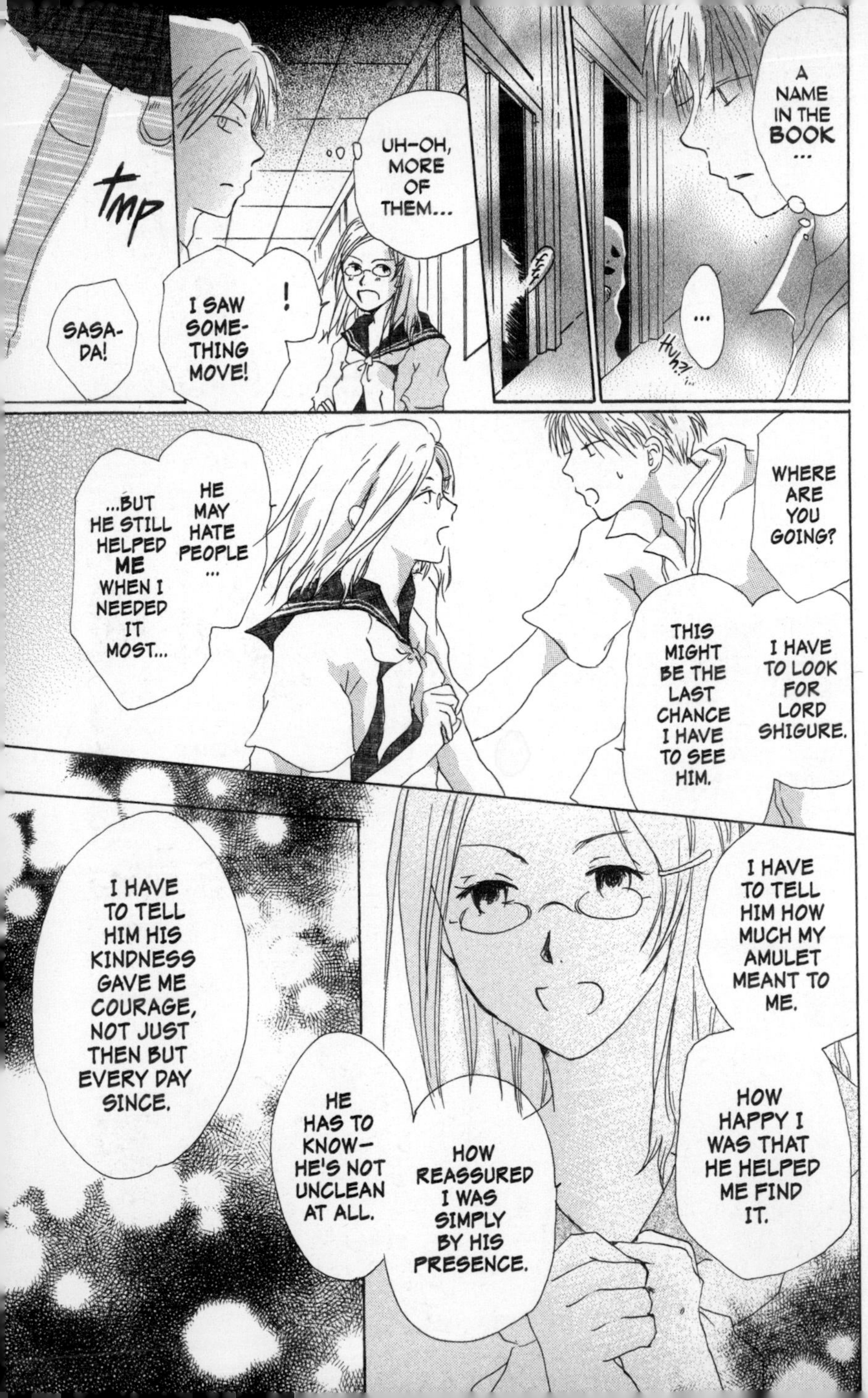
A NAME IN THE BOOK...
...
Huh?!
UH-OH, MORE OF THEM...
tmp
I SAW SOMETHING MOVE!
!
SASA-DA!
WHERE ARE YOU GOING?
I HAVE TO LOOK FOR LORD SHIGURE.
THIS MIGHT BE THE LAST CHANCE I HAVE TO SEE HIM.
HE MAY HATE PEOPLE...
...BUT HE STILL HELPED ME WHEN I NEEDED IT MOST...
I HAVE TO TELL HIM HOW MUCH MY AMULET MEANT TO ME.
HOW HAPPY I WAS THAT HE HELPED ME FIND IT.
HOW REASSURED I WAS SIMPLY BY HIS PRESENCE.
HE HAS TO KNOW—HE'S NOT UNCLEAN AT ALL.
I HAVE TO TELL HIM HIS KINDNESS GAVE ME COURAGE, NOT JUST THEN BUT EVERY DAY SINCE.

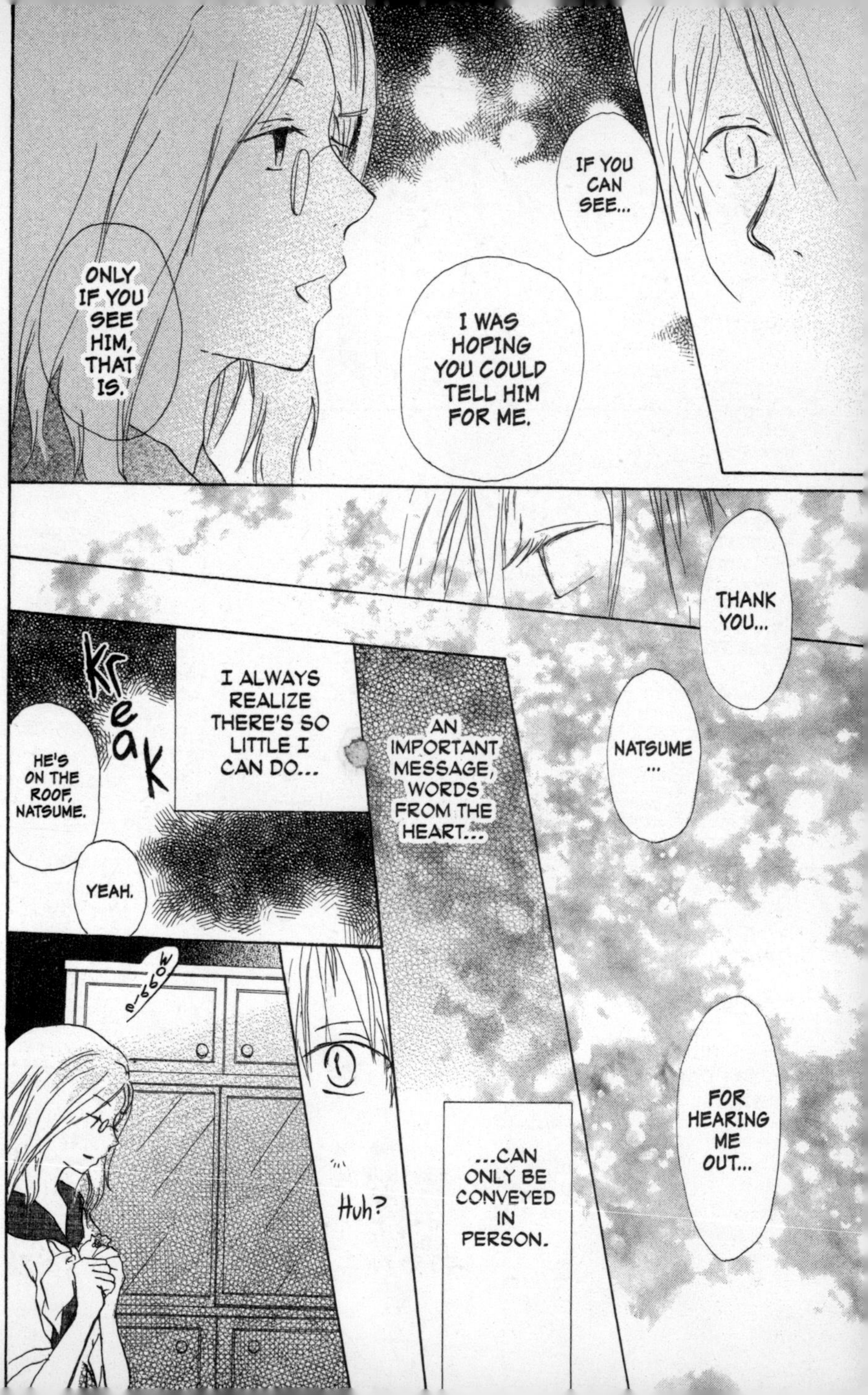
IF YOU CAN SEE...
I WAS HOPING YOU COULD TELL HIM FOR ME.
ONLY IF YOU SEE HIM, THAT IS.
THANK YOU...
NATSUME...
FOR HEARING ME OUT...
AN IMPORTANT MESSAGE, WORDS FROM THE HEART...
I ALWAYS REALIZE THERE'S SO LITTLE I CAN DO...
Kreak
HE'S ON THE ROOF, NATSUME.
YEAH.
...CAN ONLY BE CONVEYED IN PERSON.
Huh?

02

❋ Natsume's Book of Friends: Part 1

The second volume is published, thanks to everyone. Serial stories aren't often done in a bimonthly magazine, but I pretty much ignored any such consideration in the manga I worked on before Natsume. So I made an extra effort this time to make it friendly even to first-time readers in every episode.

I tackle Natsume practically as a one-shot stand-alone story each time, which means I've discovered various difficulties that I've never experienced before. But I'm slowly gaining more and more readers, so I'm happy that I'm finally doing my job right. I hope people can feel like they're reading not a story but a diary of a boy who happens to be able to see yokai.

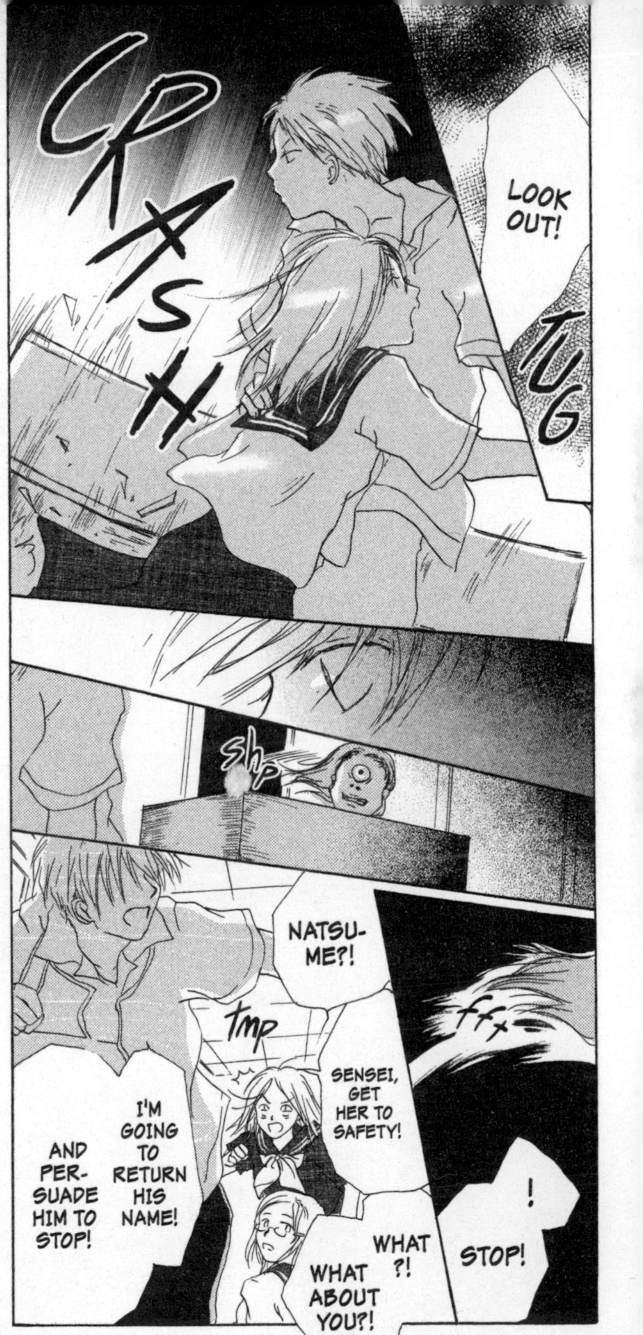
LOOK OUT!
TUG
CRASH
shp
!
STOP!
NATSUME?!
tmp
SENSEI, GET HER TO SAFETY!
I'M GOING TO RETURN HIS NAME!
AND PERSUADE HIM TO STOP!
WHAT?!
WHAT ABOUT YOU?!

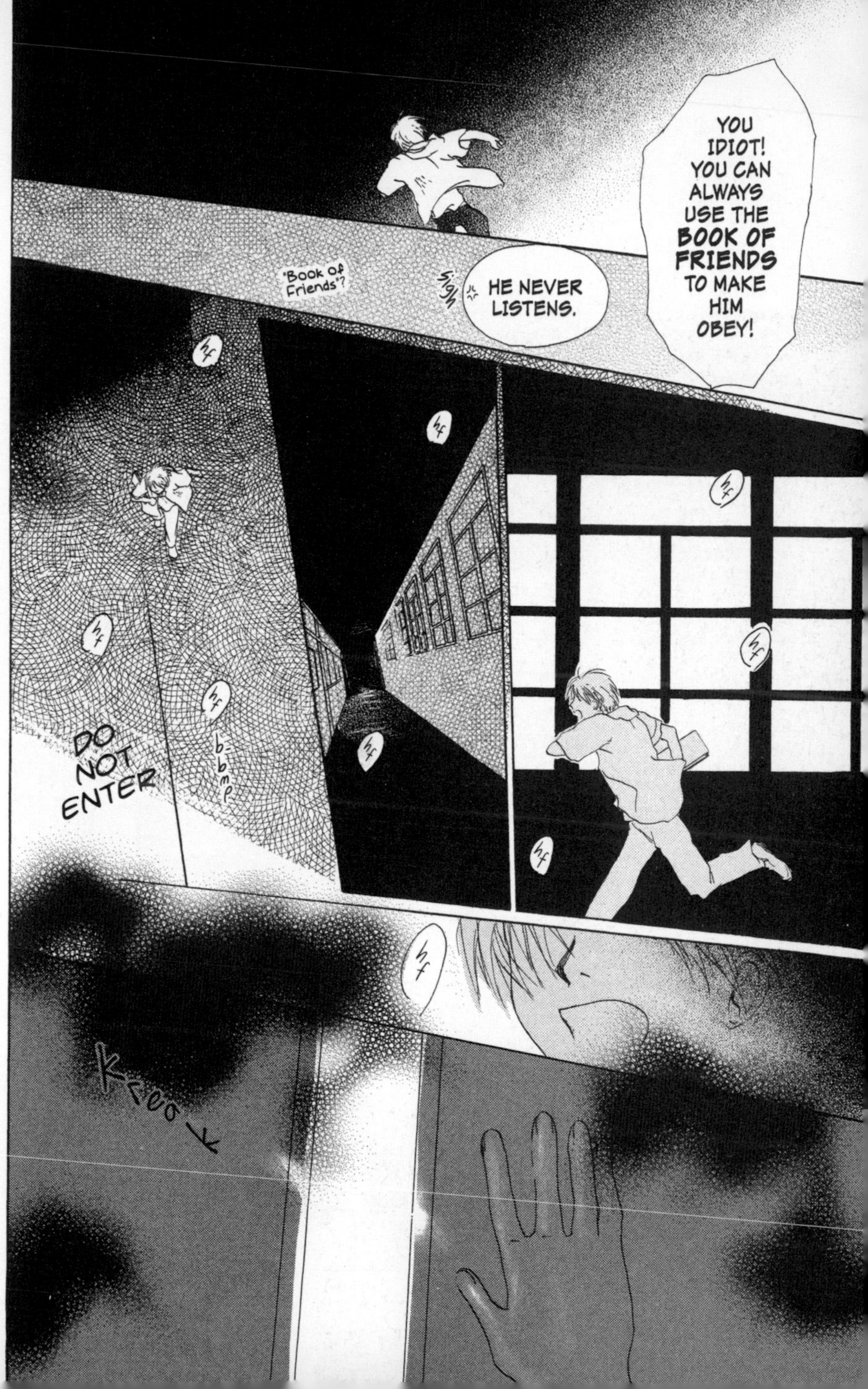
YOU IDIOT! YOU CAN ALWAYS USE THE BOOK OF FRIENDS TO MAKE HIM OBEY!
sigh
HE NEVER LISTENS.
"Book of Friends"?
hf
hf
hf
hf
hf
hf
hf
hf
b-bmp
DO NOT ENTER
hf
Kreeak

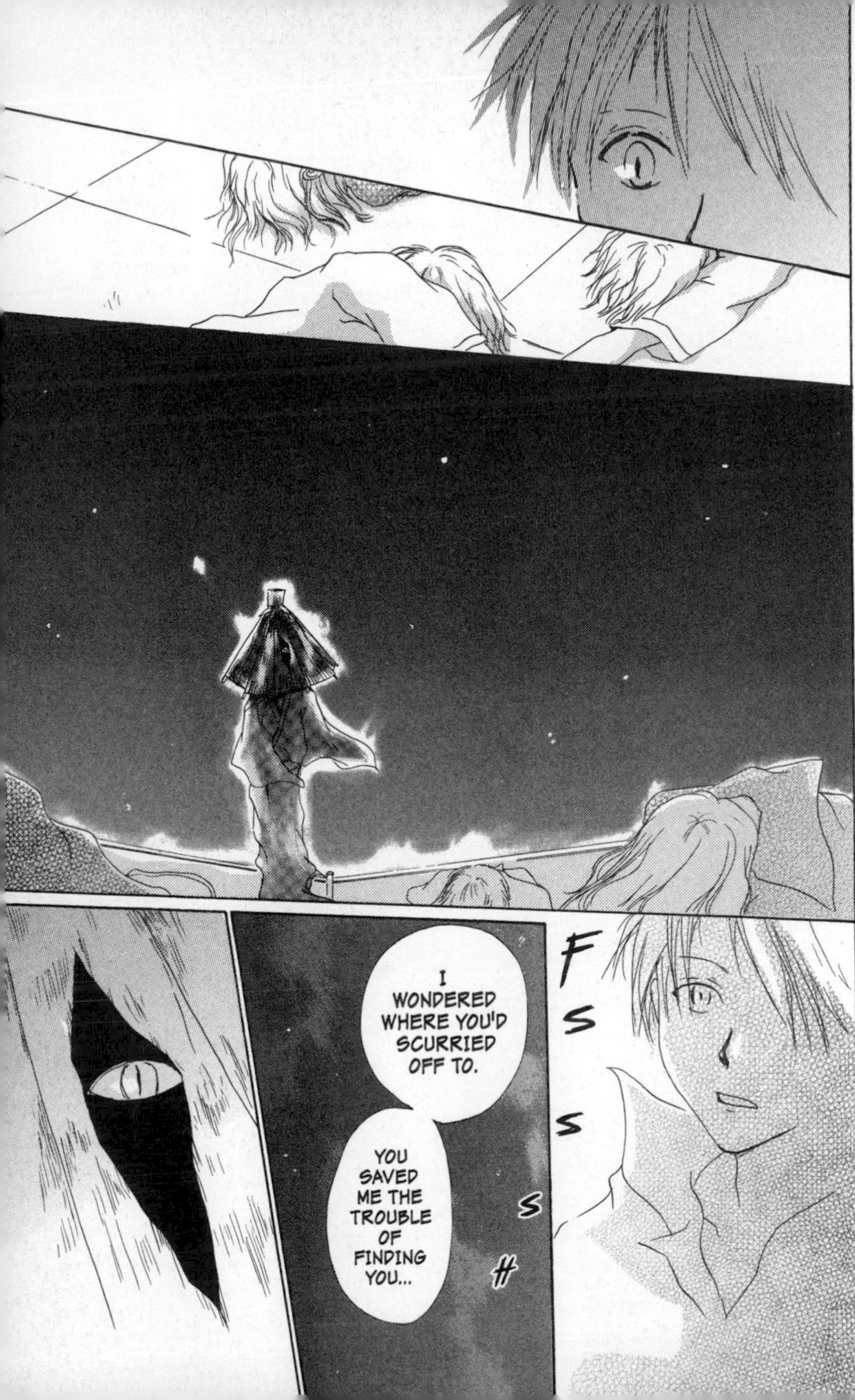
FSSSH
I WONDERED WHERE YOU'D SCURRIED OFF TO.
YOU SAVED ME THE TROUBLE OF FINDING YOU...

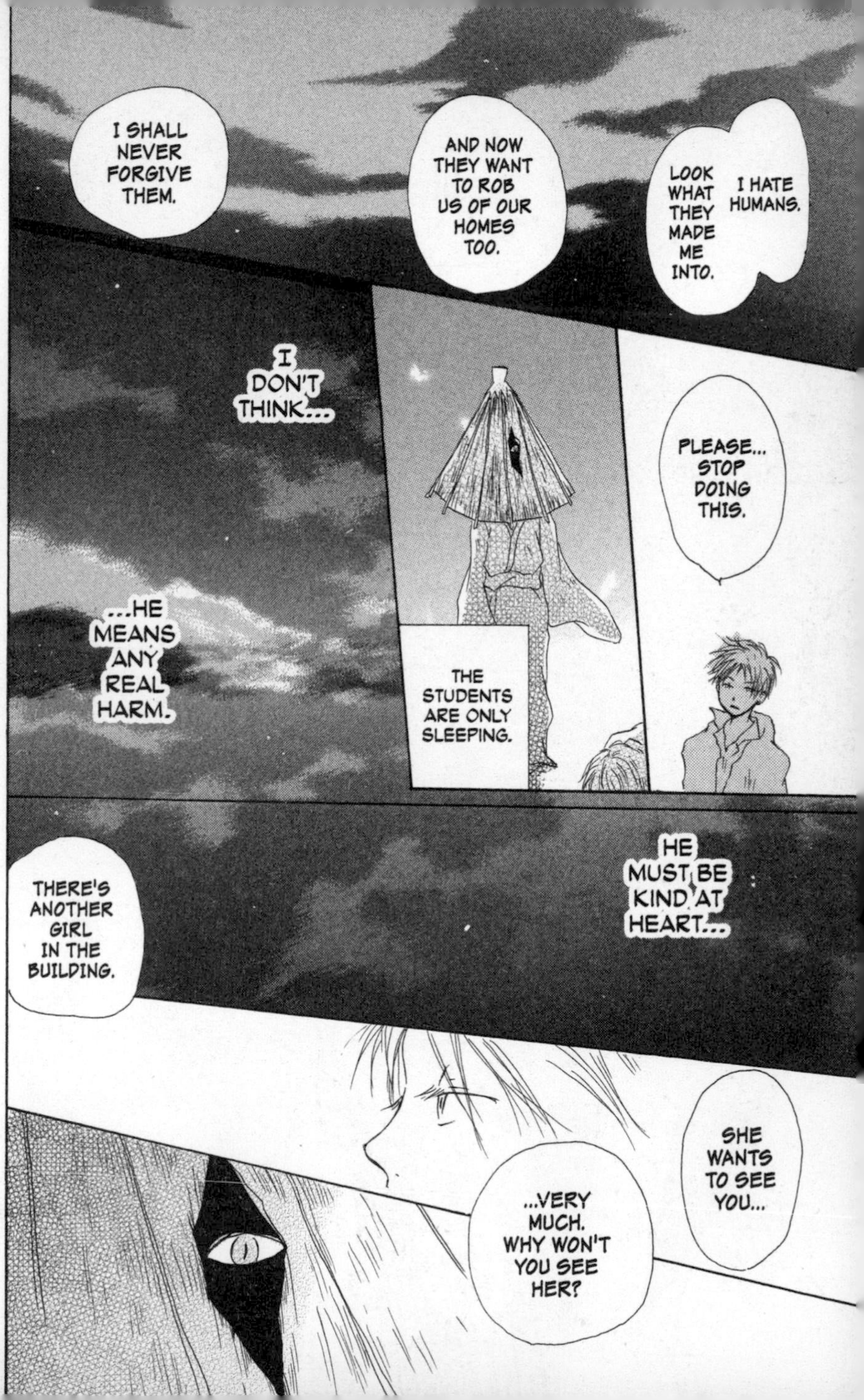
I HATE HUMANS.
LOOK WHAT THEY MADE ME INTO.
AND NOW THEY WANT TO ROB US OF OUR HOMES TOO.
I SHALL NEVER FORGIVE THEM.
PLEASE... STOP DOING THIS.
THE STUDENTS ARE ONLY SLEEPING.
I DON'T THINK...
...HE MEANS ANY REAL HARM.
HE MUST BE KIND AT HEART...
THERE'S ANOTHER GIRL IN THE BUILDING.
SHE WANTS TO SEE YOU...
...VERY MUCH. WHY WON'T YOU SEE HER?

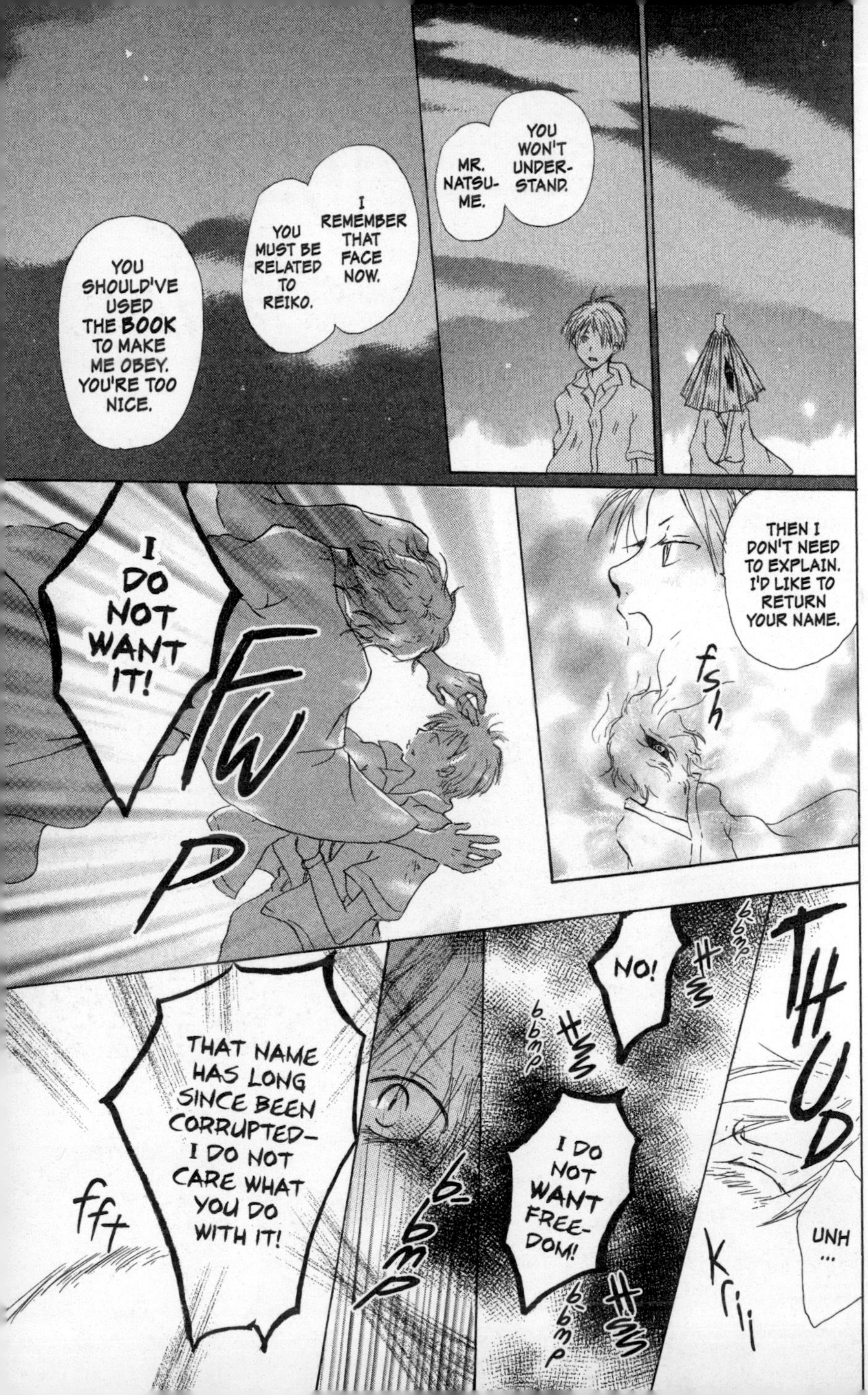
YOU WON'T UNDERSTAND.
MR. NATSUME.
I REMEMBER THAT FACE NOW.
YOU MUST BE RELATED TO REIKO.
YOU SHOULD'VE USED THE BOOK TO MAKE ME OBEY. YOU'RE TOO NICE.
THEN I DON'T NEED TO EXPLAIN. I'D LIKE TO RETURN YOUR NAME.
fsh
I DO NOT WANT IT!
FWP
THUD
b-bmp
NO!
UNH...
Kriii
b-bmp
I DO NOT WANT FREEDOM!
b-bmp
b-bmp
THAT NAME HAS LONG SINCE BEEN CORRUPTED— I DO NOT CARE WHAT YOU DO WITH IT!
fft

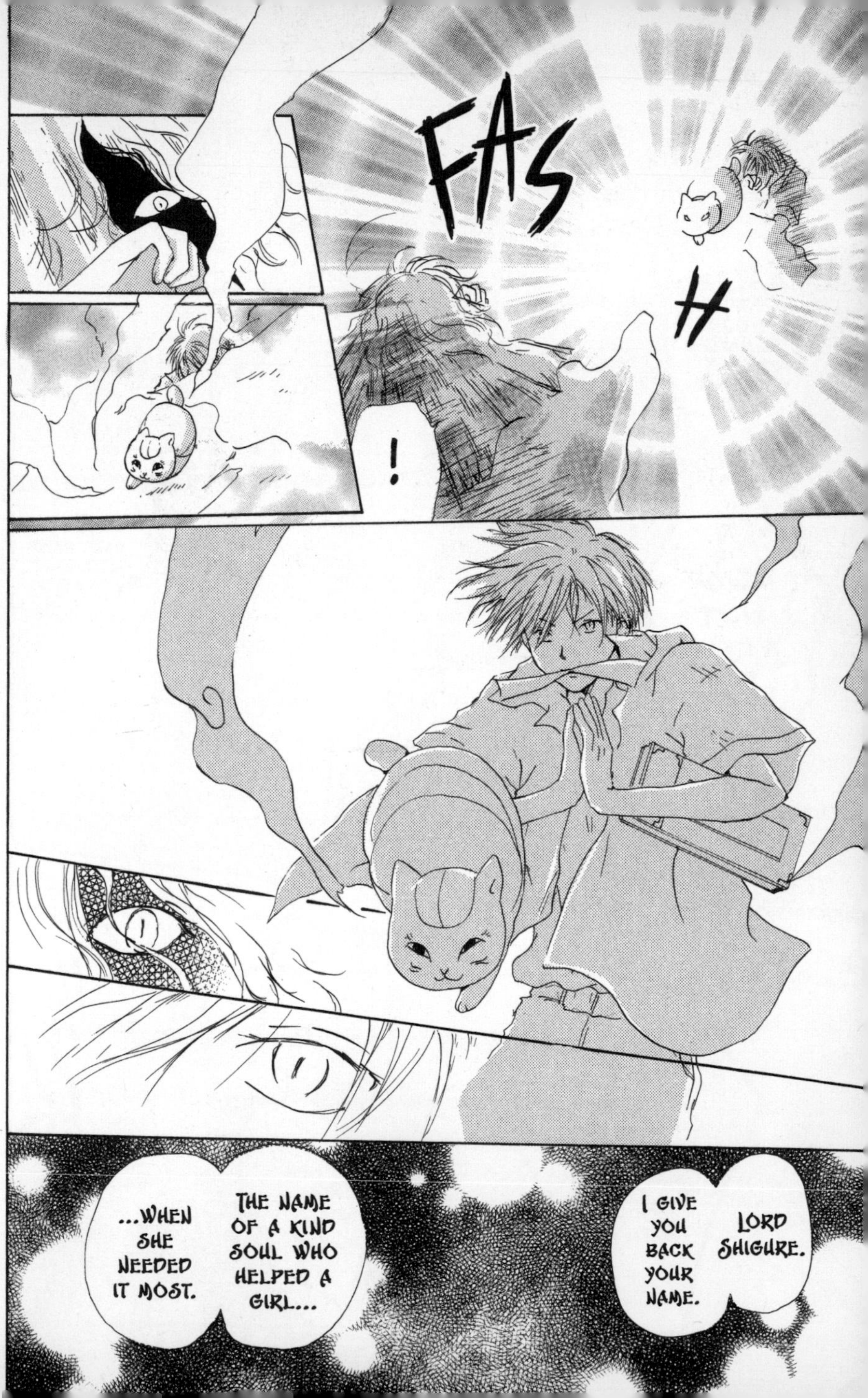
FASH
!
LORD SHIGURE.
I GIVE YOU BACK YOUR NAME.
THE NAME OF A KIND SOUL WHO HELPED A GIRL...
...WHEN SHE NEEDED IT MOST.

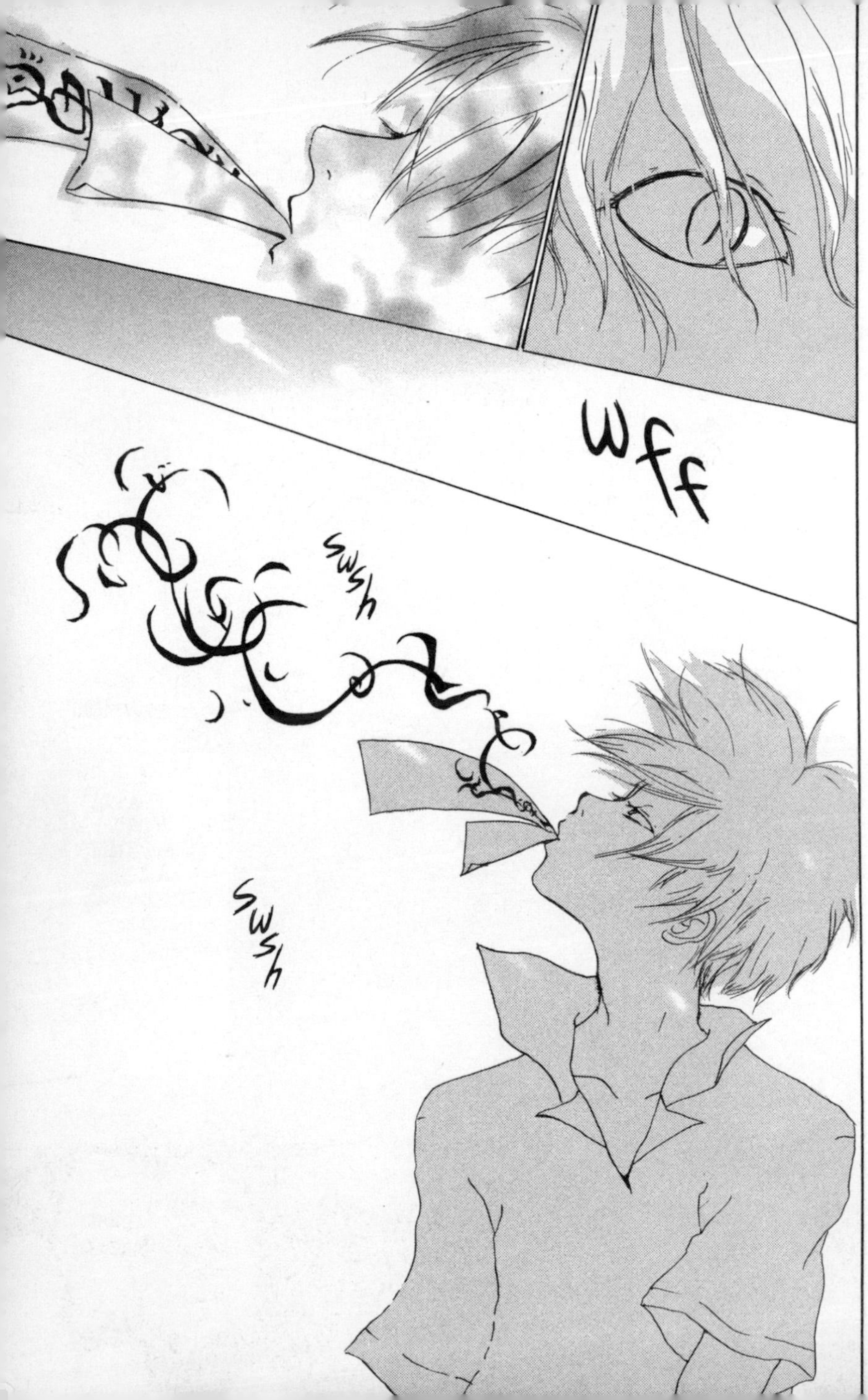
wff
swsh
swsh

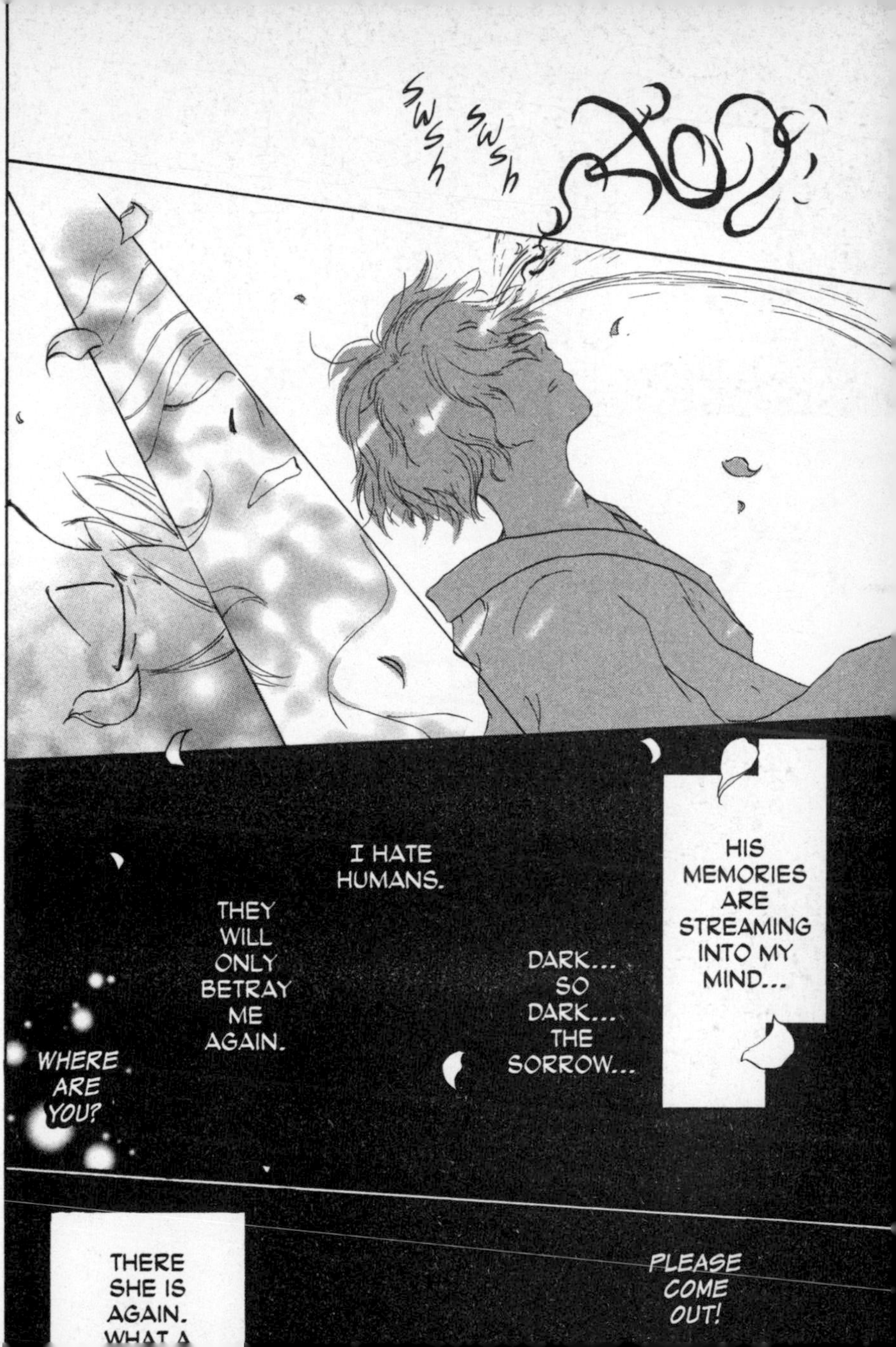
SWSH
SWSH
HIS MEMORIES ARE STREAMING INTO MY MIND...
DARK... SO DARK... THE SORROW...
I HATE HUMANS.
THEY WILL ONLY BETRAY ME AGAIN.
WHERE ARE YOU?
PLEASE COME OUT!
THERE SHE IS AGAIN. WHAT A

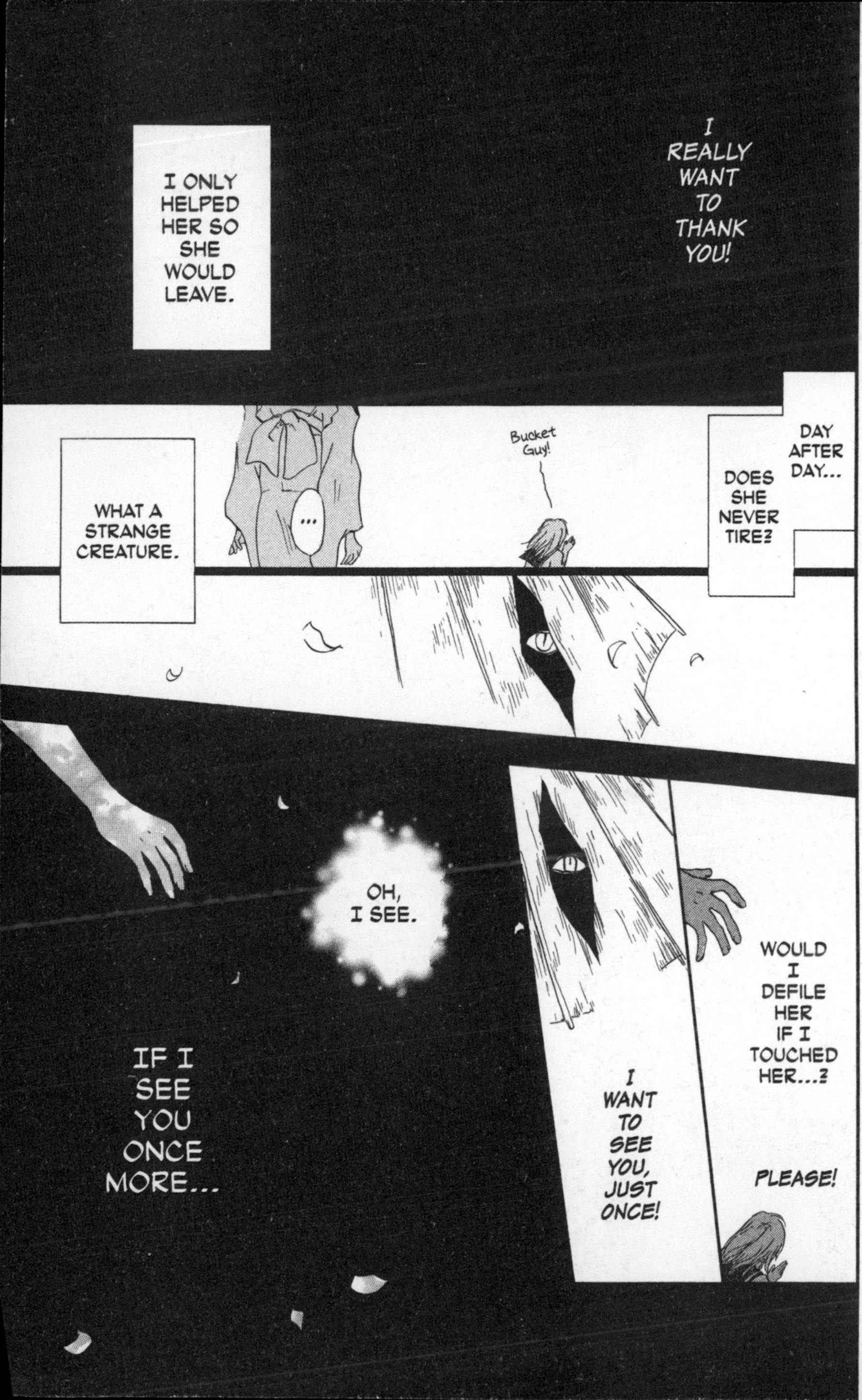
I REALLY WANT TO THANK YOU!
I ONLY HELPED HER SO SHE WOULD LEAVE.
DAY AFTER DAY...
DOES SHE NEVER TIRE?
Bucket Guy!
...
WHAT A STRANGE CREATURE.
WOULD I DEFILE HER IF I TOUCHED HER...?
PLEASE!
I WANT TO SEE YOU, JUST ONCE!
OH, I SEE.
IF I SEE YOU ONCE MORE...

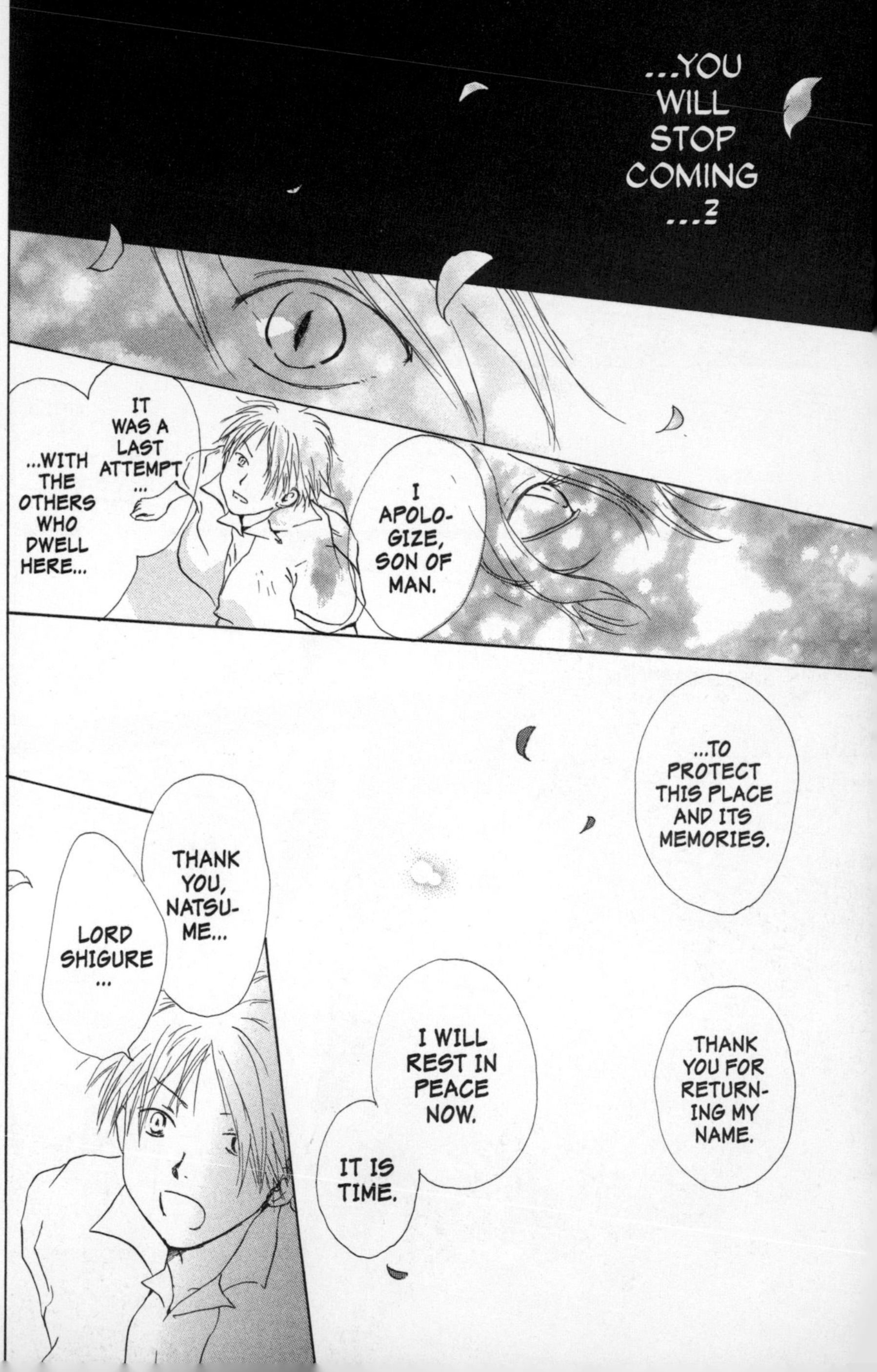
...YOU WILL STOP COMING...?
I APOLOGIZE, SON OF MAN.
IT WAS A LAST ATTEMPT...
...WITH THE OTHERS WHO DWELL HERE...
...TO PROTECT THIS PLACE AND ITS MEMORIES.
THANK YOU FOR RETURNING MY NAME.
I WILL REST IN PEACE NOW.
IT IS TIME.
THANK YOU, NATSUME...
LORD SHIGURE...

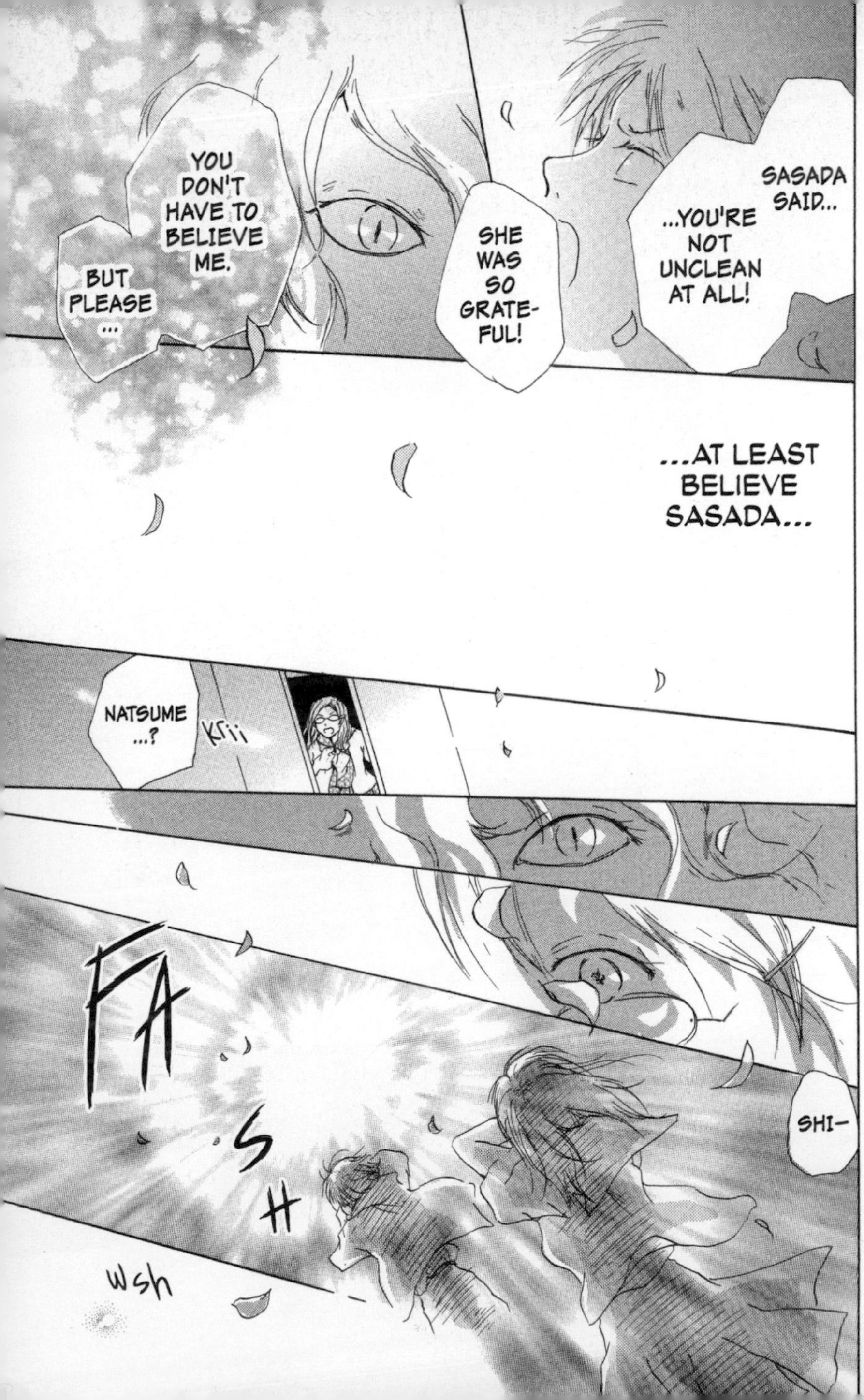
SASADA SAID...
...YOU'RE NOT UNCLEAN AT ALL!
SHE WAS SO GRATE-FUL!
YOU DON'T HAVE TO BELIEVE ME.
BUT PLEASE ...
...AT LEAST BELIEVE SASADA...
NATSUME ...?
Krii
SHI-
FASH
wsh

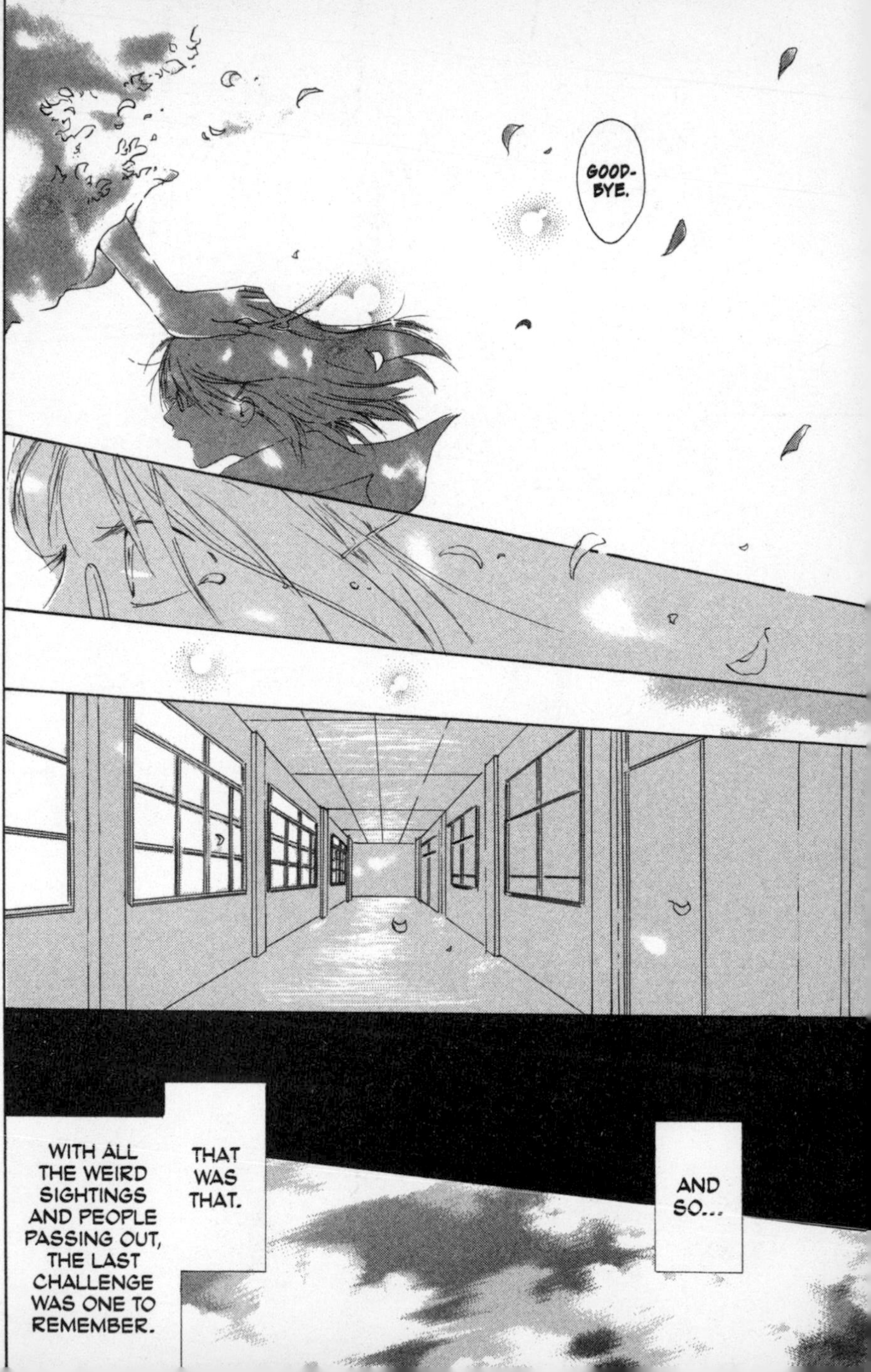
GOOD-BYE.
AND SO...
THAT WAS THAT.
WITH ALL THE WEIRD SIGHTINGS AND PEOPLE PASSING OUT, THE LAST CHALLENGE WAS ONE TO REMEMBER.

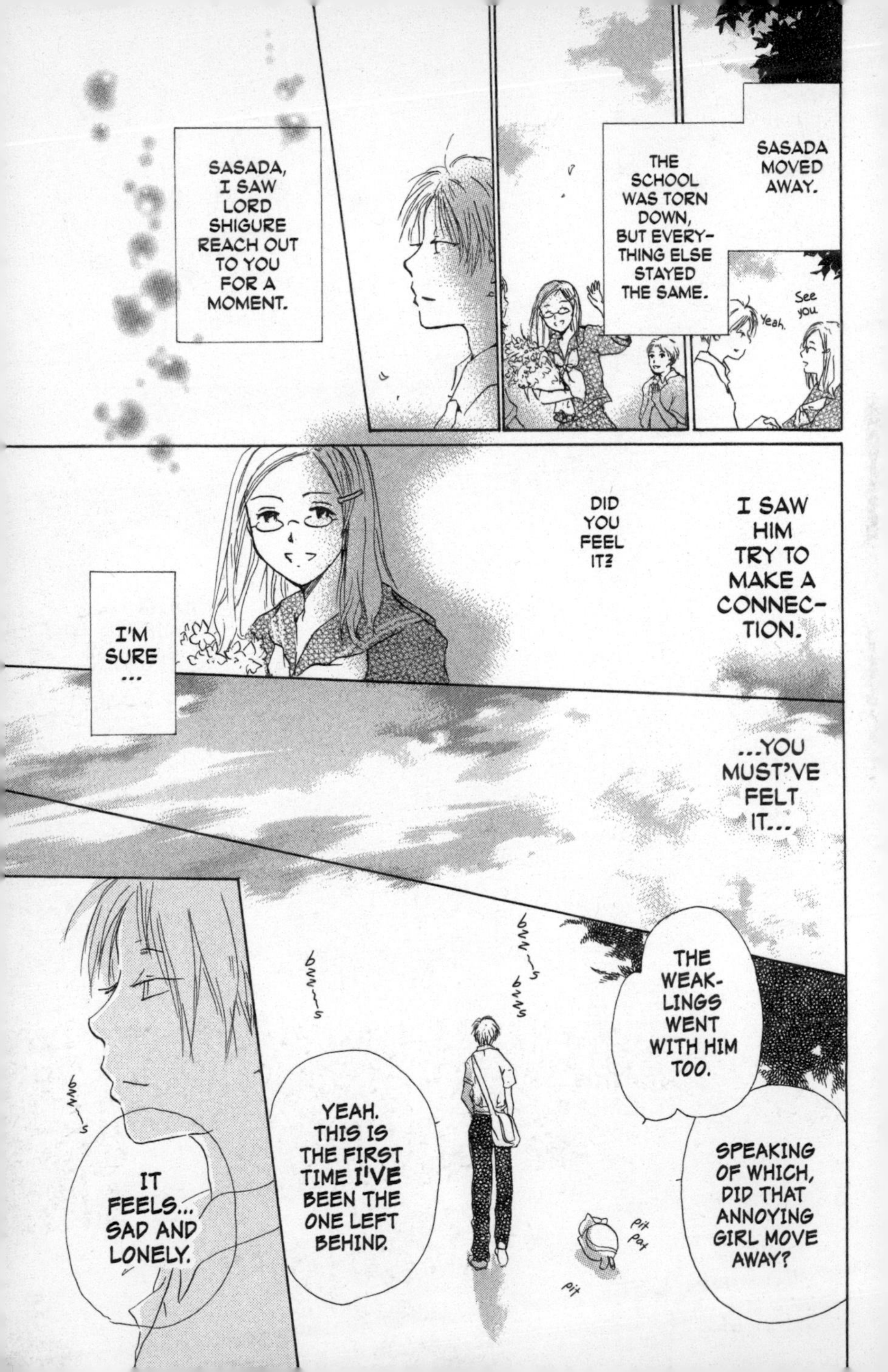
SASADA MOVED AWAY.
See you.
Yeah.
THE SCHOOL WAS TORN DOWN, BUT EVERY-THING ELSE STAYED THE SAME.
SASADA, I SAW LORD SHIGURE REACH OUT TO YOU FOR A MOMENT.
I SAW HIM TRY TO MAKE A CONNEC-TION.
DID YOU FEEL IT?
I'M SURE...
...YOU MUST'VE FELT IT...
THE WEAK-LINGS WENT WITH HIM TOO.
SPEAKING OF WHICH, DID THAT ANNOYING GIRL MOVE AWAY?
pit pat
pit
bzzz
bzzz
bzzz
YEAH. THIS IS THE FIRST TIME I'VE BEEN THE ONE LEFT BEHIND.
bzzz
IT FEELS... SAD AND LONELY.

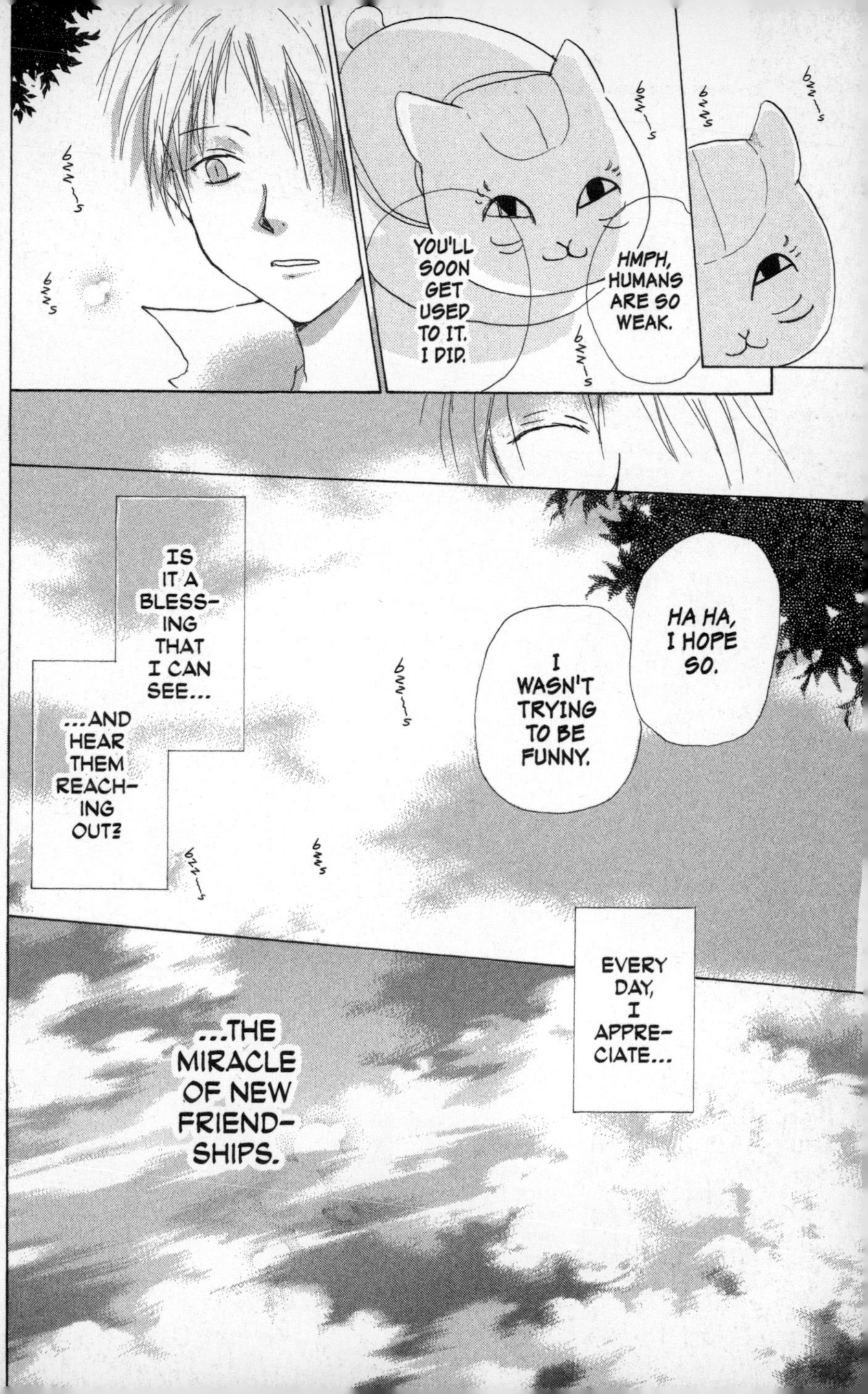
HMPH, HUMANS ARE SO WEAK.
YOU'LL SOON GET USED TO IT. I DID.
HA HA, I HOPE SO.
I WASN'T TRYING TO BE FUNNY.
IS IT A BLESSING THAT I CAN SEE...
...AND HEAR THEM REACHING OUT?
EVERY DAY, I APPRECIATE...
...THE MIRACLE OF NEW FRIENDSHIPS.

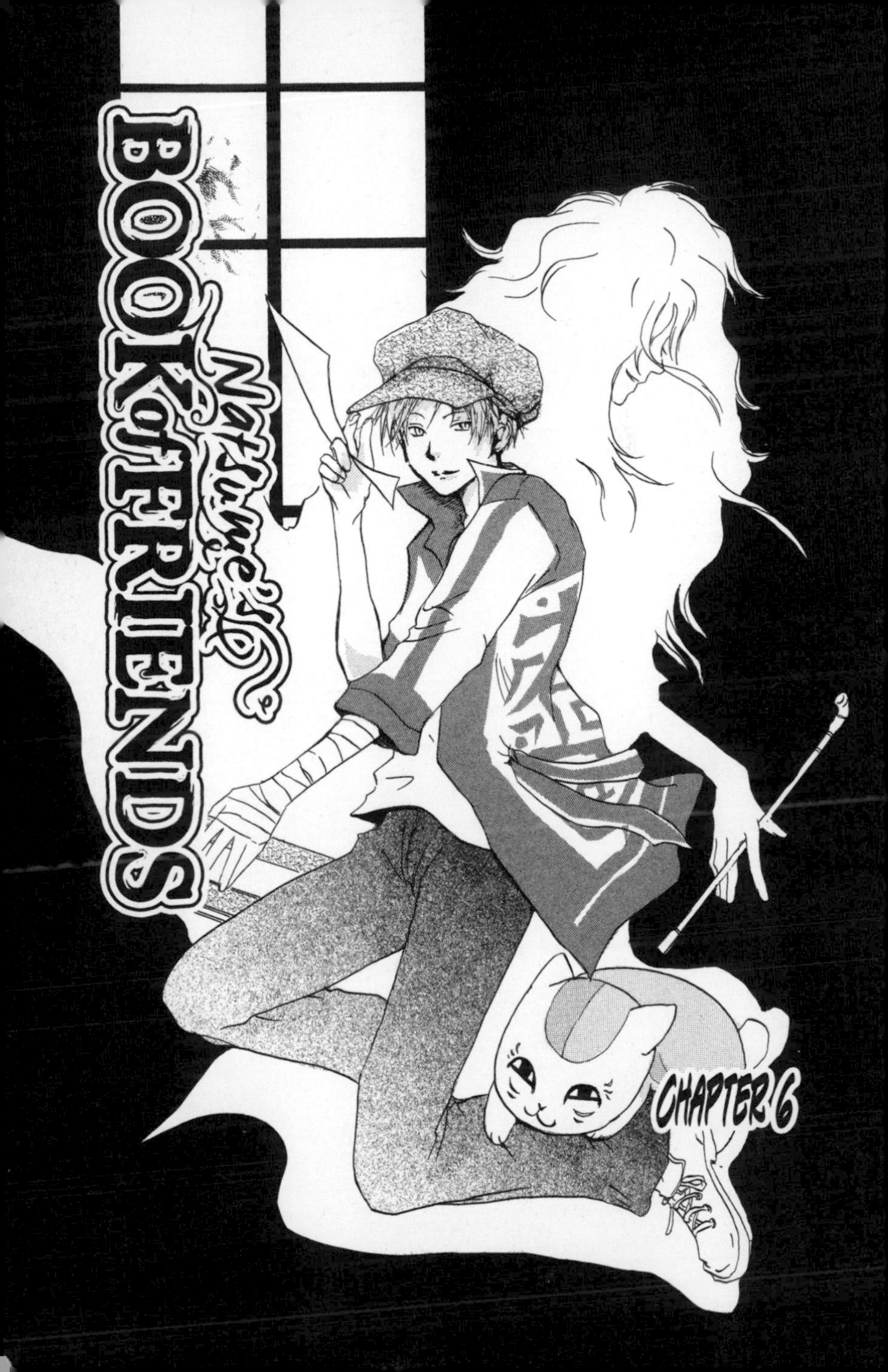
Natsume's
BOOK of FRIENDS
CHAPTER 6

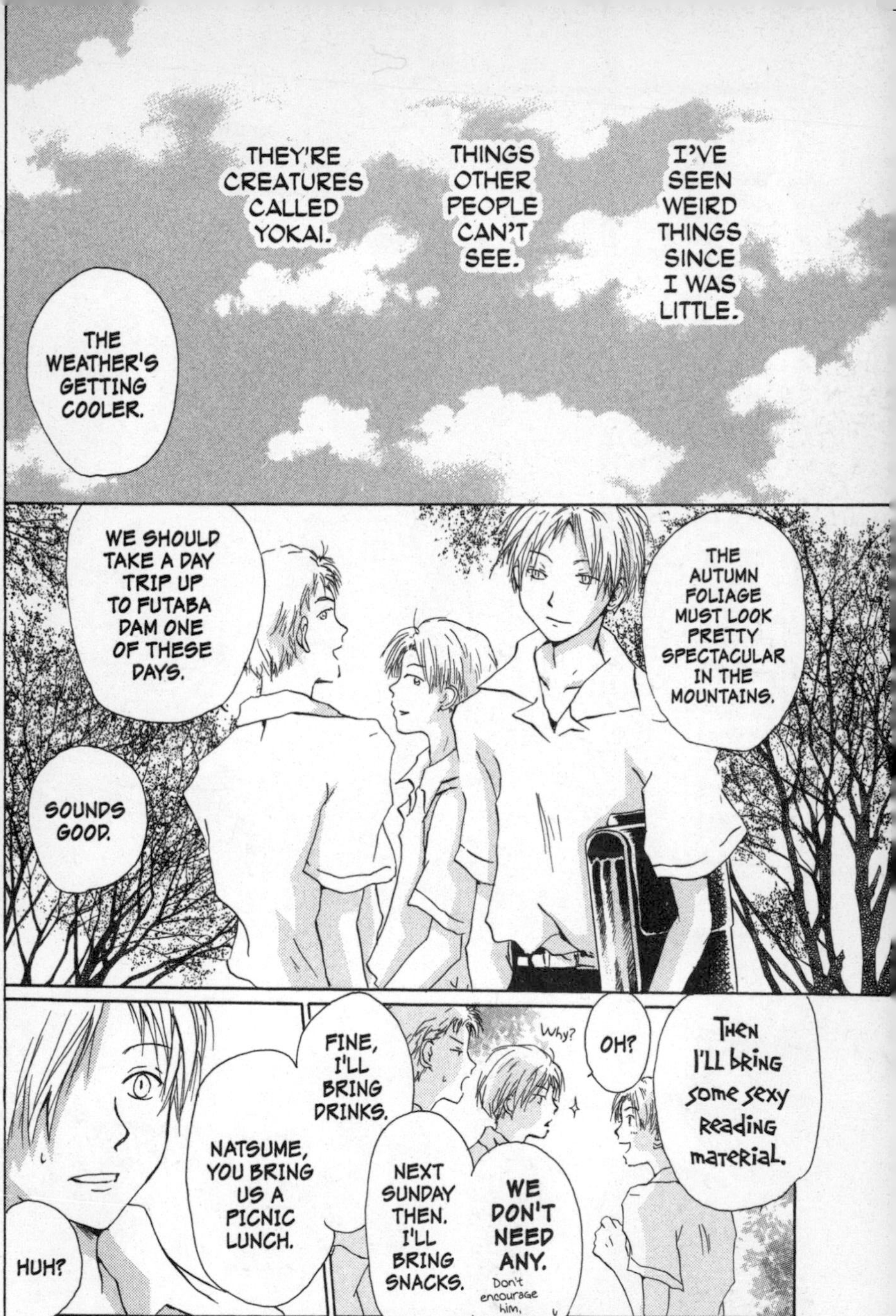
I'VE SEEN WEIRD THINGS SINCE I WAS LITTLE.
THINGS OTHER PEOPLE CAN'T SEE.
THEY'RE CREATURES CALLED YOKAI.
THE WEATHER'S GETTING COOLER.
THE AUTUMN FOLIAGE MUST LOOK PRETTY SPECTACULAR IN THE MOUNTAINS.
WE SHOULD TAKE A DAY TRIP UP TO FUTABA DAM ONE OF THESE DAYS.
SOUNDS GOOD.
Then I'll bring some sexy reading material.
OH?
Why?
WE DON'T NEED ANY.
Don't encourage him, Natsume.
NEXT SUNDAY THEN. I'LL BRING SNACKS.
FINE, I'LL BRING DRINKS.
NATSUME, YOU BRING US A PICNIC LUNCH.
HUH?

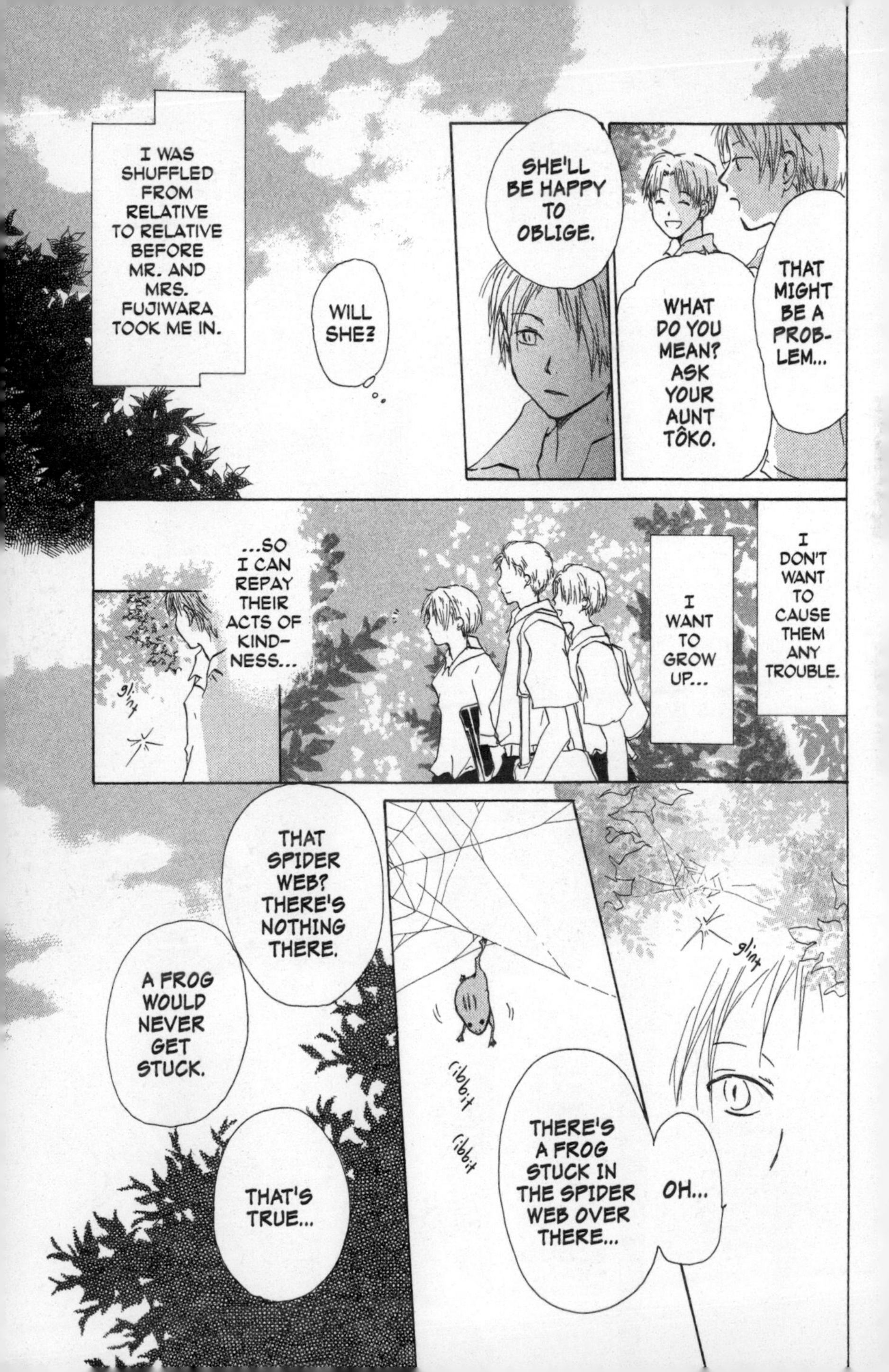
THAT MIGHT BE A PROB-LEM...
WHAT DO YOU MEAN? ASK YOUR AUNT TÔKO.
SHE'LL BE HAPPY TO OBLIGE.
WILL SHE?
I WAS SHUFFLED FROM RELATIVE TO RELATIVE BEFORE MR. AND MRS. FUJIWARA TOOK ME IN.
I DON'T WANT TO CAUSE THEM ANY TROUBLE.
I WANT TO GROW UP...
...SO I CAN REPAY THEIR ACTS OF KIND-NESS...
glint
glint
OH...
THERE'S A FROG STUCK IN THE SPIDER WEB OVER THERE...
ribbit
ribbit
THAT SPIDER WEB? THERE'S NOTHING THERE.
A FROG WOULD NEVER GET STUCK.
THAT'S TRUE...

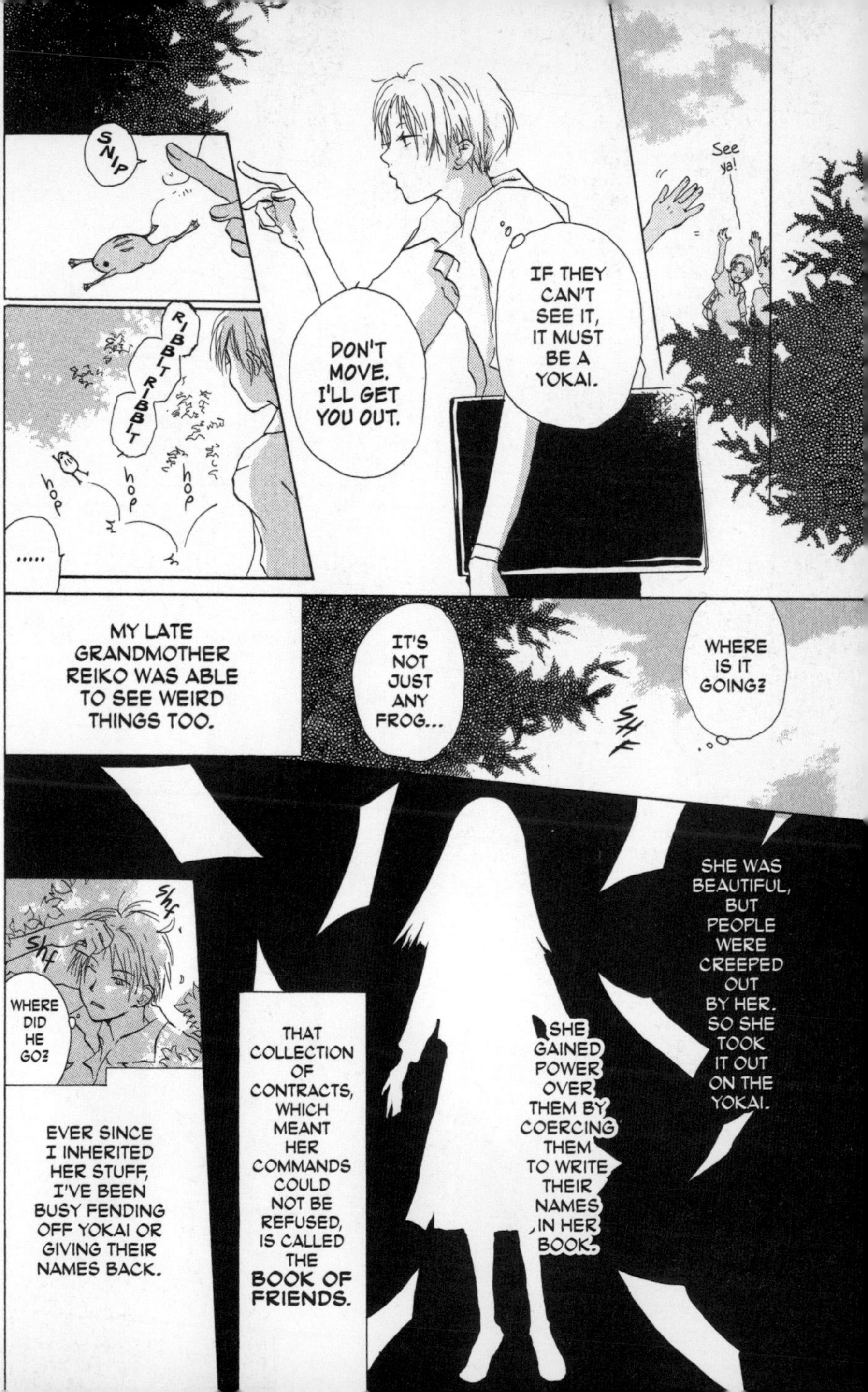
See ya!
IF THEY CAN'T SEE IT, IT MUST BE A YOKAI.
DON'T MOVE. I'LL GET YOU OUT.
SNIP
RIBBIT RIBBIT RIBBIT
hop hop hop
......
WHERE IS IT GOING?
SHF
IT'S NOT JUST ANY FROG...
MY LATE GRANDMOTHER REIKO WAS ABLE TO SEE WEIRD THINGS TOO.
SHE WAS BEAUTIFUL, BUT PEOPLE WERE CREEPED OUT BY HER. SO SHE TOOK IT OUT ON THE YOKAI.
SHE GAINED POWER OVER THEM BY COERCING THEM TO WRITE THEIR NAMES IN HER BOOK.
THAT COLLECTION OF CONTRACTS, WHICH MEANT HER COMMANDS COULD NOT BE REFUSED, IS CALLED THE BOOK OF FRIENDS.
shf
shf
WHERE DID HE GO?
EVER SINCE I INHERITED HER STUFF, I'VE BEEN BUSY FENDING OFF YOKAI OR GIVING THEIR NAMES BACK.

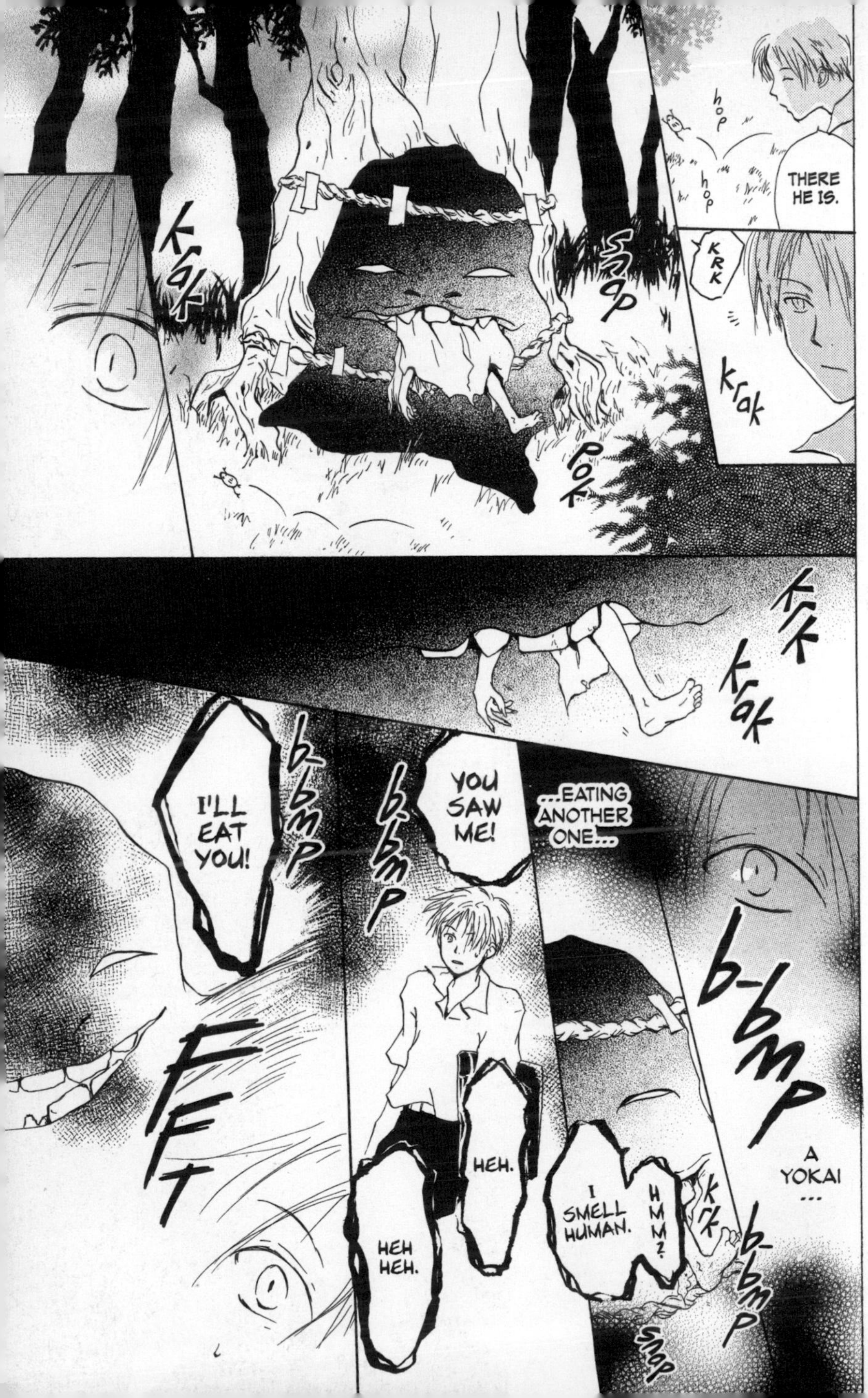
hop
hop
THERE HE IS.
KRK
krak
snap
pok
krak
krk
krak
b-bmp
A YOKAI...
b-bmp
...EATING ANOTHER ONE...
HMM?
I SMELL HUMAN.
krk
snap
YOU SAW ME!
b-bmp
HEH.
HEH HEH.
I'LL EAT YOU!
b-bmp
FFFT

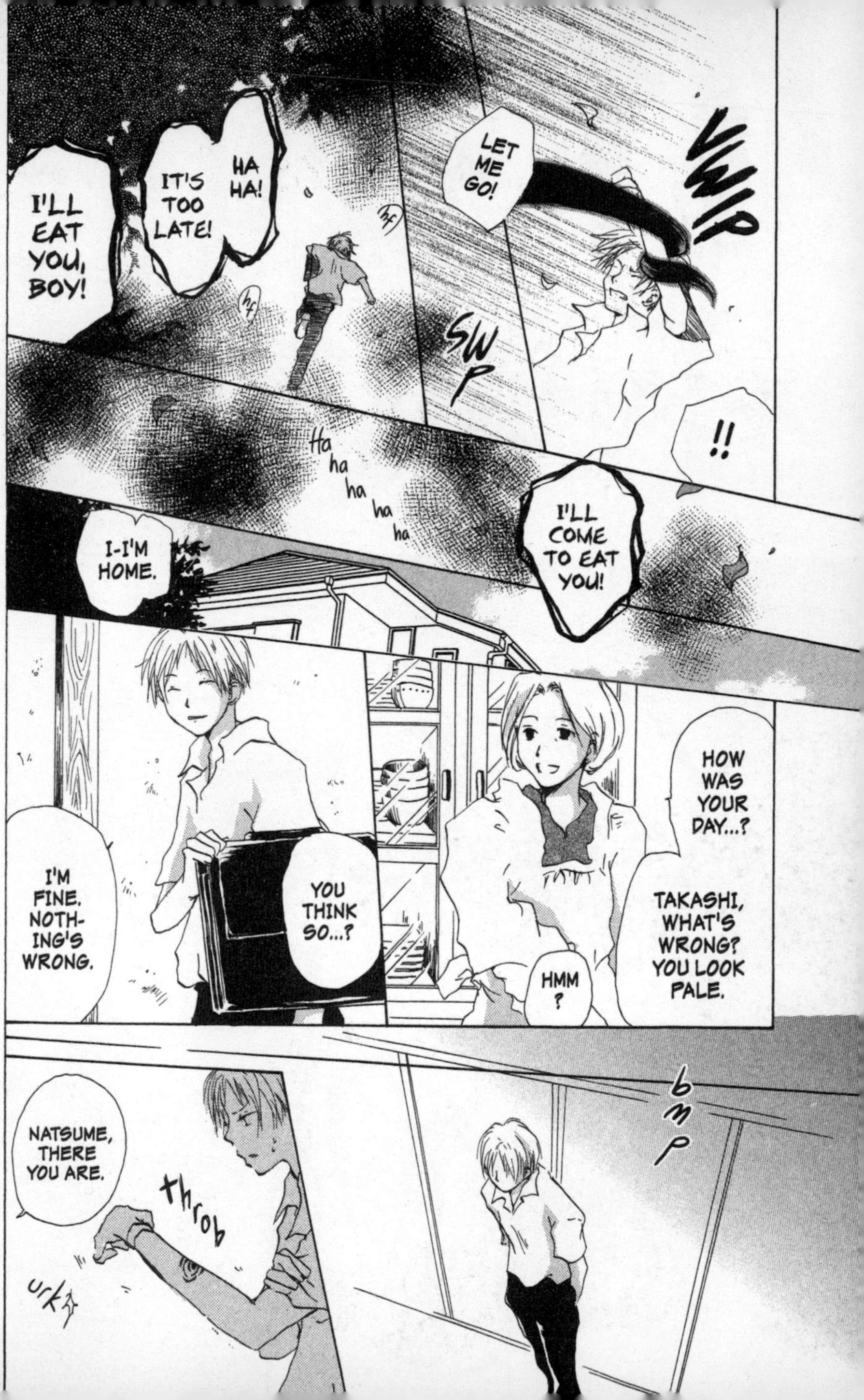
LET ME GO!
VWIP
SWP
HA HA!
IT'S TOO LATE!
I'LL EAT YOU, BOY!
hf
hf
!!
I'LL COME TO EAT YOU!
Ha ha ha ha ha
I-I'M HOME.
HOW WAS YOUR DAY...?
TAKASHI, WHAT'S WRONG? YOU LOOK PALE.
HMM?
YOU THINK SO...?
I'M FINE. NOTH-ING'S WRONG.
bmp
NATSUME, THERE YOU ARE.
throb
urk

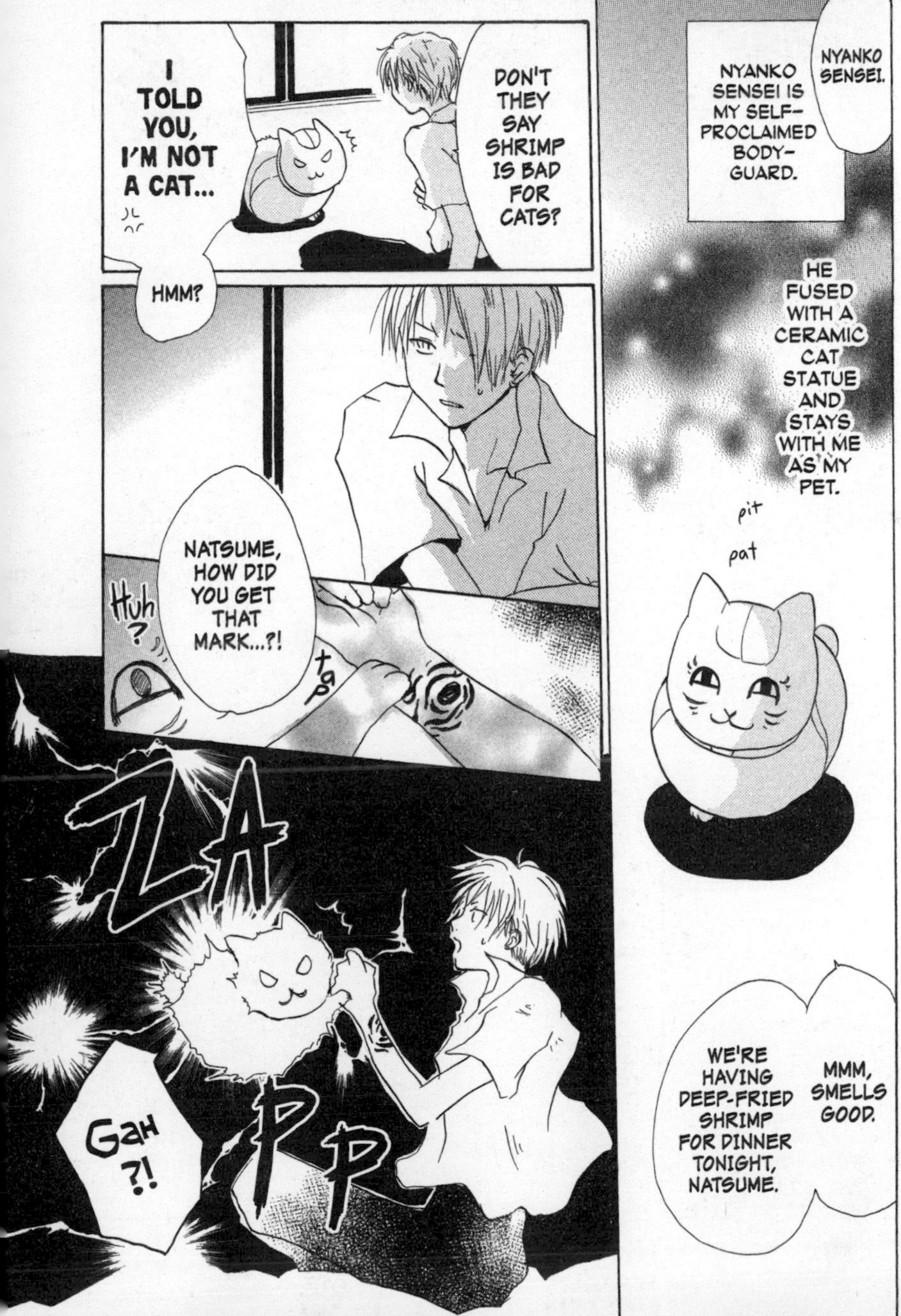
NYANKO SENSEI.
NYANKO SENSEI IS MY SELF-PROCLAIMED BODY-GUARD.
HE FUSED WITH A CERAMIC CAT STATUE AND STAYS WITH ME AS MY PET.
pit
pat
MMM, SMELLS GOOD.
WE'RE HAVING DEEP-FRIED SHRIMP FOR DINNER TONIGHT, NATSUME.
DON'T THEY SAY SHRIMP IS BAD FOR CATS?
I TOLD YOU, I'M NOT A CAT...
HMM?
NATSUME, HOW DID YOU GET THAT MARK...?!
tap
Huh?
ZAPP
Gah?!

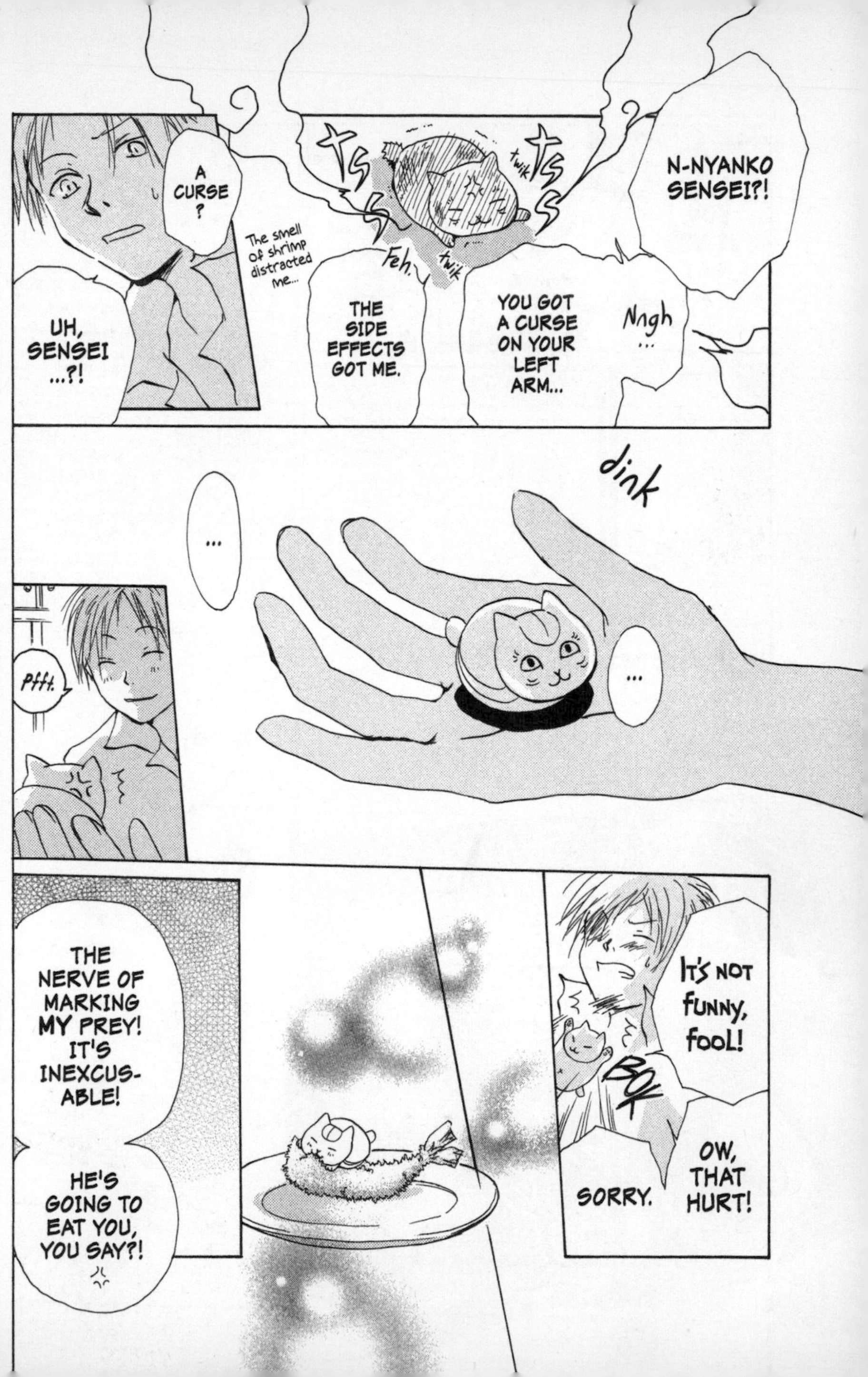

N-NYANKO SENSEI?!
Nngh...
twik
YOU GOT A CURSE ON YOUR LEFT ARM...
THE SIDE EFFECTS GOT ME.
Feh.
twik
The smell of shrimp distracted me...
A CURSE?
UH, SENSEI...?!
dink
...
...
Pfft.
IT'S NOT FUNNY, FOOL!
BOK
OW, THAT HURT!
SORRY.
THE NERVE OF MARKING MY PREY! IT'S INEXCUS-ABLE!
HE'S GOING TO EAT YOU, YOU SAY?!

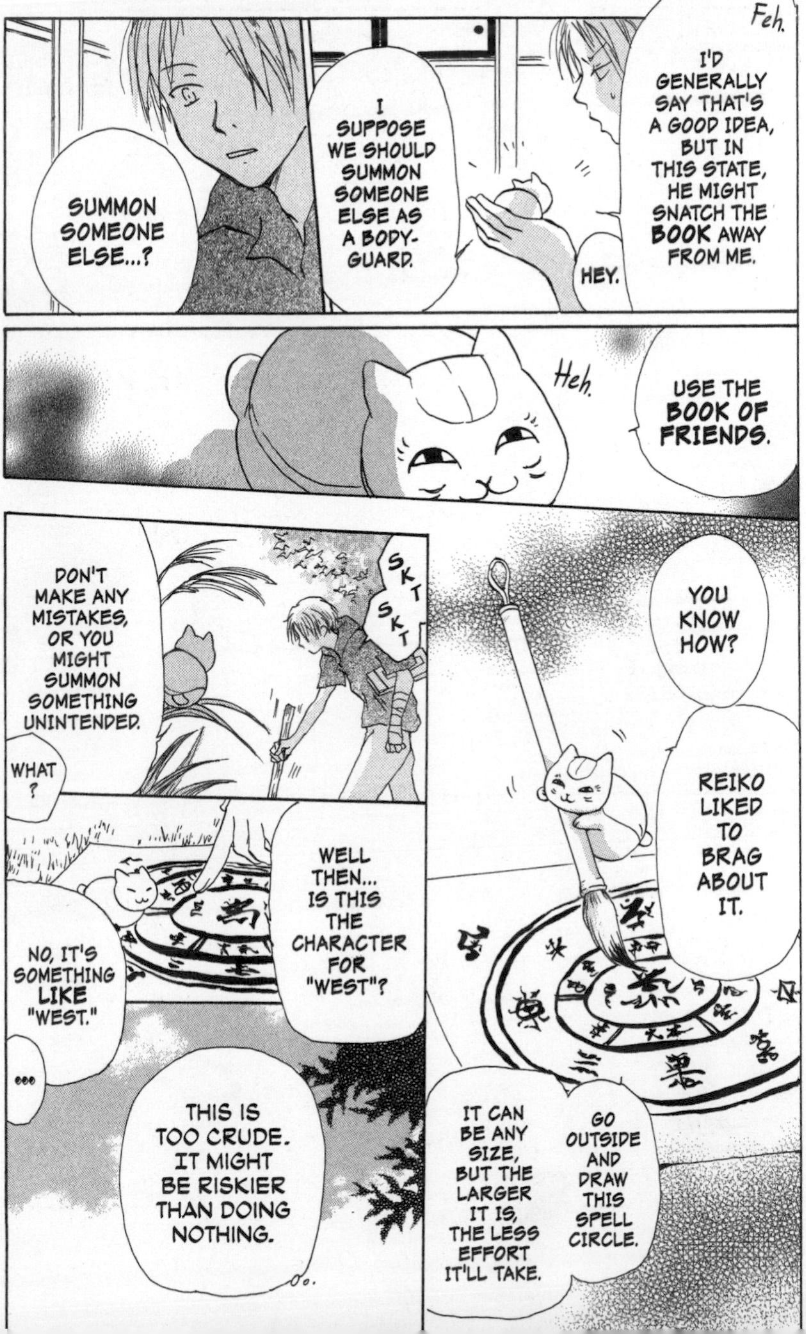
Feh.
I'D GENERALLY SAY THAT'S A GOOD IDEA, BUT IN THIS STATE, HE MIGHT SNATCH THE BOOK AWAY FROM ME.
HEY.
I SUPPOSE WE SHOULD SUMMON SOMEONE ELSE AS A BODY-GUARD.
SUMMON SOMEONE ELSE...?
USE THE BOOK OF FRIENDS.
Heh.
YOU KNOW HOW?
REIKO LIKED TO BRAG ABOUT IT.
GO OUTSIDE AND DRAW THIS SPELL CIRCLE.
IT CAN BE ANY SIZE, BUT THE LARGER IT IS, THE LESS EFFORT IT'LL TAKE.
SKT SKT
DON'T MAKE ANY MISTAKES, OR YOU MIGHT SUMMON SOMETHING UNINTENDED.
WHAT?
WELL THEN... IS THIS THE CHARACTER FOR "WEST"?
NO, IT'S SOMETHING LIKE "WEST."
THIS IS TOO CRUDE. IT MIGHT BE RISKIER THAN DOING NOTHING.
...

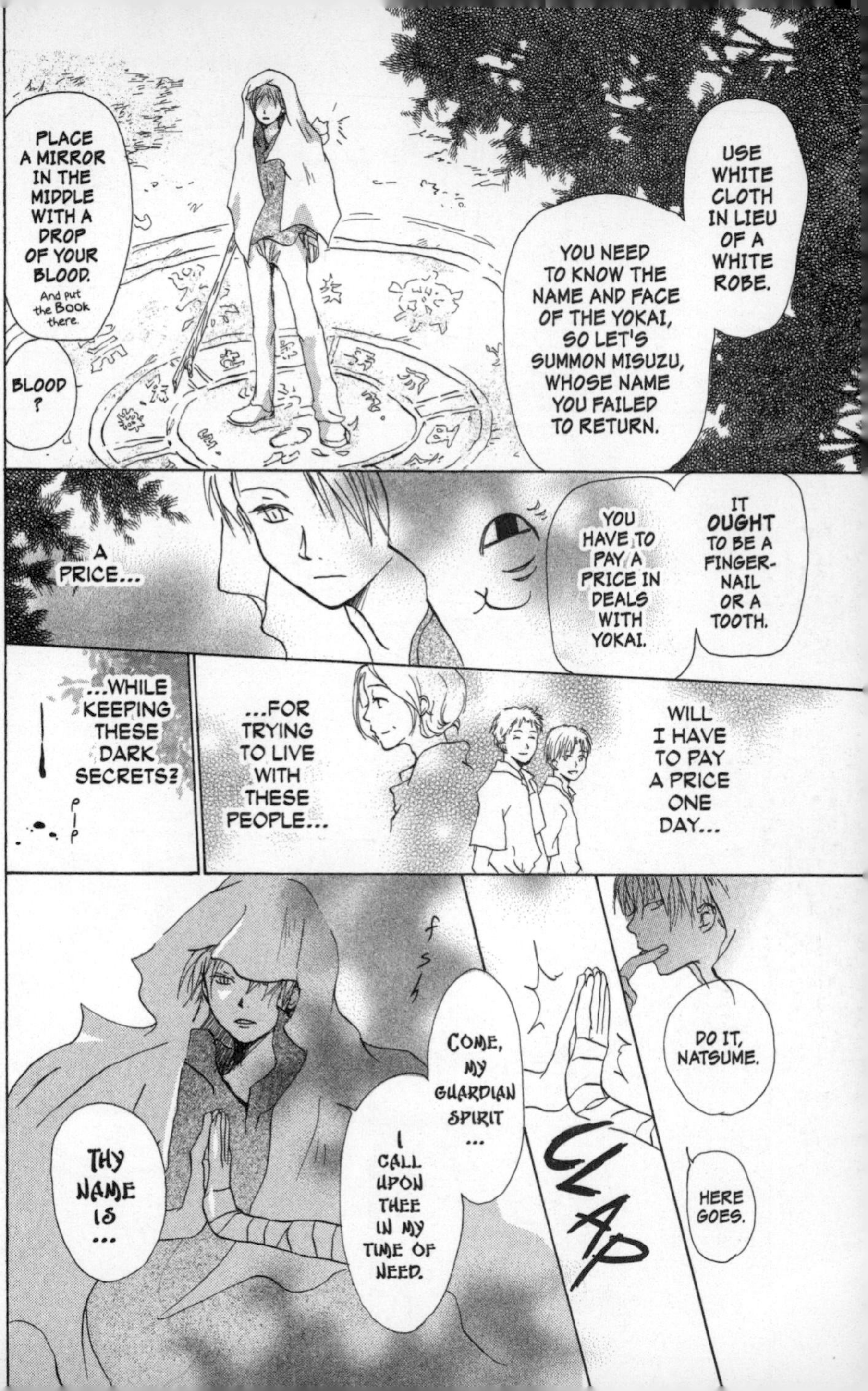
USE WHITE CLOTH IN LIEU OF A WHITE ROBE.
YOU NEED TO KNOW THE NAME AND FACE OF THE YOKAI, SO LET'S SUMMON MISUZU, WHOSE NAME YOU FAILED TO RETURN.
PLACE A MIRROR IN THE MIDDLE WITH A DROP OF YOUR BLOOD.
And put the Book there.
BLOOD?
IT OUGHT TO BE A FINGERNAIL OR A TOOTH.
YOU HAVE TO PAY A PRICE IN DEALS WITH YOKAI.
A PRICE...
WILL I HAVE TO PAY A PRICE ONE DAY...
...FOR TRYING TO LIVE WITH THESE PEOPLE...
...WHILE KEEPING THESE DARK SECRETS?
plip
DO IT, NATSUME.
HERE GOES.
CLAP
fsh
COME, MY GUARDIAN SPIRIT...
I CALL UPON THEE IN MY TIME OF NEED.
THY NAME IS...

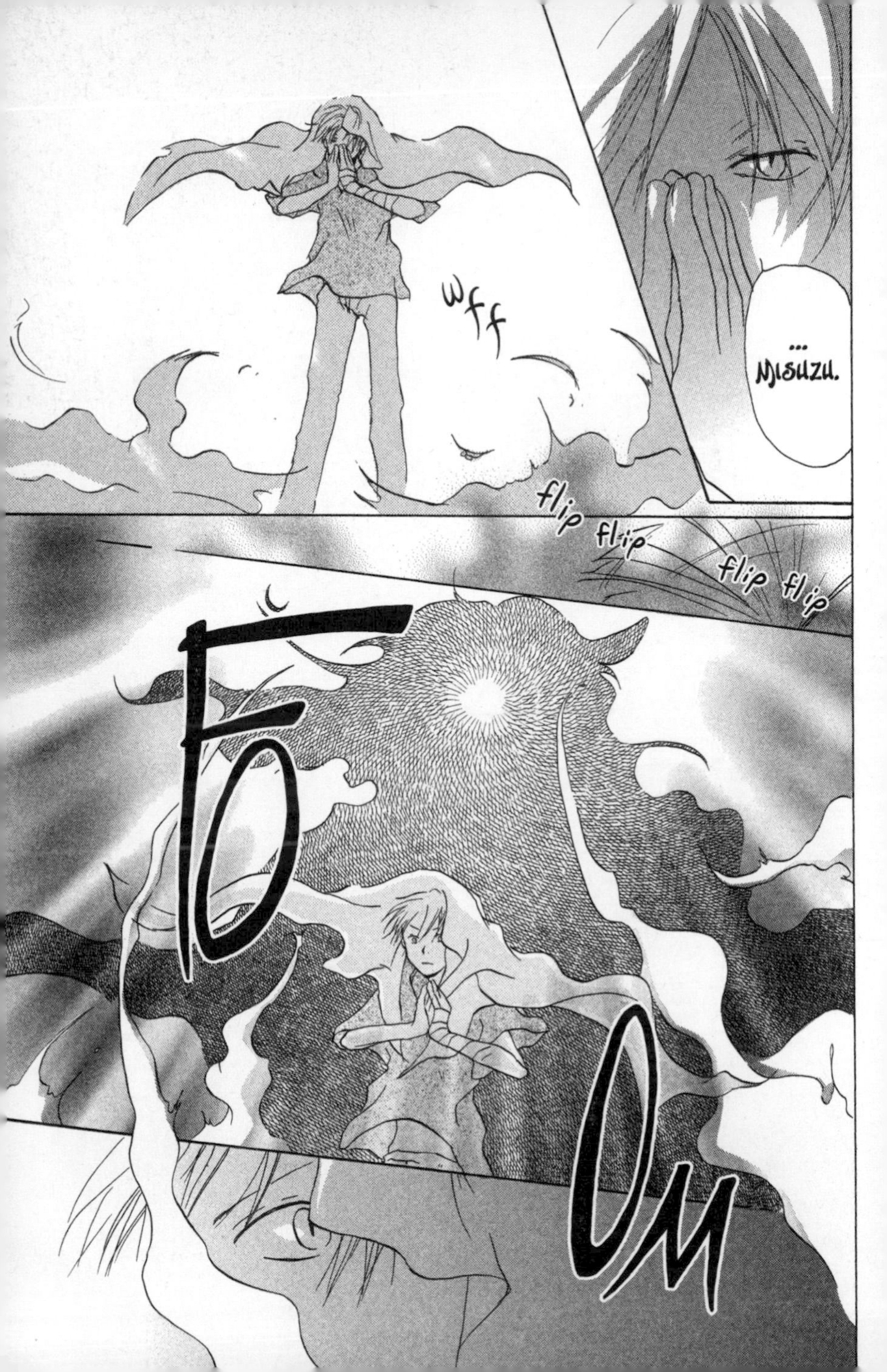
...MISUZU.
wff
flip flip flip flip
FOOM

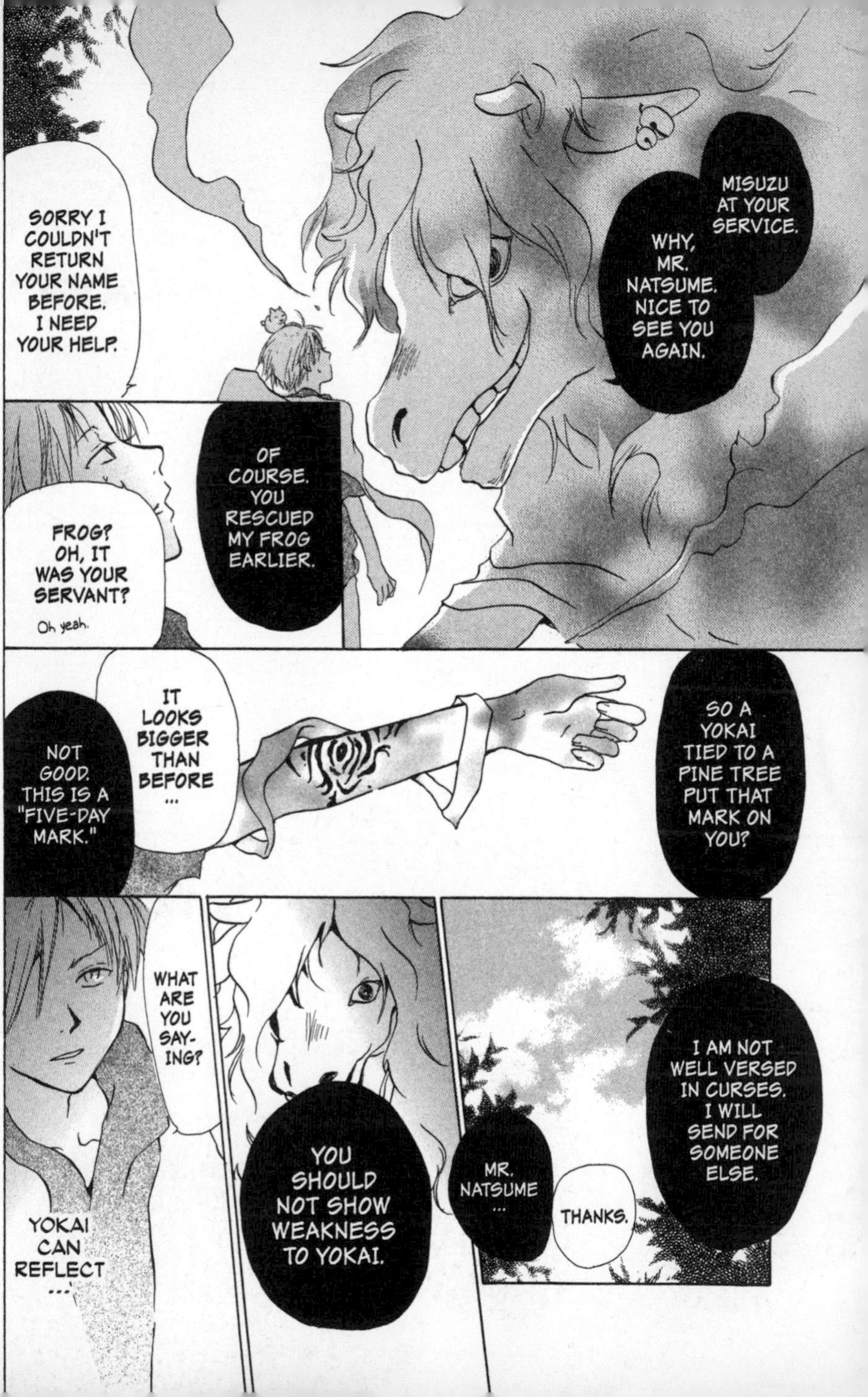
MISUZU AT YOUR SERVICE.
WHY, MR. NATSUME. NICE TO SEE YOU AGAIN.
SORRY I COULDN'T RETURN YOUR NAME BEFORE. I NEED YOUR HELP.
OF COURSE. YOU RESCUED MY FROG EARLIER.
FROG? OH, IT WAS YOUR SERVANT?
Oh yeah.
SO A YOKAI TIED TO A PINE TREE PUT THAT MARK ON YOU?
IT LOOKS BIGGER THAN BEFORE ...
NOT GOOD. THIS IS A "FIVE-DAY MARK."
I AM NOT WELL VERSED IN CURSES. I WILL SEND FOR SOMEONE ELSE.
THANKS.
MR. NATSUME ...
YOU SHOULD NOT SHOW WEAKNESS TO YOKAI.
WHAT ARE YOU SAY-ING?
YOKAI CAN REFLECT ...

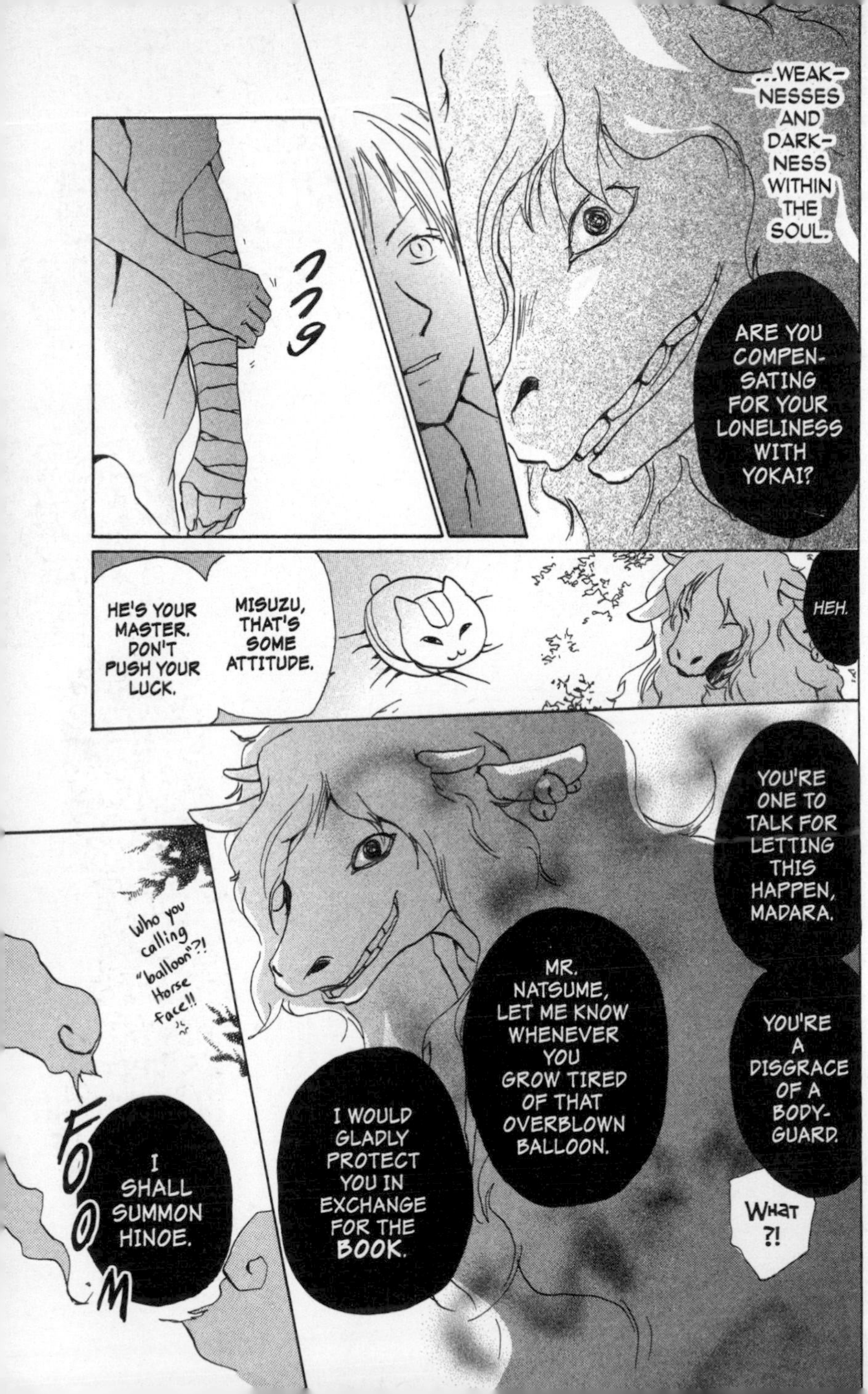
...WEAK-NESSES AND DARK-NESS WITHIN THE SOUL.
ARE YOU COMPEN-SATING FOR YOUR LONELINESS WITH YOKAI?
HEH.
MISUZU, THAT'S SOME ATTITUDE.
HE'S YOUR MASTER. DON'T PUSH YOUR LUCK.
YOU'RE ONE TO TALK FOR LETTING THIS HAPPEN, MADARA.
YOU'RE A DISGRACE OF A BODY-GUARD.
WHAT?!
MR. NATSUME, LET ME KNOW WHENEVER YOU GROW TIRED OF THAT OVERBLOWN BALLOON.
I WOULD GLADLY PROTECT YOU IN EXCHANGE FOR THE BOOK.
Who you calling "balloon"?! Horse face!!
I SHALL SUMMON HINOE.
FOOOM

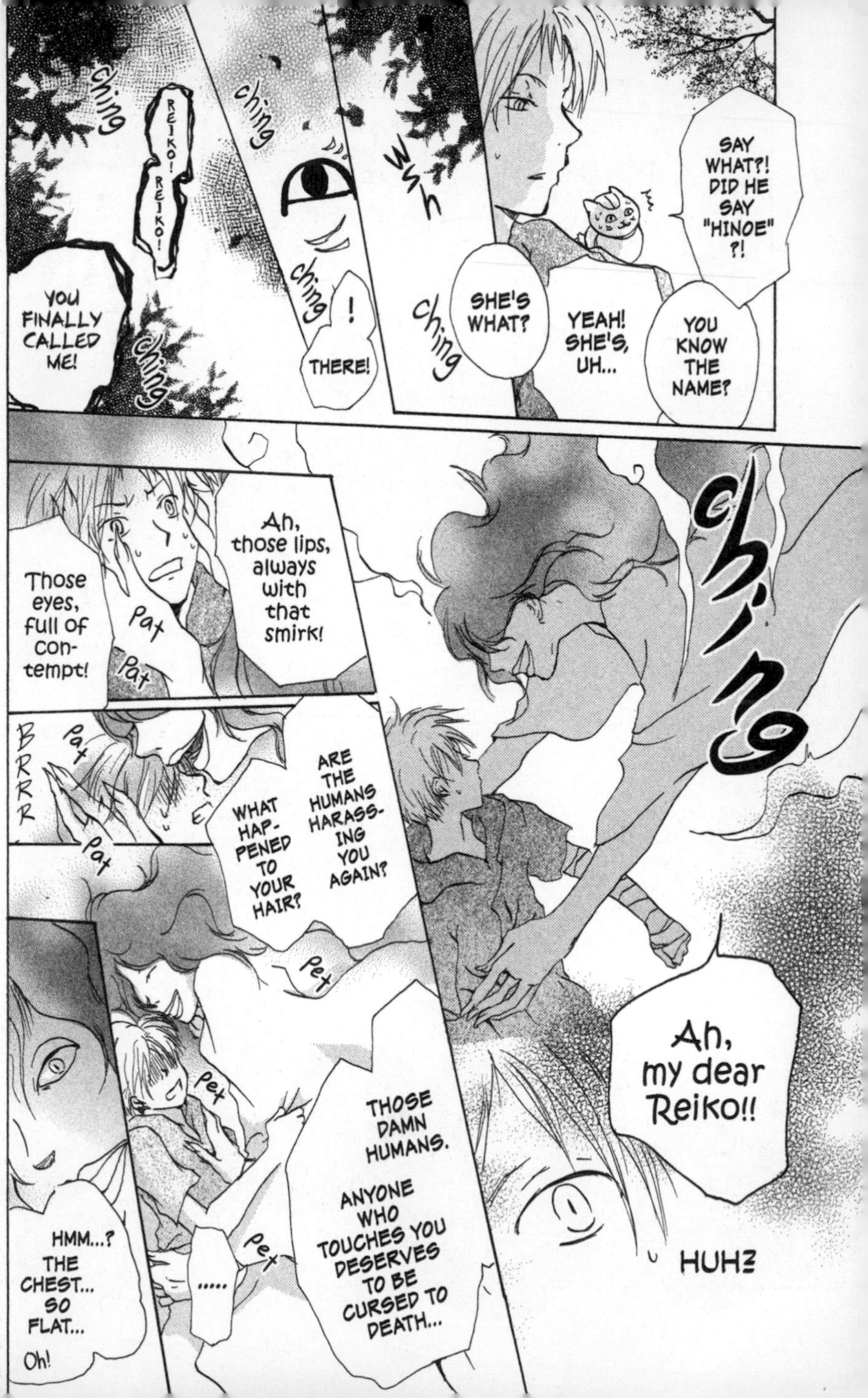
SAY WHAT?! DID HE SAY "HINOE" ?!
YOU KNOW THE NAME?
YEAH! SHE'S, UH...
SHE'S WHAT?
ching
wsh
ching
ching
!
THERE!
REIKO! REIKO! REIKO!
ching
ching
YOU FINALLY CALLED ME!
ching
Ah, my dear Reiko!!
HUH?
Ah, those lips, always with that smirk!
Those eyes, full of con-tempt!
Pat
Pat
ARE THE HUMANS HARASS-ING YOU AGAIN?
WHAT HAP-PENED TO YOUR HAIR?
BRRR
Pat
Pat
Pet
THOSE DAMN HUMANS.
ANYONE WHO TOUCHES YOU DESERVES TO BE CURSED TO DEATH...
Pet
Pet
.....
HMM...? THE CHEST... SO FLAT...
Oh!

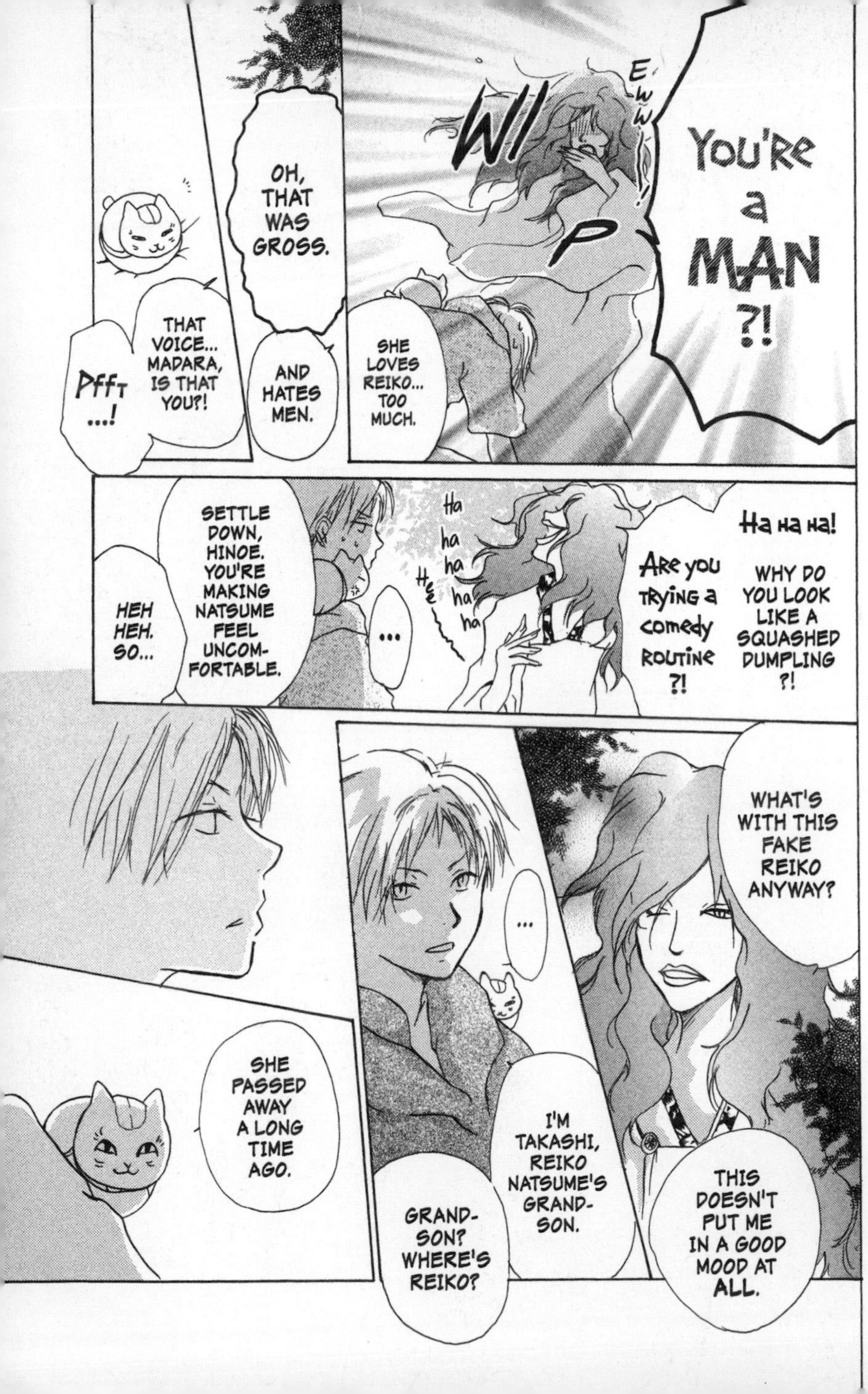
You're a MAN ?!
Eww!
WIP
SHE LOVES REIKO... TOO MUCH.
AND HATES MEN.
OH, THAT WAS GROSS.
THAT VOICE... MADARA, IS THAT YOU?!
Pfft ...!
Ha ha ha!
WHY DO YOU LOOK LIKE A SQUASHED DUMPLING ?!
Are you trying a comedy routine ?!
Ha ha ha ha ha
Hee
...
SETTLE DOWN, HINOE. YOU'RE MAKING NATSUME FEEL UNCOM-FORTABLE.
HEH HEH. SO...
WHAT'S WITH THIS FAKE REIKO ANYWAY?
...
THIS DOESN'T PUT ME IN A GOOD MOOD AT ALL.
I'M TAKASHI, REIKO NATSUME'S GRAND-SON.
GRAND-SON? WHERE'S REIKO?
SHE PASSED AWAY A LONG TIME AGO.

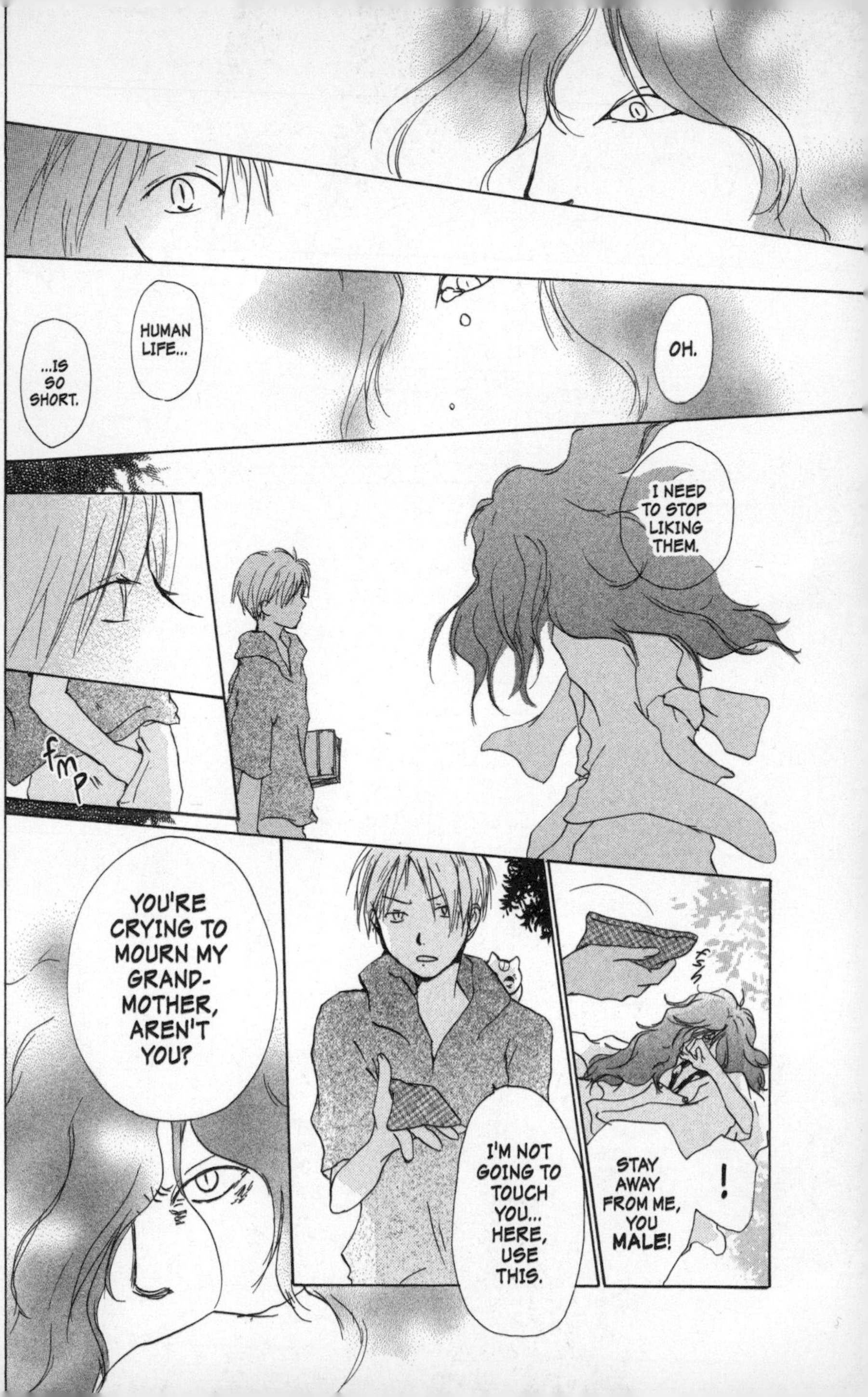
OH.
HUMAN LIFE...
...IS SO SHORT.
I NEED TO STOP LIKING THEM.
fmp
!
STAY AWAY FROM ME, YOU MALE!
I'M NOT GOING TO TOUCH YOU... HERE, USE THIS.
YOU'RE CRYING TO MOURN MY GRAND-MOTHER, AREN'T YOU?

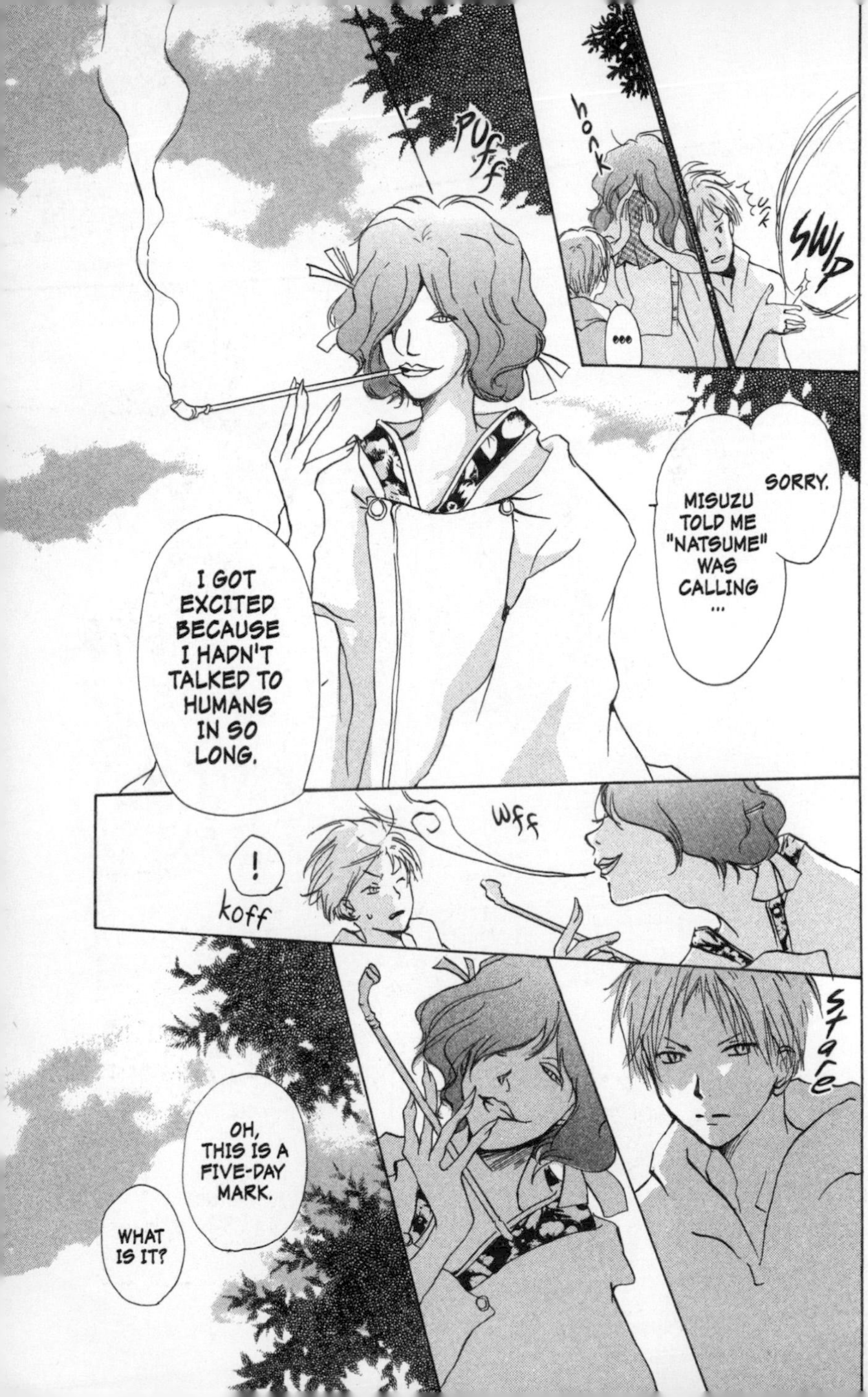
SWIP
honk
...
PUFF
SORRY.
MISUZU TOLD ME "NATSUME" WAS CALLING ...
I GOT EXCITED BECAUSE I HADN'T TALKED TO HUMANS IN SO LONG.
wff
!
koff
stare
OH, THIS IS A FIVE-DAY MARK.
WHAT IS IT?

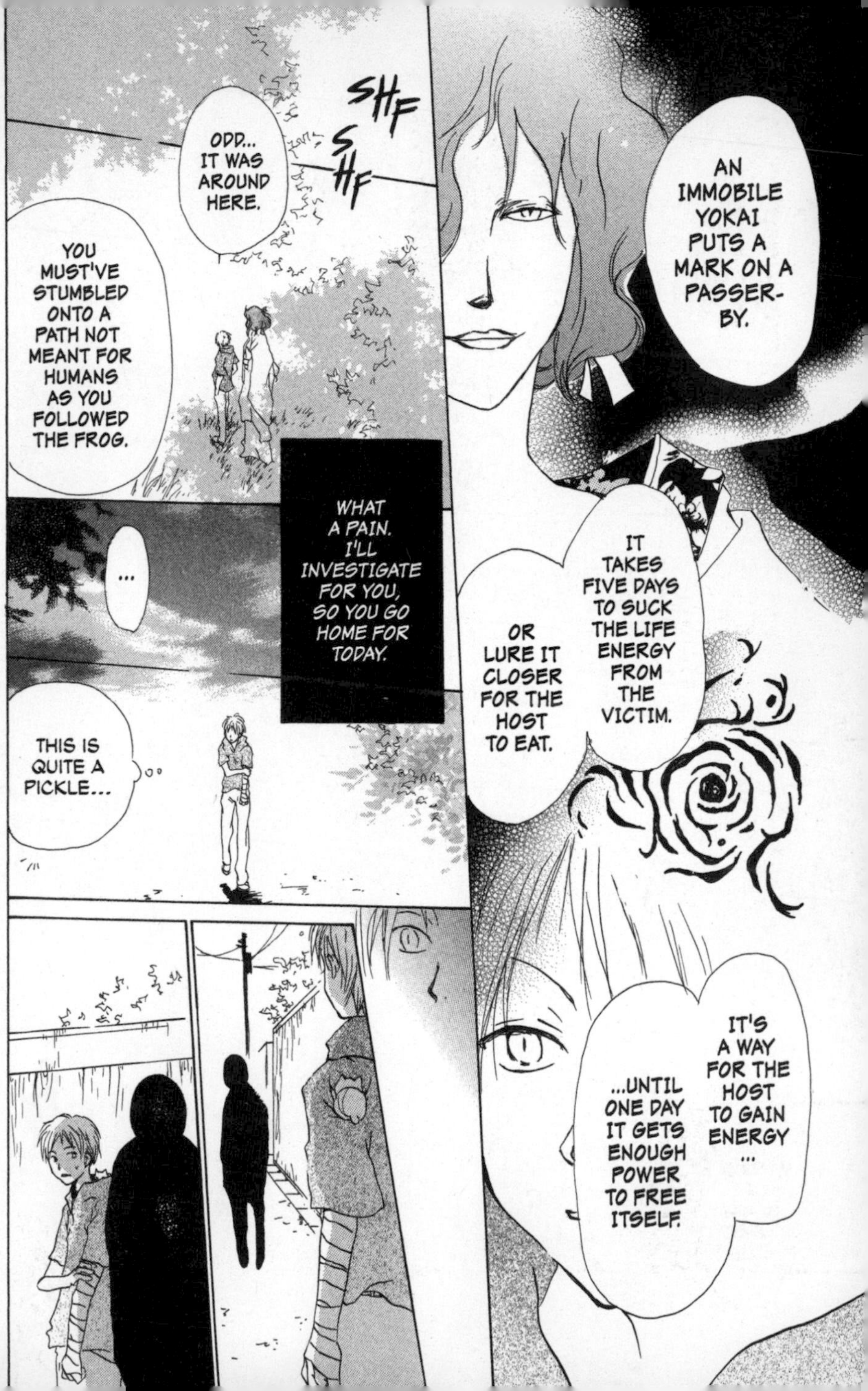

AN IMMOBILE YOKAI PUTS A MARK ON A PASSER-BY.
IT TAKES FIVE DAYS TO SUCK THE LIFE ENERGY FROM THE VICTIM.
OR LURE IT CLOSER FOR THE HOST TO EAT.
IT'S A WAY FOR THE HOST TO GAIN ENERGY...
...UNTIL ONE DAY IT GETS ENOUGH POWER TO FREE ITSELF.
SHF
SHF
ODD... IT WAS AROUND HERE.
YOU MUST'VE STUMBLED ONTO A PATH NOT MEANT FOR HUMANS AS YOU FOLLOWED THE FROG.
WHAT A PAIN. I'LL INVESTIGATE FOR YOU, SO YOU GO HOME FOR TODAY.
...
THIS IS QUITE A PICKLE...

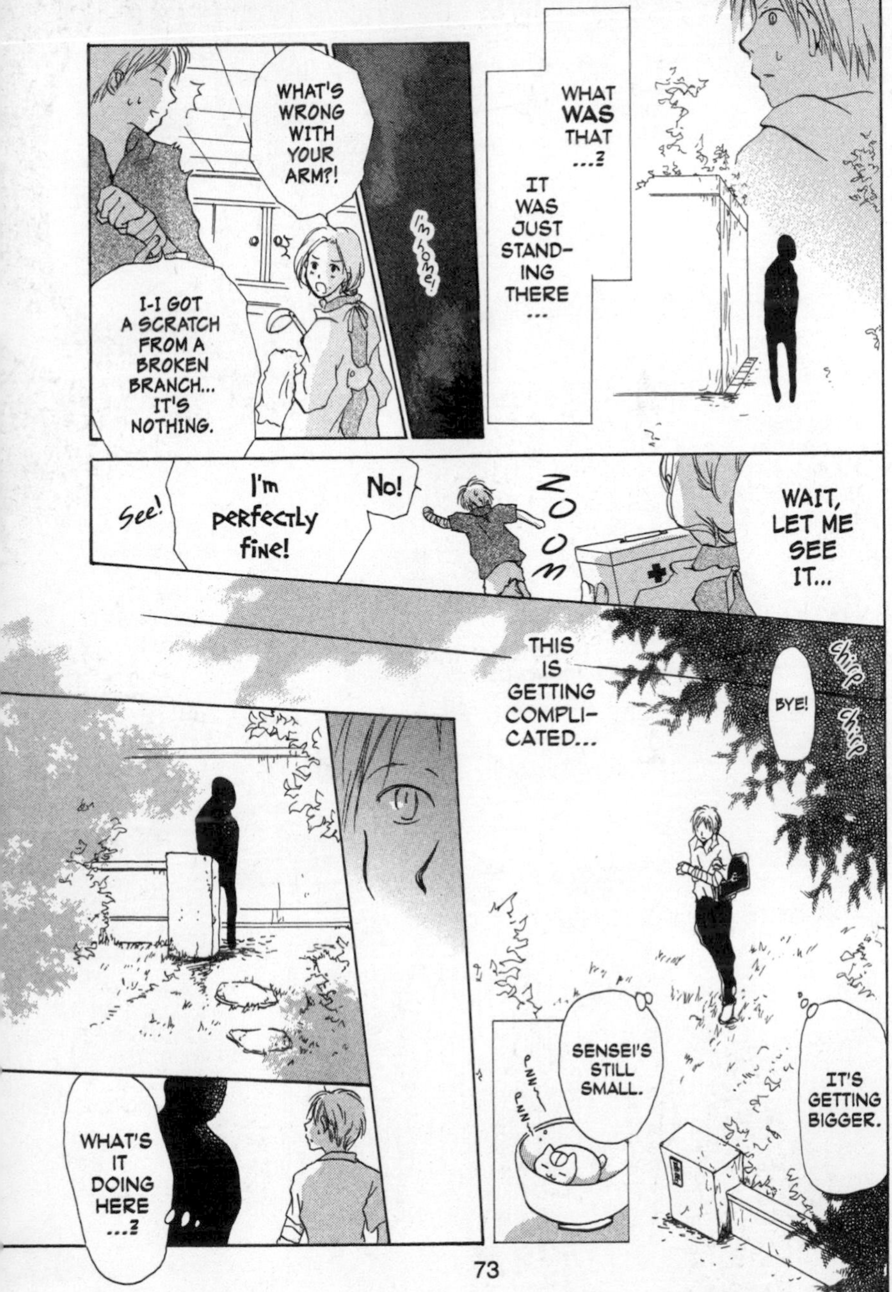
WHAT WAS THAT ...?
IT WAS JUST STANDING THERE ...
I'm home!
WHAT'S WRONG WITH YOUR ARM?!
I-I GOT A SCRATCH FROM A BROKEN BRANCH... IT'S NOTHING.
WAIT, LET ME SEE IT...
ZOOM
No!
I'm perfectly fine!
See!
chirp chirp
BYE!
THIS IS GETTING COMPLICATED...
IT'S GETTING BIGGER.
SENSEI'S STILL SMALL.
nnn nnn
WHAT'S IT DOING HERE ...?

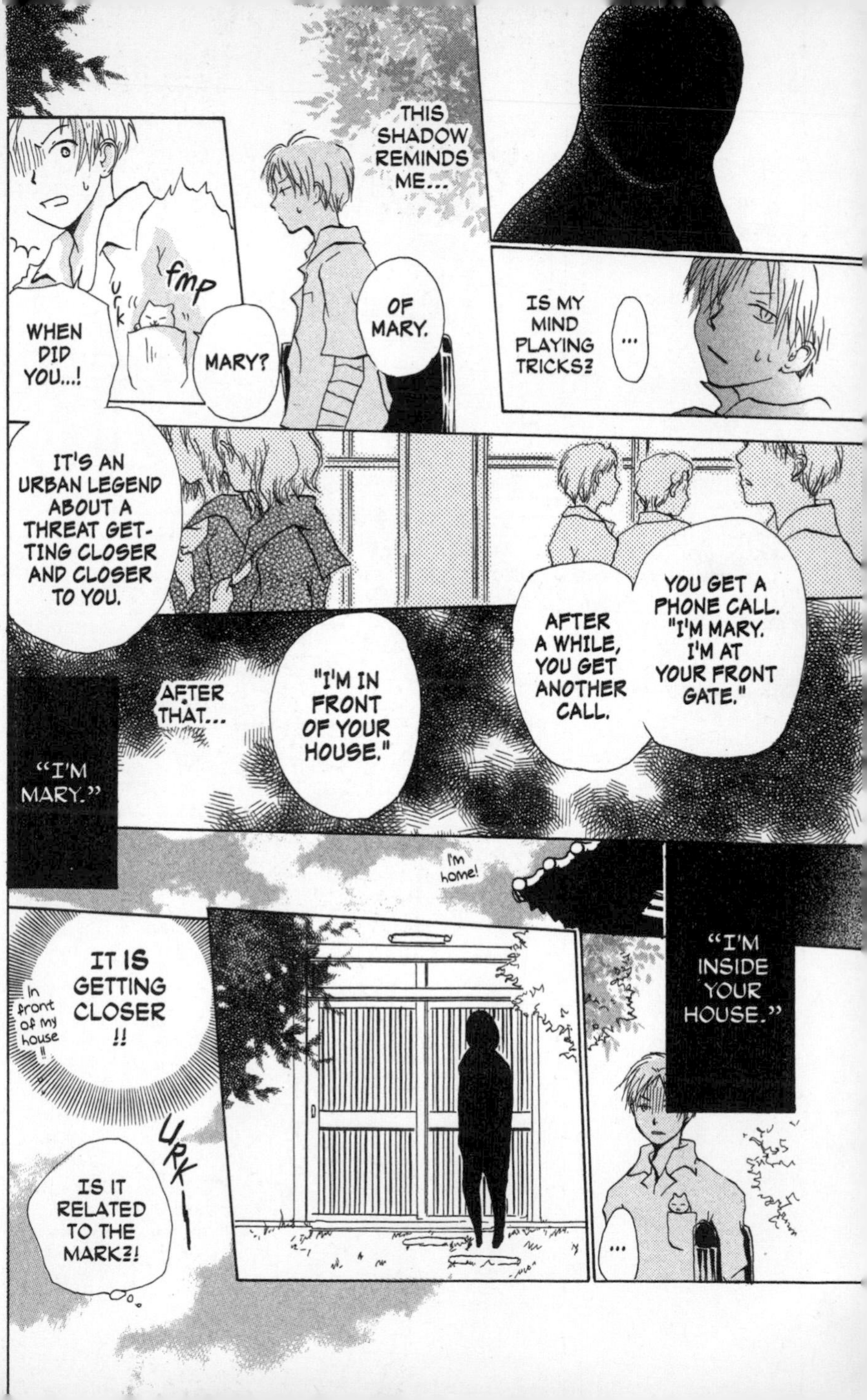
THIS SHADOW REMINDS ME...
OF MARY.
IS MY MIND PLAYING TRICKS?
...
fmp
urk
MARY?
WHEN DID YOU...!
IT'S AN URBAN LEGEND ABOUT A THREAT GET-TING CLOSER AND CLOSER TO YOU.
YOU GET A PHONE CALL. "I'M MARY. I'M AT YOUR FRONT GATE."
AFTER A WHILE, YOU GET ANOTHER CALL.
"I'M IN FRONT OF YOUR HOUSE."
AFTER THAT...
"I'M MARY."
I'm home!
"I'M INSIDE YOUR HOUSE."
...
IT IS GETTING CLOSER !!
In front of my house !!
URK
IS IT RELATED TO THE MARK?!

03

❋Natsume's Book of Friends: Part 2

My manga used to have different points of view intertwined, with flashbacks and flash-forwards and whatever else I felt like. But I wanted to try something solid that's easy to read for once. And what better place to do it than in Natsume! It seems like such basic storytelling to follow events in order and have the readers experience things at the same time as the protagonist, but it's so hard to make it interesting. Whenever I flail and flounder, my editor does his best to help me. As a result of those efforts, I think it's slowly getting easier to read.

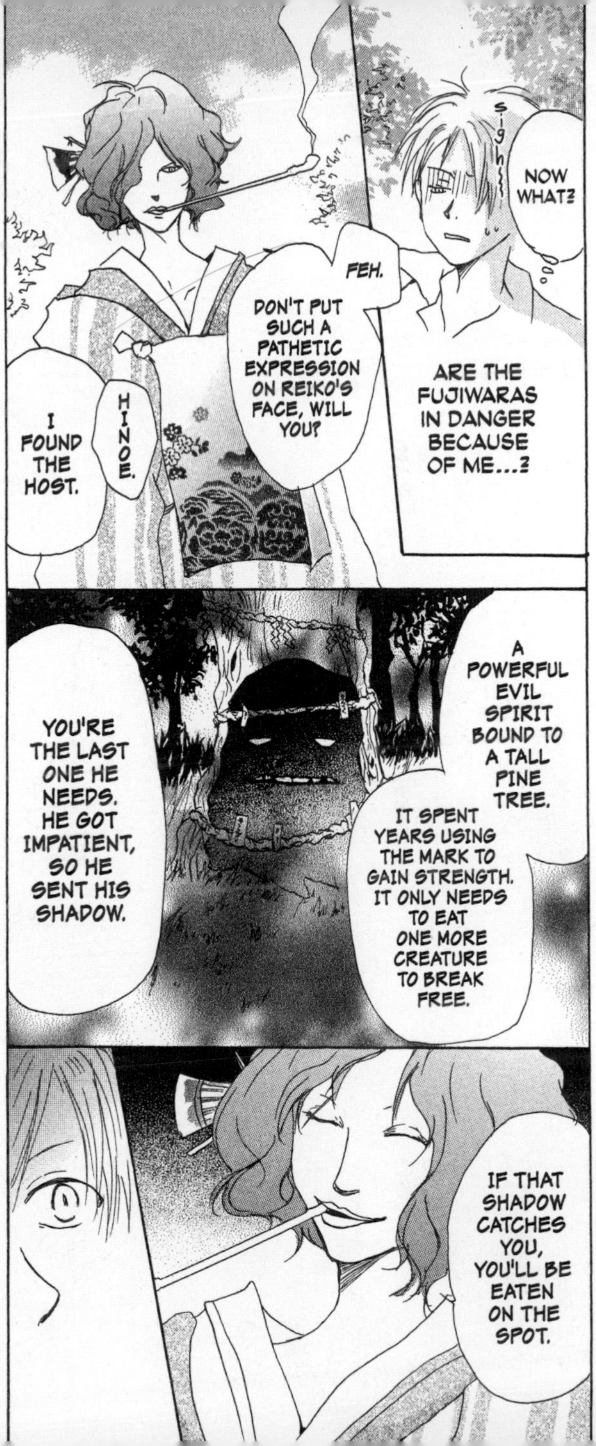
s-i-g-h
NOW WHAT?
ARE THE FUJIWARAS IN DANGER BECAUSE OF ME...?
FEH.
DON'T PUT SUCH A PATHETIC EXPRESSION ON REIKO'S FACE, WILL YOU?
HINOE.
I FOUND THE HOST.
A POWERFUL EVIL SPIRIT BOUND TO A TALL PINE TREE.
IT SPENT YEARS USING THE MARK TO GAIN STRENGTH. IT ONLY NEEDS TO EAT ONE MORE CREATURE TO BREAK FREE.
YOU'RE THE LAST ONE HE NEEDS. HE GOT IMPATIENT, SO HE SENT HIS SHADOW.
IF THAT SHADOW CATCHES YOU, YOU'LL BE EATEN ON THE SPOT.

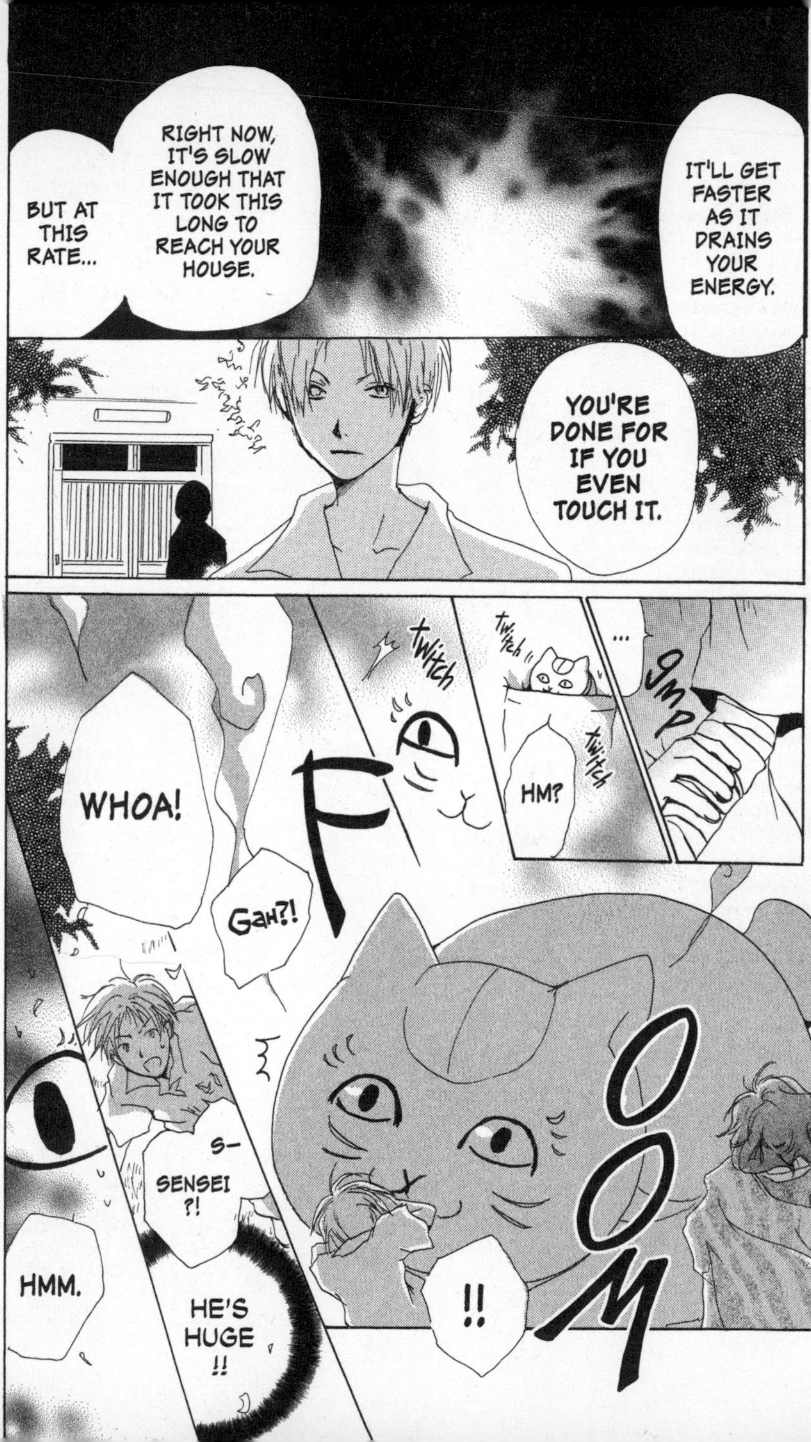
IT'LL GET FASTER AS IT DRAINS YOUR ENERGY.
RIGHT NOW, IT'S SLOW ENOUGH THAT IT TOOK THIS LONG TO REACH YOUR HOUSE.
BUT AT THIS RATE...
YOU'RE DONE FOR IF YOU EVEN TOUCH IT.
...
gmp
twitch
HM?
twitch
twitch
WHOA!
Gah?!
OOM
!!
S-SENSEI?!
HMM.
HE'S HUGE!!

04

❋Nyanko Sensei

I make him quite round and plump when he's in his feline form. And I make sure that his face is weird. My goal is a creature that's a bit too bizarre. His original form is a long, white, fluffy beast. Like a sleek mink or fox. But in hindsight, I was probably influenced by the flying fluffy beast that carried the protagonist on his back in one of my favorite movies from my childhood. The dream of climbing on the back of an animal and soaring into the sky is unforgettable, even as an adult. I also love it when large magical creatures disguise themselves as little critters.

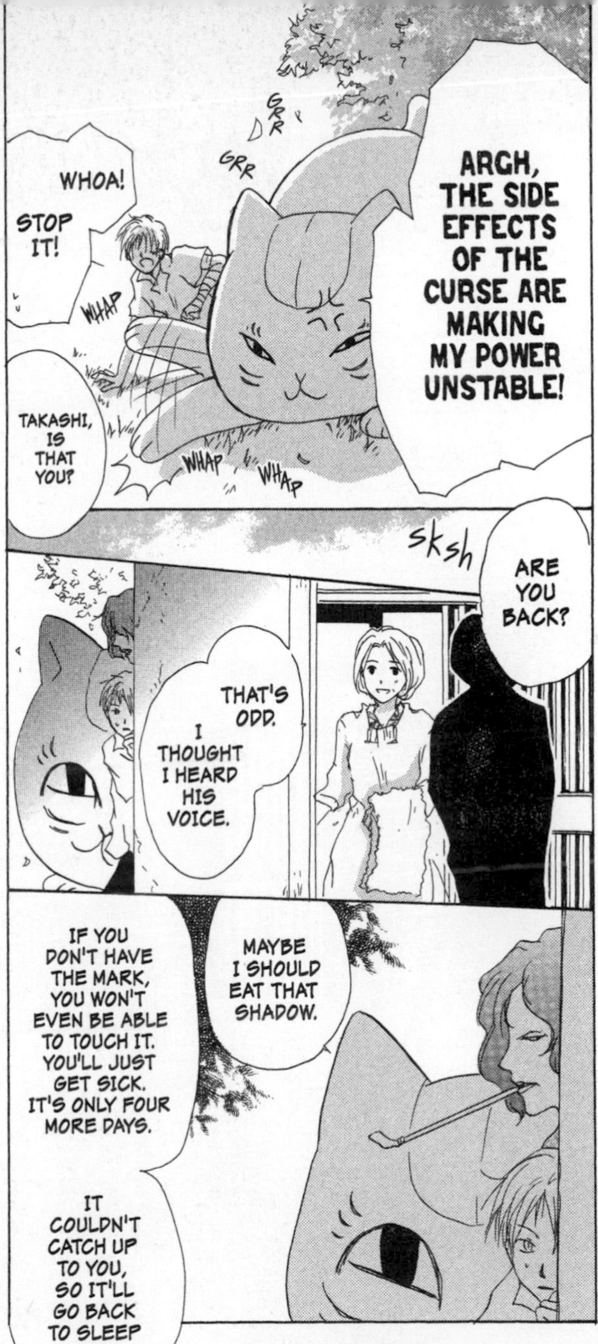
ARGH, THE SIDE EFFECTS OF THE CURSE ARE MAKING MY POWER UNSTABLE!
GRR
GRR
WHOA!
STOP IT!
WHAP
TAKASHI, IS THAT YOU?
WHAP
WHAP
sksh
ARE YOU BACK?
THAT'S ODD.
I THOUGHT I HEARD HIS VOICE.
MAYBE I SHOULD EAT THAT SHADOW.
IF YOU DON'T HAVE THE MARK, YOU WON'T EVEN BE ABLE TO TOUCH IT. YOU'LL JUST GET SICK. IT'S ONLY FOUR MORE DAYS.
IT COULDN'T CATCH UP TO YOU, SO IT'LL GO BACK TO SLEEP AGAIN.

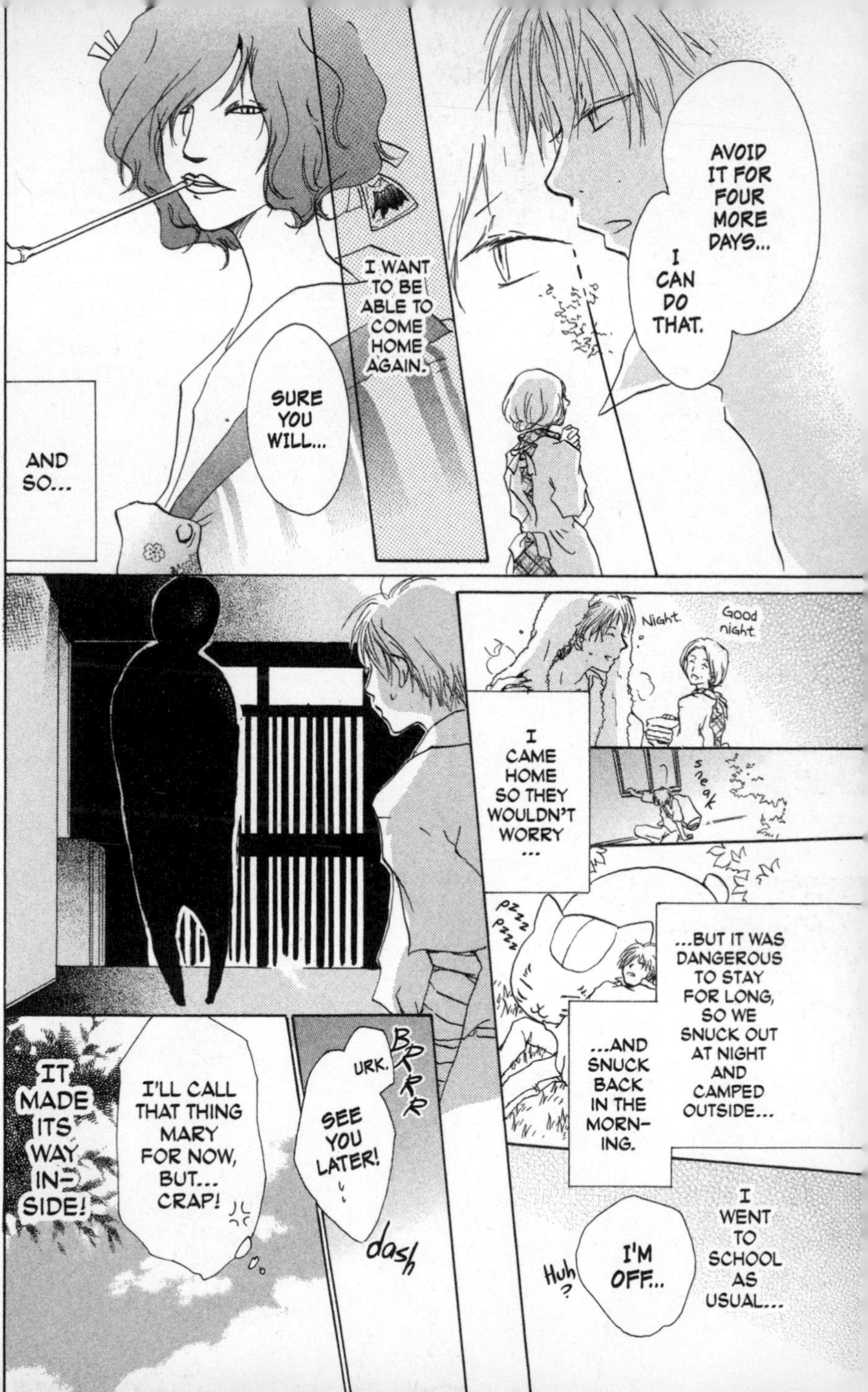
AVOID IT FOR FOUR MORE DAYS...
I CAN DO THAT.
I WANT TO BE ABLE TO COME HOME AGAIN.
SURE YOU WILL...
AND SO...
Good night.
Night.
I CAME HOME SO THEY WOULDN'T WORRY...
sneak
...BUT IT WAS DANGEROUS TO STAY FOR LONG, SO WE SNUCK OUT AT NIGHT AND CAMPED OUTSIDE...
...AND SNUCK BACK IN THE MORNING.
pzzz pzzz
I WENT TO SCHOOL AS USUAL...
I'M OFF...
Huh?
BRRR
URK.
SEE YOU LATER!
dash
I'LL CALL THAT THING MARY FOR NOW, BUT... CRAP!
IT MADE ITS WAY IN-SIDE!

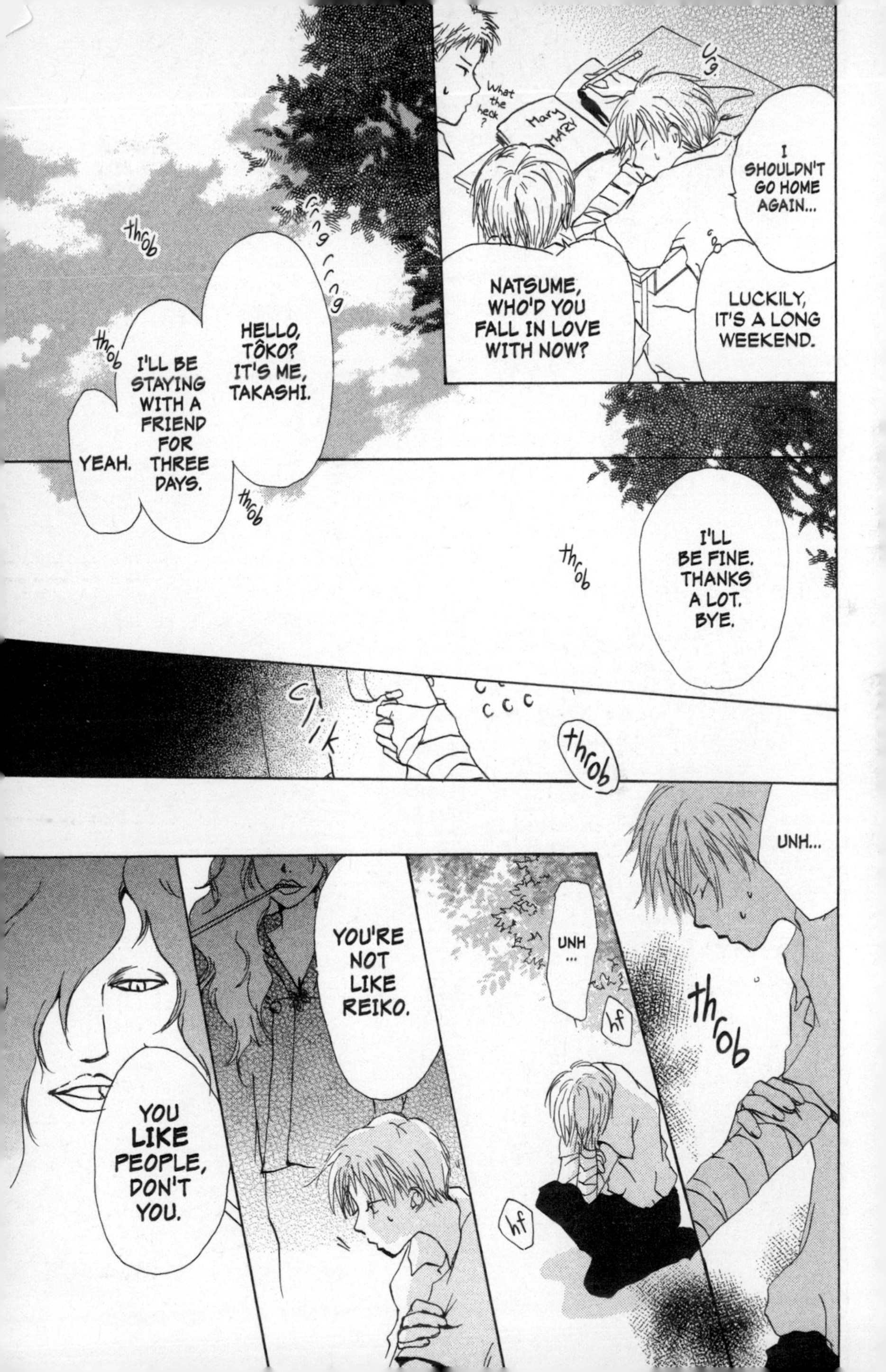
Urg.
What the heck?
Mary MARY
I SHOULDN'T GO HOME AGAIN...
LUCKILY, IT'S A LONG WEEKEND.
NATSUME, WHO'D YOU FALL IN LOVE WITH NOW?
rrng
rrng
throb
HELLO, TÔKO? IT'S ME, TAKASHI.
throb
I'LL BE STAYING WITH A FRIEND FOR THREE DAYS.
YEAH.
throb
I'LL BE FINE. THANKS A LOT. BYE.
throb
throb
clik
UNH...
throb
UNH...
hf
hf
YOU'RE NOT LIKE REIKO.
YOU LIKE PEOPLE, DON'T YOU.

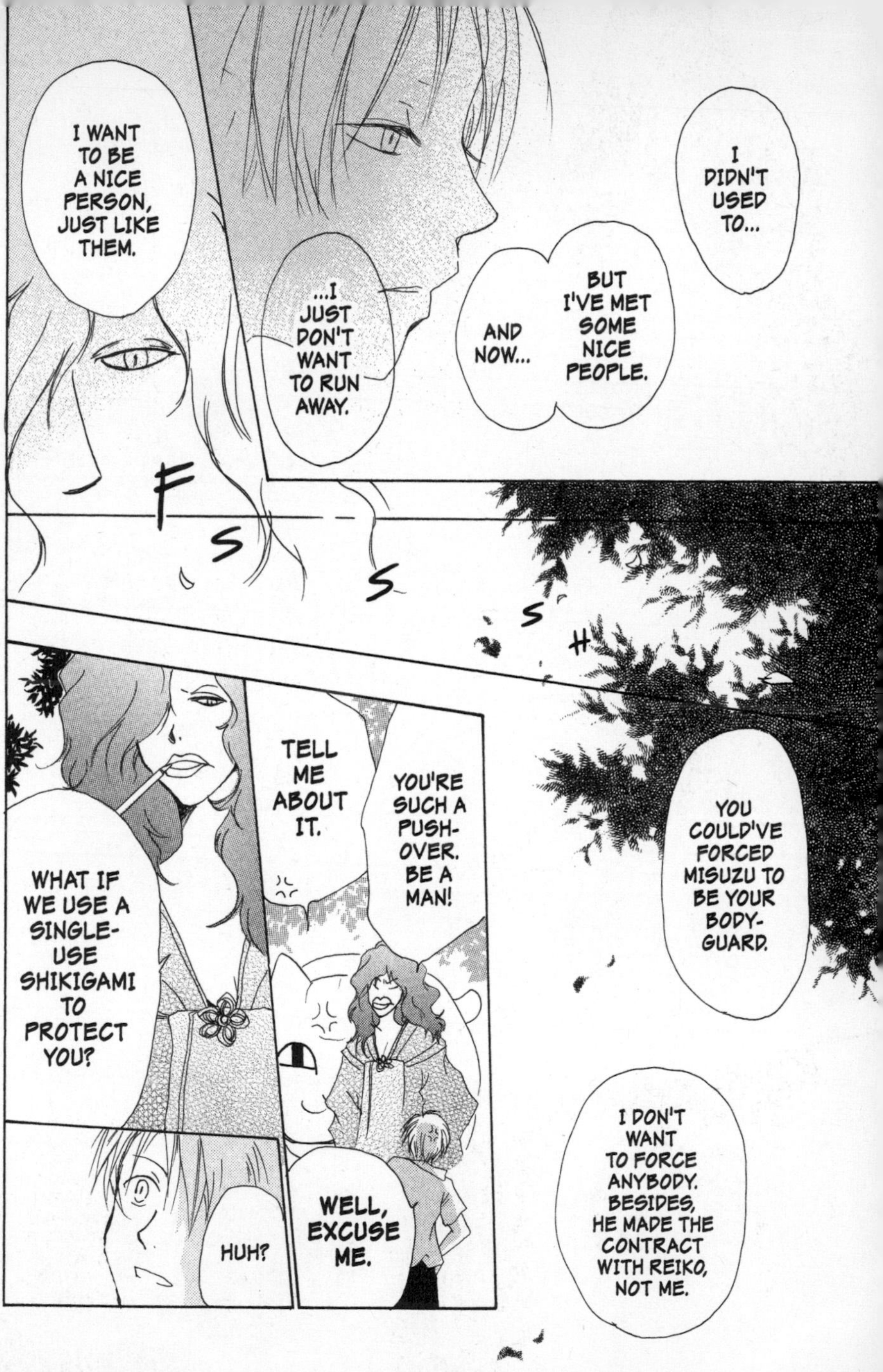
I DIDN'T USED TO...
BUT I'VE MET SOME NICE PEOPLE.
AND NOW...
...I JUST DON'T WANT TO RUN AWAY.
I WANT TO BE A NICE PERSON, JUST LIKE THEM.
FSSSH
YOU COULD'VE FORCED MISUZU TO BE YOUR BODY-GUARD.
I DON'T WANT TO FORCE ANYBODY. BESIDES, HE MADE THE CONTRACT WITH REIKO, NOT ME.
YOU'RE SUCH A PUSH-OVER. BE A MAN!
TELL ME ABOUT IT.
WELL, EXCUSE ME.
WHAT IF WE USE A SINGLE-USE SHIKIGAMI TO PROTECT YOU?
HUH?

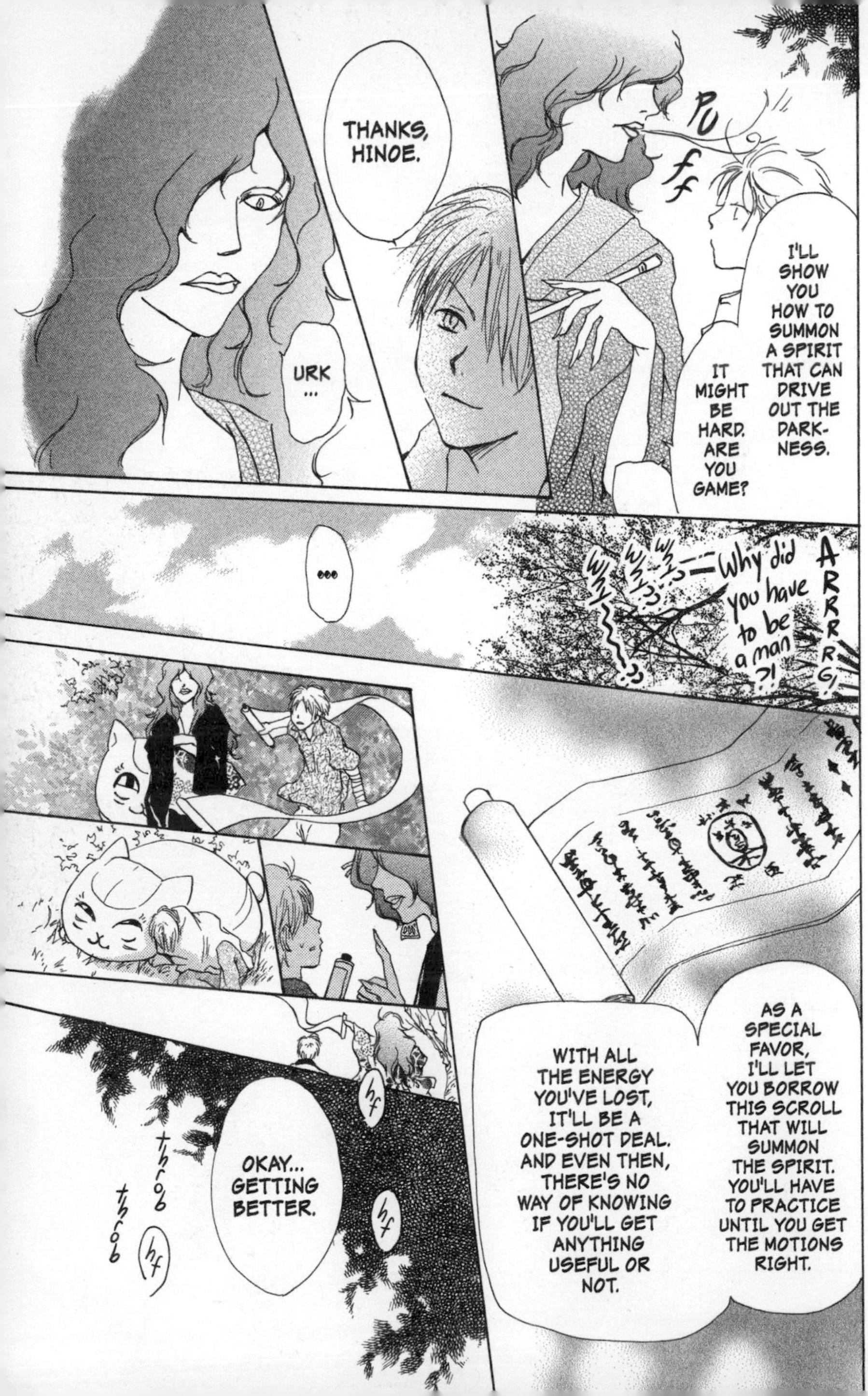
PUFFF
I'LL SHOW YOU HOW TO SUMMON A SPIRIT THAT CAN DRIVE OUT THE DARKNESS.
IT MIGHT BE HARD. ARE YOU GAME?
THANKS, HINOE.
URK...
ARRRRG!
Why did you have to be a man?!
Why? Why?? Why~~??
...
AS A SPECIAL FAVOR, I'LL LET YOU BORROW THIS SCROLL THAT WILL SUMMON THE SPIRIT. YOU'LL HAVE TO PRACTICE UNTIL YOU GET THE MOTIONS RIGHT.
WITH ALL THE ENERGY YOU'VE LOST, IT'LL BE A ONE-SHOT DEAL. AND EVEN THEN, THERE'S NO WAY OF KNOWING IF YOU'LL GET ANYTHING USEFUL OR NOT.
hf
hf
OKAY... GETTING BETTER.
hf
throb throb

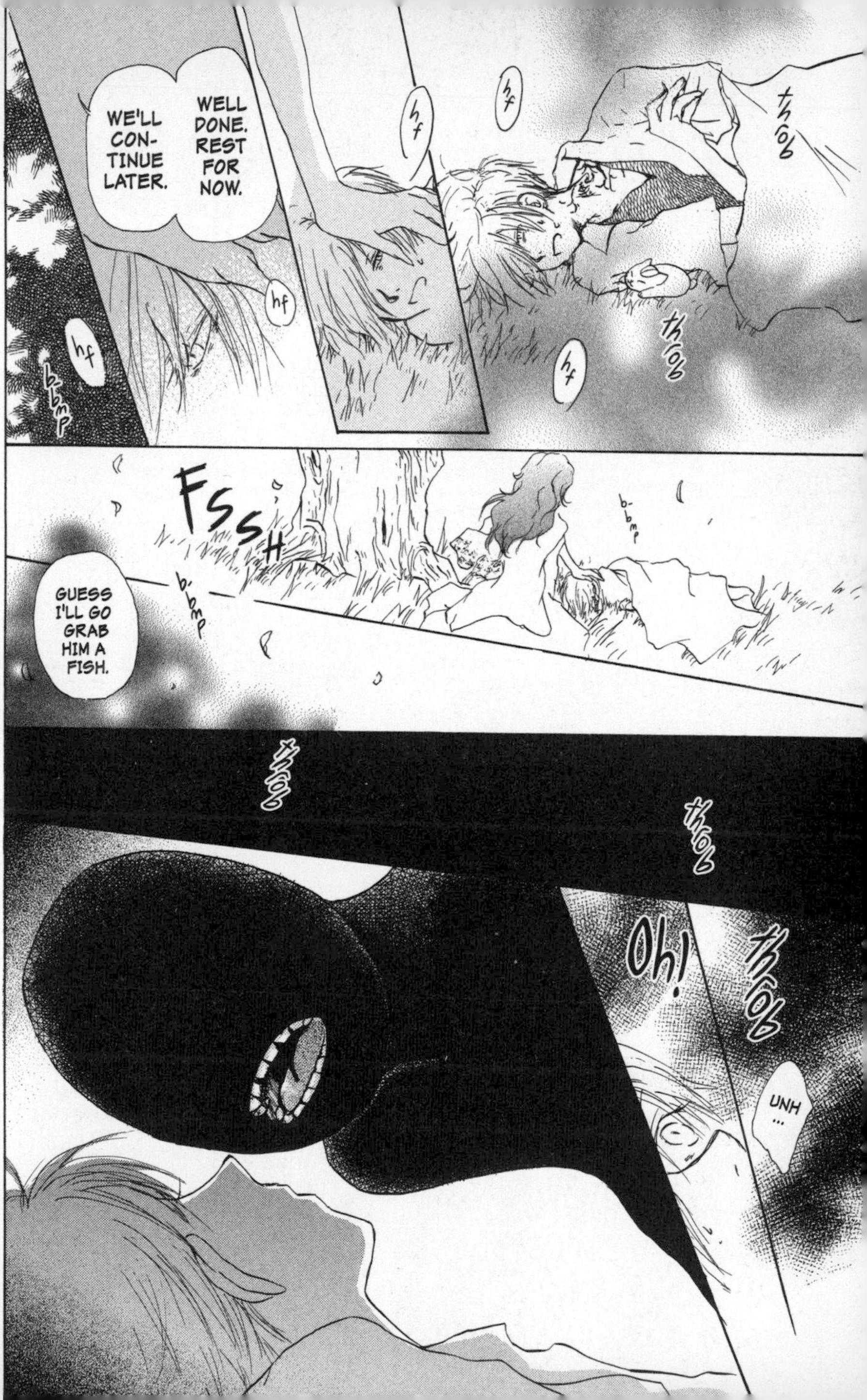
throb
hf
throb
hf
hf
hf
WELL DONE. REST FOR NOW.
WE'LL CON-TINUE LATER.
hf
b-bmp
b-bmp
FSSH
b-bmp
GUESS I'LL GO GRAB HIM A FISH.
throb
throb
Oh!
throb
UNH ...

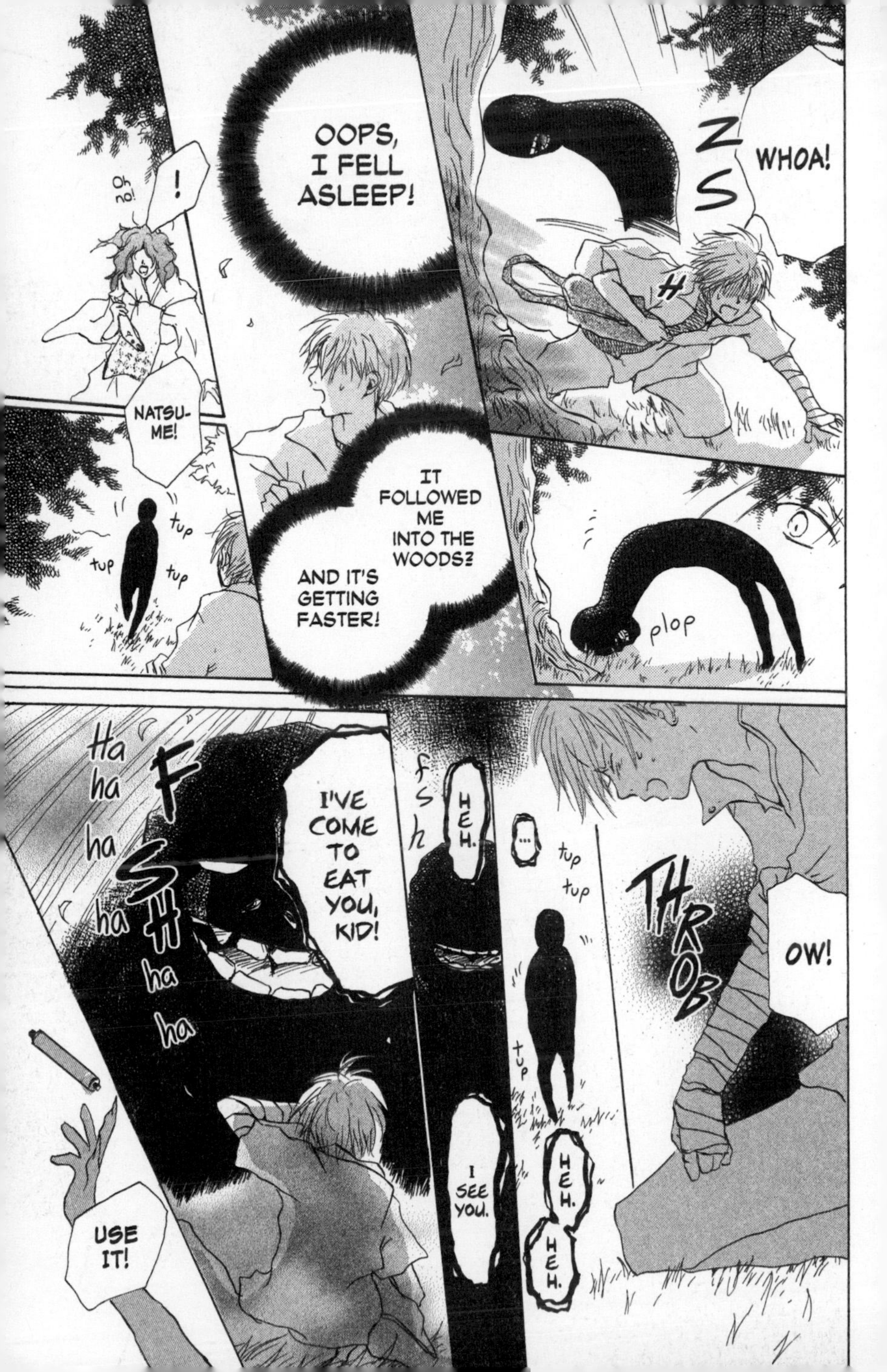
ZS
WHOA!
H
!
Oh no!
OOPS, I FELL ASLEEP!
plop
NATSU-ME!
IT FOLLOWED ME INTO THE WOODS?
AND IT'S GETTING FASTER!
tup
tup
tup
OW!
THROB
...
tup
tup
tup
HEH. HEH.
HEH. HEH.
I SEE YOU.
fsh
HEH.
I'VE COME TO EAT YOU, KID!
F
SH
Ha ha ha ha ha ha
USE IT!

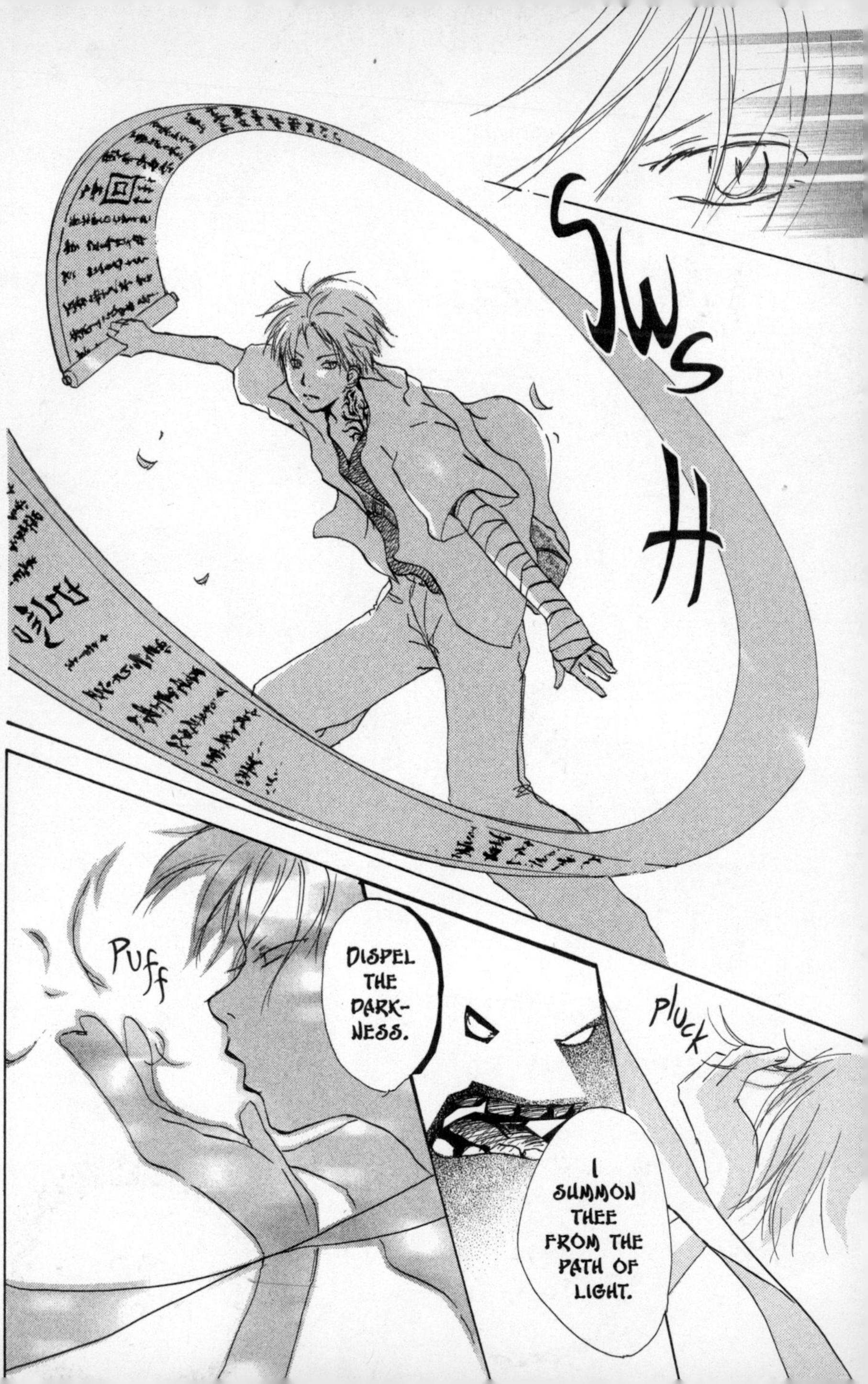

SWSH
PLUCK
I SUMMON THEE FROM THE PATH OF LIGHT.
DISPEL THE DARK-NESS.
PUFF

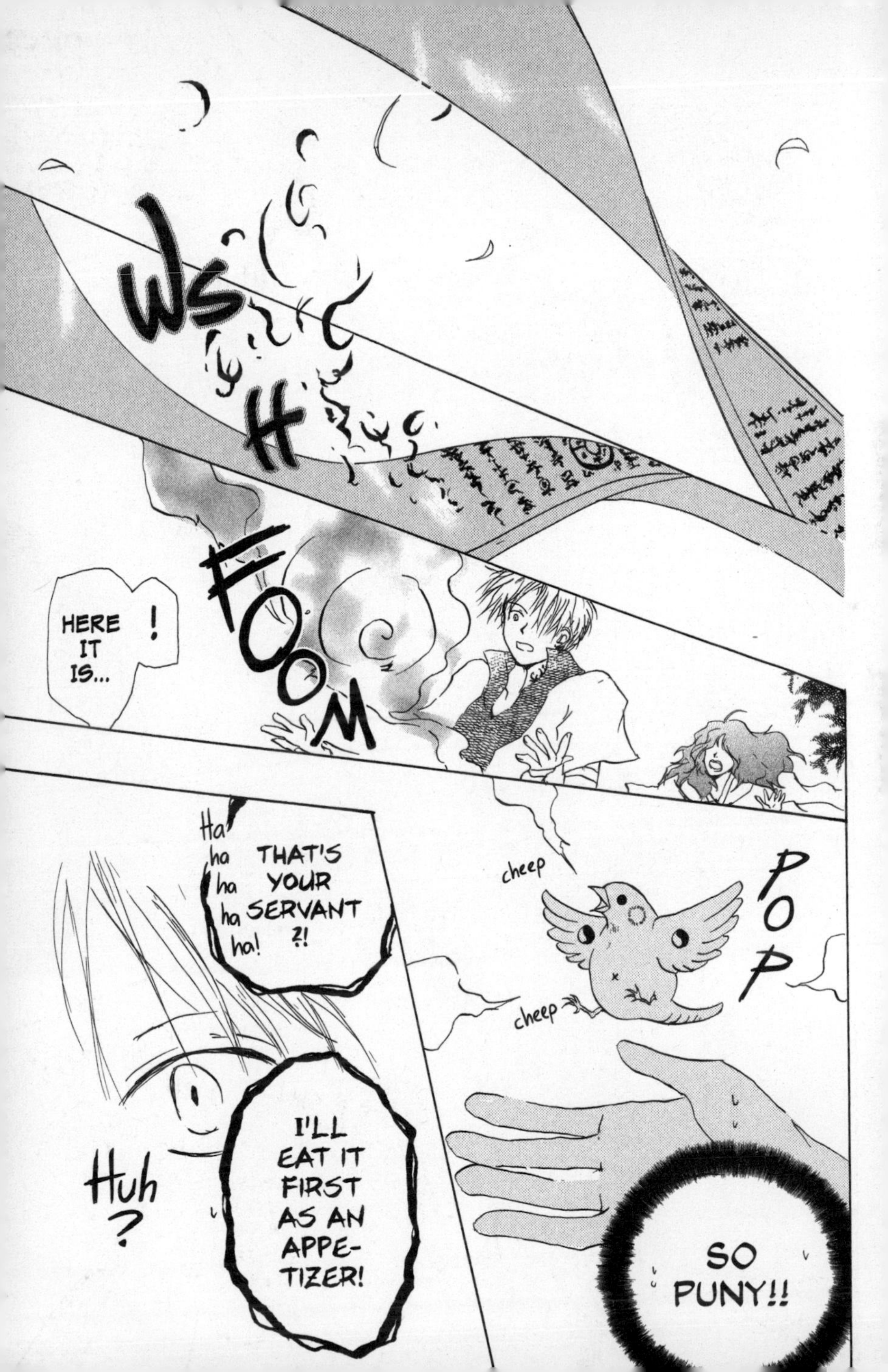
WSH
FOOM
HERE IT IS... !
POP
cheep
cheep
SO PUNY!!
Ha ha ha ha ha!
THAT'S YOUR SERVANT ?!
I'LL EAT IT FIRST AS AN APPE-TIZER!
Huh?

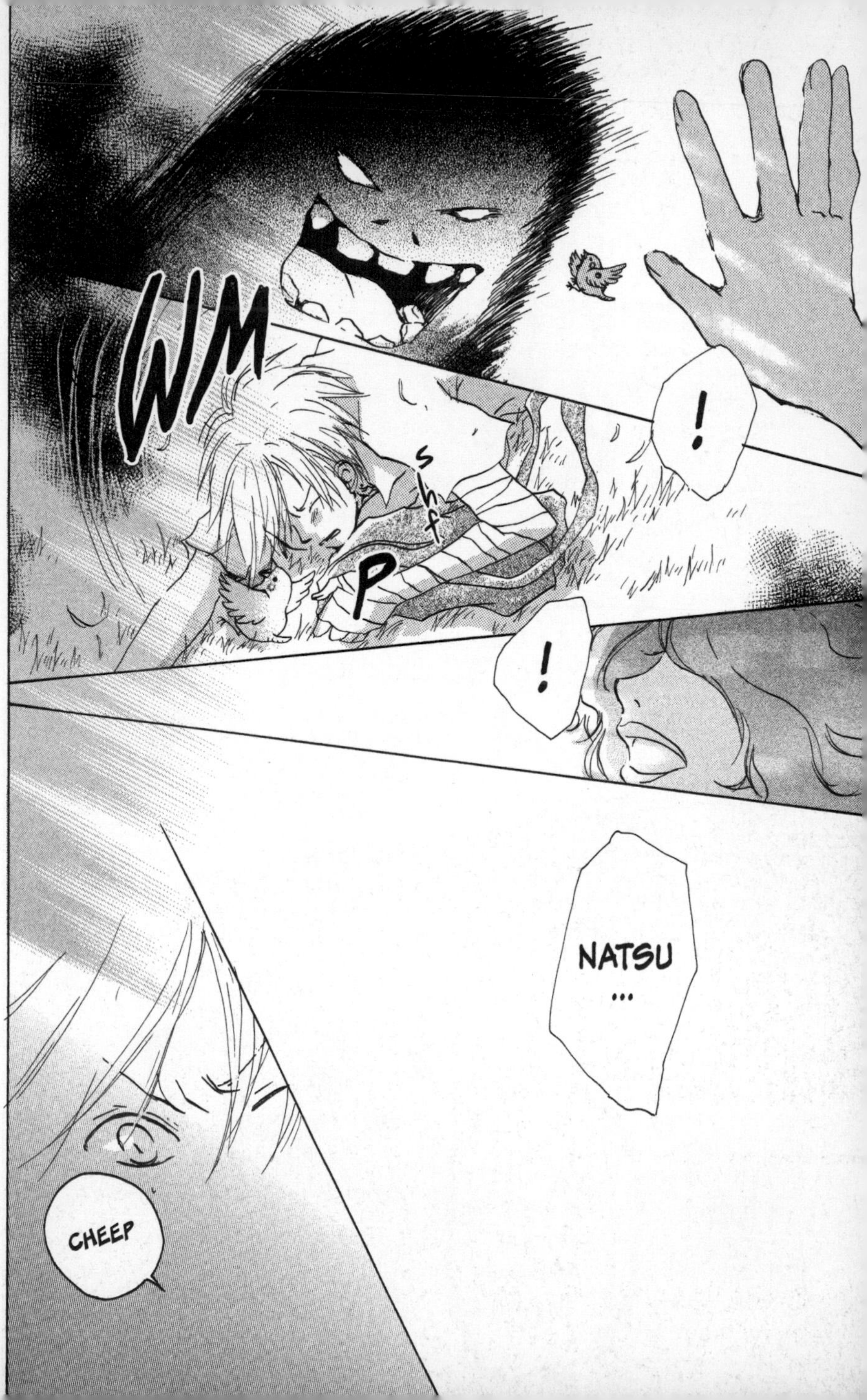
!
WM
shif
P
!
NATSU ...
CHEEP

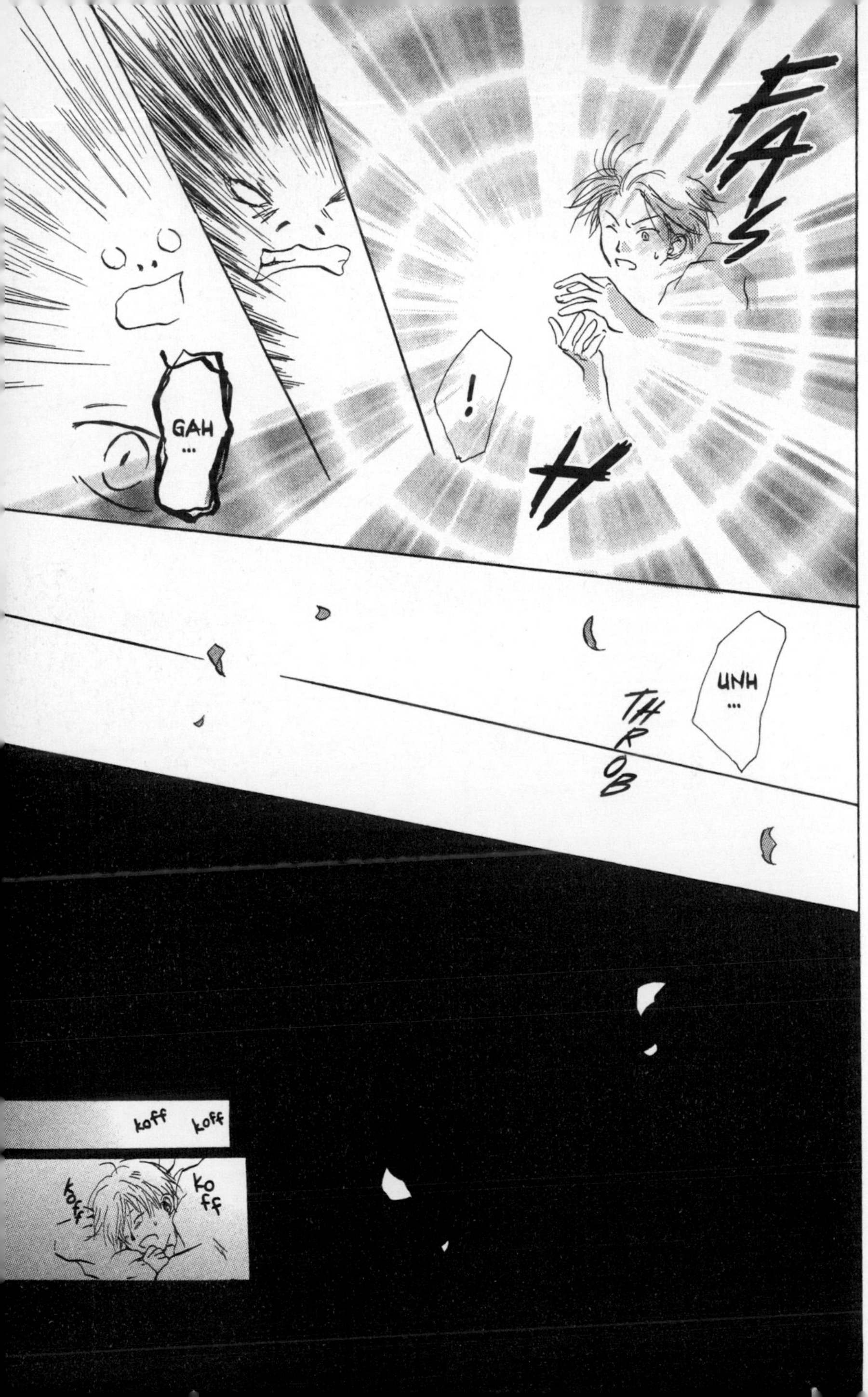
FLASH
!
GAH...
UNH...
THROB
koff koff
koff
koff

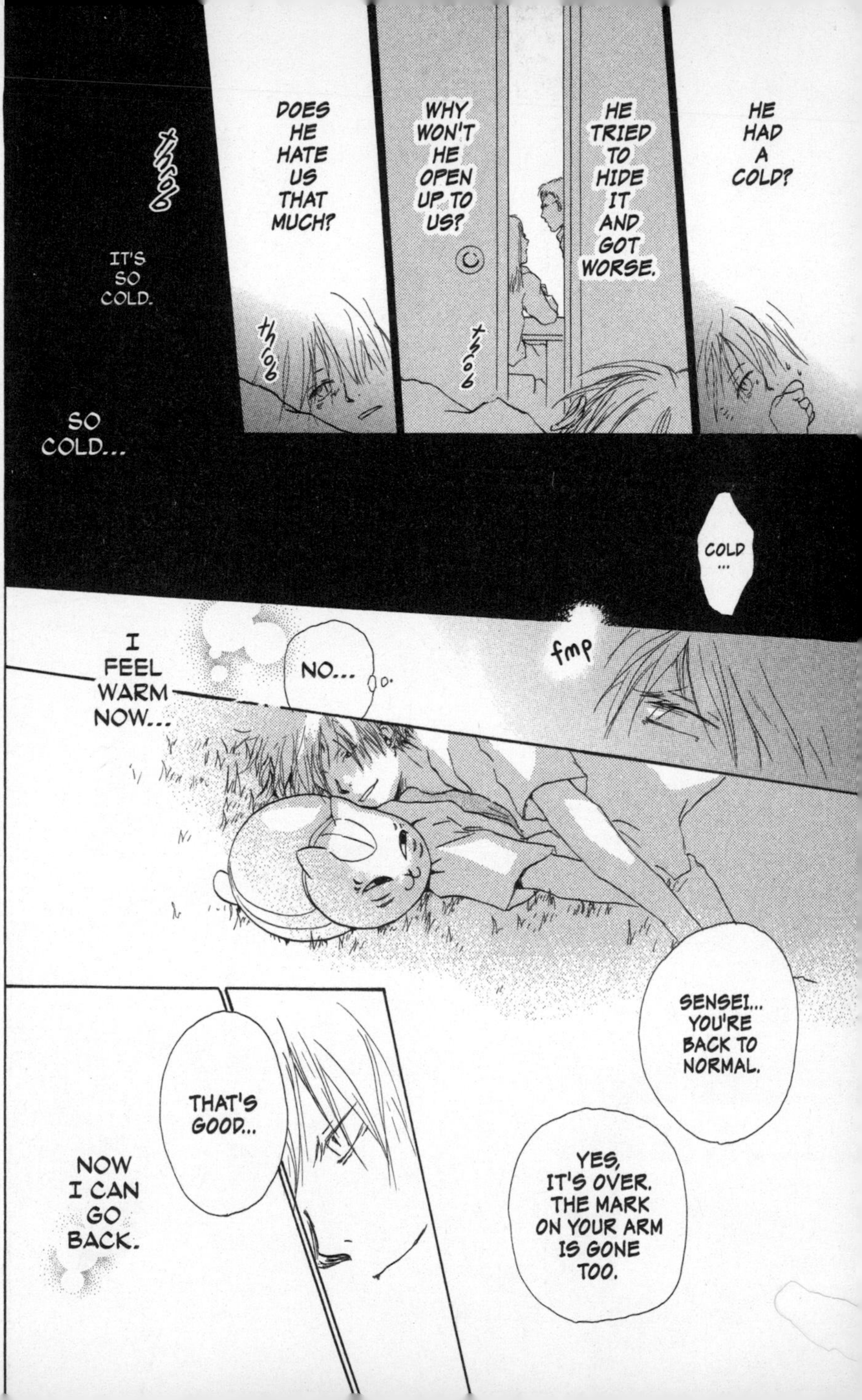
HE HAD A COLD?
HE TRIED TO HIDE IT AND GOT WORSE.
throb
WHY WON'T HE OPEN UP TO US?
throb
DOES HE HATE US THAT MUCH?
throb
IT'S SO COLD.
SO COLD...
COLD...
fmp
NO...
I FEEL WARM NOW...
SENSEI... YOU'RE BACK TO NORMAL.
YES, IT'S OVER. THE MARK ON YOUR ARM IS GONE TOO.
THAT'S GOOD...
NOW I CAN GO BACK.

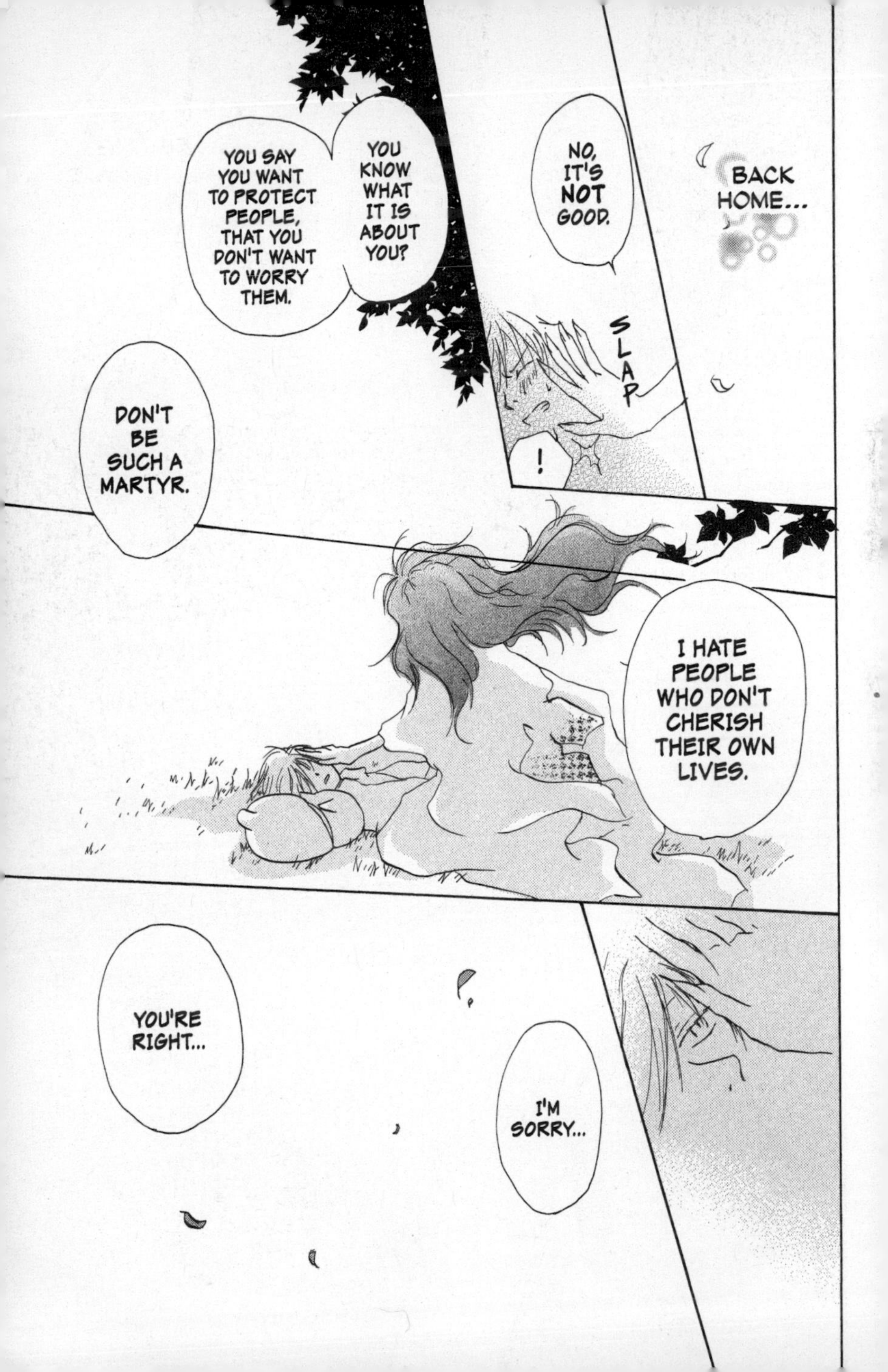
BACK HOME...
NO, IT'S NOT GOOD.
SLAP
!
YOU KNOW WHAT IT IS ABOUT YOU?
YOU SAY YOU WANT TO PROTECT PEOPLE, THAT YOU DON'T WANT TO WORRY THEM.
DON'T BE SUCH A MARTYR.
I HATE PEOPLE WHO DON'T CHERISH THEIR OWN LIVES.
YOU'RE RIGHT...
I'M SORRY...

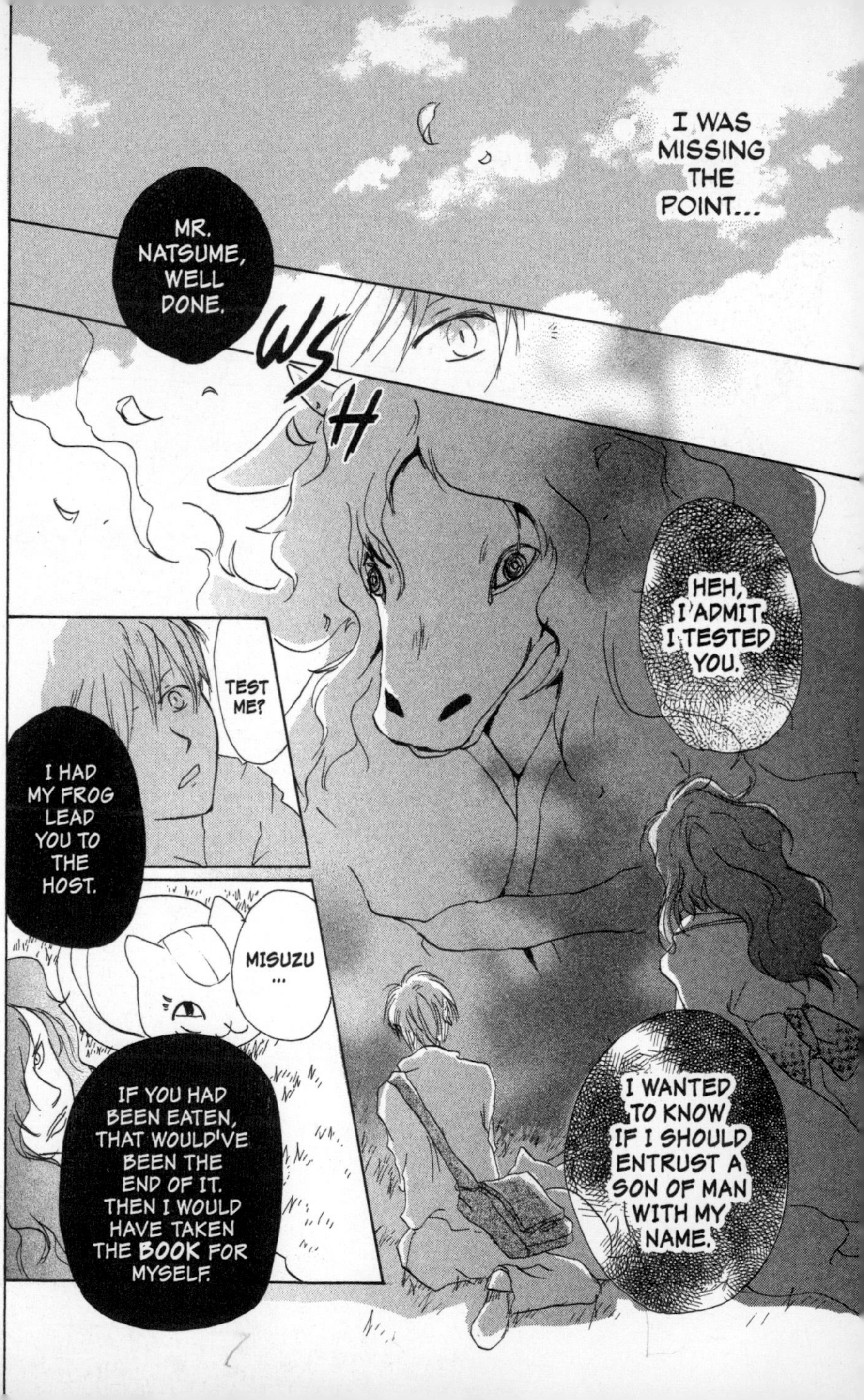
I WAS MISSING THE POINT...
MR. NATSUME, WELL DONE.
WSH
HEH, I ADMIT I TESTED YOU.
I WANTED TO KNOW IF I SHOULD ENTRUST A SON OF MAN WITH MY NAME.
TEST ME?
I HAD MY FROG LEAD YOU TO THE HOST.
MISUZU...
IF YOU HAD BEEN EATEN, THAT WOULD'VE BEEN THE END OF IT. THEN I WOULD HAVE TAKEN THE BOOK FOR MYSELF.

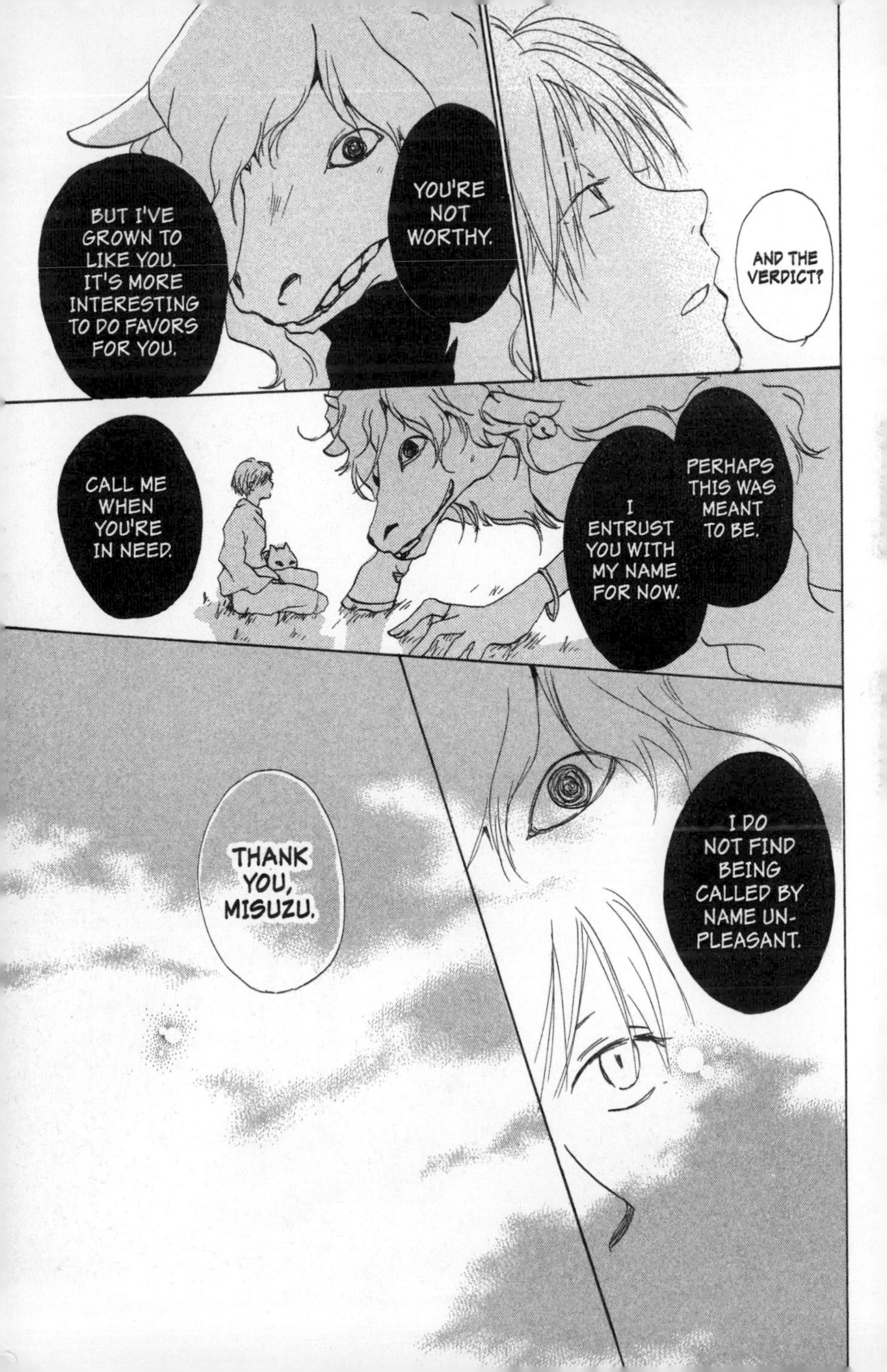
AND THE VERDICT?
YOU'RE NOT WORTHY.
BUT I'VE GROWN TO LIKE YOU. IT'S MORE INTERESTING TO DO FAVORS FOR YOU.
PERHAPS THIS WAS MEANT TO BE.
I ENTRUST YOU WITH MY NAME FOR NOW.
CALL ME WHEN YOU'RE IN NEED.
I DO NOT FIND BEING CALLED BY NAME UN-PLEASANT.
THANK YOU, MISUZU.

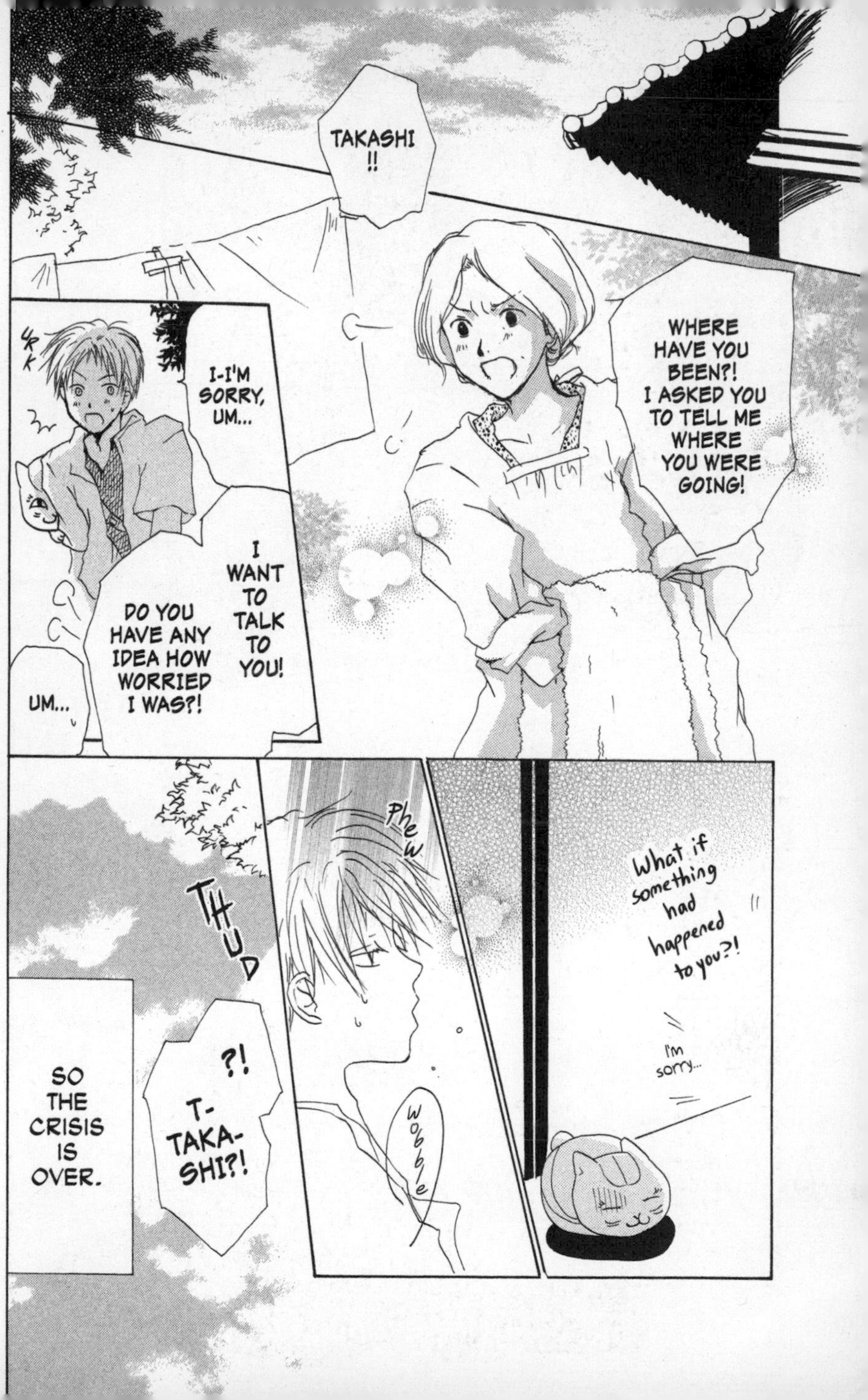
TAKASHI!!
WHERE HAVE YOU BEEN?! I ASKED YOU TO TELL ME WHERE YOU WERE GOING!
URK
I-I'M SORRY, UM...
I WANT TO TALK TO YOU!
DO YOU HAVE ANY IDEA HOW WORRIED I WAS?!
UM...
What if something had happened to you?!
I'm sorry...
Phew
Wobble
THUD
?!
T-TAKA-SHI?!
SO THE CRISIS IS OVER.

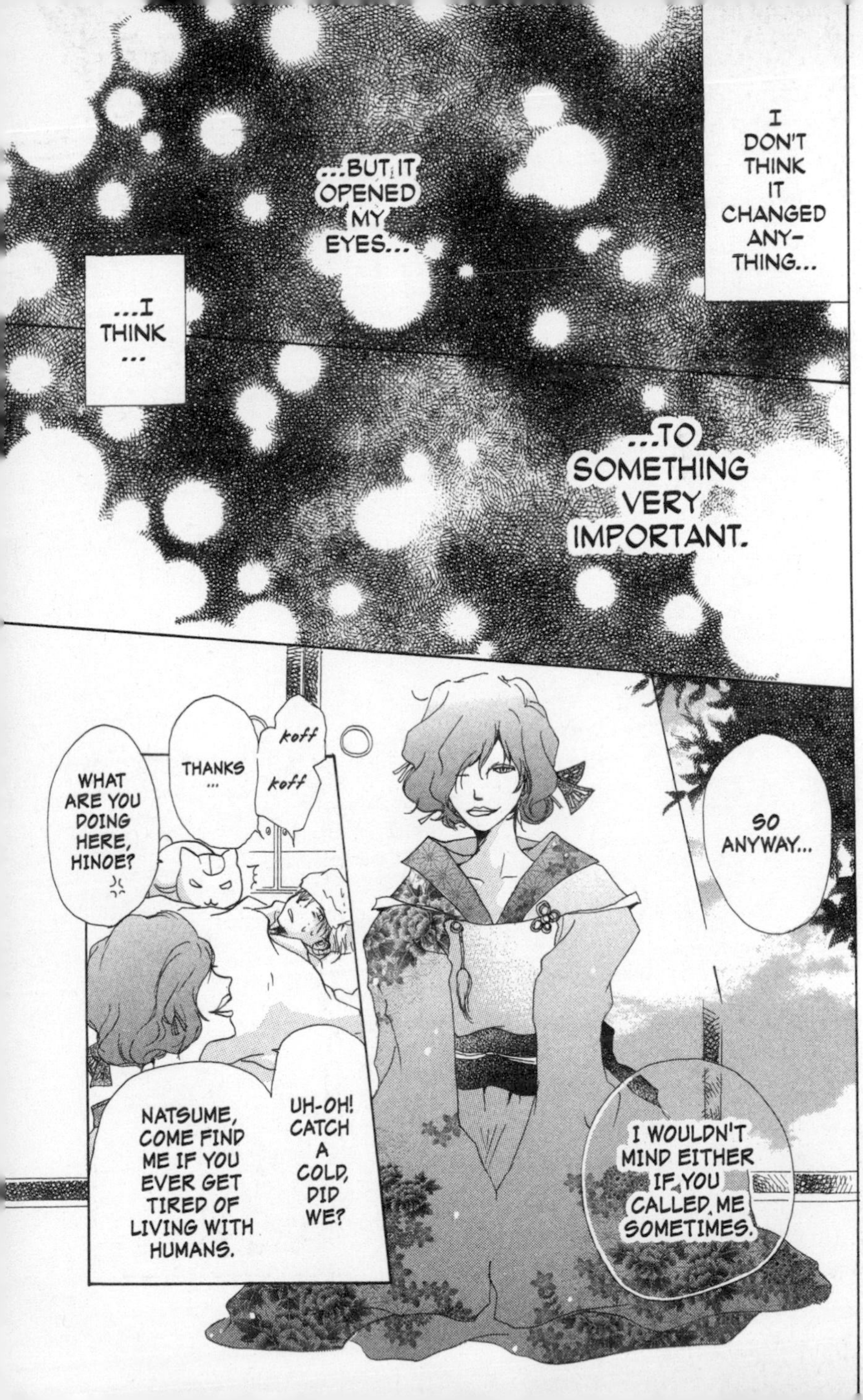
I DON'T THINK IT CHANGED ANYTHING...
...BUT IT OPENED MY EYES...
...I THINK...
...TO SOMETHING VERY IMPORTANT.
SO ANYWAY...
I WOULDN'T MIND EITHER IF YOU CALLED ME SOMETIMES.
koff koff
THANKS...
WHAT ARE YOU DOING HERE, HINOE?
UH-OH! CATCH A COLD, DID WE?
NATSUME, COME FIND ME IF YOU EVER GET TIRED OF LIVING WITH HUMANS.

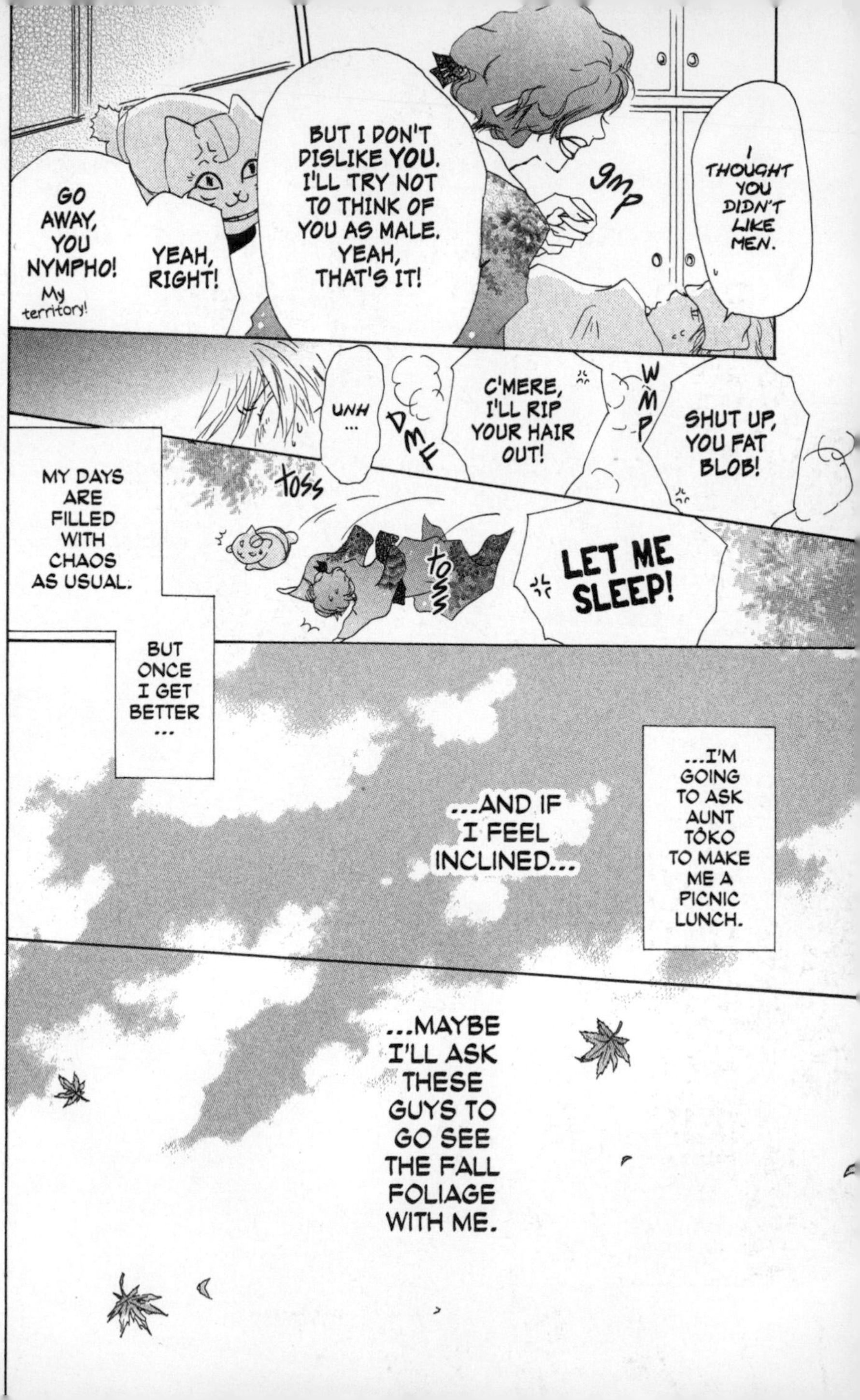
I THOUGHT YOU DIDN'T LIKE MEN.
gmp
BUT I DON'T DISLIKE YOU. I'LL TRY NOT TO THINK OF YOU AS MALE. YEAH, THAT'S IT!
YEAH, RIGHT!
GO AWAY, YOU NYMPHO!
My territory!
SHUT UP, YOU FAT BLOB!
WMP
C'MERE, I'LL RIP YOUR HAIR OUT!
DMF
UNH ...
LET ME SLEEP!
TOSS
TOSS
MY DAYS ARE FILLED WITH CHAOS AS USUAL.
BUT ONCE I GET BETTER ...
...I'M GOING TO ASK AUNT TÔKO TO MAKE ME A PICNIC LUNCH.
...AND IF I FEEL INCLINED...
...MAYBE I'LL ASK THESE GUYS TO GO SEE THE FALL FOLIAGE WITH ME.

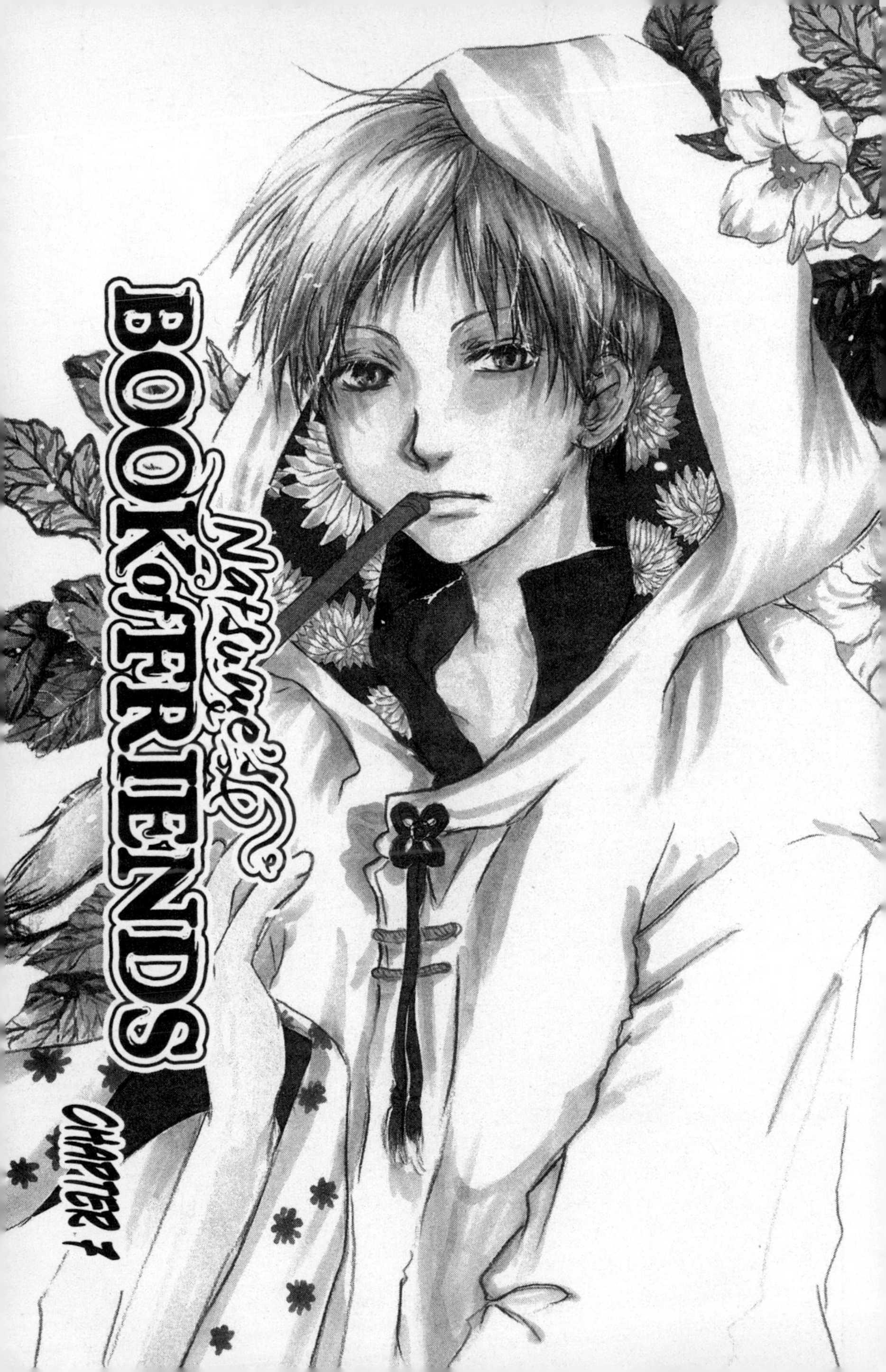
Natsume's
BOOK of FRIENDS
CHAPTER 7

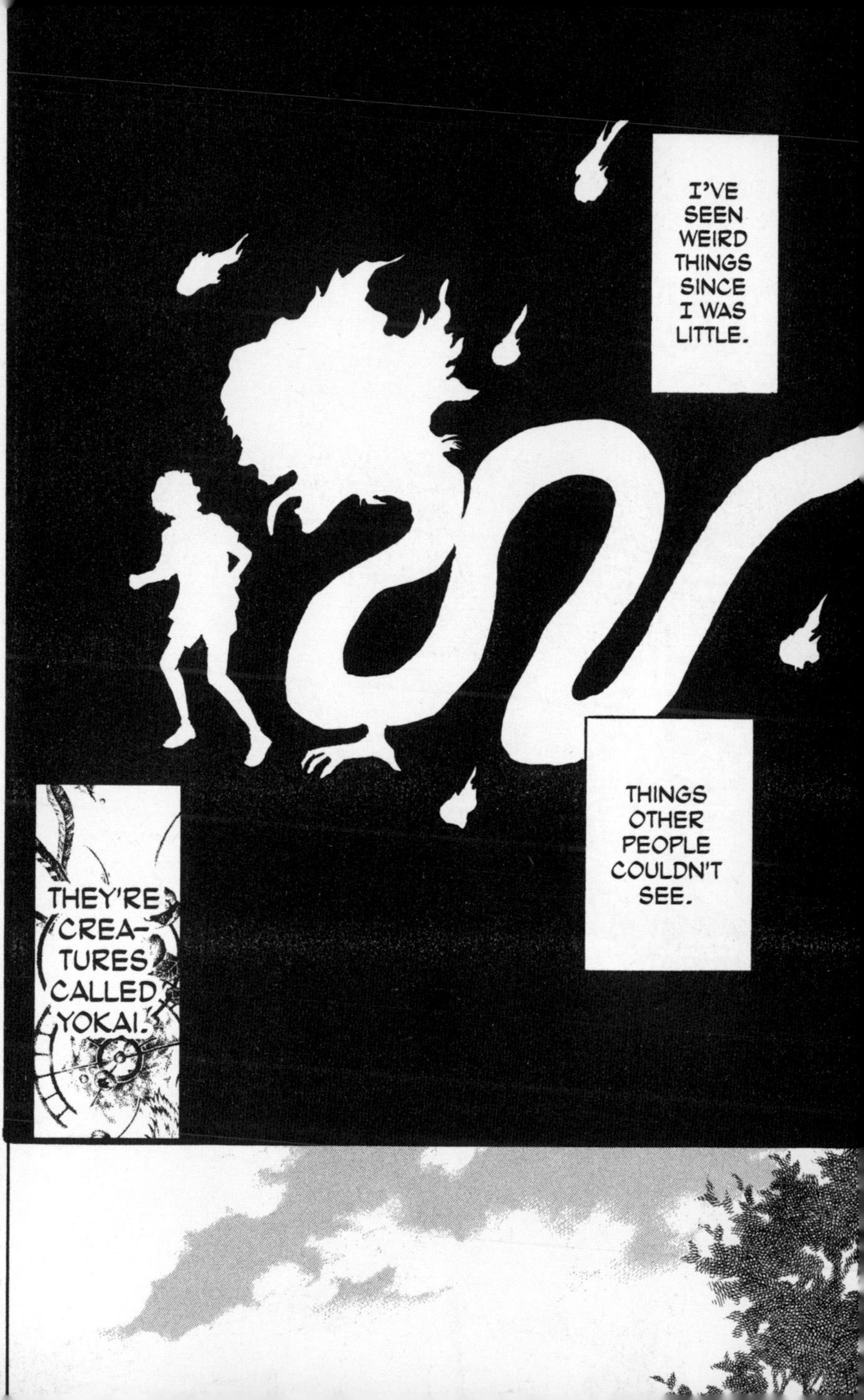
I'VE SEEN WEIRD THINGS SINCE I WAS LITTLE.
THINGS OTHER PEOPLE COULDN'T SEE.
THEY'RE CREA-TURES CALLED YOKAI.

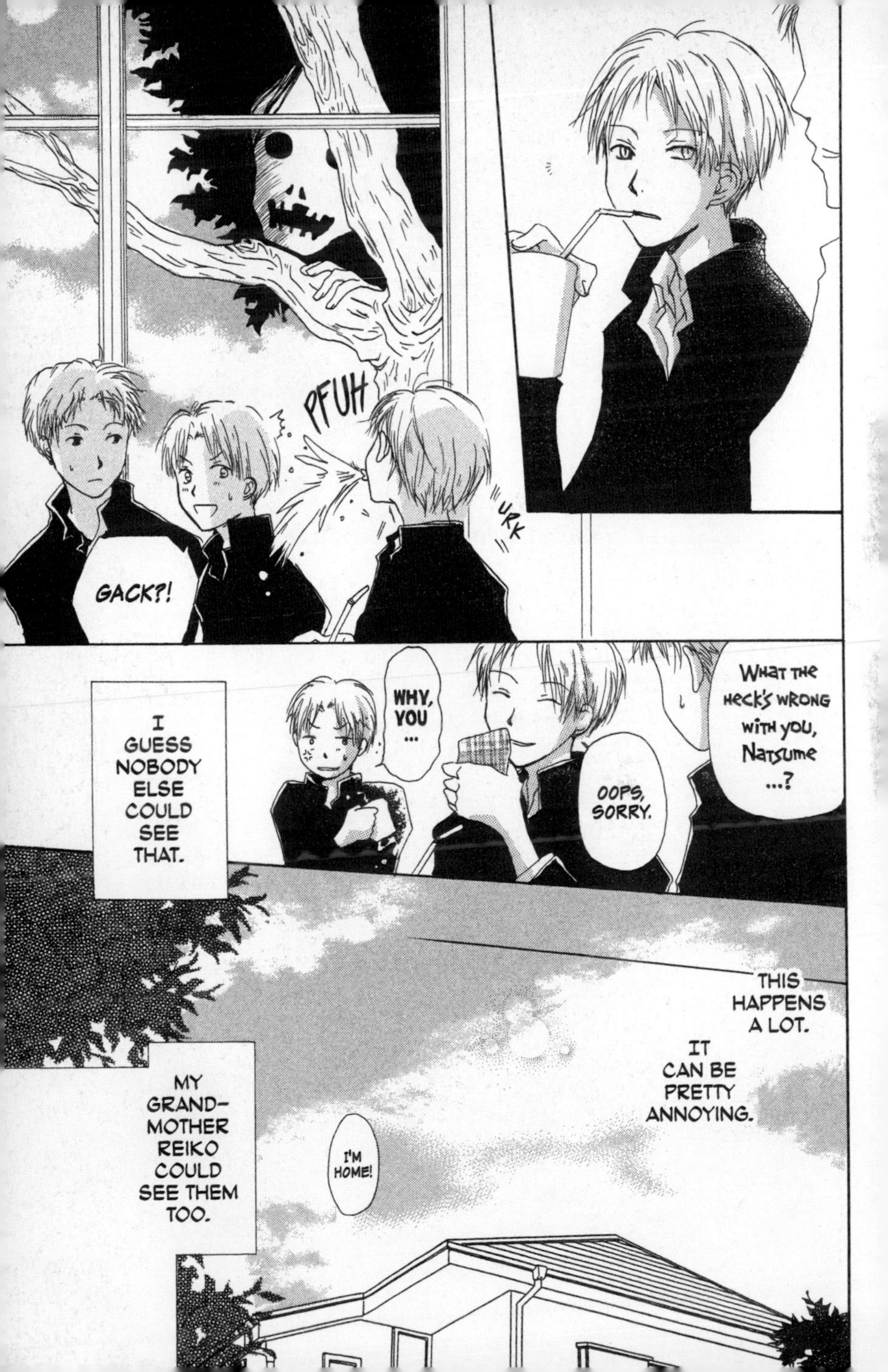
PFUH
URK
GACK?!
What the heck's wrong with you, Natsume ...?
OOPS, SORRY.
WHY, YOU ...
I GUESS NOBODY ELSE COULD SEE THAT.
THIS HAPPENS A LOT.
IT CAN BE PRETTY ANNOYING.
I'M HOME!
MY GRAND-MOTHER REIKO COULD SEE THEM TOO.

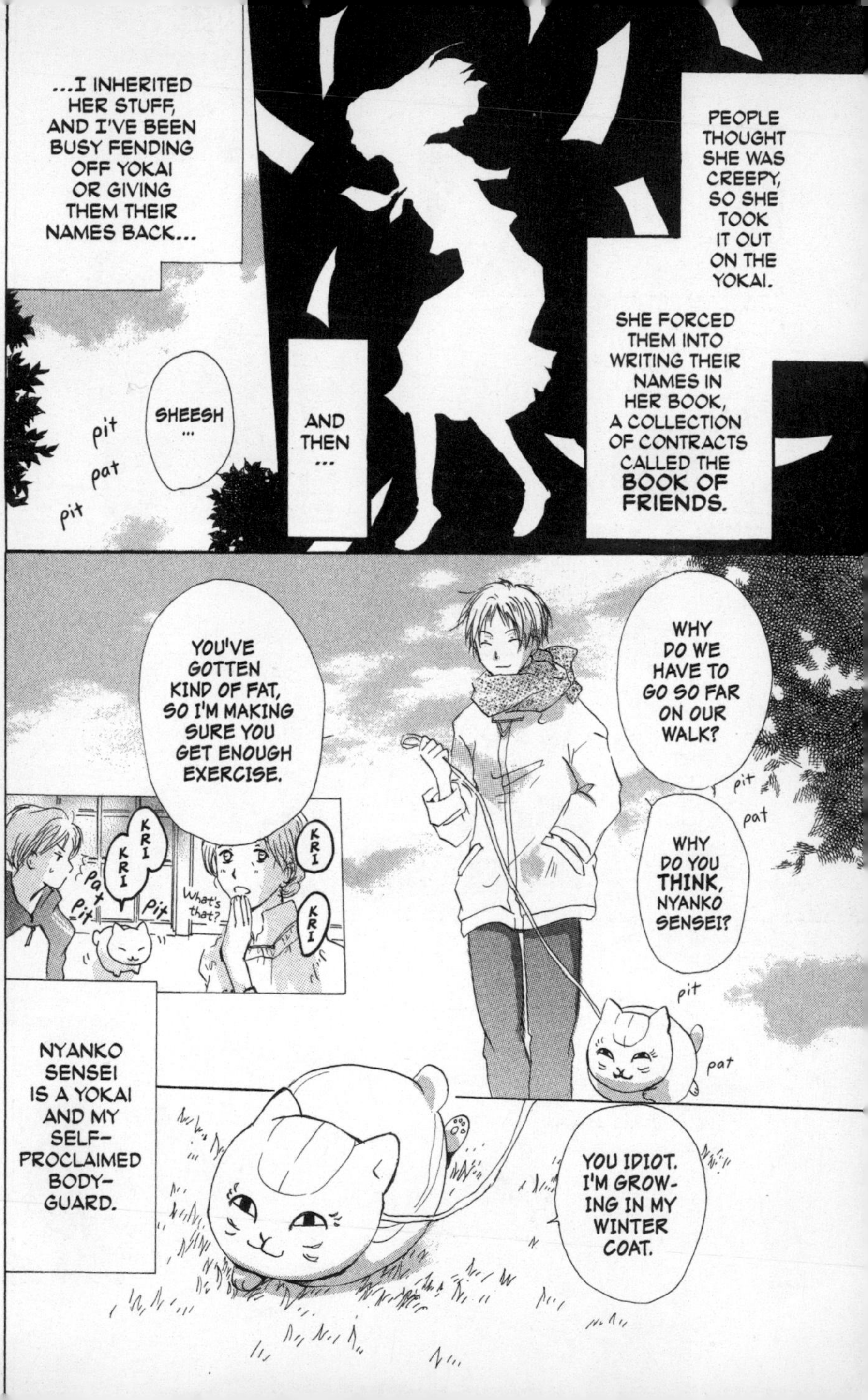
PEOPLE THOUGHT SHE WAS CREEPY, SO SHE TOOK IT OUT ON THE YOKAI.
SHE FORCED THEM INTO WRITING THEIR NAMES IN HER BOOK, A COLLECTION OF CONTRACTS CALLED THE BOOK OF FRIENDS.
AND THEN...
...I INHERITED HER STUFF, AND I'VE BEEN BUSY FENDING OFF YOKAI OR GIVING THEM THEIR NAMES BACK...
SHEESH...
pit
pat
pit
WHY DO WE HAVE TO GO SO FAR ON OUR WALK?
YOU'VE GOTTEN KIND OF FAT, SO I'M MAKING SURE YOU GET ENOUGH EXERCISE.
KRI KRI
KRI
KRI
Pat
pit
pit
What's that?
pit
pat
WHY DO YOU THINK, NYANKO SENSEI?
pit
pat
YOU IDIOT. I'M GROWING IN MY WINTER COAT.
NYANKO SENSEI IS A YOKAI AND MY SELF-PROCLAIMED BODY-GUARD.

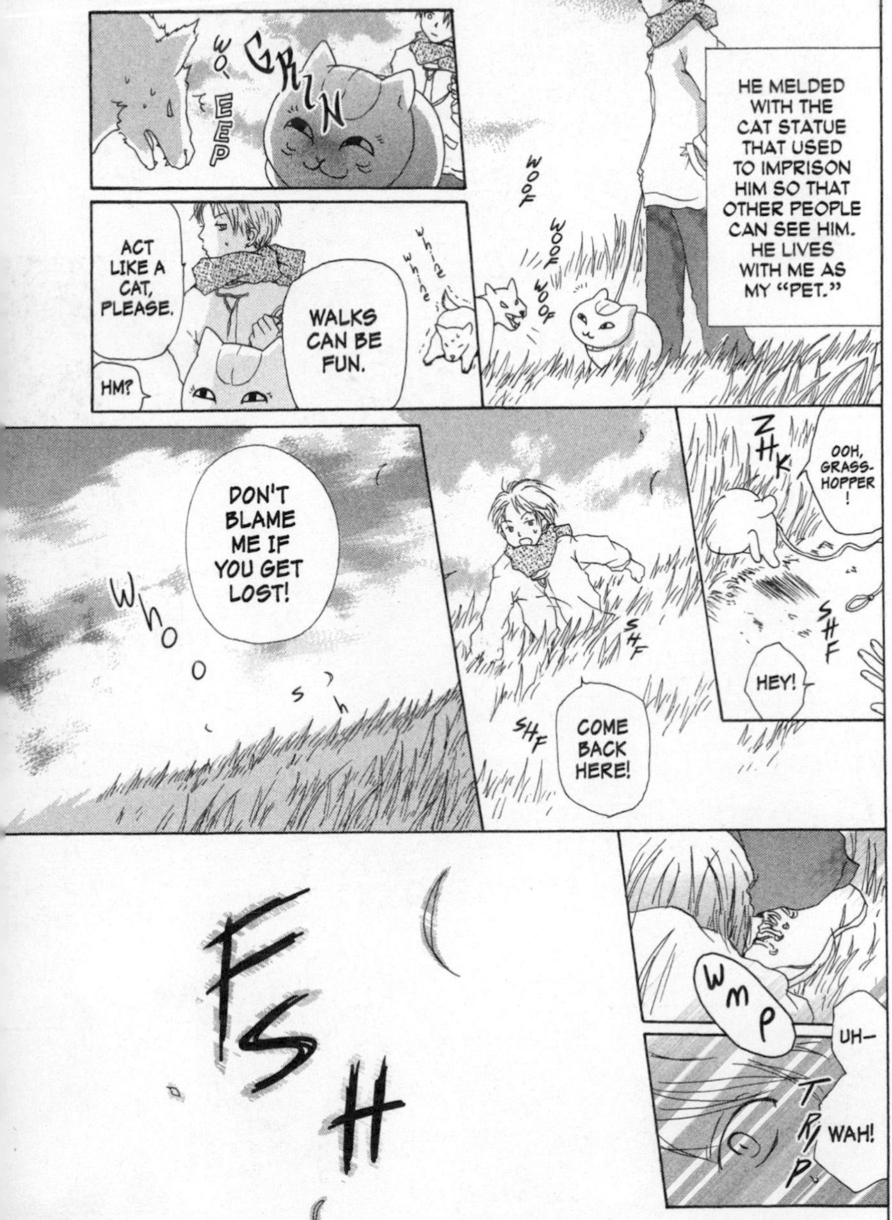
HE MELDED WITH THE CAT STATUE THAT USED TO IMPRISON HIM SO THAT OTHER PEOPLE CAN SEE HIM. HE LIVES WITH ME AS MY "PET."
WOOF
WOOF
WOOF
GRIN
WO-EEP
whine whine
WALKS CAN BE FUN.
ACT LIKE A CAT, PLEASE.
HM?
ZHK
OOH, GRASS-HOPPER!
SHF
HEY!
SHF
COME BACK HERE!
DON'T BLAME ME IF YOU GET LOST!
Whoosh
WMP
UH–
TRIP
WAH!
FSH

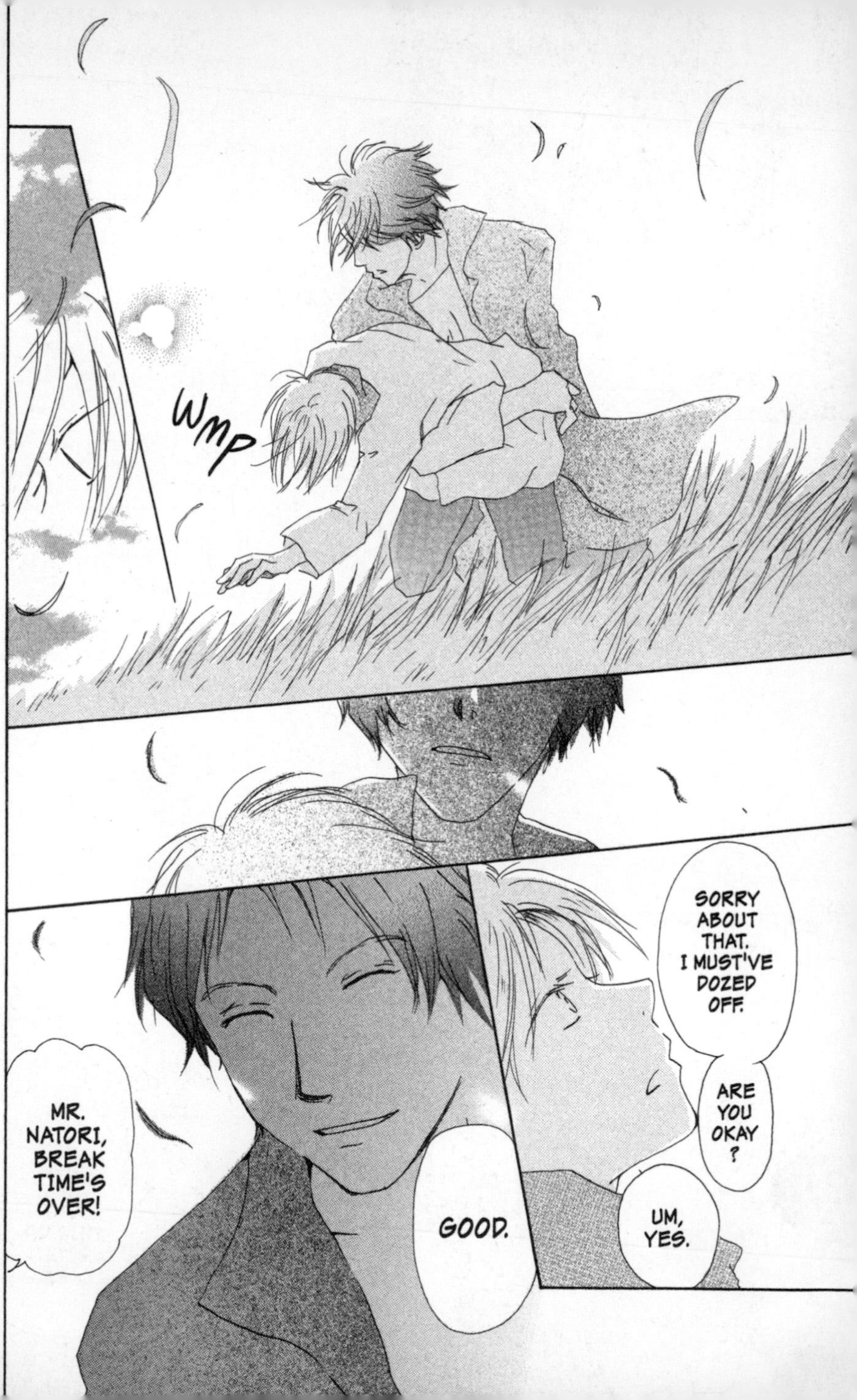
WMP
SORRY ABOUT THAT. I MUST'VE DOZED OFF.
ARE YOU OKAY?
UM, YES.
GOOD.
MR. NATORI, BREAK TIME'S OVER!

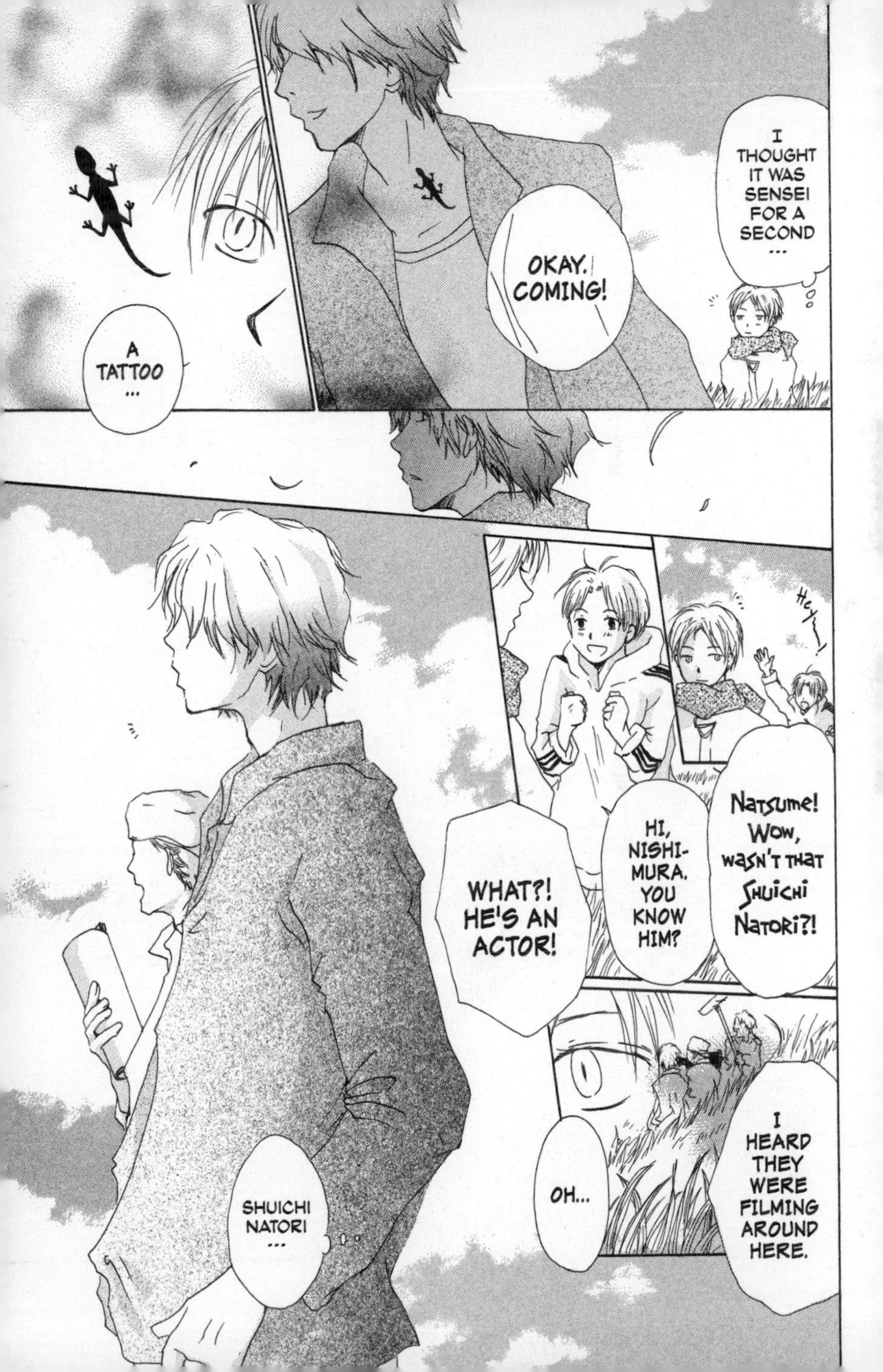
I THOUGHT IT WAS SENSEI FOR A SECOND ...
OKAY. COMING!
A TATTOO ...
Hey—!
Natsume! Wow, wasn't that Shuichi Natori?!
HI, NISHIMURA. YOU KNOW HIM?
WHAT?! HE'S AN ACTOR!
I HEARD THEY WERE FILMING AROUND HERE.
OH...
SHUICHI NATORI ...

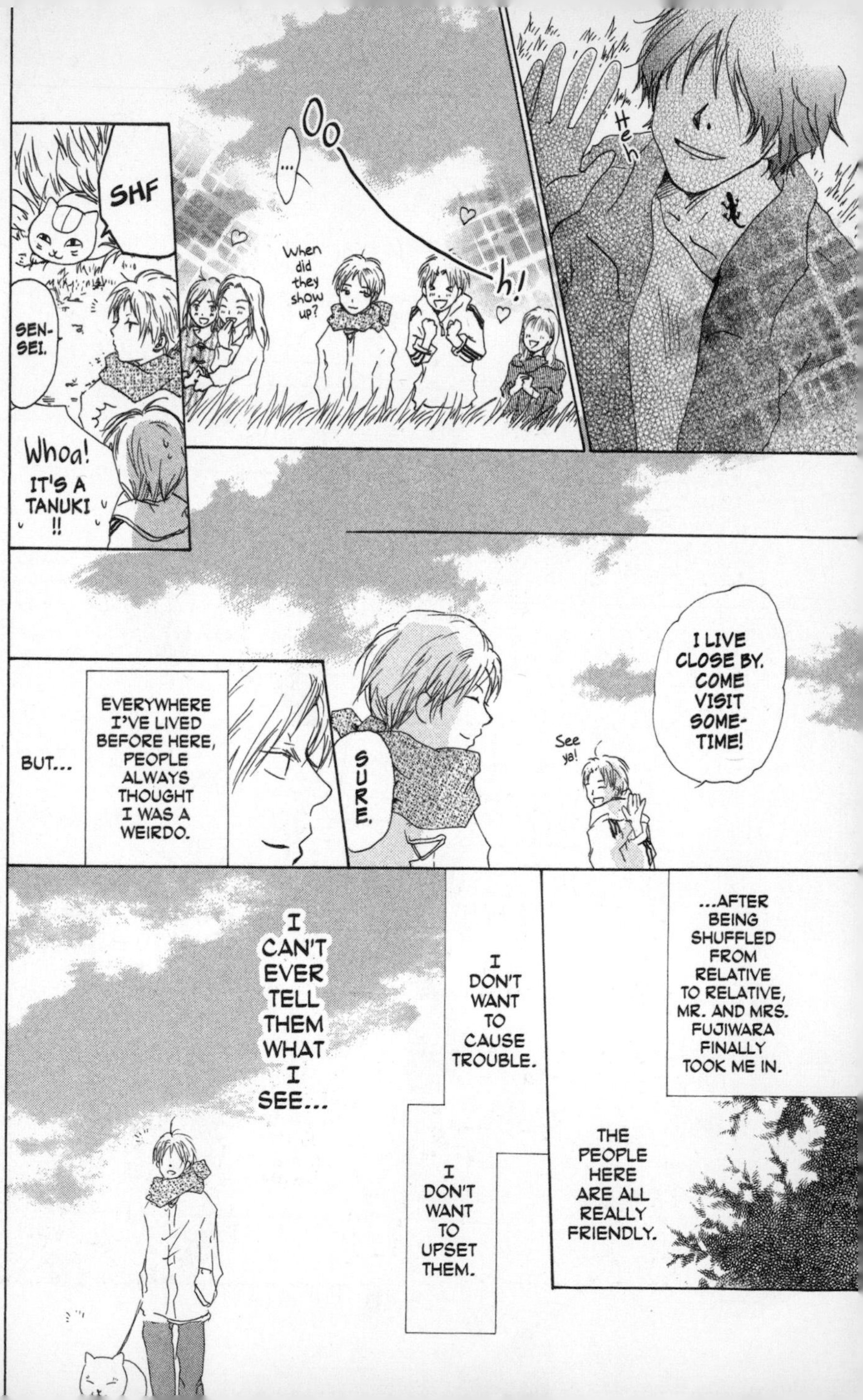
Heh
Oo...h!
...
When did they show up?
SHF
SEN-SEI.
Whoa! IT'S A TANUKI!!
I LIVE CLOSE BY. COME VISIT SOME-TIME!
See ya!
SURE.
EVERYWHERE I'VE LIVED BEFORE HERE, PEOPLE ALWAYS THOUGHT I WAS A WEIRDO.
BUT...
...AFTER BEING SHUFFLED FROM RELATIVE TO RELATIVE, MR. AND MRS. FUJIWARA FINALLY TOOK ME IN.
THE PEOPLE HERE ARE ALL REALLY FRIENDLY.
I DON'T WANT TO CAUSE TROUBLE.
I DON'T WANT TO UPSET THEM.
I CAN'T EVER TELL THEM WHAT I SEE...

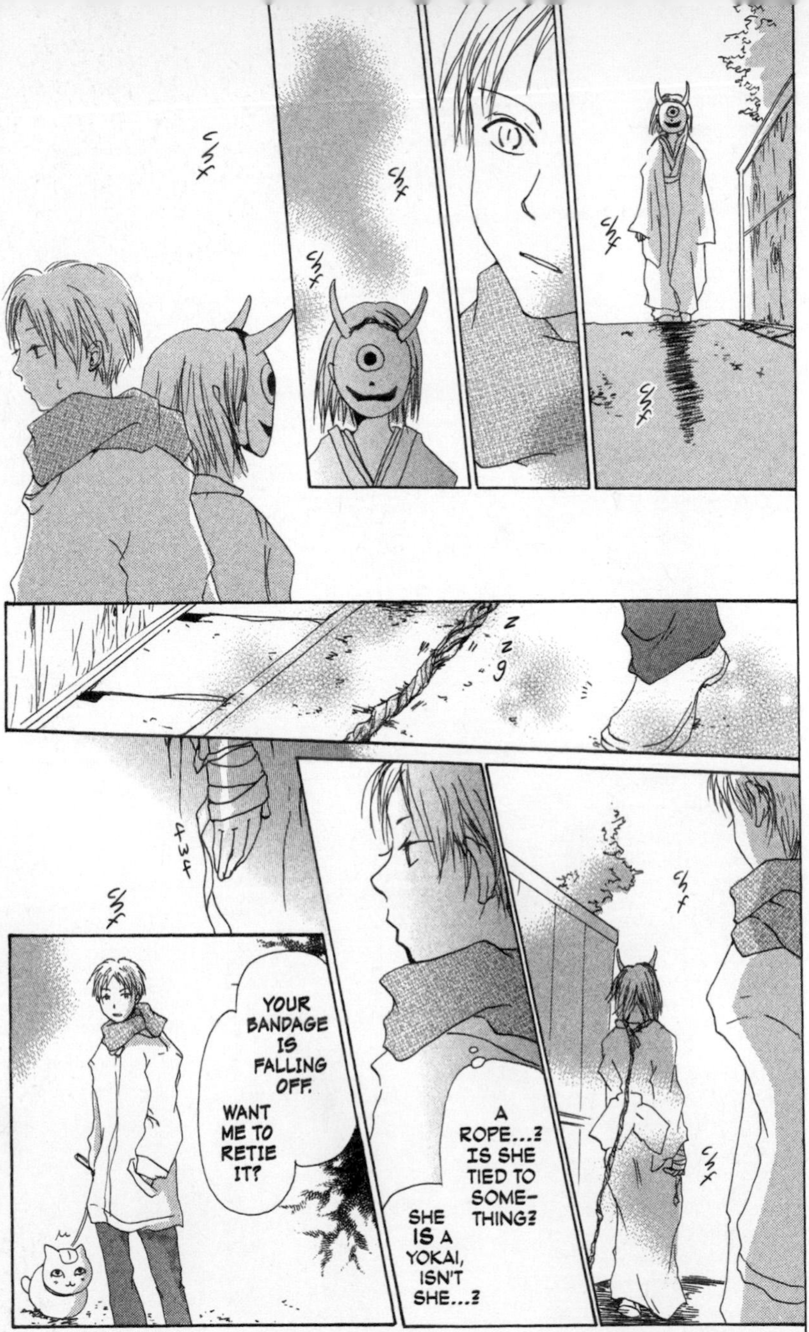
A ROPE...? IS SHE TIED TO SOMETHING?
SHE IS A YOKAI, ISN'T SHE...?
YOUR BANDAGE IS FALLING OFF.
WANT ME TO RETIE IT?

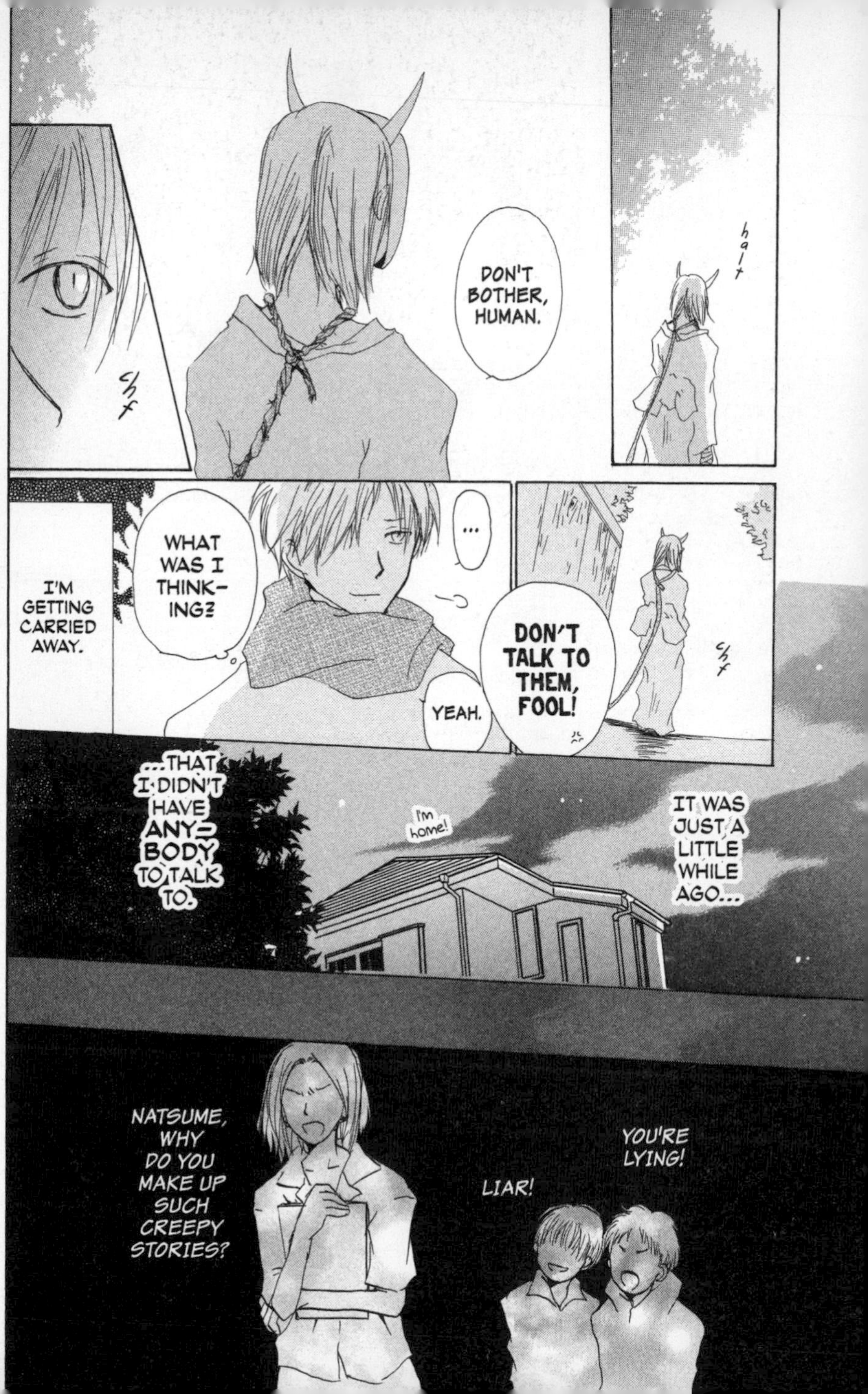
halt
DON'T BOTHER, HUMAN.
chf
DON'T TALK TO THEM, FOOL!
chf
...
YEAH.
WHAT WAS I THINKING?
I'M GETTING CARRIED AWAY.
IT WAS JUST A LITTLE WHILE AGO...
I'm home!
...THAT I DIDN'T HAVE ANYBODY TO TALK TO.
YOU'RE LYING!
LIAR!
NATSUME, WHY DO YOU MAKE UP SUCH CREEPY STORIES?

05

❋ Large yokai

When I was little, I was smitten by the beauty of horses. So I'm happy every time I draw Misuzu. And his fluffy mane. But he's so huge (just like Nyanko Sensei's true form) his entire body doesn't fit into the panel. That's my only regret. I keep thinking I should use bigger panels in my layout, at least when I have big creatures, but I have this habit of scrimping and saving space. I hope I learn to use large panels for my bigger characters one of these days. When I was working on the title page for chapter 7, I realized it was my first time coloring such a large face. It's something I have to work on.

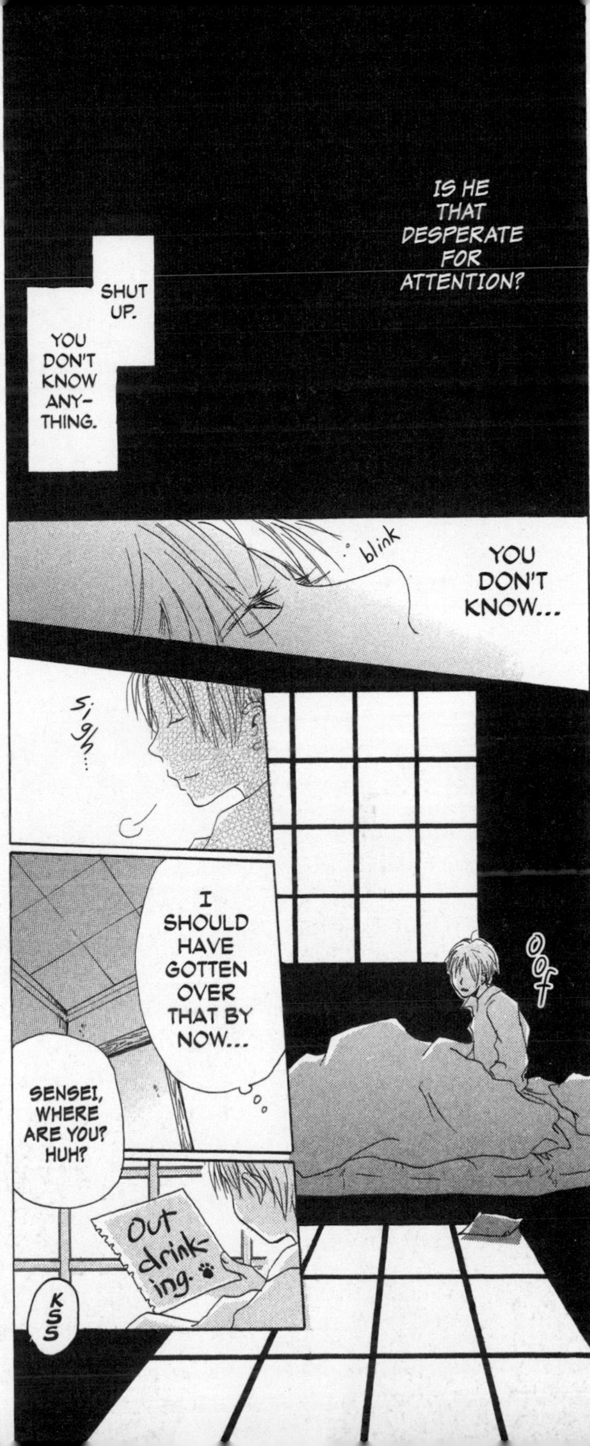
IS HE THAT DESPERATE FOR ATTENTION?
SHUT UP.
YOU DON'T KNOW ANYTHING.
blink
YOU DON'T KNOW...
sigh...
oof
I SHOULD HAVE GOTTEN OVER THAT BY NOW...
SENSEI, WHERE ARE YOU? HUH?
Out drinking.
KSS

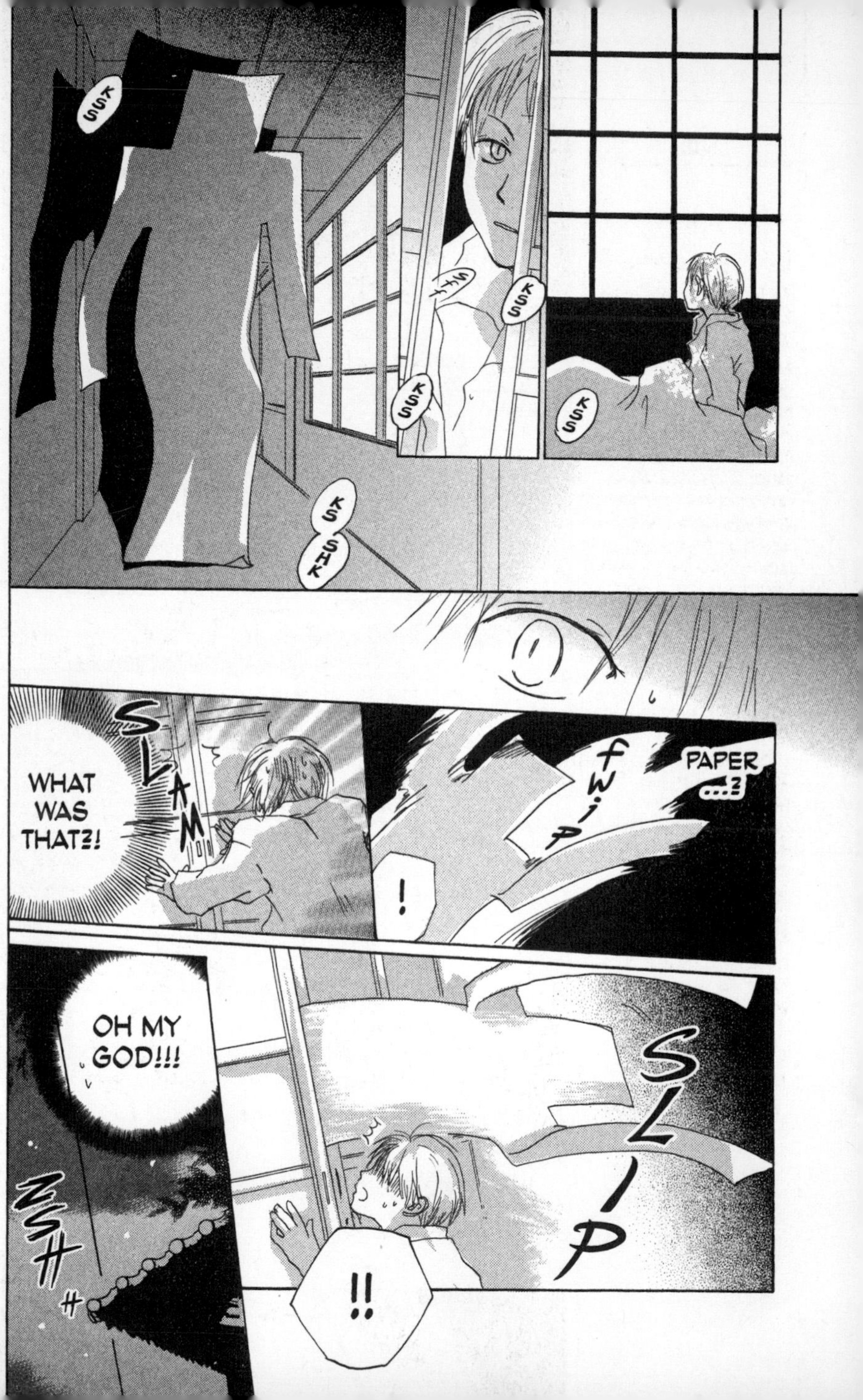
KSS
KSS
SFF
KSS
KSS
KS SHK
PAPER ...?
FWIP
!
SLAM
WHAT WAS THAT?!
SLIP
!!
OH MY GOD!!!
ZSHH

06

❋Goldfish

Besides horses, I've always loved goldfish. I still can't resist the goldfish-patterned products that appear every summer. There was a period of my life when I loved them so much that I was amazed at the amount of adrenaline pumping through my body just at the sight of a crimson fish under crystal clear water. There's also a type of Japanese confection where a candy fish floats inside a piece of translucent agar. That just makes me squirm with joy. Why is that?!

Probably by extension, I love ponds, lakes and generally bodies of water of any size surrounded by nature. Why is that? Because it looks like Jell-O?

On an unrelated note...

← Continued in part 07

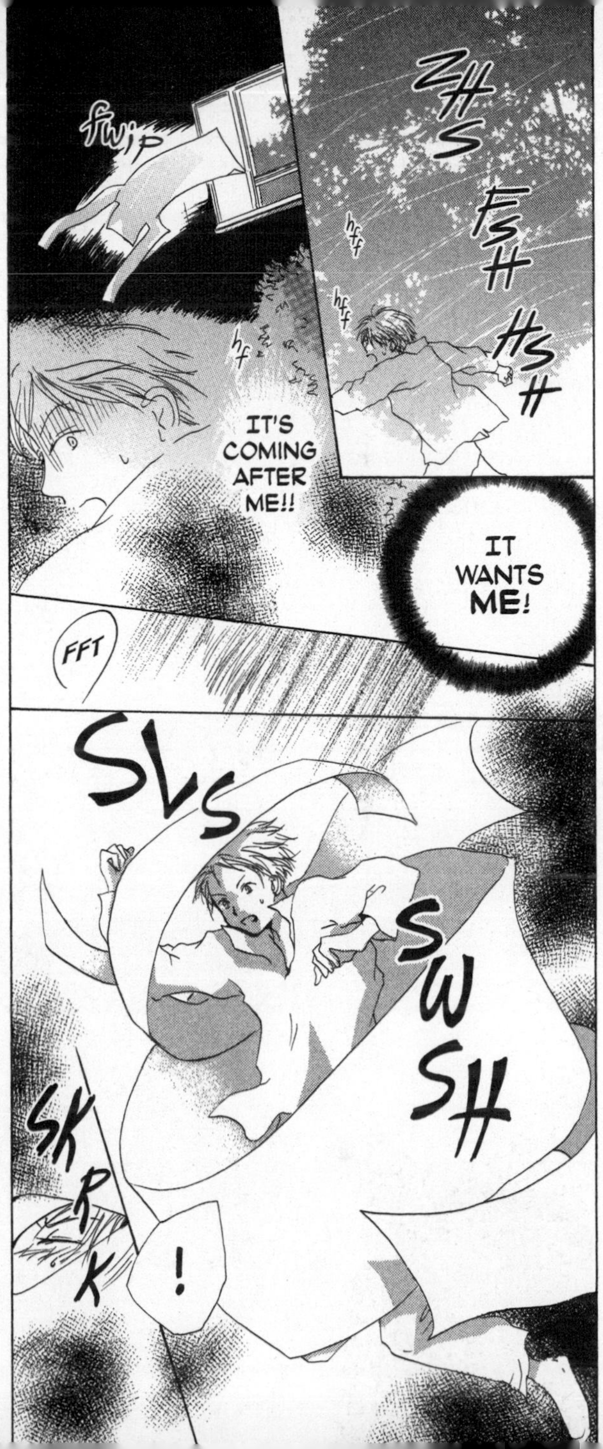
ZHS
FSH
HSH
hff
hff
fwip
hf
IT'S COMING AFTER ME!!
IT WANTS ME!
FFT
SWSH
SVS
SKRK
!

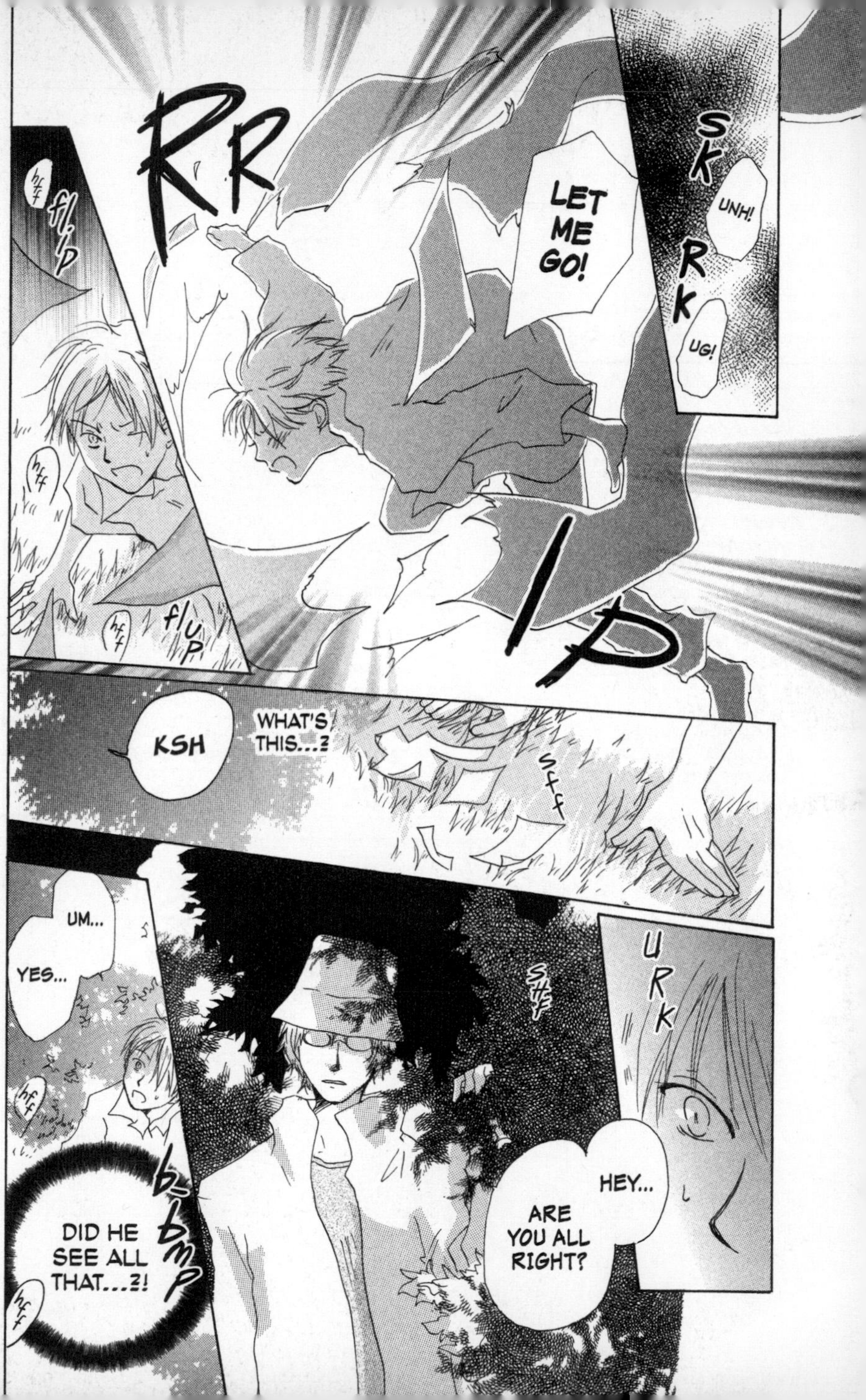
SKRK
UNH!
UG!
LET ME GO!
RR
IP
flip
hff
hff
flup
hff
sff
WHAT'S THIS...?
KSH
URK
HEY...
ARE YOU ALL RIGHT?
sff
UM...
YES...
hff
DID HE SEE ALL THAT...?!
b-bmp
hff

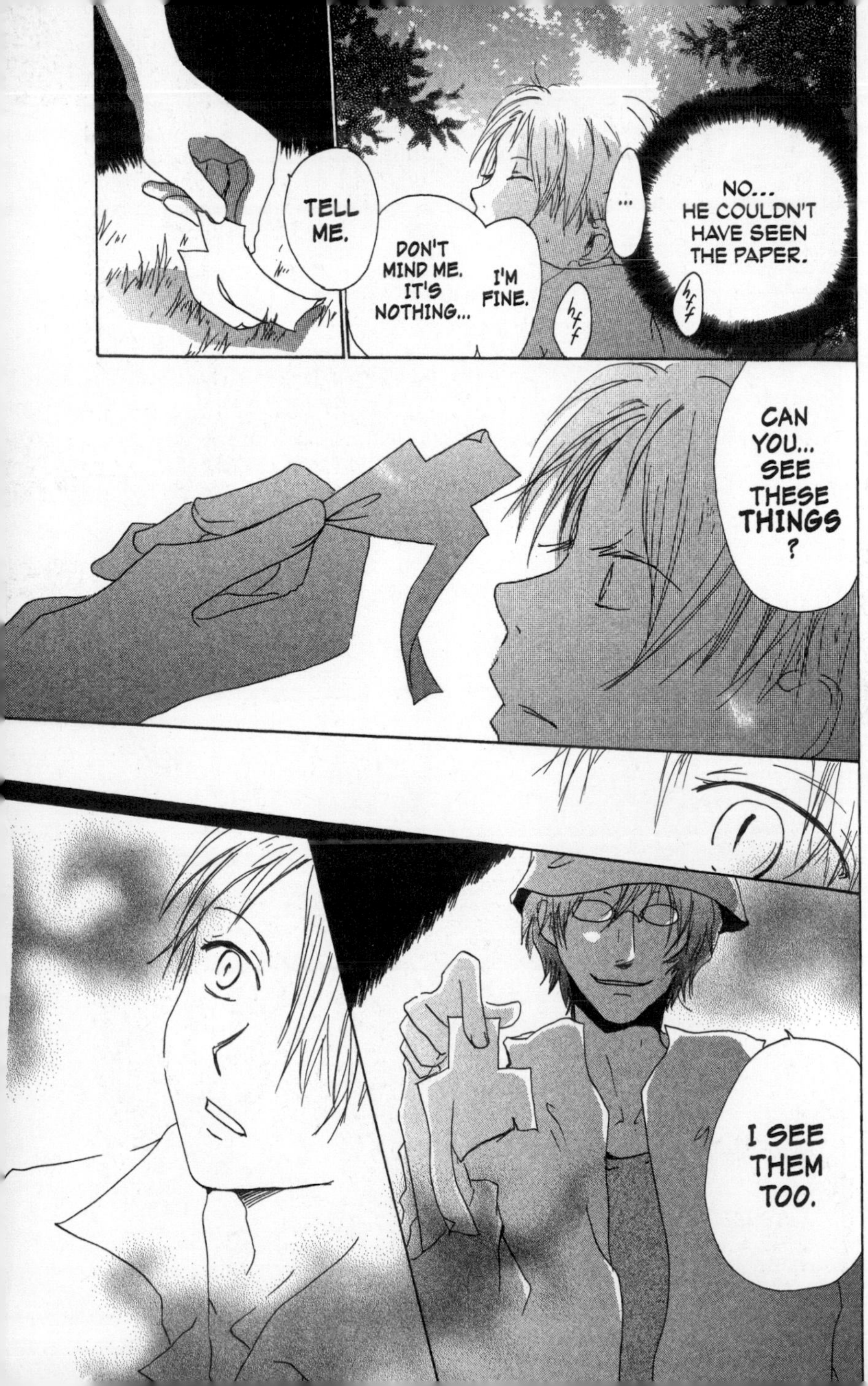
NO... HE COULDN'T HAVE SEEN THE PAPER.
...
hff
hff
I'M FINE.
DON'T MIND ME. IT'S NOTHING...
TELL ME.
CAN YOU... SEE THESE THINGS?
I SEE THEM TOO.

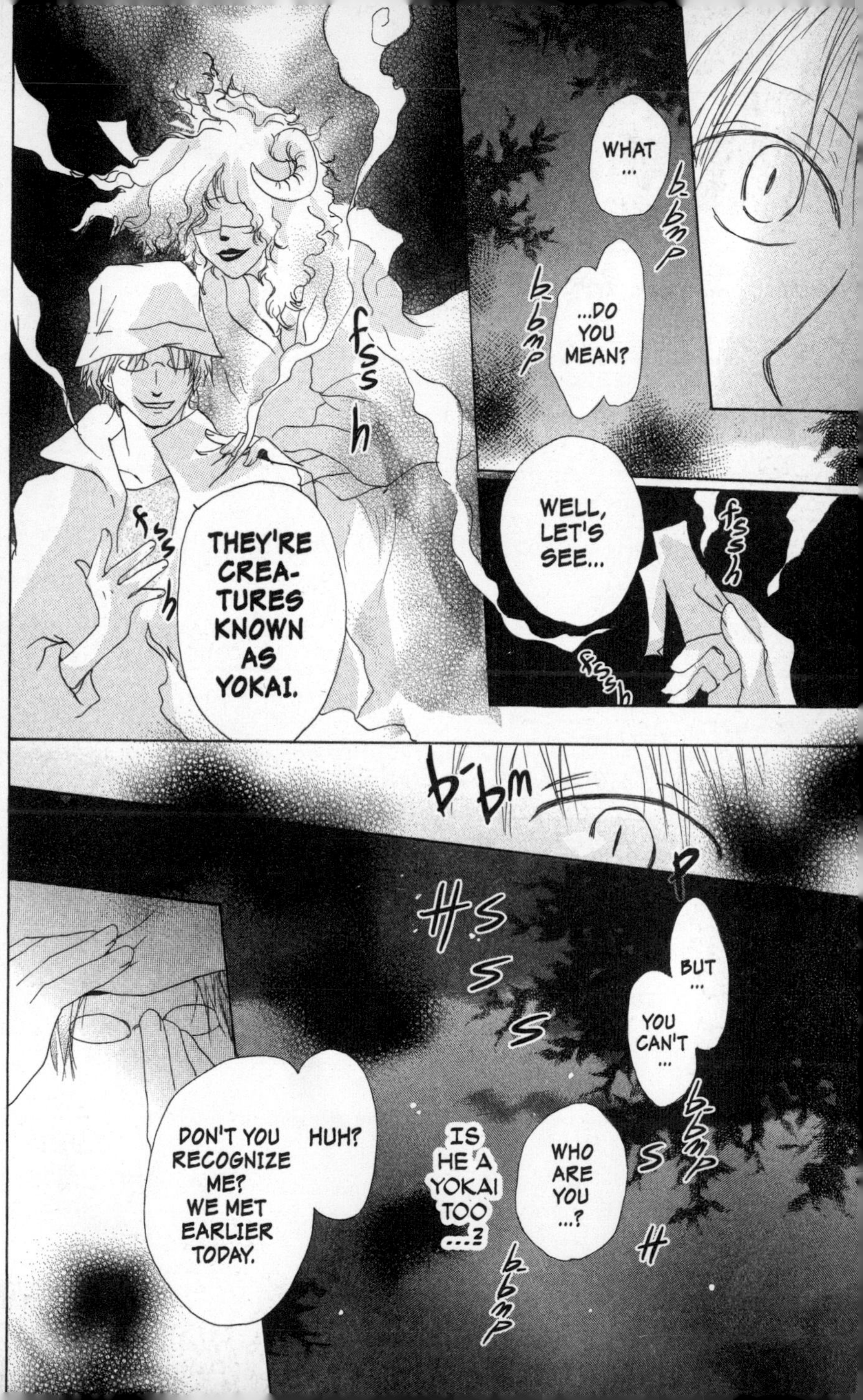
WHAT ...
b-bmp
...DO YOU MEAN?
b-bmp
WELL, LET'S SEE...
fssh
fssh
fssh
THEY'RE CREA-TURES KNOWN AS YOKAI.
fssh
b-bmp
BUT ...
YOU CAN'T ...
b-bmp
WHO ARE YOU ...?
HSSSSH
IS HE A YOKAI TOO ...?
b-bmp
HUH?
DON'T YOU RECOGNIZE ME? WE MET EARLIER TODAY.

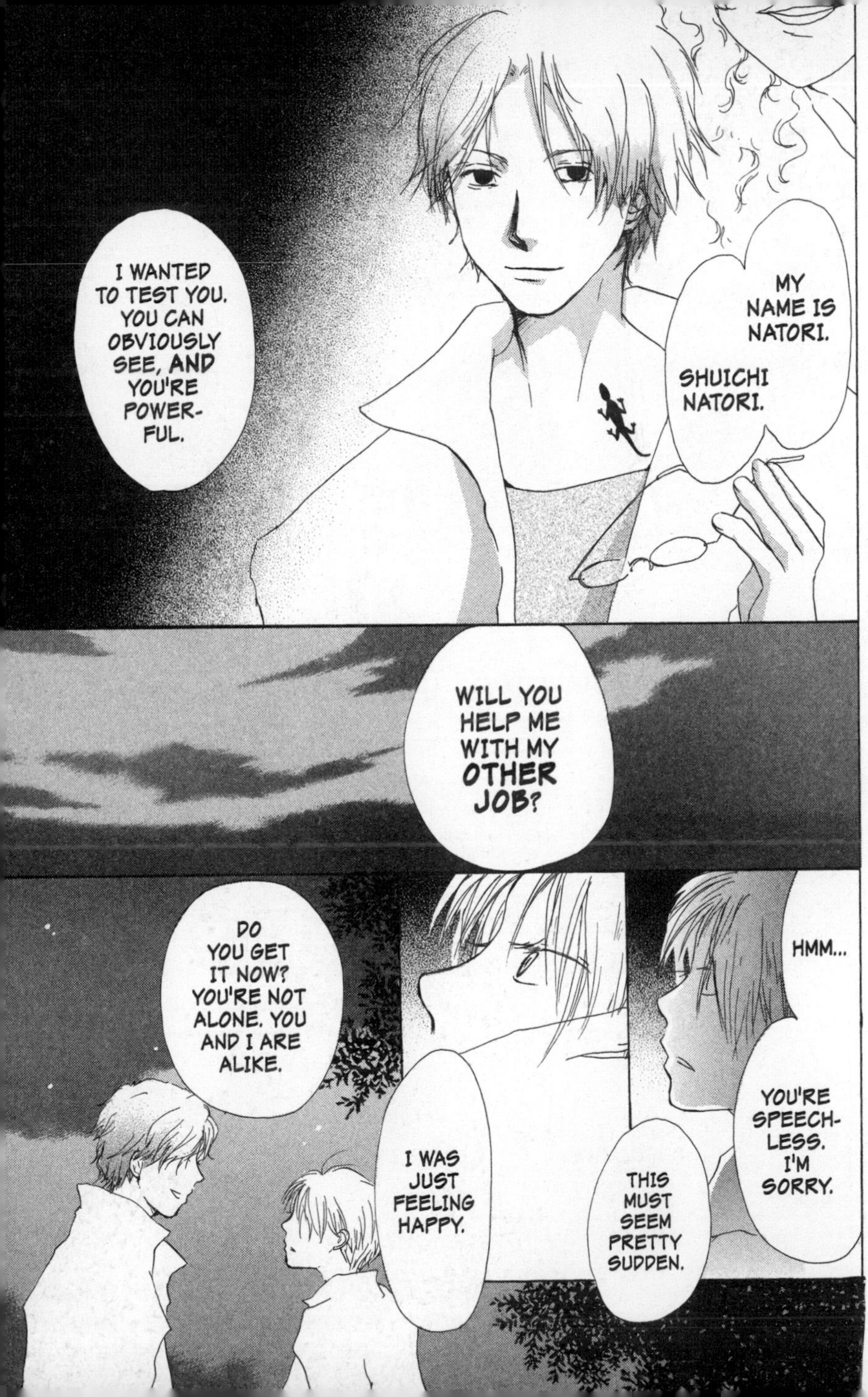
MY NAME IS NATORI.
SHUICHI NATORI.
I WANTED TO TEST YOU. YOU CAN OBVIOUSLY SEE, AND YOU'RE POWER-FUL.
WILL YOU HELP ME WITH MY OTHER JOB?
HMM...
YOU'RE SPEECH-LESS. I'M SORRY.
THIS MUST SEEM PRETTY SUDDEN.
I WAS JUST FEELING HAPPY.
DO YOU GET IT NOW? YOU'RE NOT ALONE. YOU AND I ARE ALIKE.

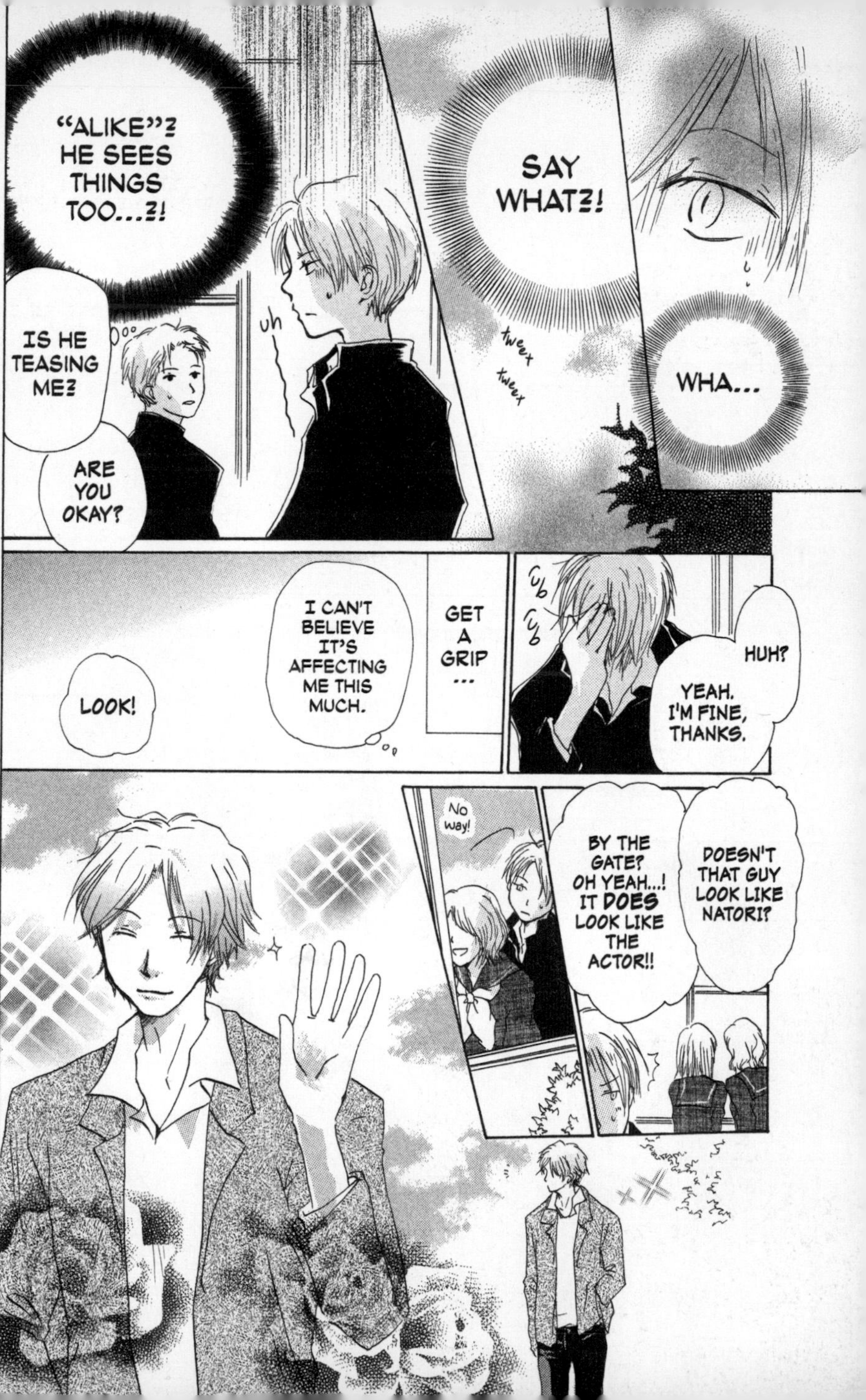
WHA...
SAY WHAT?!
tweet tweet
"ALIKE"? HE SEES THINGS TOO...?!
uh
IS HE TEASING ME?
ARE YOU OKAY?
rub rub
HUH?
YEAH. I'M FINE, THANKS.
GET A GRIP...
I CAN'T BELIEVE IT'S AFFECTING ME THIS MUCH.
LOOK!
DOESN'T THAT GUY LOOK LIKE NATORI?
BY THE GATE? OH YEAH...! IT DOES LOOK LIKE THE ACTOR!!
No way!

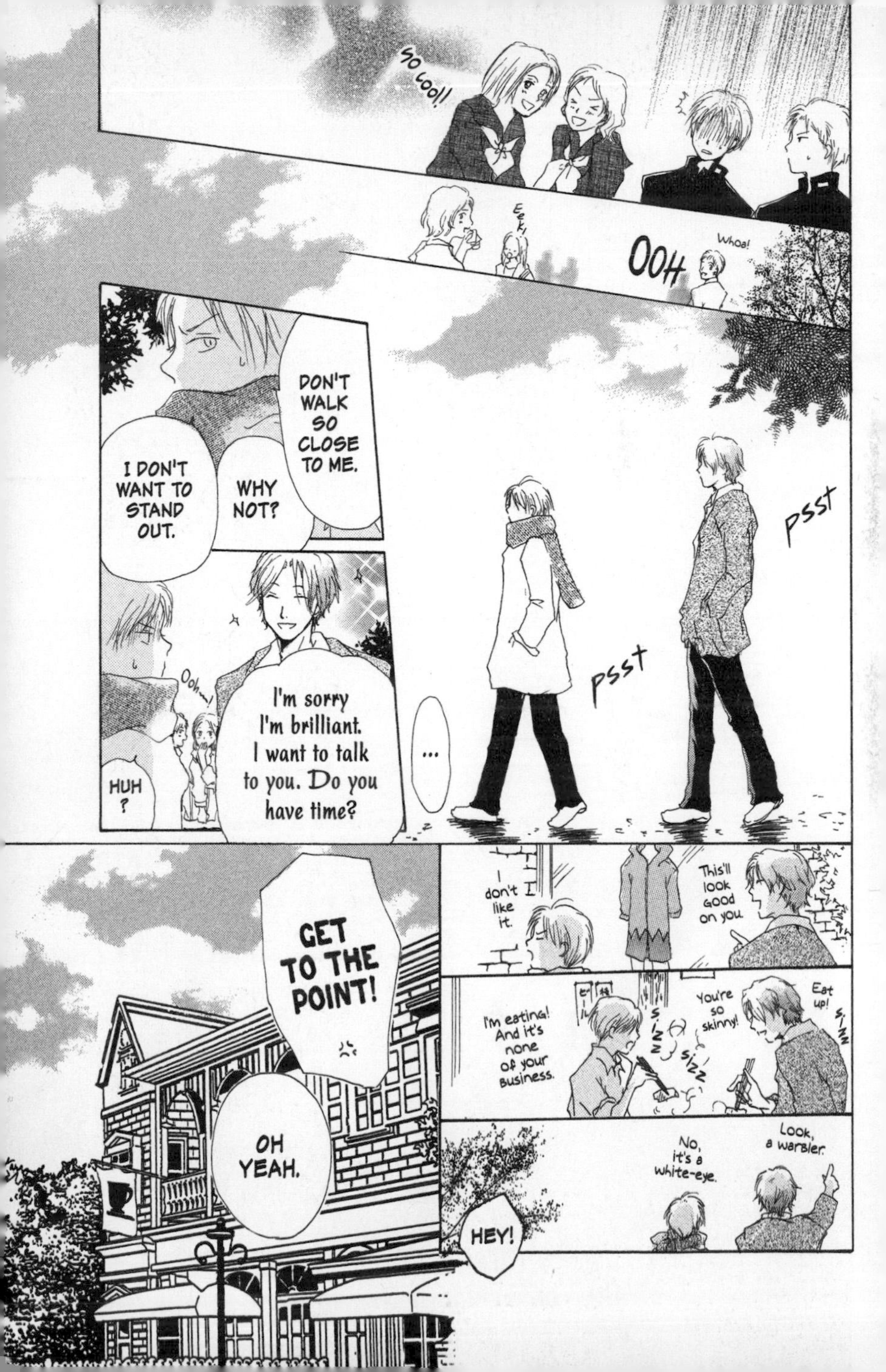
So cool!
Whoa!
OOH
Eek!
psst
psst
...
DON'T WALK SO CLOSE TO ME.
WHY NOT?
I DON'T WANT TO STAND OUT.
I'm sorry I'm brilliant. I want to talk to you. Do you have time?
Ooh...!
HUH?
This'll look good on you.
I don't like it.
Eat up!
You're so skinny!
I'm eating! And it's none of your business.
SIZZ
SIZZ
SIZZ
Look, a warbler.
No, it's a white-eye.
HEY!
GET TO THE POINT!
OH YEAH.

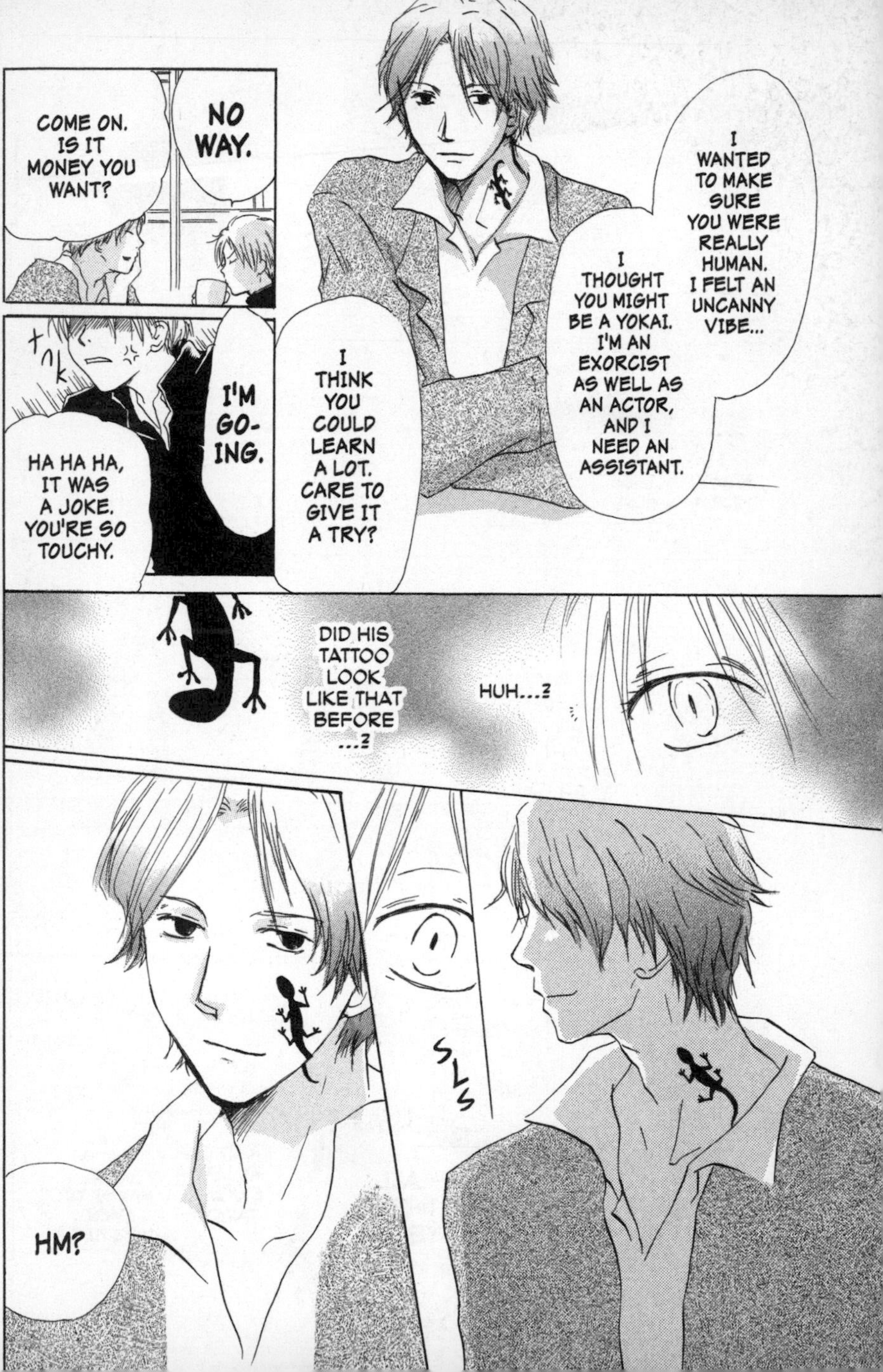
I WANTED TO MAKE SURE YOU WERE REALLY HUMAN. I FELT AN UNCANNY VIBE...
I THOUGHT YOU MIGHT BE A YOKAI. I'M AN EXORCIST AS WELL AS AN ACTOR, AND I NEED AN ASSISTANT.
I THINK YOU COULD LEARN A LOT. CARE TO GIVE IT A TRY?
NO WAY.
COME ON. IS IT MONEY YOU WANT?
I'M GO-ING.
HA HA HA, IT WAS A JOKE. YOU'RE SO TOUCHY.
HUH...?
DID HIS TATTOO LOOK LIKE THAT BEFORE ...?
SLS
HM?

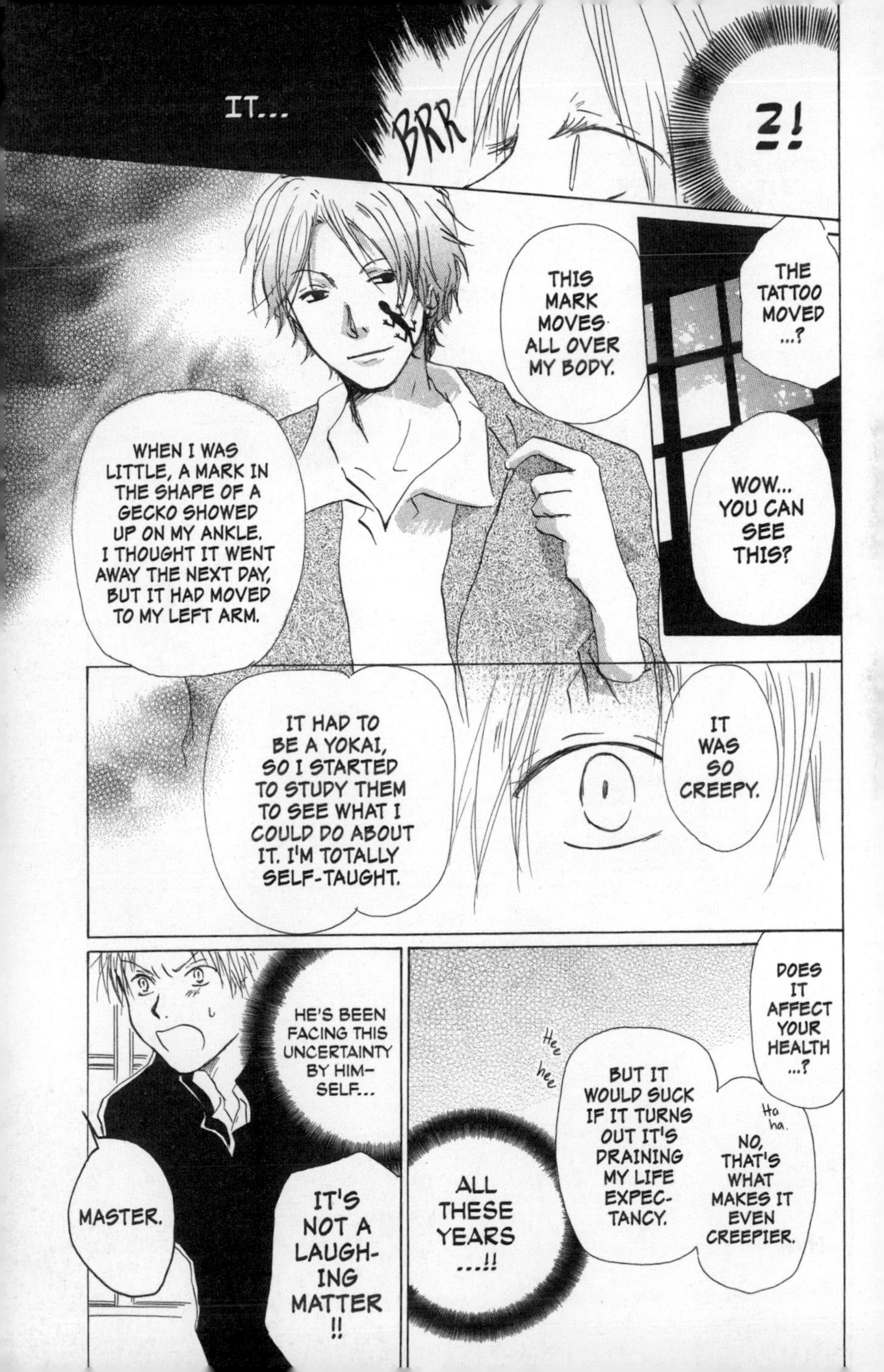
Z!
BRR
IT...
THE TATTOO MOVED ...?
WOW... YOU CAN SEE THIS?
THIS MARK MOVES ALL OVER MY BODY.
WHEN I WAS LITTLE, A MARK IN THE SHAPE OF A GECKO SHOWED UP ON MY ANKLE. I THOUGHT IT WENT AWAY THE NEXT DAY, BUT IT HAD MOVED TO MY LEFT ARM.
IT WAS SO CREEPY.
IT HAD TO BE A YOKAI, SO I STARTED TO STUDY THEM TO SEE WHAT I COULD DO ABOUT IT. I'M TOTALLY SELF-TAUGHT.
DOES IT AFFECT YOUR HEALTH ...?
Ha ha.
NO, THAT'S WHAT MAKES IT EVEN CREEPIER.
BUT IT WOULD SUCK IF IT TURNS OUT IT'S DRAINING MY LIFE EXPEC-TANCY.
Hee hee
ALL THESE YEARS ...!!
HE'S BEEN FACING THIS UNCERTAINTY BY HIM-SELF...
IT'S NOT A LAUGH-ING MATTER !!
MASTER.

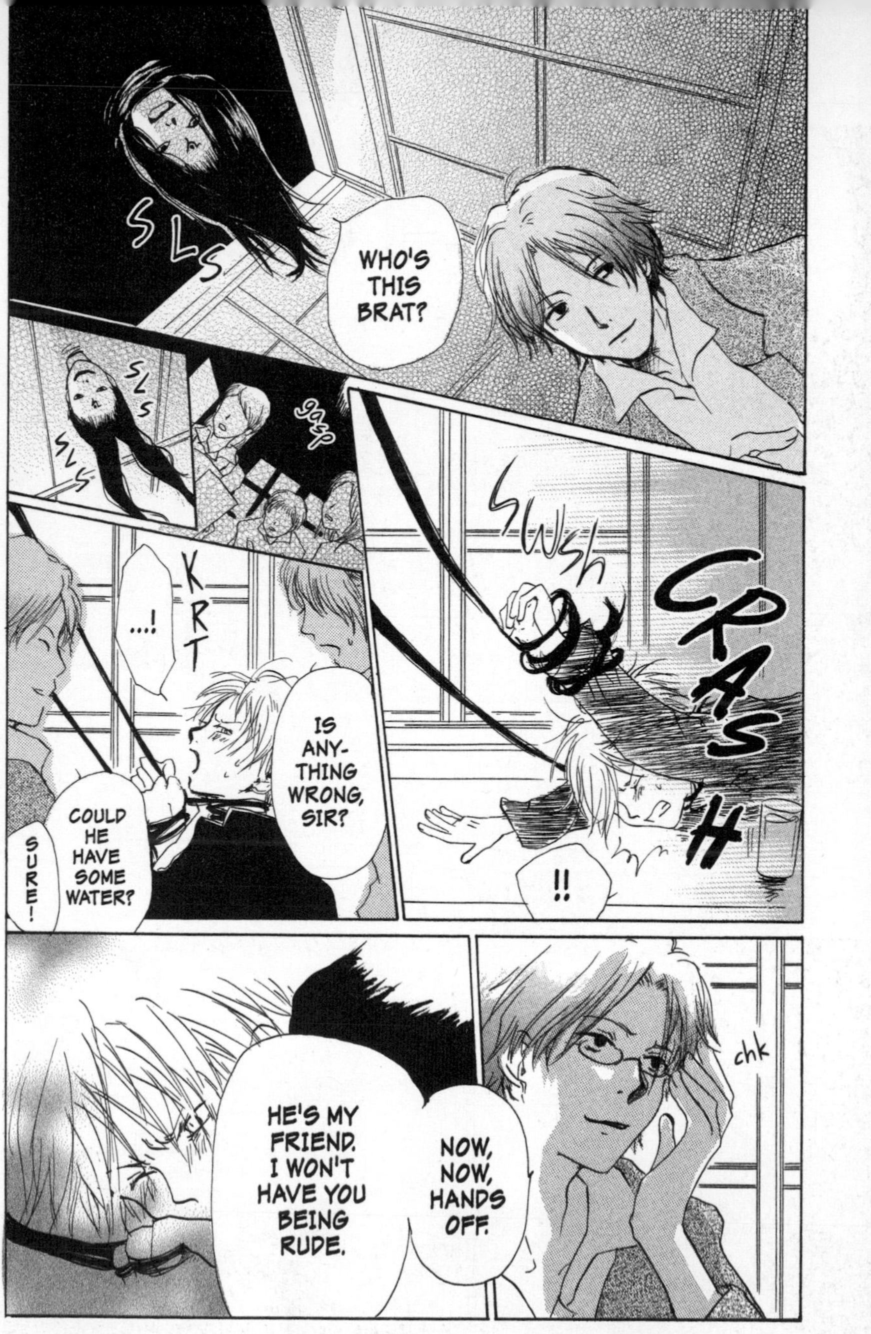
SLS
WHO'S THIS BRAT?
SWSH
CRASH
!!
SLS
SLS
gasp
KRT
...!
IS ANYTHING WRONG, SIR?
COULD HE HAVE SOME WATER?
SURE!
chk
NOW, NOW, HANDS OFF.
HE'S MY FRIEND. I WON'T HAVE YOU BEING RUDE.

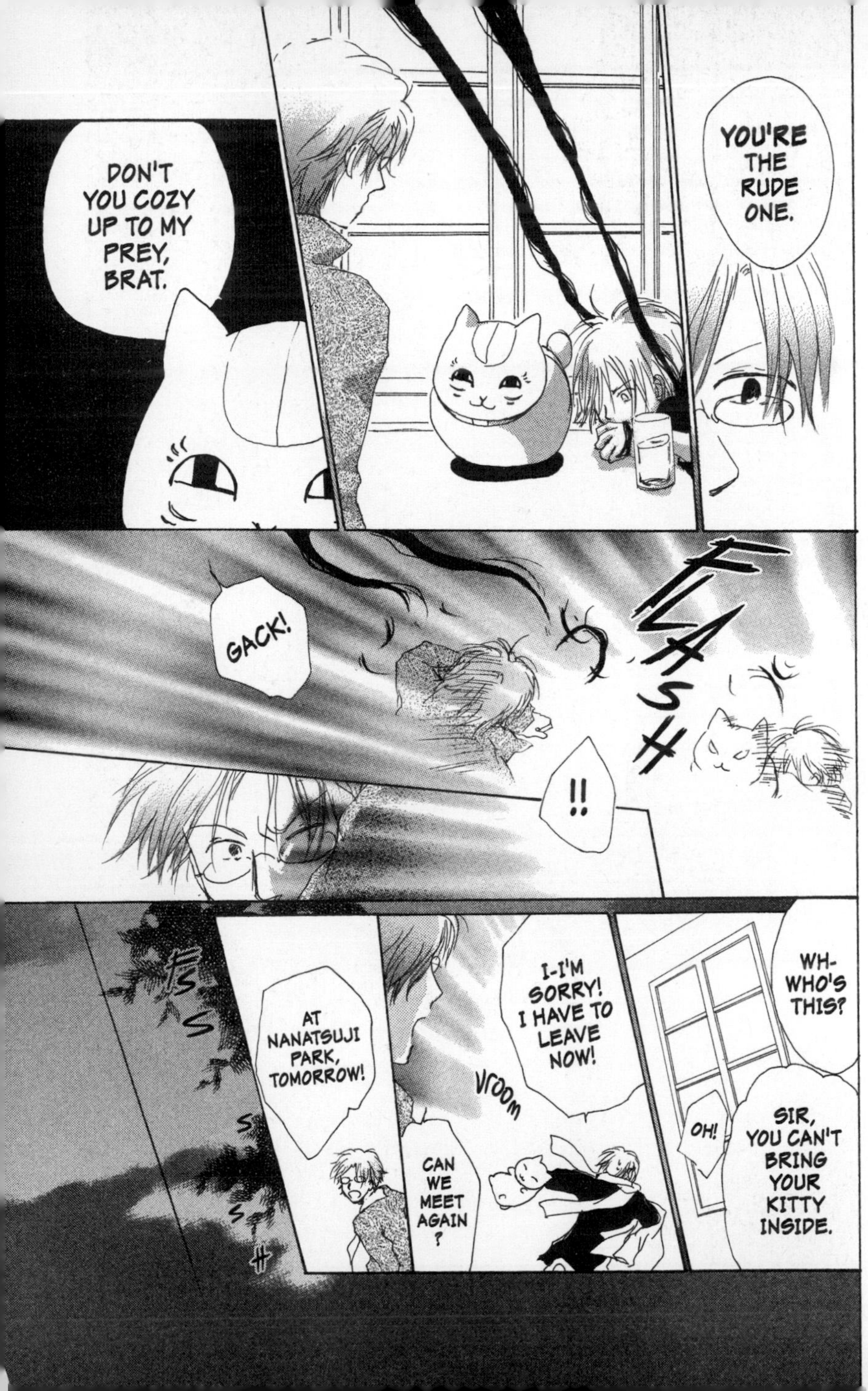
YOU'RE THE RUDE ONE.
DON'T YOU COZY UP TO MY PREY, BRAT.
FLASH
GACK!
!!
WH-WHO'S THIS?
SIR, YOU CAN'T BRING YOUR KITTY INSIDE.
OH!
I-I'M SORRY! I HAVE TO LEAVE NOW!
VROOM
AT NANATSUJI PARK, TOMORROW!
CAN WE MEET AGAIN?

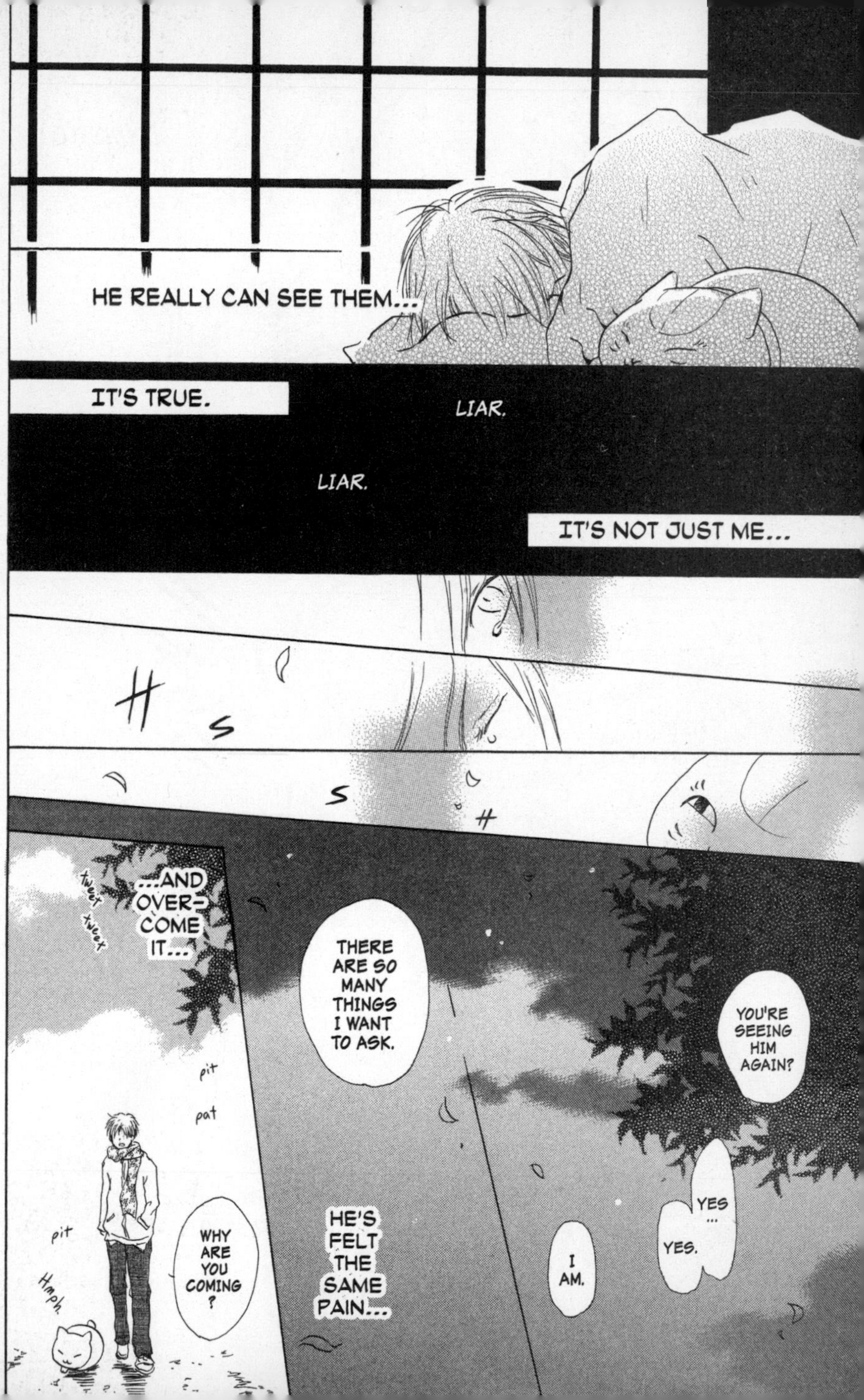

HE REALLY CAN SEE THEM...
IT'S TRUE.
LIAR.
LIAR.
IT'S NOT JUST ME...
H
S
S
H
YOU'RE SEEING HIM AGAIN?
YES...
YES.
I AM.
THERE ARE SO MANY THINGS I WANT TO ASK.
HE'S FELT THE SAME PAIN...
...AND OVER-COME IT...
tweet tweet
pit
pat
pit
WHY ARE YOU COMING?
Hmph.

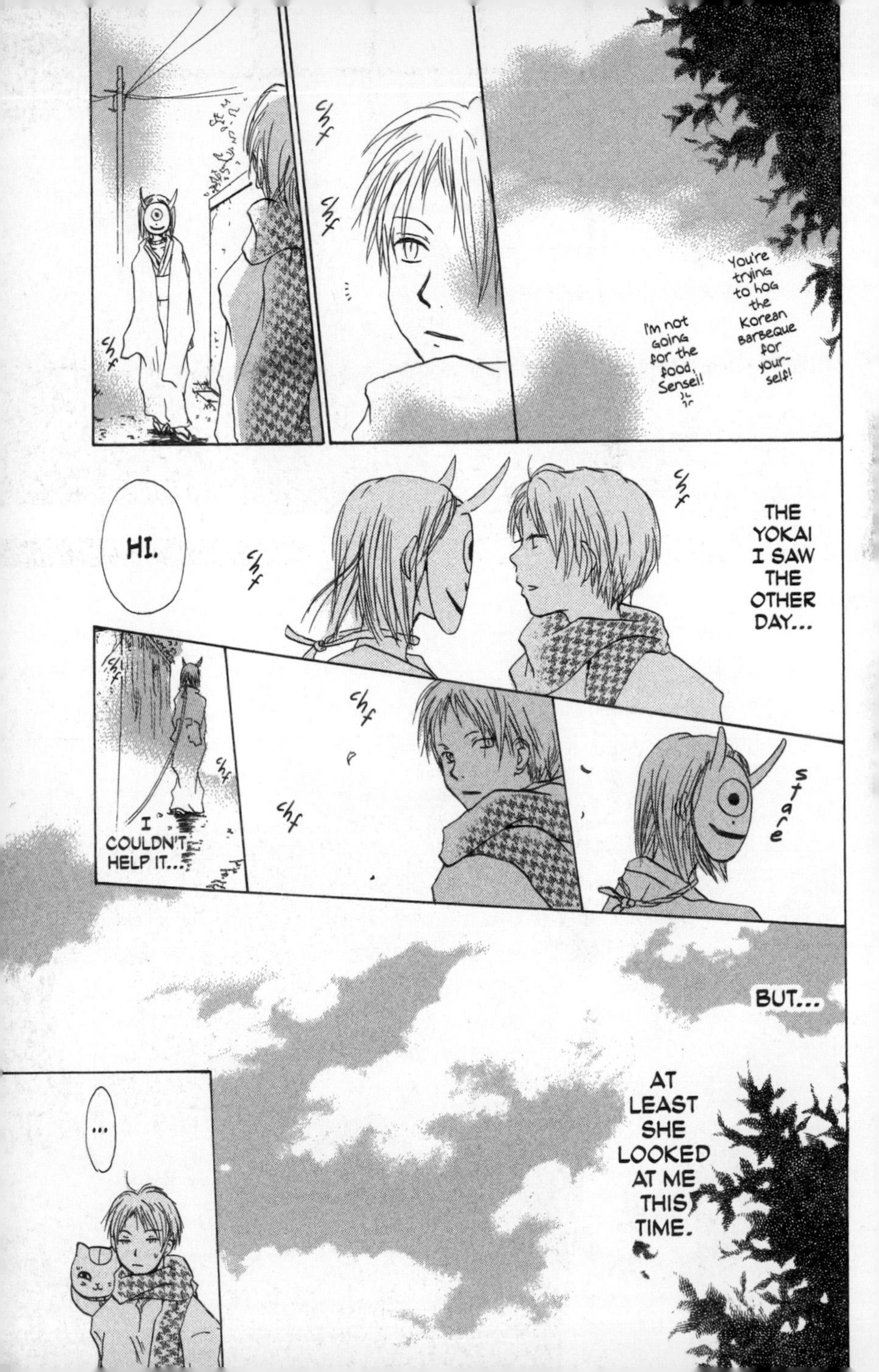
You're trying to hog the Korean Barbeque for your-self!
I'm not going for the food, Sensei!
chf
chf
...
chf
THE YOKAI I SAW THE OTHER DAY...
chf
chf
HI.
stare
chf
chf
I COULDN'T HELP IT...
chf
chf
BUT...
AT LEAST SHE LOOKED AT ME THIS TIME.
...

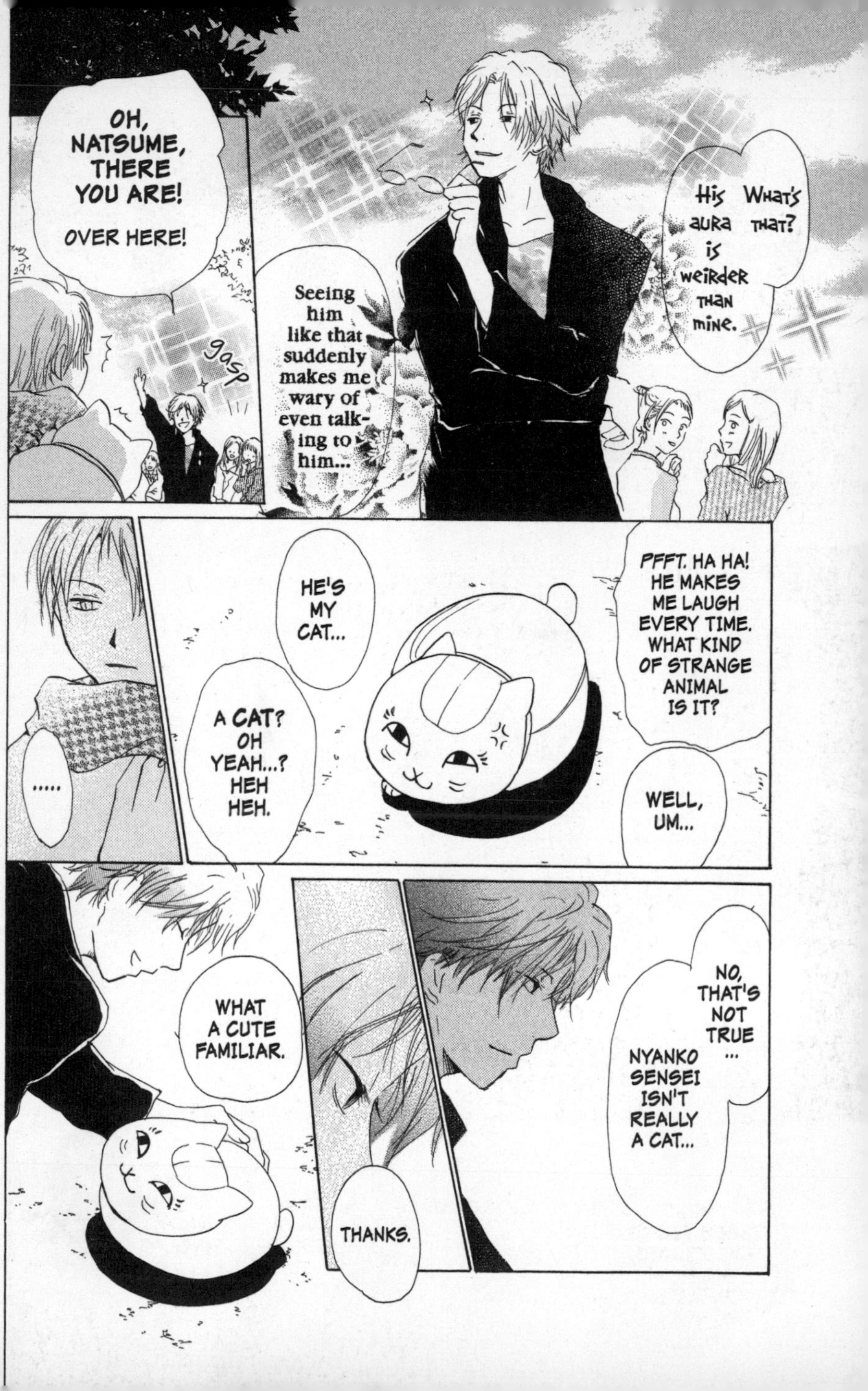
What's that?
His aura is weirder than mine.
Seeing him like that suddenly makes me wary of even talking to him...
OH, NATSUME, THERE YOU ARE!
OVER HERE!
gasp
PFFT. HA HA! HE MAKES ME LAUGH EVERY TIME. WHAT KIND OF STRANGE ANIMAL IS IT?
WELL, UM...
HE'S MY CAT...
A CAT? OH YEAH...? HEH HEH.
.....
NO, THAT'S NOT TRUE ...
NYANKO SENSEI ISN'T REALLY A CAT...
THANKS.
WHAT A CUTE FAMILIAR.

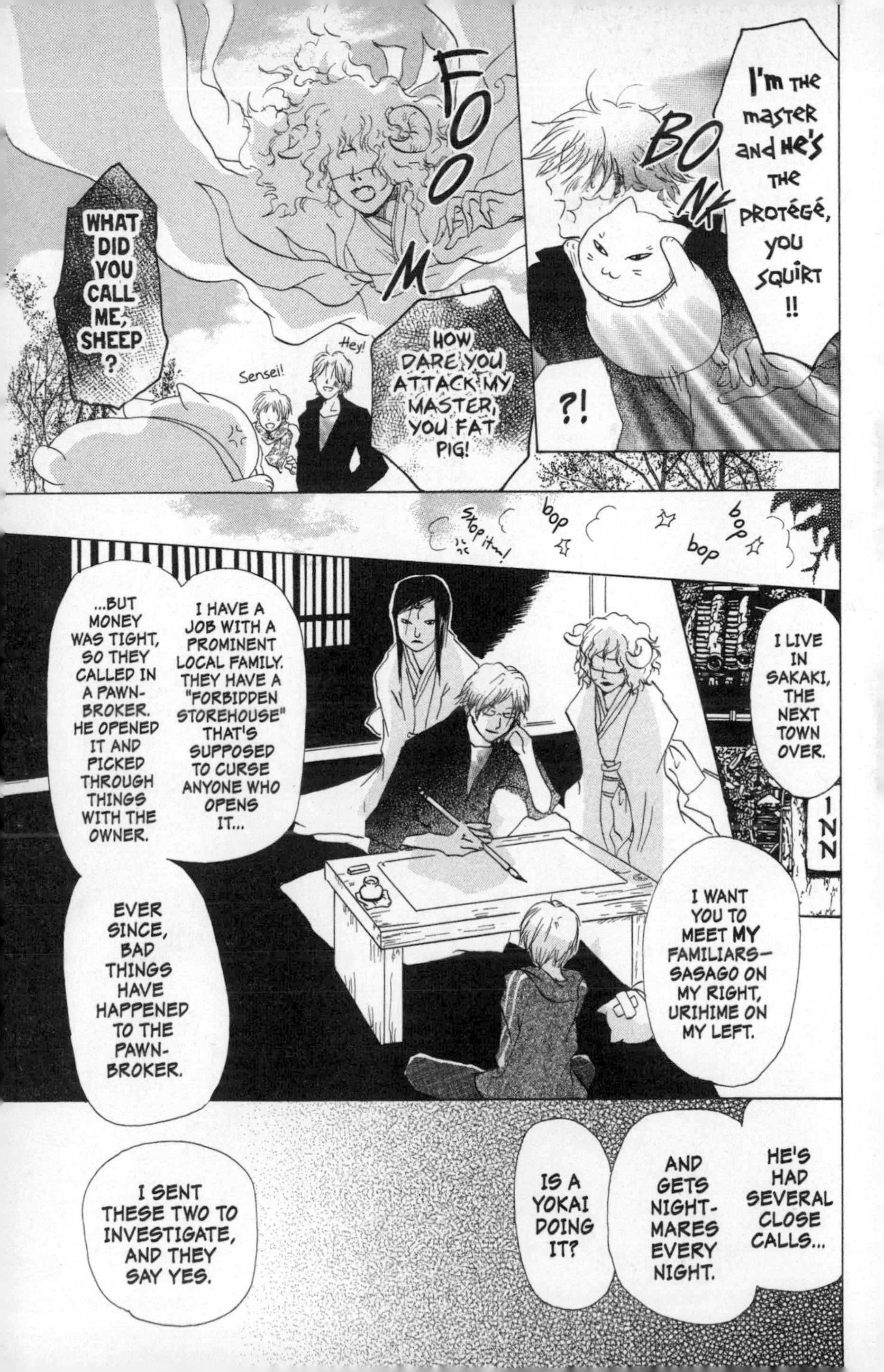
I'm the master and he's the protégé, you squirt!!
BONK
?!
FOOOM
HOW DARE YOU ATTACK MY MASTER, YOU FAT PIG!
Hey!
Sensei!
WHAT DID YOU CALL ME, SHEEP?
bop
bop
bop
Stop it!
I LIVE IN SAKAKI, THE NEXT TOWN OVER.
INN
I WANT YOU TO MEET MY FAMILIARS—SASAGO ON MY RIGHT, URIHIME ON MY LEFT.
I HAVE A JOB WITH A PROMINENT LOCAL FAMILY. THEY HAVE A "FORBIDDEN STOREHOUSE" THAT'S SUPPOSED TO CURSE ANYONE WHO OPENS IT...
...BUT MONEY WAS TIGHT, SO THEY CALLED IN A PAWN-BROKER. HE OPENED IT AND PICKED THROUGH THINGS WITH THE OWNER.
EVER SINCE, BAD THINGS HAVE HAPPENED TO THE PAWN-BROKER.
HE'S HAD SEVERAL CLOSE CALLS...
AND GETS NIGHT-MARES EVERY NIGHT.
IS A YOKAI DOING IT?
I SENT THESE TWO TO INVESTIGATE, AND THEY SAY YES.

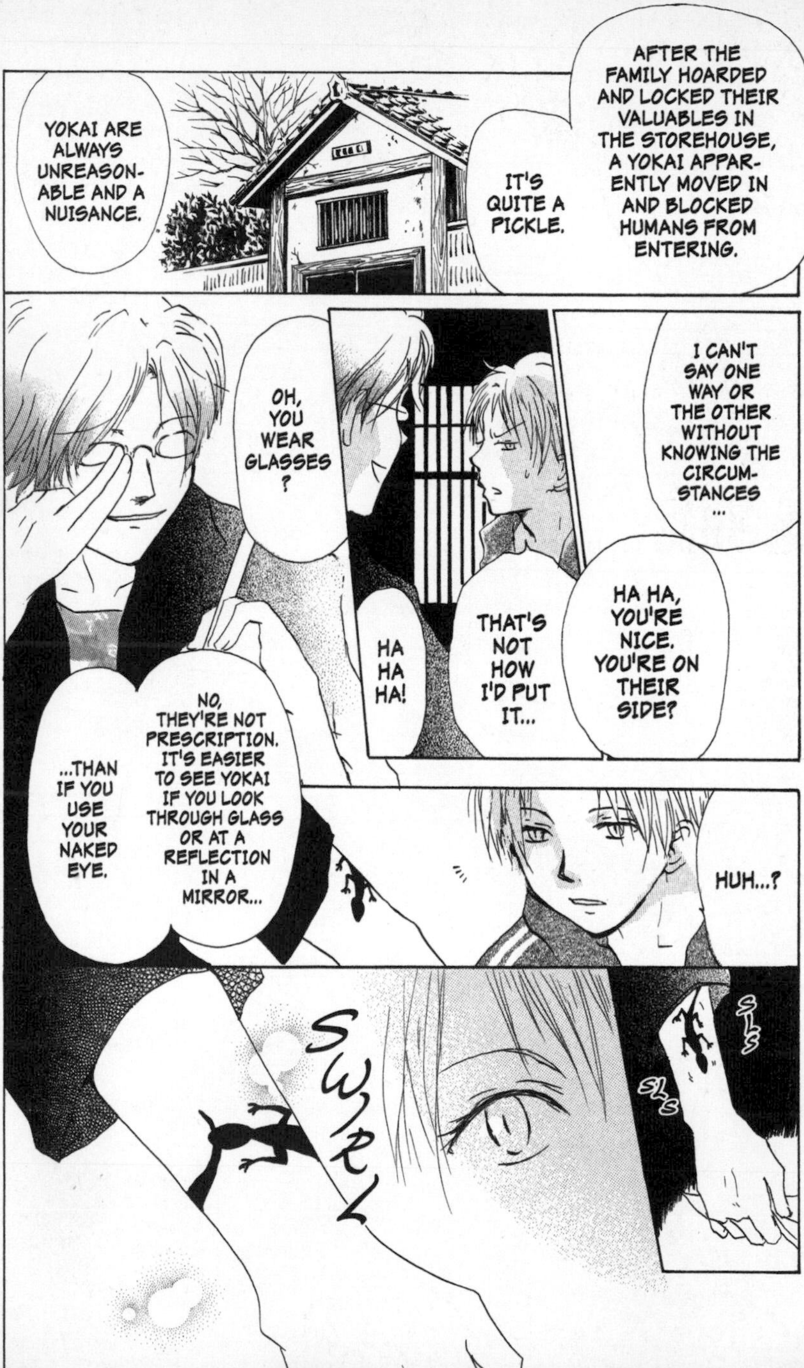
AFTER THE FAMILY HOARDED AND LOCKED THEIR VALUABLES IN THE STOREHOUSE, A YOKAI APPARENTLY MOVED IN AND BLOCKED HUMANS FROM ENTERING.
IT'S QUITE A PICKLE.
YOKAI ARE ALWAYS UNREASONABLE AND A NUISANCE.
I CAN'T SAY ONE WAY OR THE OTHER WITHOUT KNOWING THE CIRCUMSTANCES...
HA HA, YOU'RE NICE. YOU'RE ON THEIR SIDE?
THAT'S NOT HOW I'D PUT IT...
HA HA HA!
OH, YOU WEAR GLASSES?
NO, THEY'RE NOT PRESCRIPTION. IT'S EASIER TO SEE YOKAI IF YOU LOOK THROUGH GLASS OR AT A REFLECTION IN A MIRROR...
...THAN IF YOU USE YOUR NAKED EYE.
HUH...?
SLS
SLS
SWIRL

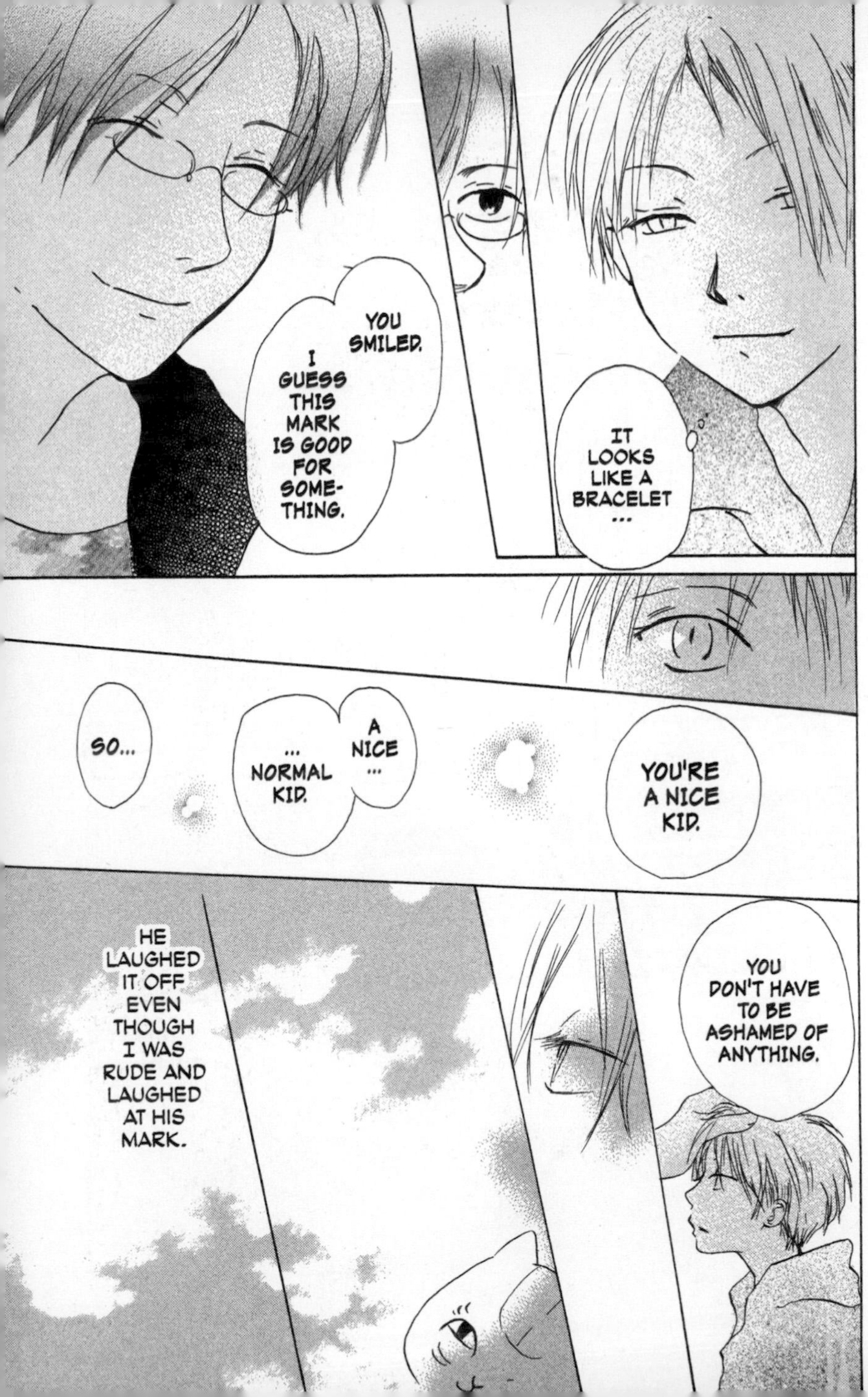
IT LOOKS LIKE A BRACELET ...
YOU SMILED.
I GUESS THIS MARK IS GOOD FOR SOMETHING.
YOU'RE A NICE KID.
A NICE ...
... NORMAL KID.
SO...
YOU DON'T HAVE TO BE ASHAMED OF ANYTHING.
HE LAUGHED IT OFF EVEN THOUGH I WAS RUDE AND LAUGHED AT HIS MARK.

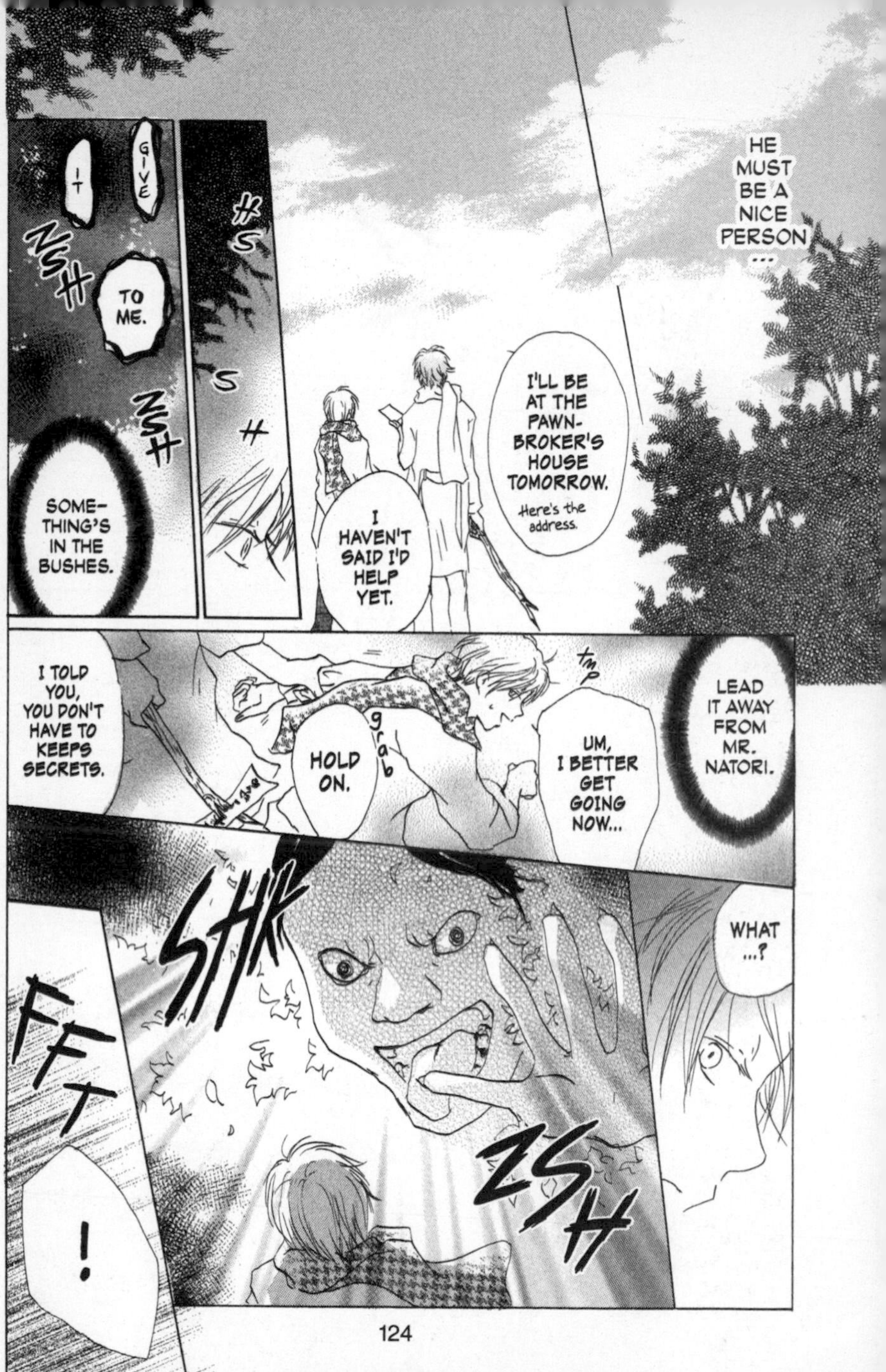
HE MUST BE A NICE PERSON...
I'LL BE AT THE PAWNBROKER'S HOUSE TOMORROW.
Here's the address.
I HAVEN'T SAID I'D HELP YET.
SH
S
H
GIVE IT
TO ME.
ZSH
ZSH
SOMETHING'S IN THE BUSHES.
LEAD IT AWAY FROM MR. NATORI.
xmp
UM, I BETTER GET GOING NOW...
grab
HOLD ON.
I TOLD YOU, YOU DON'T HAVE TO KEEPS SECRETS.
WHAT...?
SHK
ZSH
FFT
!

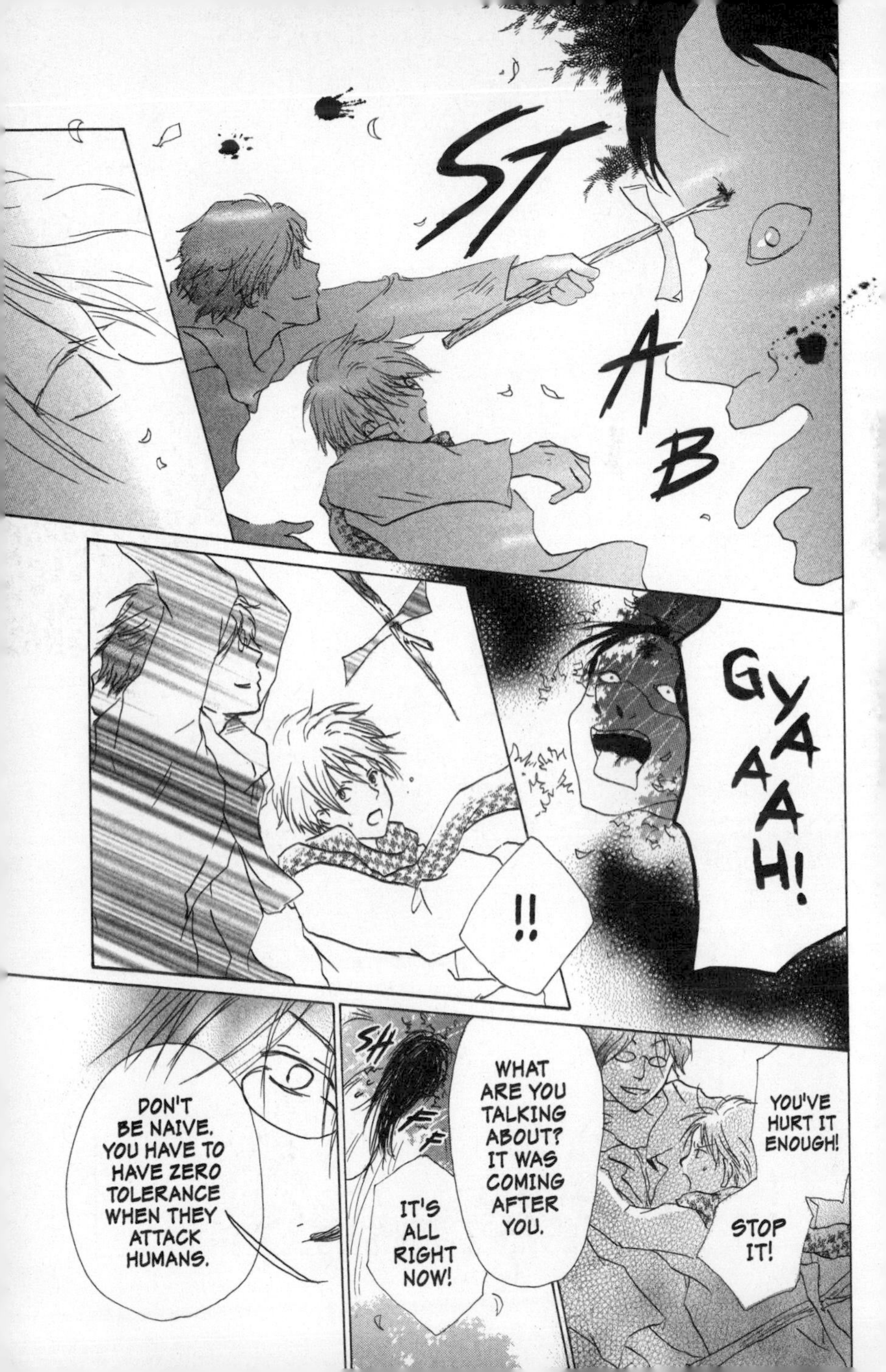
STAB
GYAAAAH!
!!
YOU'VE HURT IT ENOUGH!
STOP IT!
WHAT ARE YOU TALKING ABOUT? IT WAS COMING AFTER YOU.
SHFF
IT'S ALL RIGHT NOW!
DON'T BE NAIVE. YOU HAVE TO HAVE ZERO TOLERANCE WHEN THEY ATTACK HUMANS.

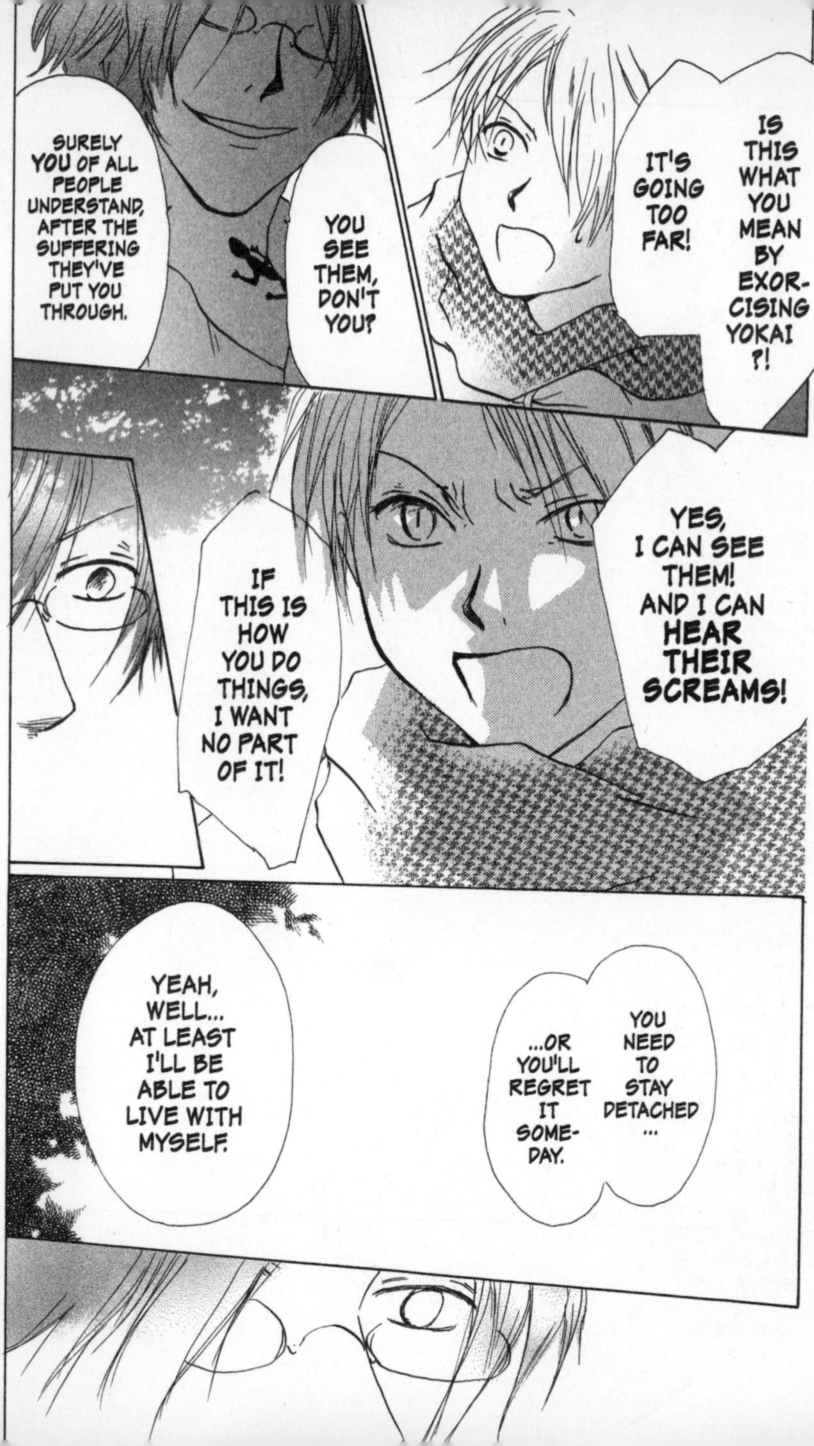
IS THIS WHAT YOU MEAN BY EXORCISING YOKAI?!
IT'S GOING TOO FAR!
YOU SEE THEM, DON'T YOU?
SURELY YOU OF ALL PEOPLE UNDERSTAND, AFTER THE SUFFERING THEY'VE PUT YOU THROUGH.
YES, I CAN SEE THEM! AND I CAN **HEAR THEIR SCREAMS!**
IF THIS IS HOW YOU DO THINGS, I WANT NO PART OF IT!
YOU NEED TO STAY DETACHED...
...OR YOU'LL REGRET IT SOMEDAY.
YEAH, WELL... AT LEAST I'LL BE ABLE TO LIVE WITH MYSELF.

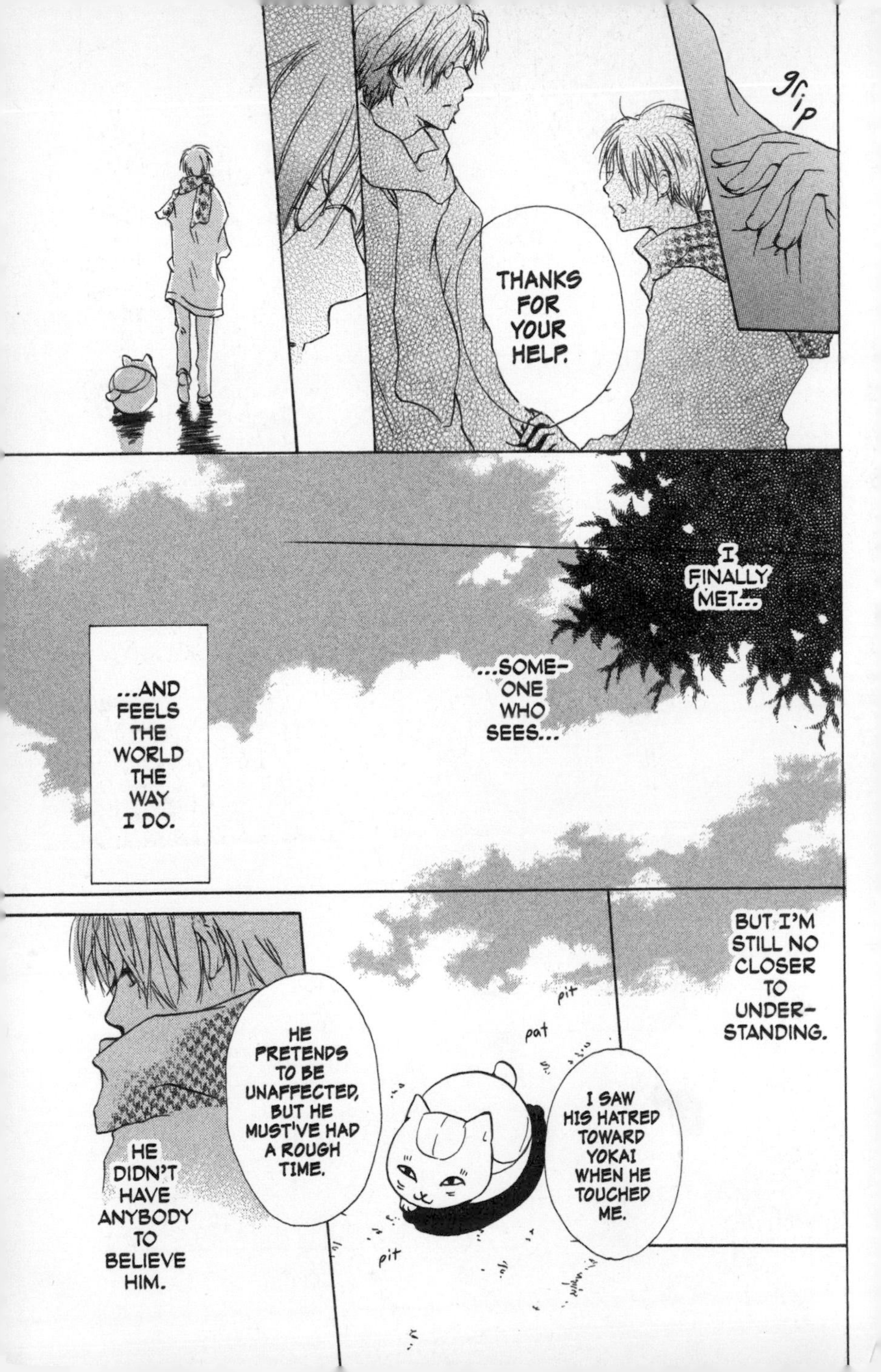

grip
THANKS FOR YOUR HELP.
I FINALLY MET...
...SOME-ONE WHO SEES...
...AND FEELS THE WORLD THE WAY I DO.
BUT I'M STILL NO CLOSER TO UNDER-STANDING.
pit
pat
I SAW HIS HATRED TOWARD YOKAI WHEN HE TOUCHED ME.
HE PRETENDS TO BE UNAFFECTED, BUT HE MUST'VE HAD A ROUGH TIME.
HE DIDN'T HAVE ANYBODY TO BELIEVE HIM.
pit

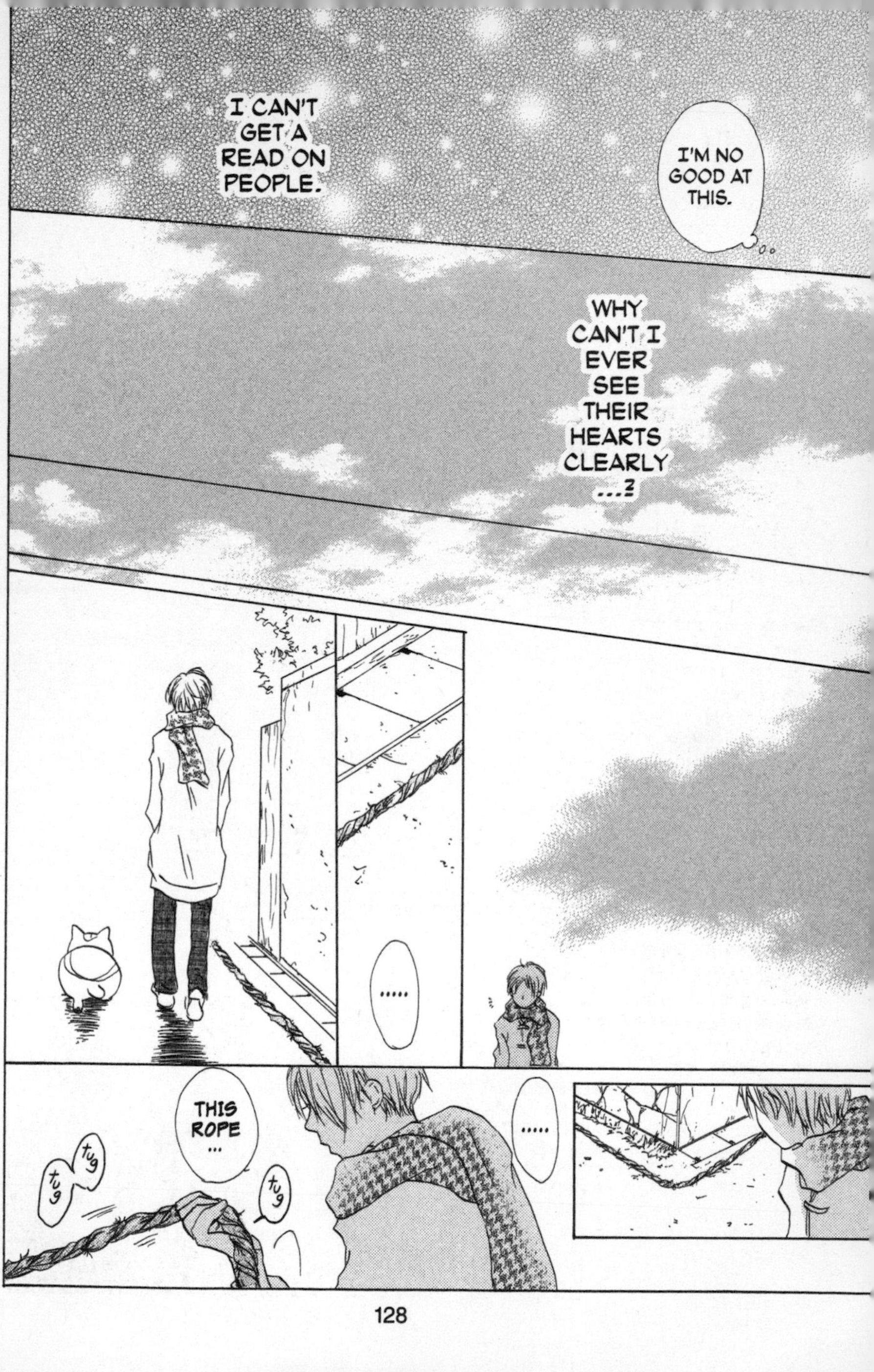
I'M NO GOOD AT THIS.
I CAN'T GET A READ ON PEOPLE.
WHY CAN'T I EVER SEE THEIR HEARTS CLEARLY ...?
......
......
THIS ROPE ...
tug
tug tug

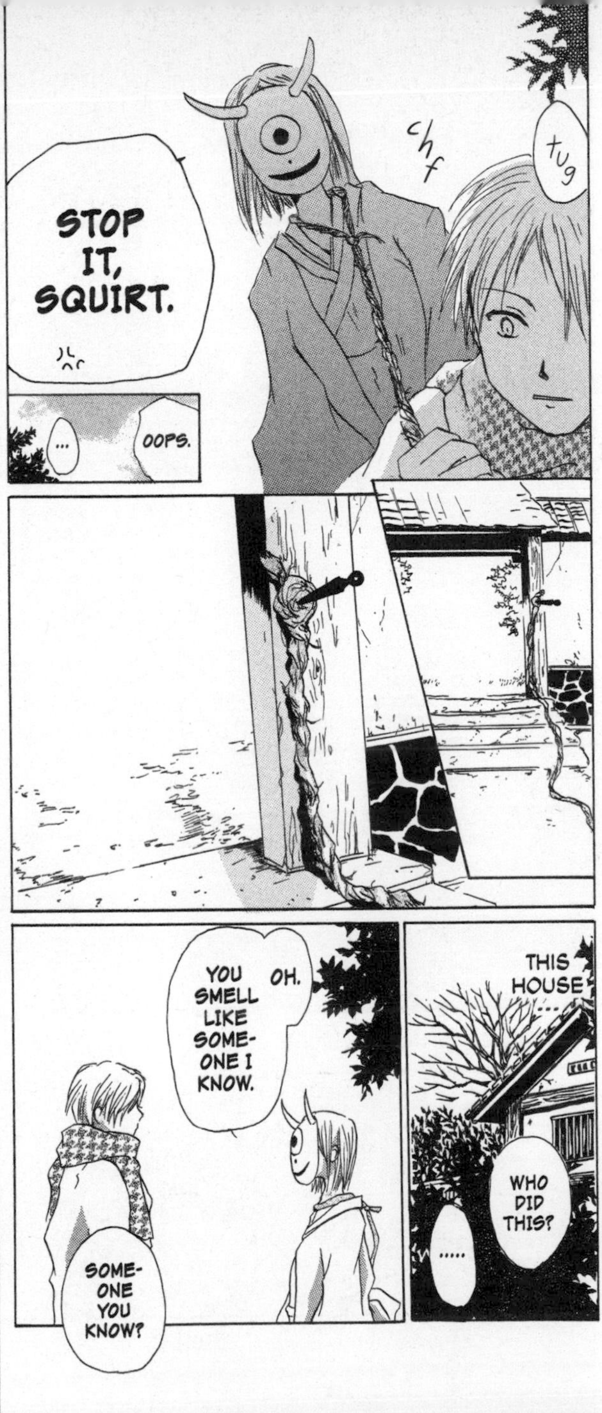
tug
chf
STOP IT, SQUIRT.
OOPS.
...
THIS HOUSE...
WHO DID THIS?
.....
OH.
YOU SMELL LIKE SOME-ONE I KNOW.
SOME-ONE YOU KNOW?

07

→Continued from 06

We used to have an artificial pond in our small yard. It was plain and surrounded by large rocks, about the size of two bathtubs, built by the people who had lived there previously. But it was empty, so I always used to imagine it filled with water. I begged my parents to fill it up once, but it wouldn't stay filled for some reason. I used to make pretend cement from wet sand in the hope of filling the cracks between the rocks. I really wanted some real cement.

Even without water, there were a lot of frogs and moss. How I dreamed of it being filled with swimming goldfish and carp. It's still there, just the way it was back then.

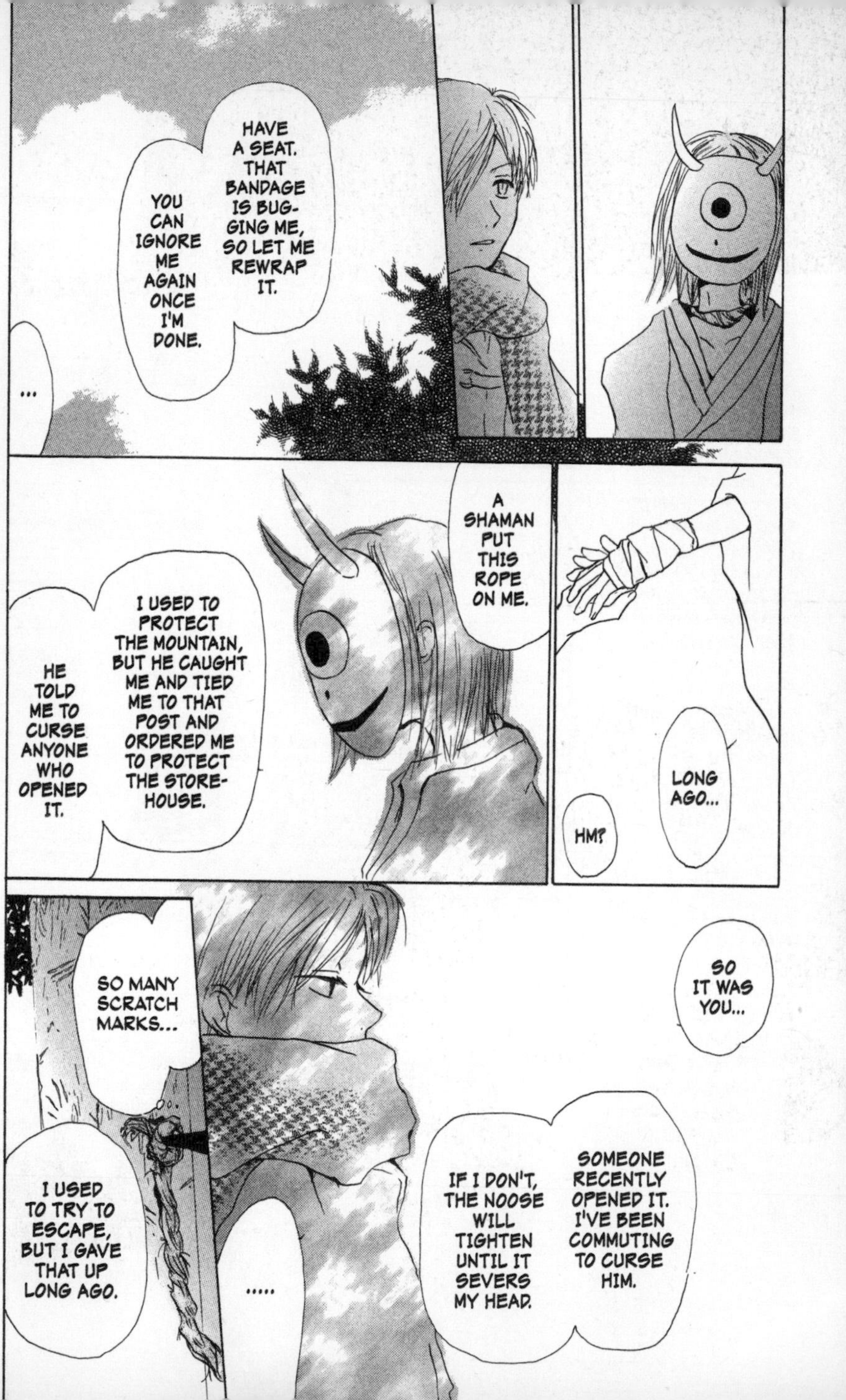
HAVE A SEAT. THAT BANDAGE IS BUG-GING ME, SO LET ME REWRAP IT.
YOU CAN IGNORE ME AGAIN ONCE I'M DONE.
...
LONG AGO...
HM?
A SHAMAN PUT THIS ROPE ON ME.
I USED TO PROTECT THE MOUNTAIN, BUT HE CAUGHT ME AND TIED ME TO THAT POST AND ORDERED ME TO PROTECT THE STORE-HOUSE.
HE TOLD ME TO CURSE ANYONE WHO OPENED IT.
SO IT WAS YOU...
SOMEONE RECENTLY OPENED IT. I'VE BEEN COMMUTING TO CURSE HIM.
IF I DON'T, THE NOOSE WILL TIGHTEN UNTIL IT SEVERS MY HEAD.
......
SO MANY SCRATCH MARKS...
I USED TO TRY TO ESCAPE, BUT I GAVE THAT UP LONG AGO.

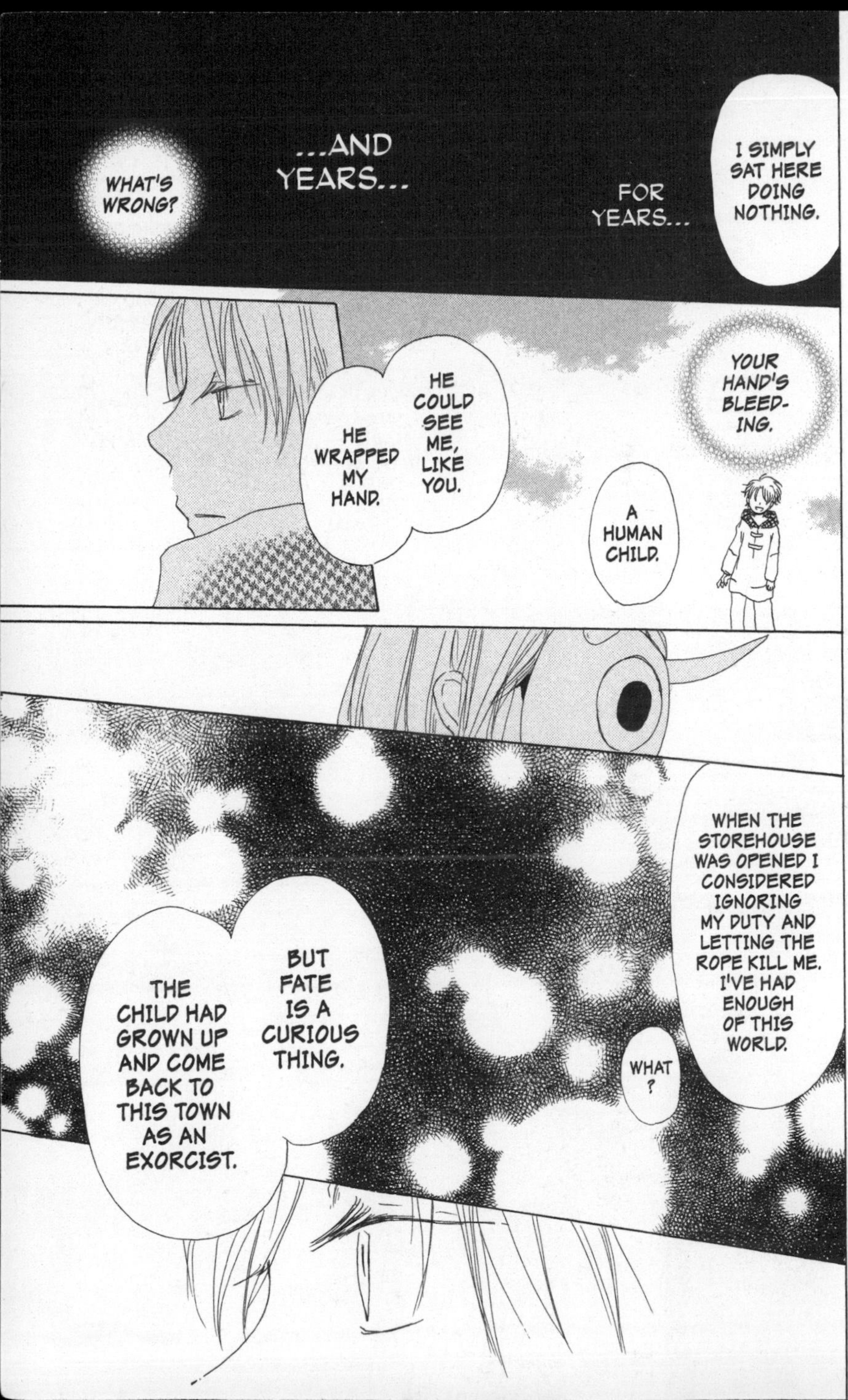
I SIMPLY SAT HERE DOING NOTHING.
FOR YEARS...
...AND YEARS...
WHAT'S WRONG?
YOUR HAND'S BLEED- ING.
A HUMAN CHILD.
HE COULD SEE ME, LIKE YOU.
HE WRAPPED MY HAND.
WHEN THE STOREHOUSE WAS OPENED I CONSIDERED IGNORING MY DUTY AND LETTING THE ROPE KILL ME. I'VE HAD ENOUGH OF THIS WORLD.
WHAT ?
BUT FATE IS A CURIOUS THING.
THE CHILD HAD GROWN UP AND COME BACK TO THIS TOWN AS AN EXORCIST.

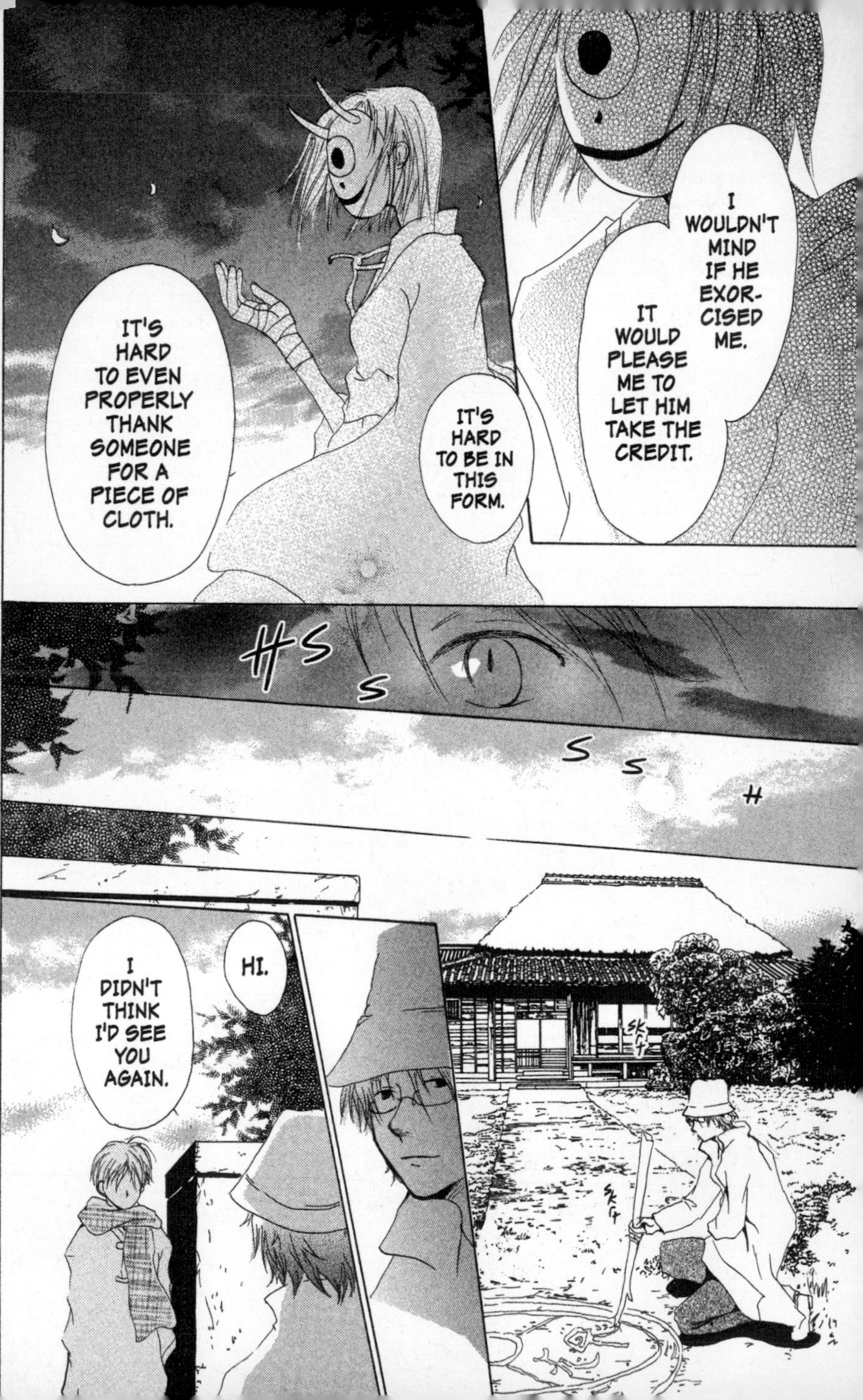
I WOULDN'T MIND IF HE EXORCISED ME.
IT WOULD PLEASE ME TO LET HIM TAKE THE CREDIT.
IT'S HARD TO BE IN THIS FORM.
IT'S HARD TO EVEN PROPERLY THANK SOMEONE FOR A PIECE OF CLOTH.
HSS
SSH
SKRT
HI.
I DIDN'T THINK I'D SEE YOU AGAIN.
SKRT

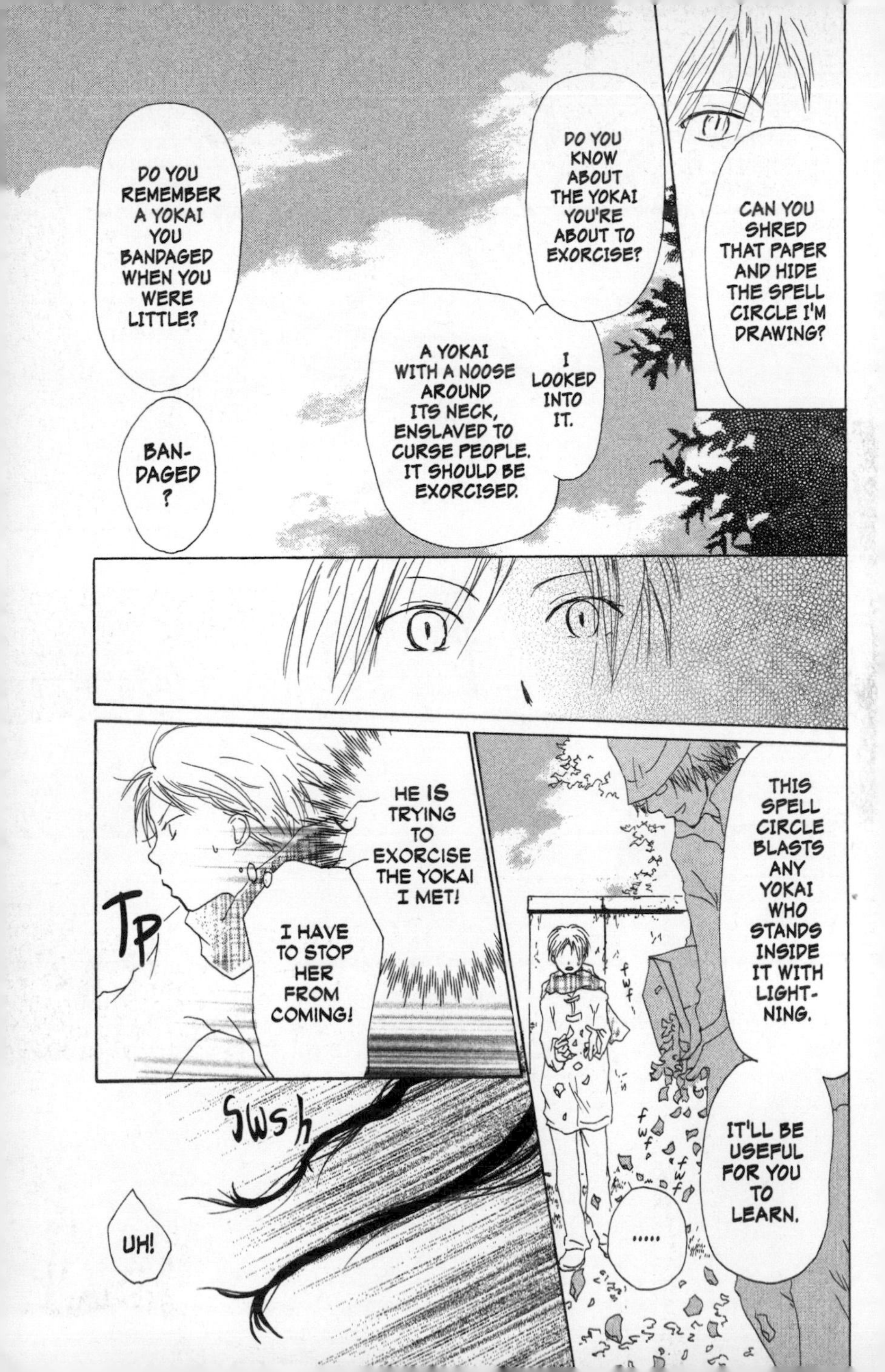
CAN YOU SHRED THAT PAPER AND HIDE THE SPELL CIRCLE I'M DRAWING?
DO YOU KNOW ABOUT THE YOKAI YOU'RE ABOUT TO EXORCISE?
I LOOKED INTO IT.
A YOKAI WITH A NOOSE AROUND ITS NECK, ENSLAVED TO CURSE PEOPLE. IT SHOULD BE EXORCISED.
DO YOU REMEMBER A YOKAI YOU BANDAGED WHEN YOU WERE LITTLE?
BAN-DAGED?
THIS SPELL CIRCLE BLASTS ANY YOKAI WHO STANDS INSIDE IT WITH LIGHT-NING.
fwf
IT'LL BE USEFUL FOR YOU TO LEARN.
fwf
fwf
......
HE IS TRYING TO EXORCISE THE YOKAI I MET!
I HAVE TO STOP HER FROM COMING!
TP
SWSH
UH!

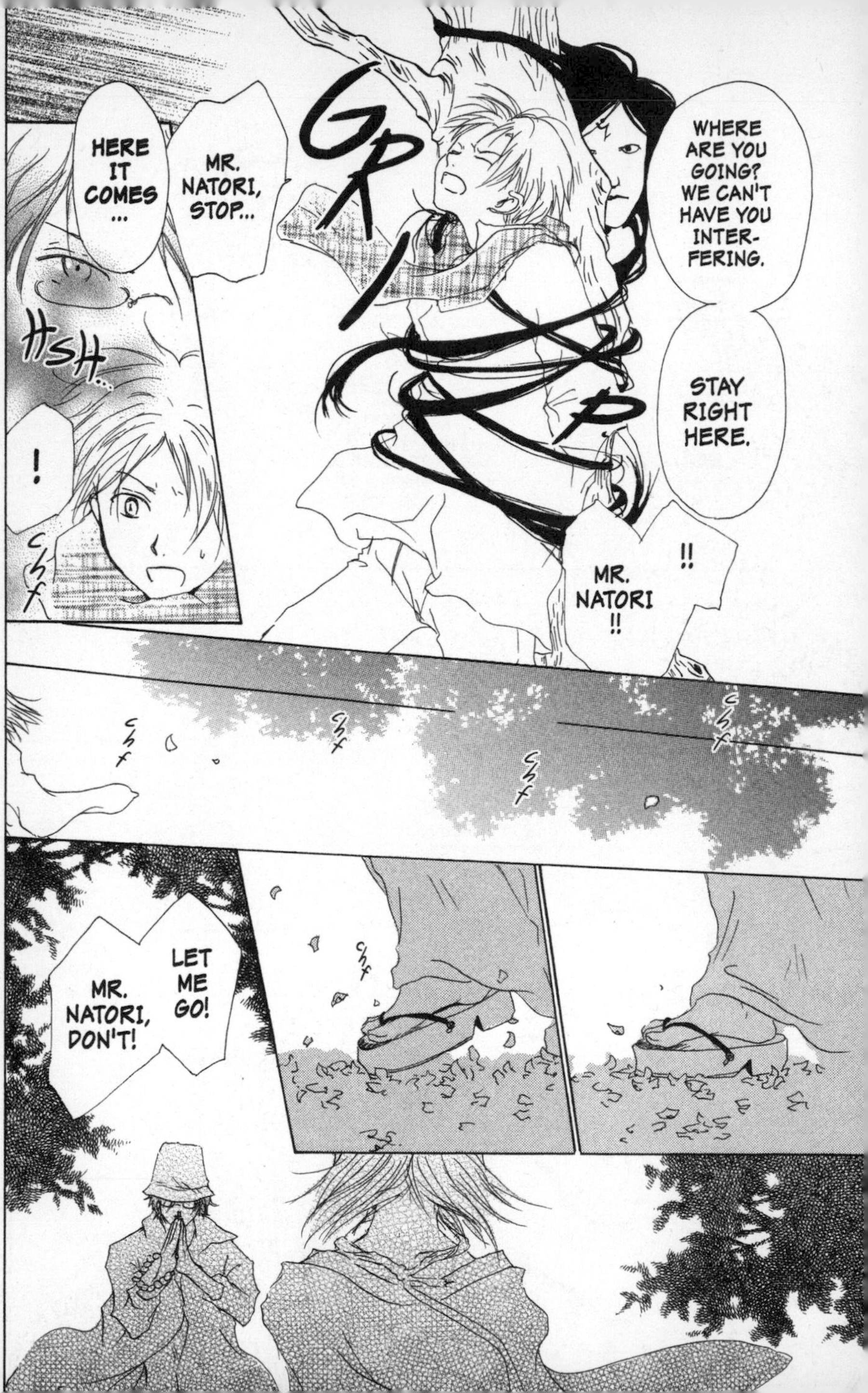
GRIP
WHERE ARE YOU GOING? WE CAN'T HAVE YOU INTERFERING.
STAY RIGHT HERE.
!!
MR. NATORI !!
MR. NATORI, STOP...
HERE IT COMES ...
HSH...
!
chf
chf
chf
chf
chf
chf
LET ME GO!
MR. NATORI, DON'T!

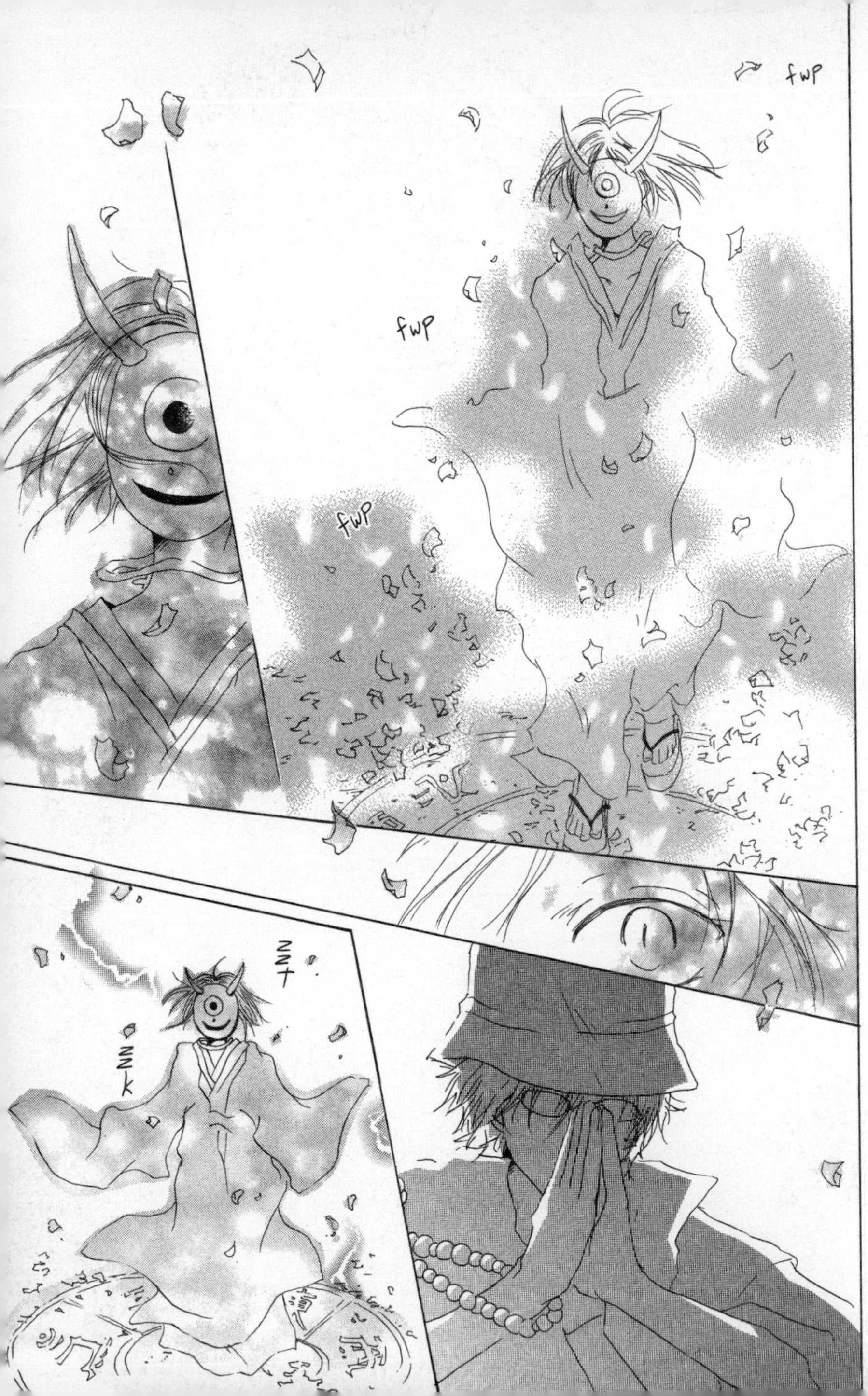
fwp
fwp
fwp
ZZT
ZZK

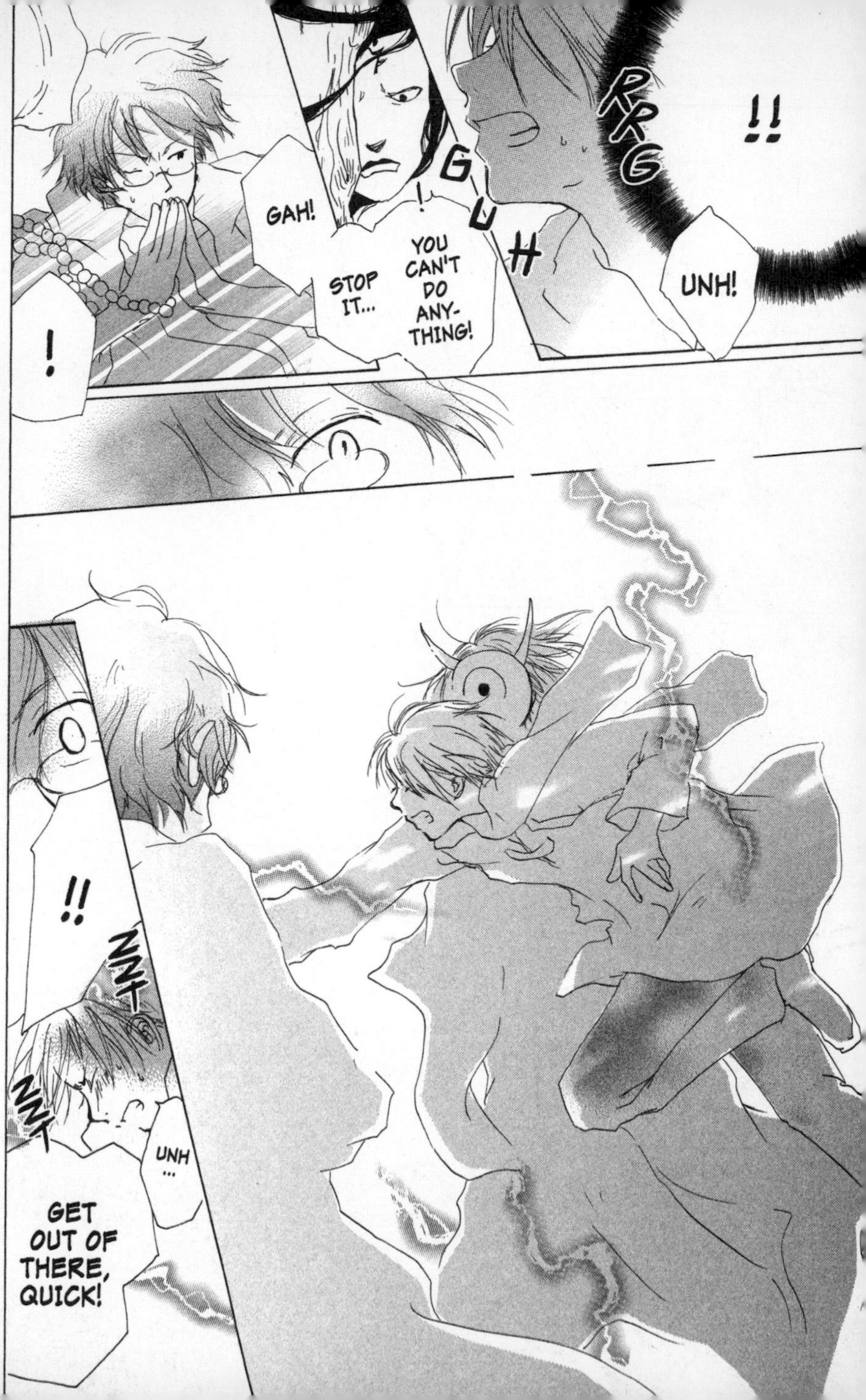

RRG
!!
GUH
UNH!
!
GAH!
YOU CAN'T DO ANYTHING!
STOP IT...
!
!!
ZZZT
ZZZT
UNH ...
GET OUT OF THERE, QUICK!

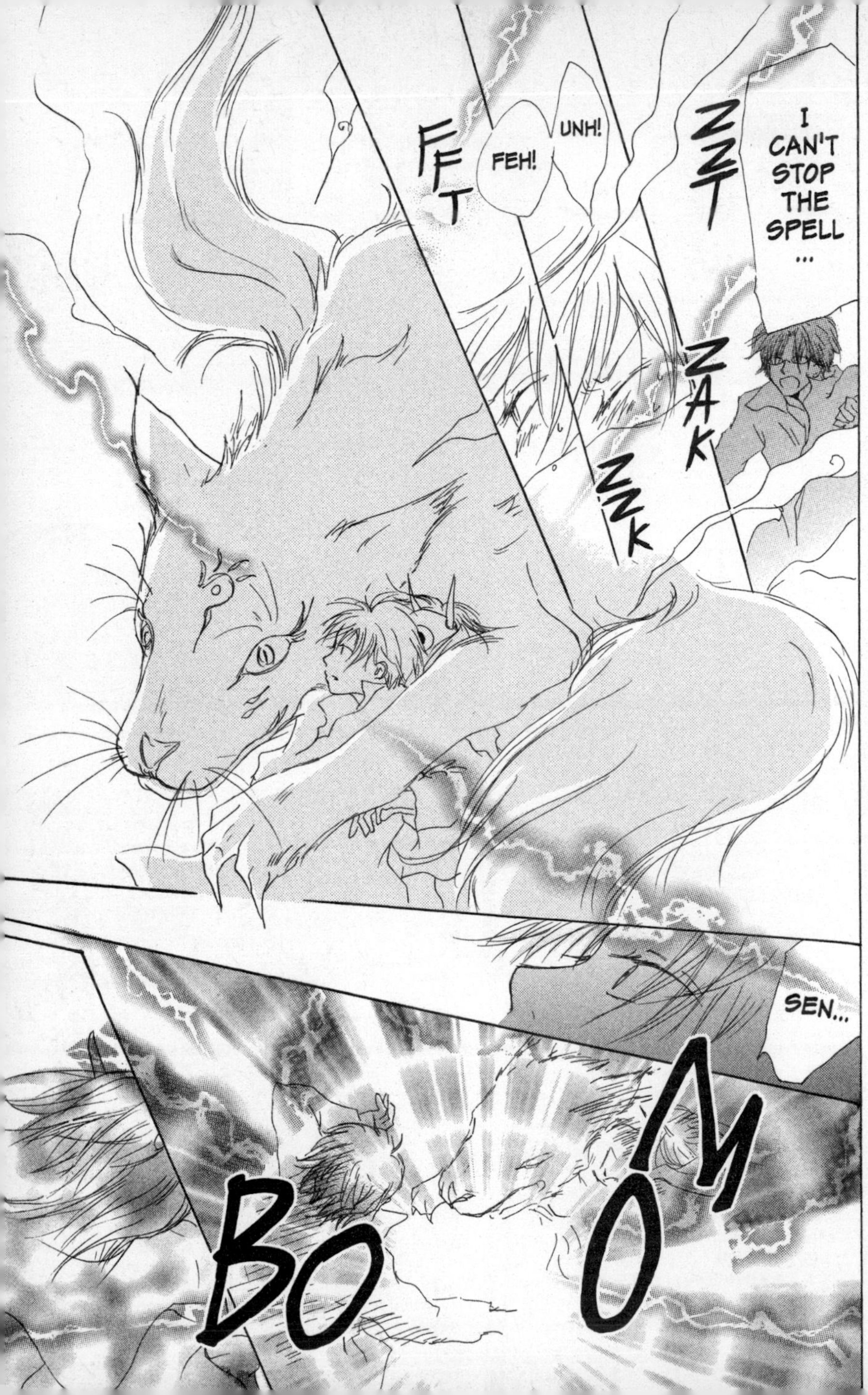
I CAN'T STOP THE SPELL ...
ZZT
UNH!
FEH!
FFT
ZAK
ZZK
SEN...
BOOM

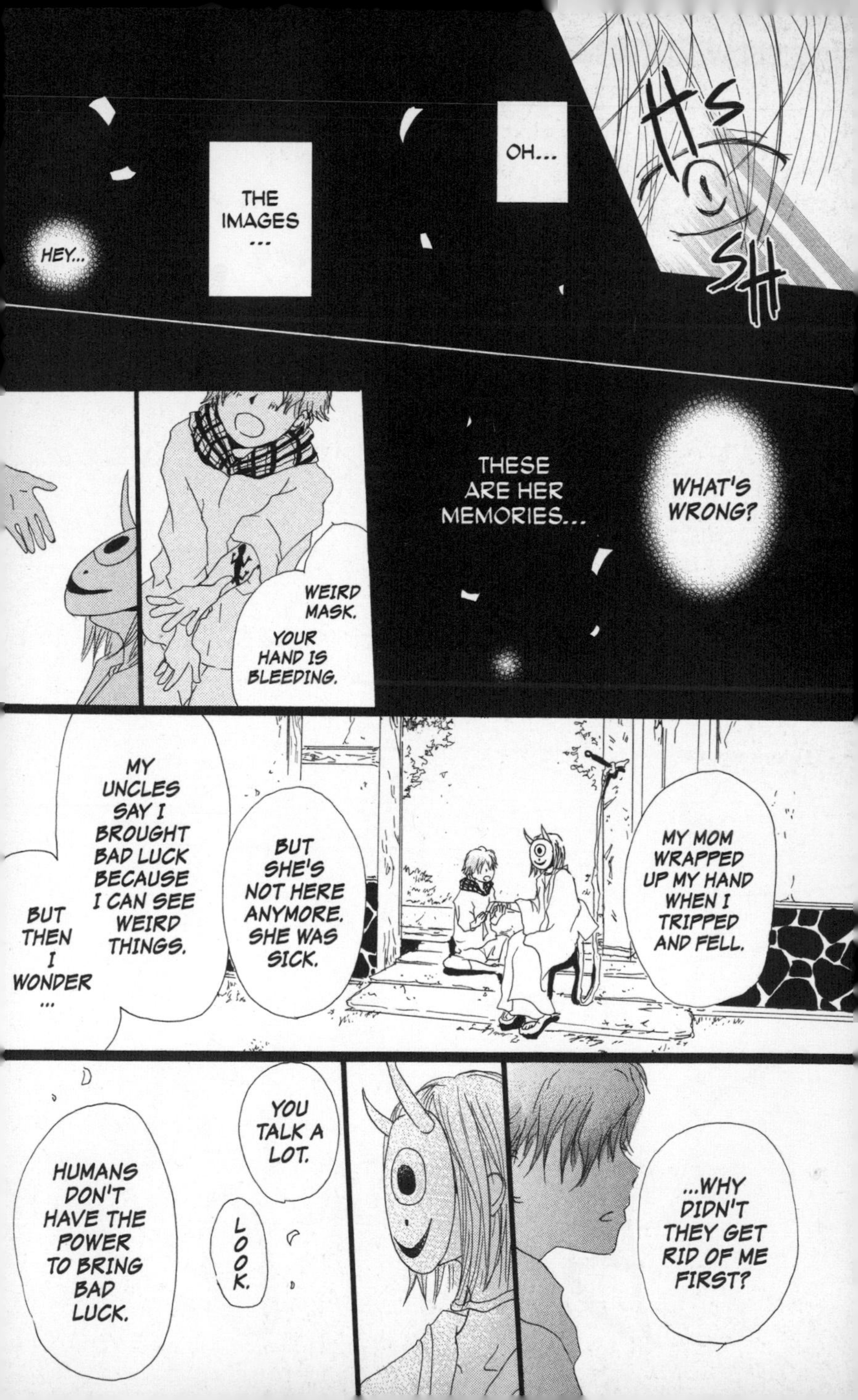
HS
SH
OH...
THE IMAGES...
HEY...
WHAT'S WRONG?
THESE ARE HER MEMORIES...
WEIRD MASK.
YOUR HAND IS BLEEDING.
MY MOM WRAPPED UP MY HAND WHEN I TRIPPED AND FELL.
BUT SHE'S NOT HERE ANYMORE. SHE WAS SICK.
MY UNCLES SAY I BROUGHT BAD LUCK BECAUSE I CAN SEE WEIRD THINGS.
BUT THEN I WONDER...
...WHY DIDN'T THEY GET RID OF ME FIRST?
YOU TALK A LOT.
LOOK.
HUMANS DON'T HAVE THE POWER TO BRING BAD LUCK.

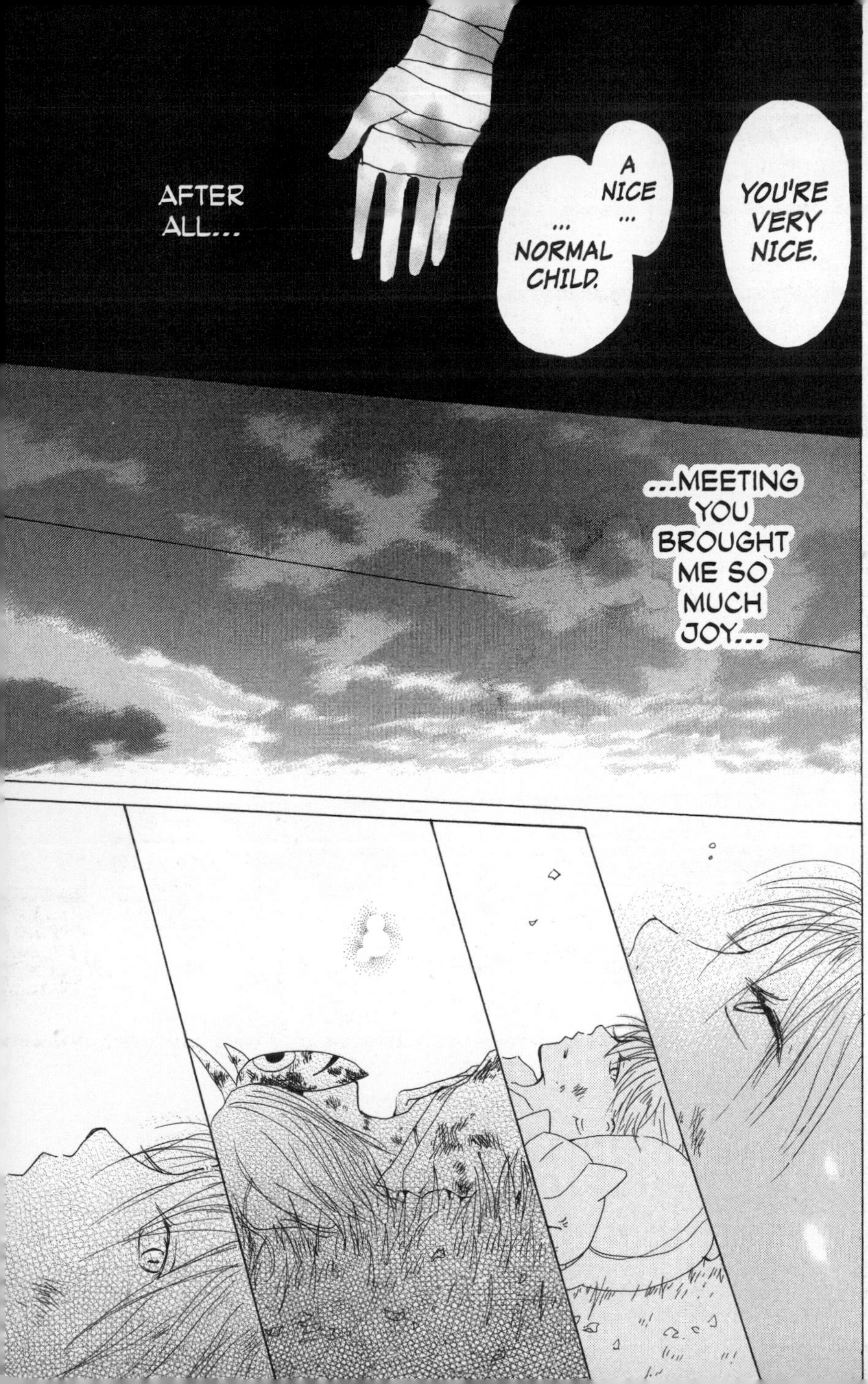
YOU'RE VERY NICE.
A NICE ... ... NORMAL CHILD.
AFTER ALL...
...MEETING YOU BROUGHT ME SO MUCH JOY...

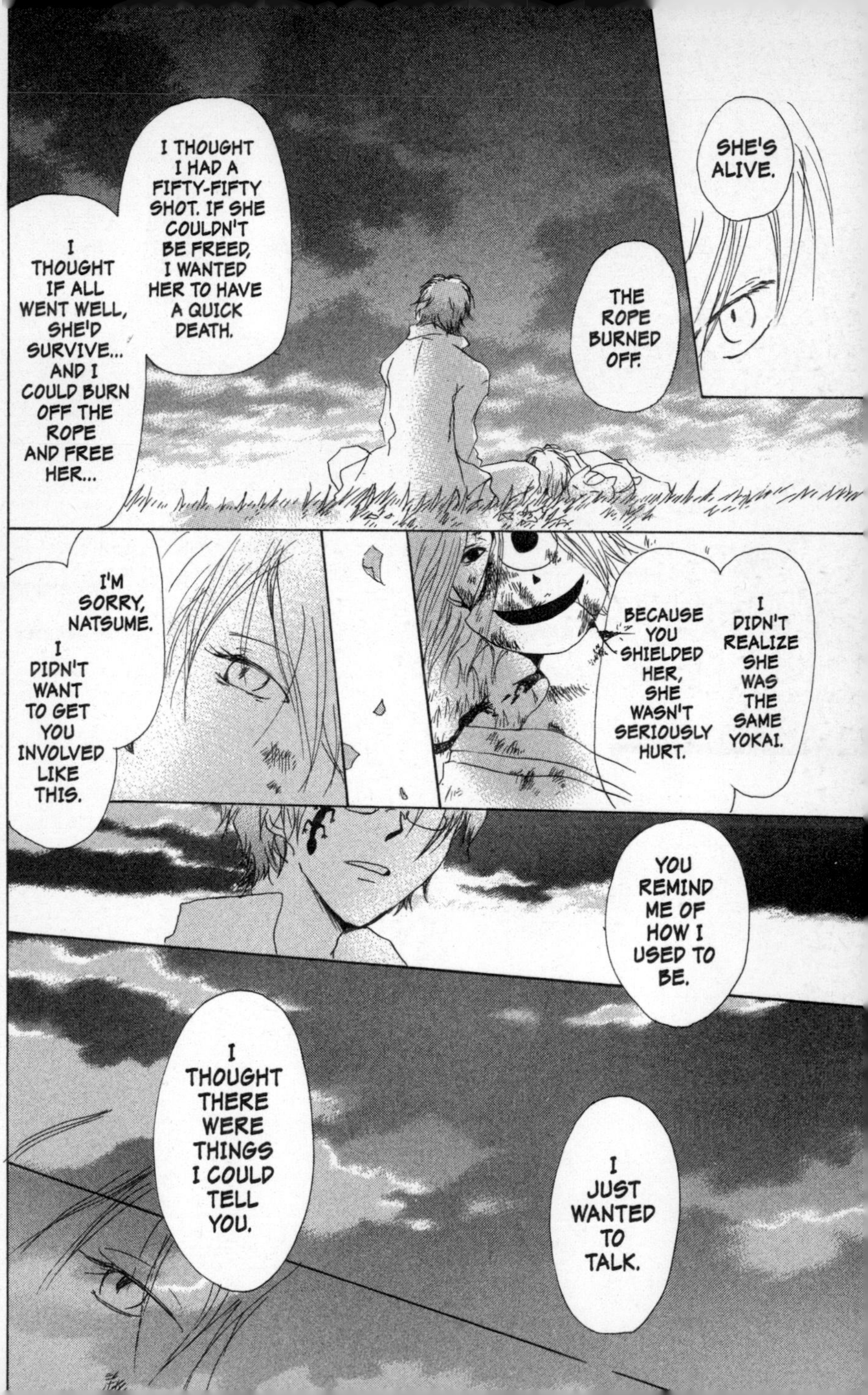
SHE'S ALIVE.
THE ROPE BURNED OFF.
I THOUGHT I HAD A FIFTY-FIFTY SHOT. IF SHE COULDN'T BE FREED, I WANTED HER TO HAVE A QUICK DEATH.
I THOUGHT IF ALL WENT WELL, SHE'D SURVIVE... AND I COULD BURN OFF THE ROPE AND FREE HER...
I DIDN'T REALIZE SHE WAS THE SAME YOKAI.
BECAUSE YOU SHIELDED HER, SHE WASN'T SERIOUSLY HURT.
I'M SORRY, NATSUME.
I DIDN'T WANT TO GET YOU INVOLVED LIKE THIS.
YOU REMIND ME OF HOW I USED TO BE.
I JUST WANTED TO TALK.
I THOUGHT THERE WERE THINGS I COULD TELL YOU.

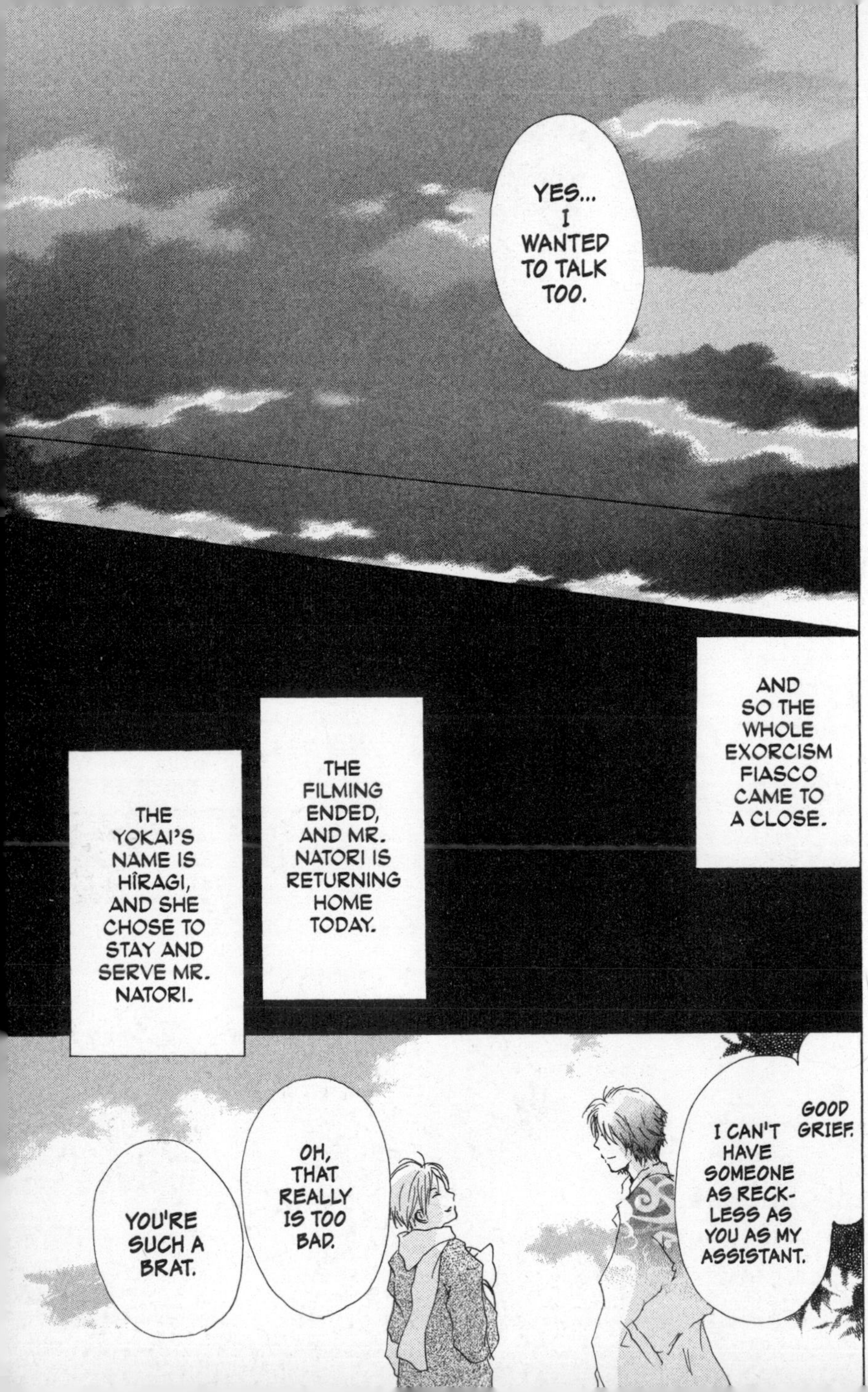
YES... I WANTED TO TALK TOO.
AND SO THE WHOLE EXORCISM FIASCO CAME TO A CLOSE.
THE FILMING ENDED, AND MR. NATORI IS RETURNING HOME TODAY.
THE YOKAI'S NAME IS HÎRAGI, AND SHE CHOSE TO STAY AND SERVE MR. NATORI.
GOOD GRIEF.
I CAN'T HAVE SOMEONE AS RECK-LESS AS YOU AS MY ASSISTANT.
OH, THAT REALLY IS TOO BAD.
YOU'RE SUCH A BRAT.

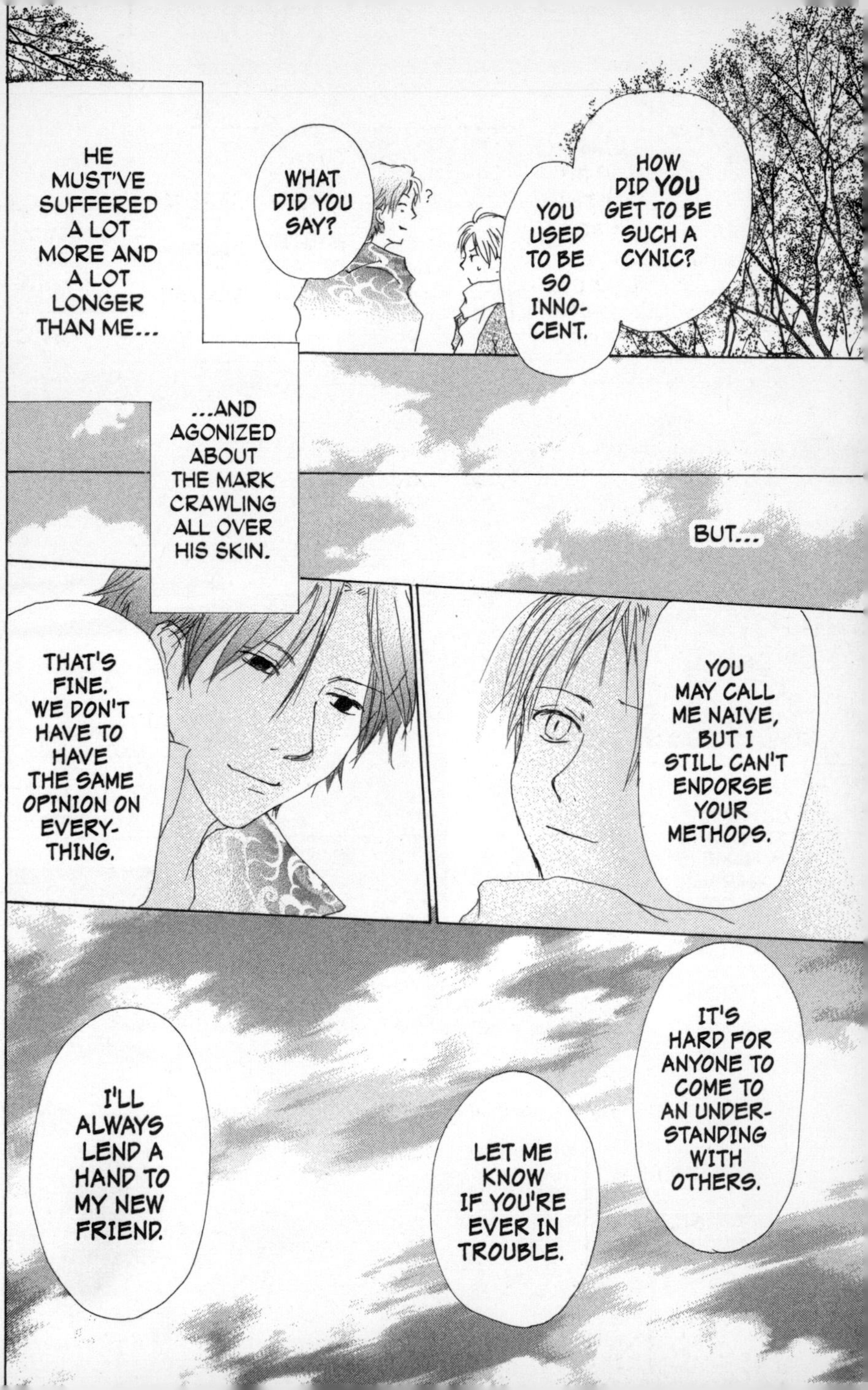
HOW DID YOU GET TO BE SUCH A CYNIC?
YOU USED TO BE SO INNO-CENT.
WHAT DID YOU SAY?
HE MUST'VE SUFFERED A LOT MORE AND A LOT LONGER THAN ME...
...AND AGONIZED ABOUT THE MARK CRAWLING ALL OVER HIS SKIN.
BUT...
YOU MAY CALL ME NAIVE, BUT I STILL CAN'T ENDORSE YOUR METHODS.
THAT'S FINE. WE DON'T HAVE TO HAVE THE SAME OPINION ON EVERY-THING.
IT'S HARD FOR ANYONE TO COME TO AN UNDER-STANDING WITH OTHERS.
LET ME KNOW IF YOU'RE EVER IN TROUBLE.
I'LL ALWAYS LEND A HAND TO MY NEW FRIEND.

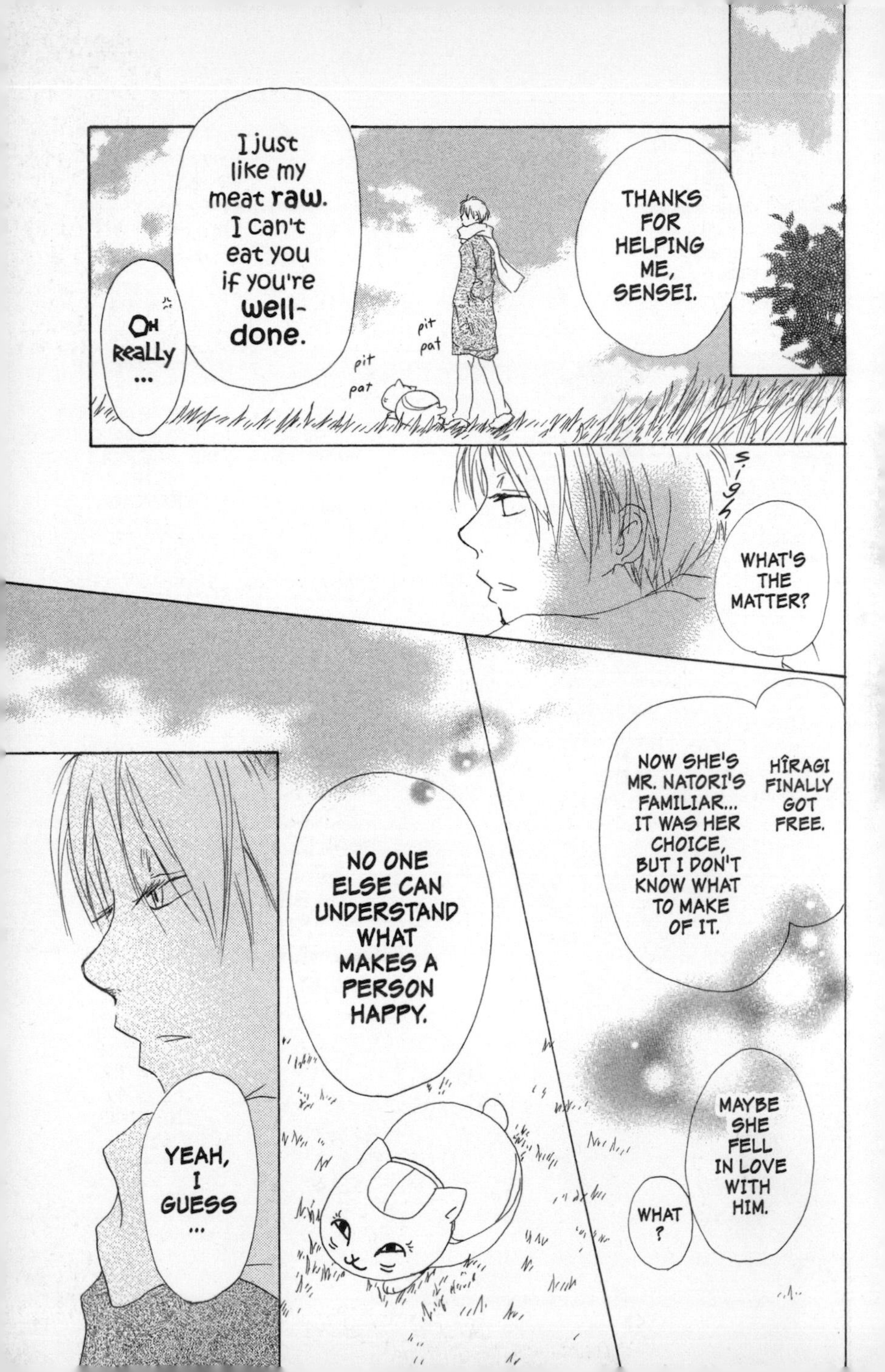
THANKS FOR HELPING ME, SENSEI.
I just like my meat raw. I can't eat you if you're well-done.
pit pat
pit pat
Oh really...
s-i-g-h
WHAT'S THE MATTER?
HÎRAGI FINALLY GOT FREE.
NOW SHE'S MR. NATORI'S FAMILIAR... IT WAS HER CHOICE, BUT I DON'T KNOW WHAT TO MAKE OF IT.
MAYBE SHE FELL IN LOVE WITH HIM.
WHAT?
NO ONE ELSE CAN UNDERSTAND WHAT MAKES A PERSON HAPPY.
YEAH, I GUESS...

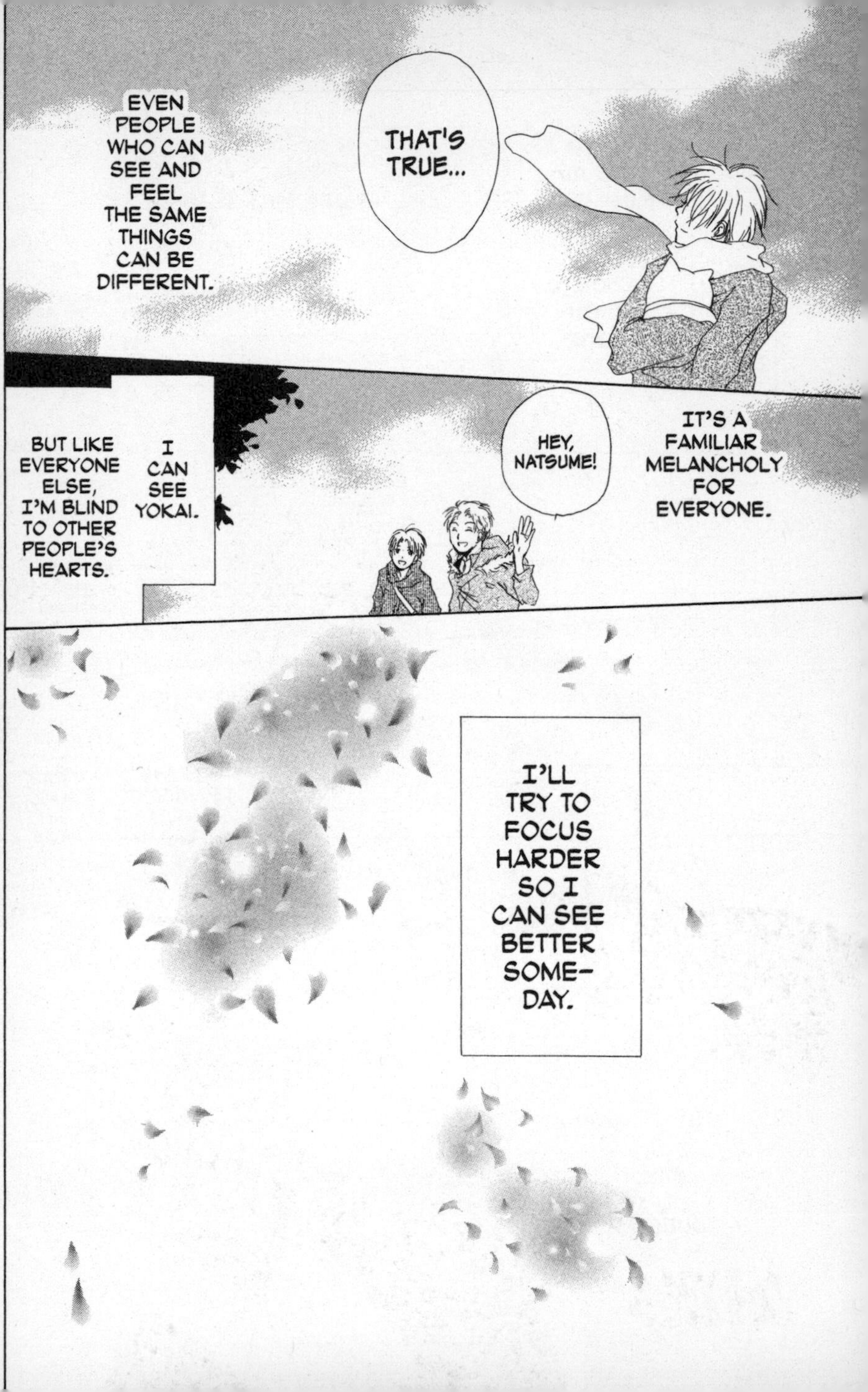
THAT'S TRUE...
EVEN PEOPLE WHO CAN SEE AND FEEL THE SAME THINGS CAN BE DIFFERENT.
IT'S A FAMILIAR MELANCHOLY FOR EVERYONE.
HEY, NATSUME!
I CAN SEE YOKAI.
BUT LIKE EVERYONE ELSE, I'M BLIND TO OTHER PEOPLE'S HEARTS.
I'LL TRY TO FOCUS HARDER SO I CAN SEE BETTER SOME-DAY.

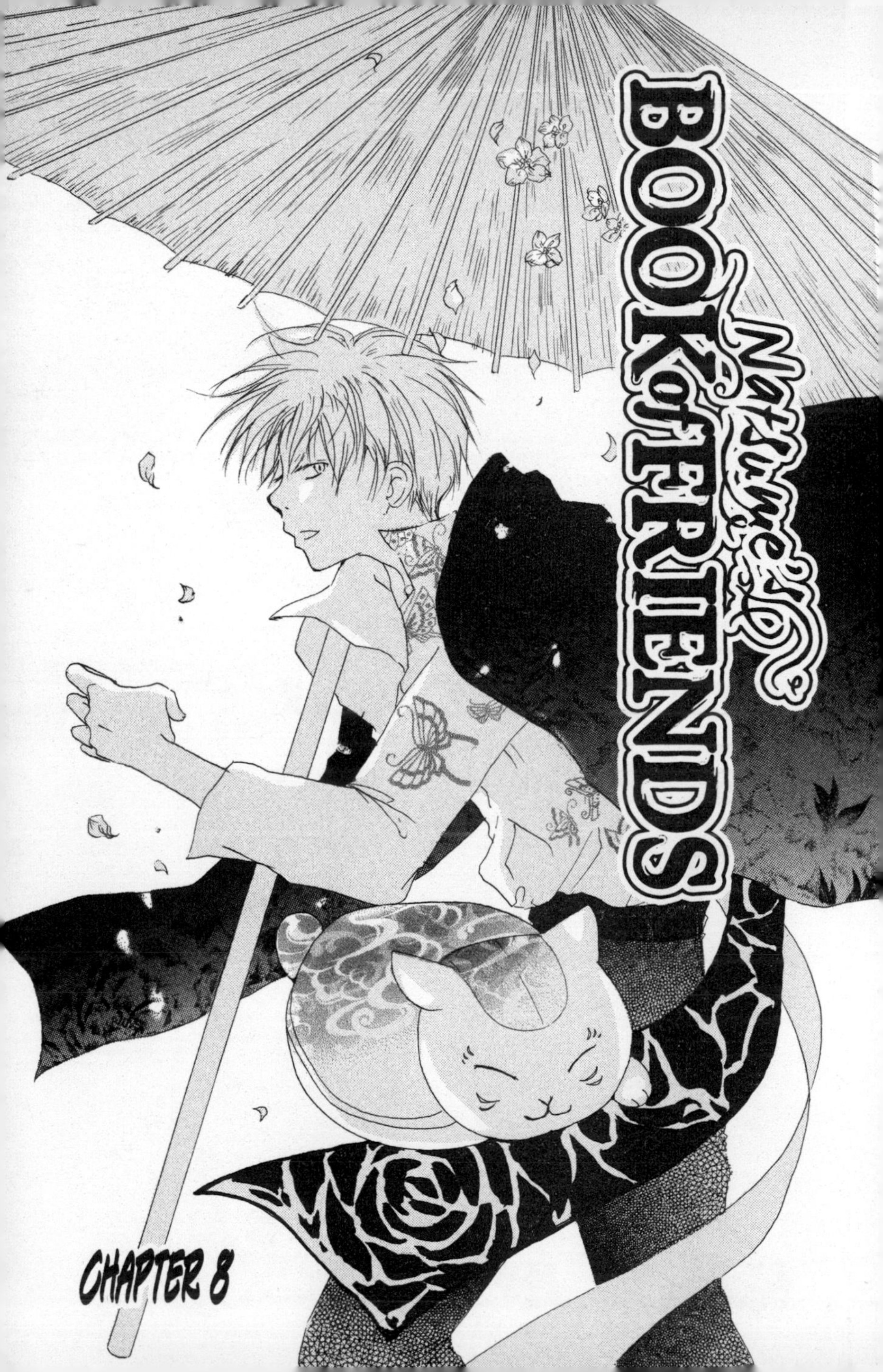
Natsume's
BOOK of FRIENDS
CHAPTER 8

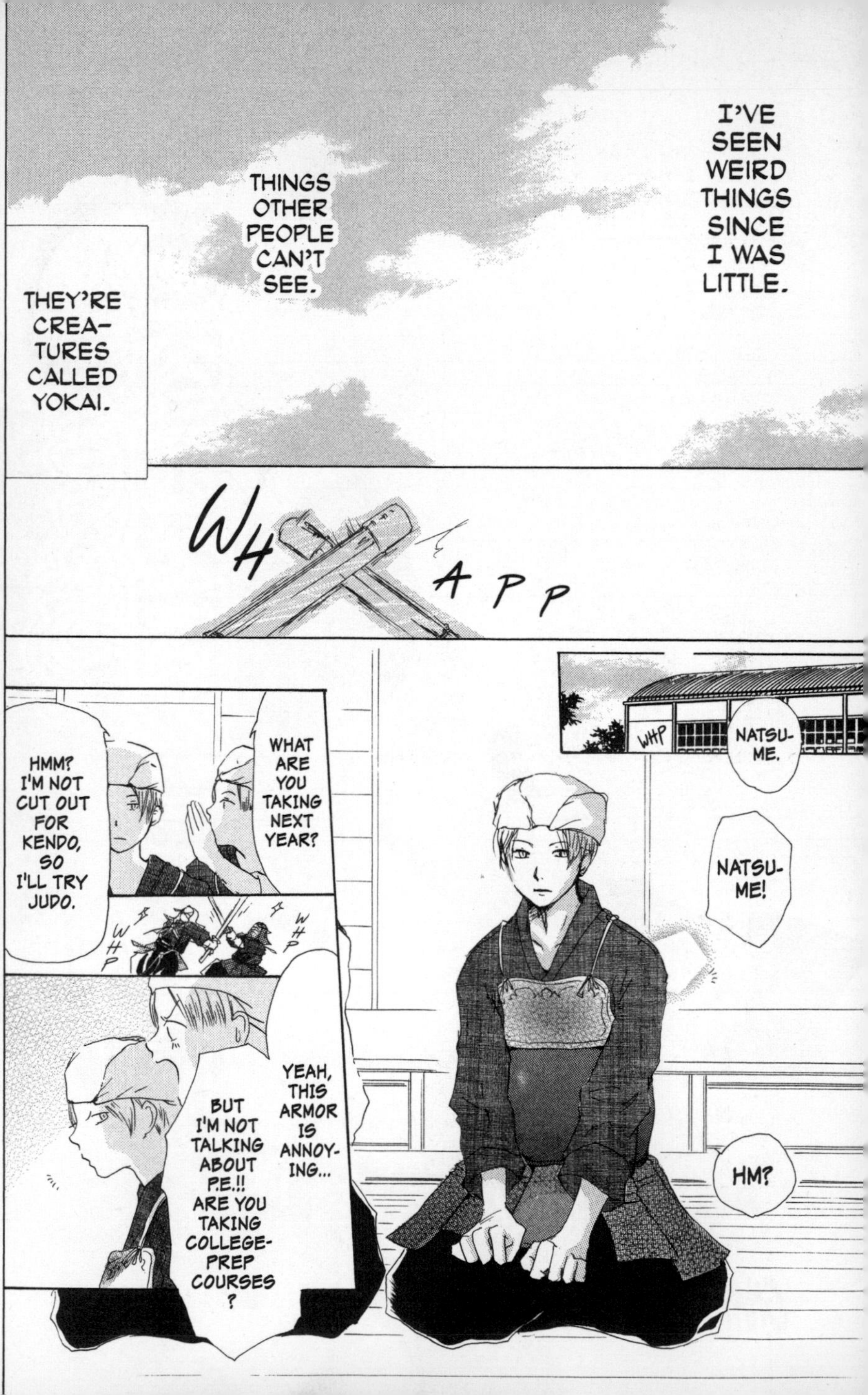

I'VE SEEN WEIRD THINGS SINCE I WAS LITTLE.
THINGS OTHER PEOPLE CAN'T SEE.
THEY'RE CREA-TURES CALLED YOKAI.
WHAPP
WHP
NATSU-ME.
NATSU-ME!
HM?
WHAT ARE YOU TAKING NEXT YEAR?
HMM? I'M NOT CUT OUT FOR KENDO, SO I'LL TRY JUDO.
WHP
WHP
YEAH, THIS ARMOR IS ANNOY-ING...
BUT I'M NOT TALKING ABOUT P.E.!! ARE YOU TAKING COLLEGE-PREP COURSES?

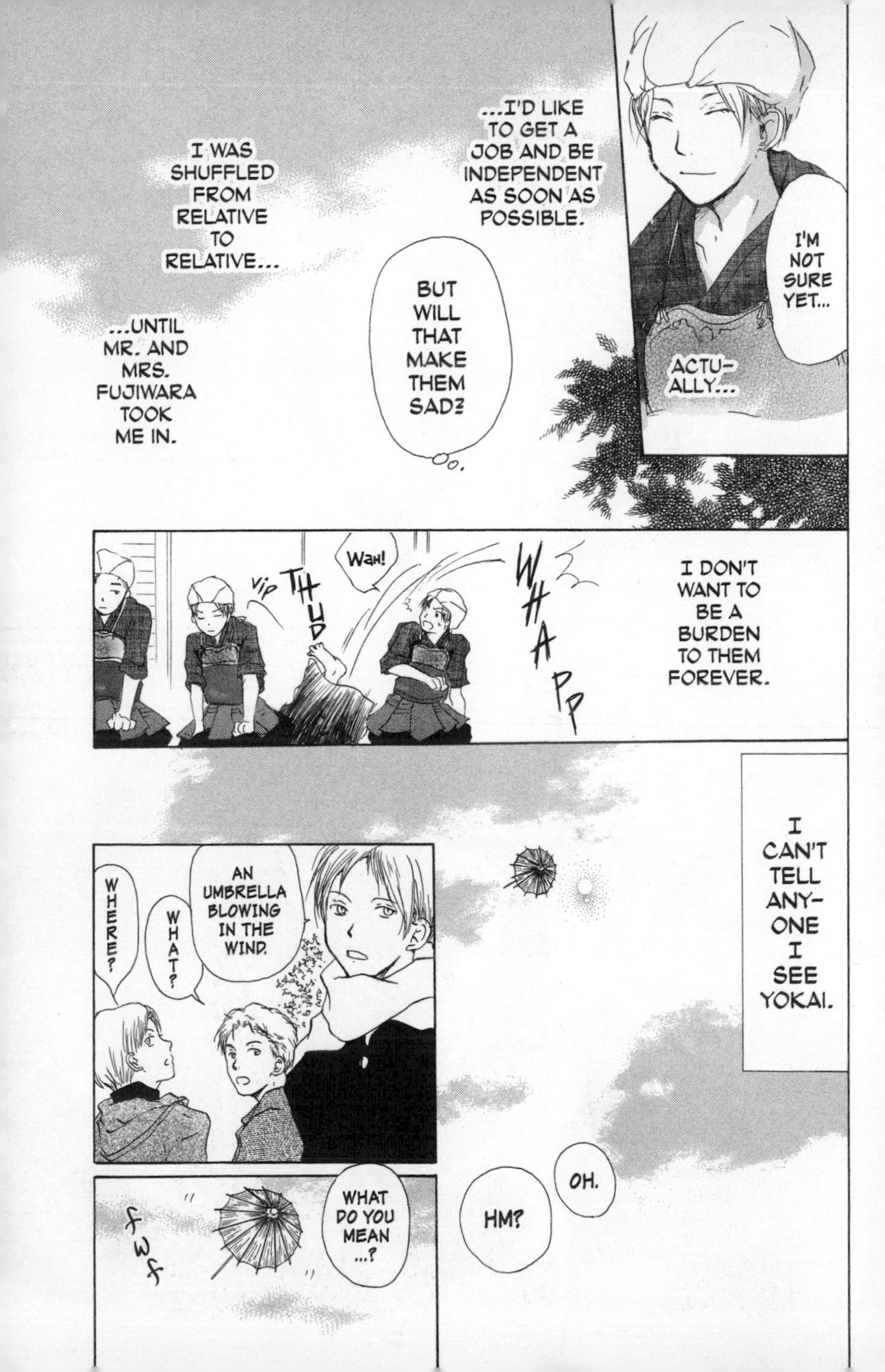
I'M NOT SURE YET...
ACTU-ALLY...
...I'D LIKE TO GET A JOB AND BE INDEPENDENT AS SOON AS POSSIBLE.
BUT WILL THAT MAKE THEM SAD?
I WAS SHUFFLED FROM RELATIVE TO RELATIVE...
...UNTIL MR. AND MRS. FUJIWARA TOOK ME IN.
I DON'T WANT TO BE A BURDEN TO THEM FOREVER.
WHAPP
Wah!
THUD
vip
I CAN'T TELL ANYONE I SEE YOKAI.
AN UMBRELLA BLOWING IN THE WIND.
WHAT?
WHERE?
OH.
HM?
WHAT DO YOU MEAN ...?
fwf

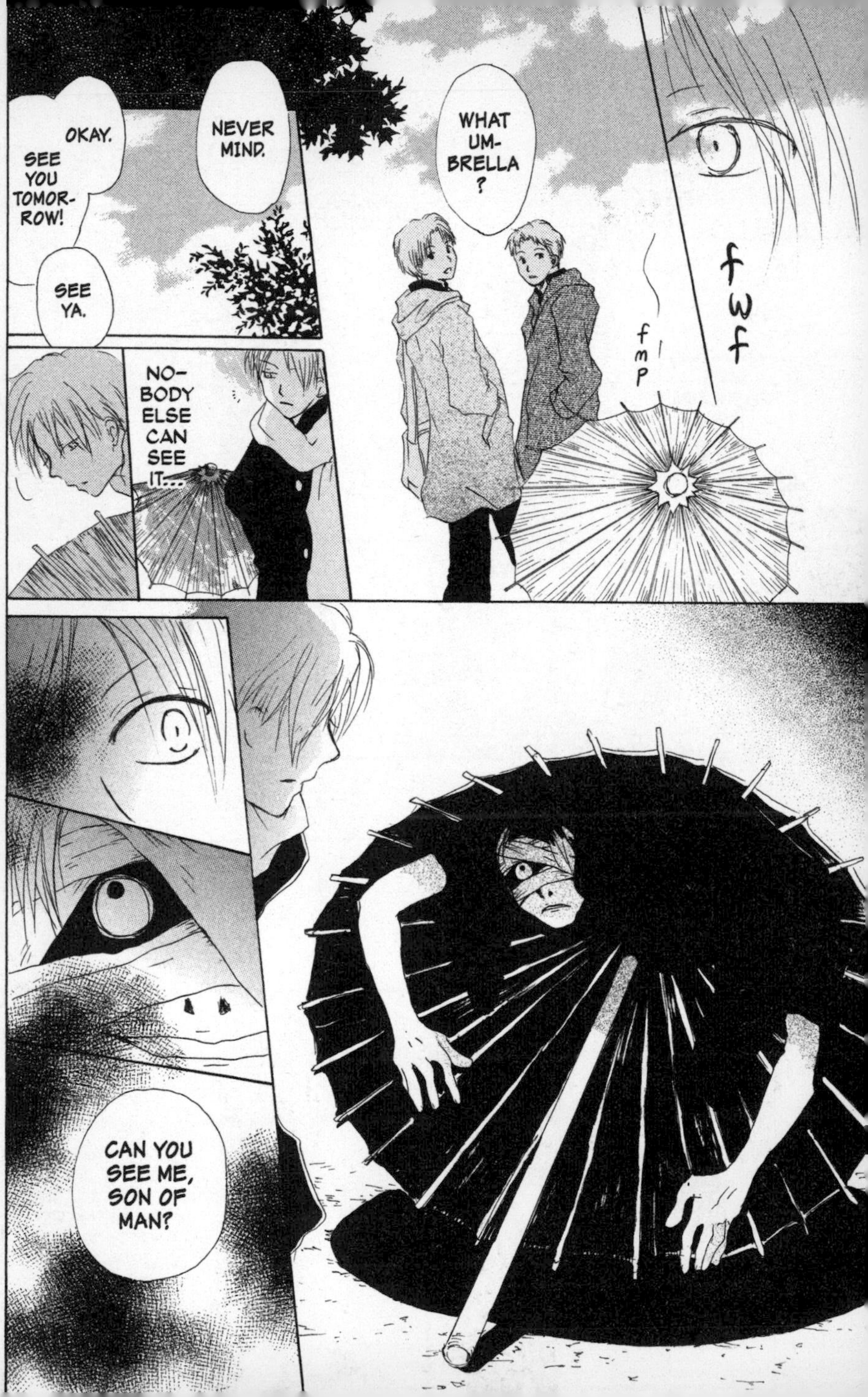
fwf
fmp
WHAT UM-BRELLA?
NEVER MIND.
OKAY. SEE YOU TOMOR-ROW!
SEE YA.
NO-BODY ELSE CAN SEE IT...
CAN YOU SEE ME, SON OF MAN?

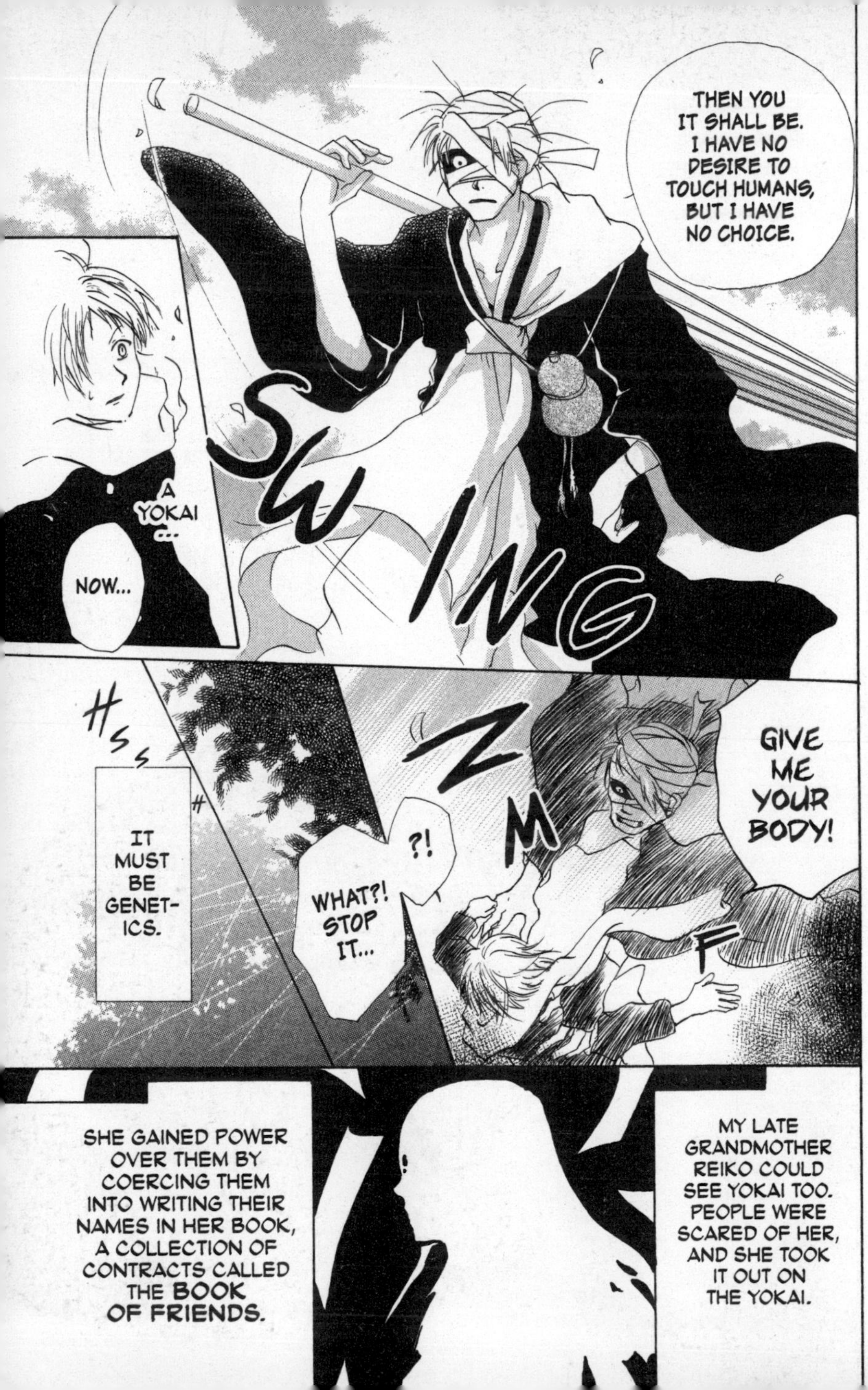
THEN YOU IT SHALL BE. I HAVE NO DESIRE TO TOUCH HUMANS, BUT I HAVE NO CHOICE.
SWING
A YOKAI ...
NOW...
GIVE ME YOUR BODY!
ZM
?!
WHAT?! STOP IT...
F
HSS
IT MUST BE GENET-ICS.
MY LATE GRANDMOTHER REIKO COULD SEE YOKAI TOO. PEOPLE WERE SCARED OF HER, AND SHE TOOK IT OUT ON THE YOKAI.
SHE GAINED POWER OVER THEM BY COERCING THEM INTO WRITING THEIR NAMES IN HER BOOK, A COLLECTION OF CONTRACTS CALLED THE BOOK OF FRIENDS.

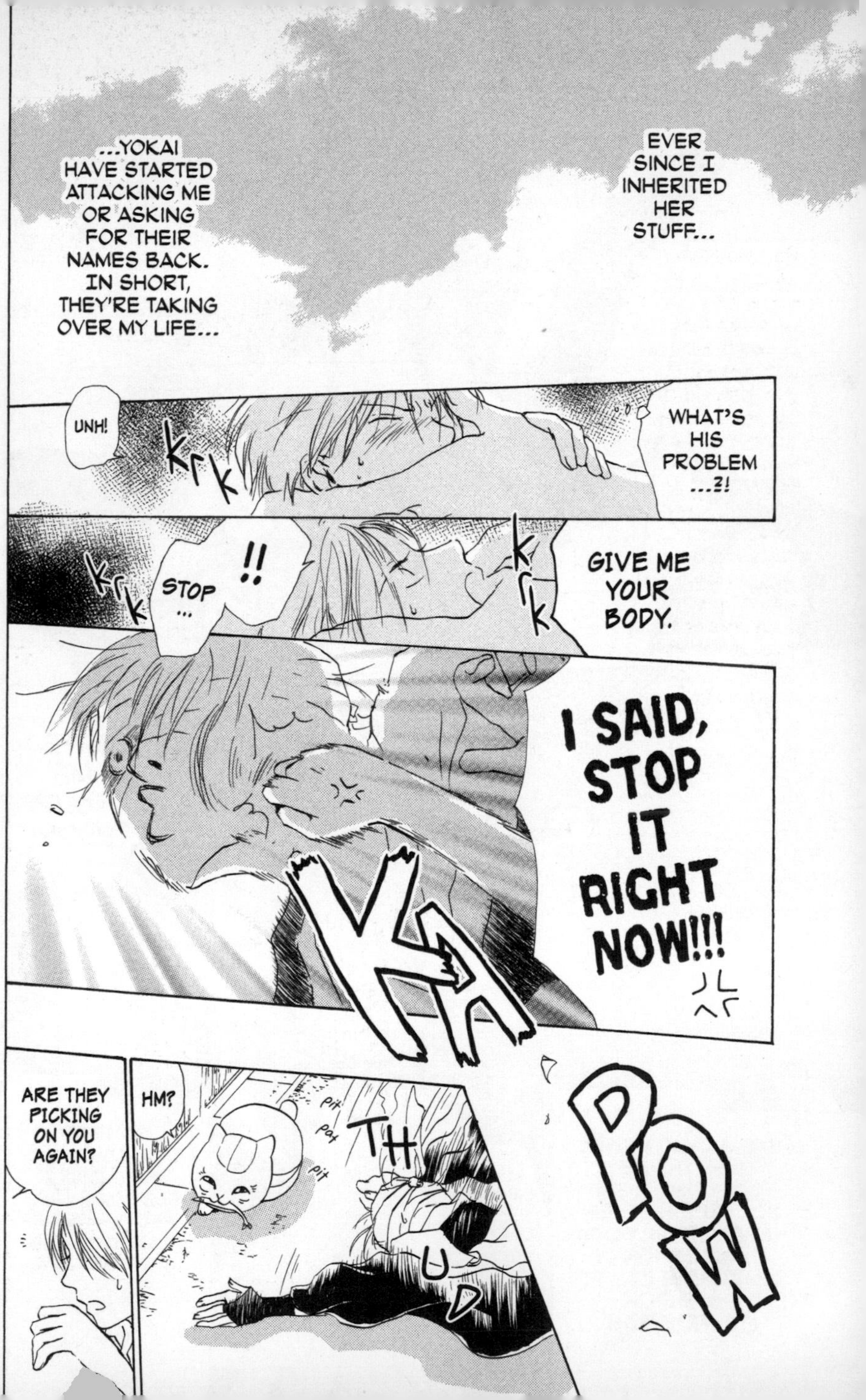
EVER SINCE I INHERITED HER STUFF...
...YOKAI HAVE STARTED ATTACKING ME OR ASKING FOR THEIR NAMES BACK. IN SHORT, THEY'RE TAKING OVER MY LIFE...
WHAT'S HIS PROBLEM ...?!
KRK
UNH!
GIVE ME YOUR BODY.
KRK
!!
STOP ...
KRK
I SAID, STOP IT RIGHT NOW!!!
KA
POW
THUD
pit
pat
pit
HM?
ARE THEY PICKING ON YOU AGAIN?

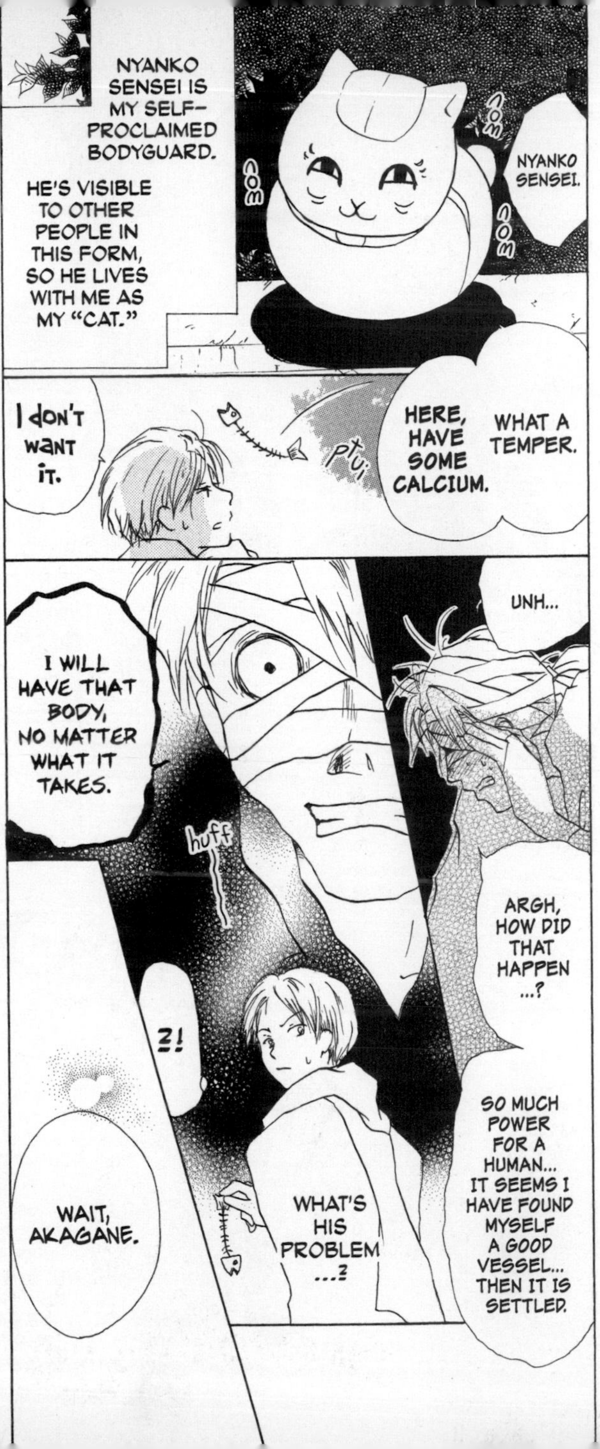
mow
mow
NYANKO SENSEI.
mow
NYANKO SENSEI IS MY SELF-PROCLAIMED BODYGUARD.
HE'S VISIBLE TO OTHER PEOPLE IN THIS FORM, SO HE LIVES WITH ME AS MY "CAT."
WHAT A TEMPER.
HERE, HAVE SOME CALCIUM.
ptui
I DON'T WANT IT.
UNH...
ARGH, HOW DID THAT HAPPEN ...?
SO MUCH POWER FOR A HUMAN... IT SEEMS I HAVE FOUND MYSELF A GOOD VESSEL... THEN IT IS SETTLED.
I WILL HAVE THAT BODY, NO MATTER WHAT IT TAKES.
huff
WHAT'S HIS PROBLEM ...?
?!
WAIT, AKAGANE.

08

❋Hinoe

Perhaps because she's not supposed to be beautiful, she was very easy to draw. I try to use screentone to put patterns on clothing, but I keep peeling them off again because I prefer the black-and-white look. But Hinoe is supposed to be fashionable and wears glamorous kimonos, so my assistant and I discussed and tried out different patterns. It was fun.

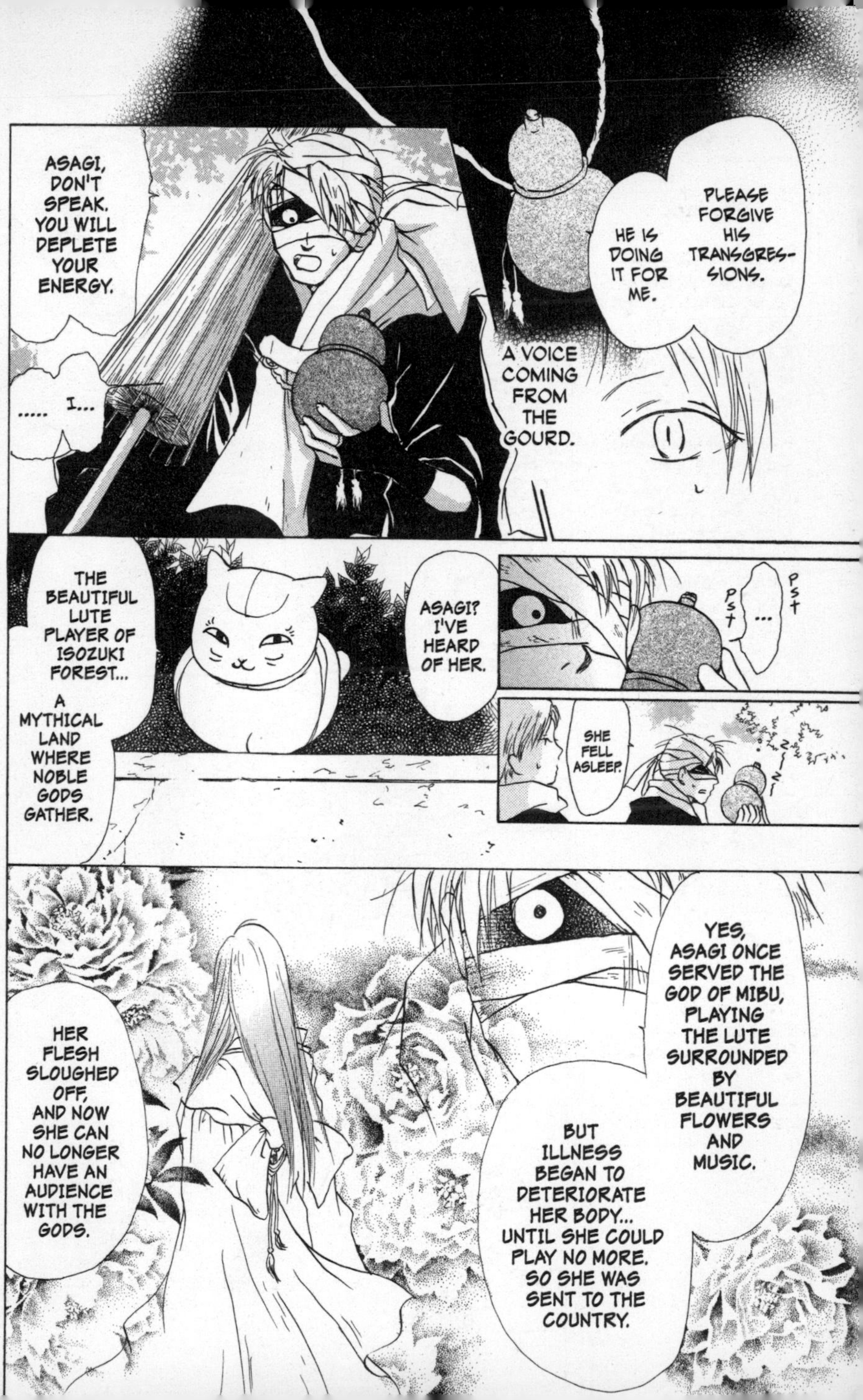
PLEASE FORGIVE HIS TRANSGRES-SIONS.
HE IS DOING IT FOR ME.
A VOICE COMING FROM THE GOURD.
ASAGI, DON'T SPEAK. YOU WILL DEPLETE YOUR ENERGY.
..... I...
Pst ... Pst
SHE FELL ASLEEP.
ASAGI? I'VE HEARD OF HER.
THE BEAUTIFUL LUTE PLAYER OF ISOZUKI FOREST...
A MYTHICAL LAND WHERE NOBLE GODS GATHER.
YES, ASAGI ONCE SERVED THE GOD OF MIBU, PLAYING THE LUTE SURROUNDED BY BEAUTIFUL FLOWERS AND MUSIC.
BUT ILLNESS BEGAN TO DETERIORATE HER BODY... UNTIL SHE COULD PLAY NO MORE. SO SHE WAS SENT TO THE COUNTRY.
HER FLESH SLOUGHED OFF, AND NOW SHE CAN NO LONGER HAVE AN AUDIENCE WITH THE GODS.

09

❋ Names

We have new characters and yokai every episode, so it's fun to come up with new names. I pick them carefully when it's important, but usually I simply wait for ideas to appear in my mind. "I want a name that begins with an S," for example. Even after I start using a name, I change it right away if it's not working for me. They often work out once changed. Natsume's first name was "Takeshi" at first, but I changed it and it was perfect. A boy in one of my previous manga was called Karashima, but he was a "Sakamoto" when I first showed it to my editor. I feel like the character really came alive after I changed his name. So I have to really be sure before it gets finalized in a preview.

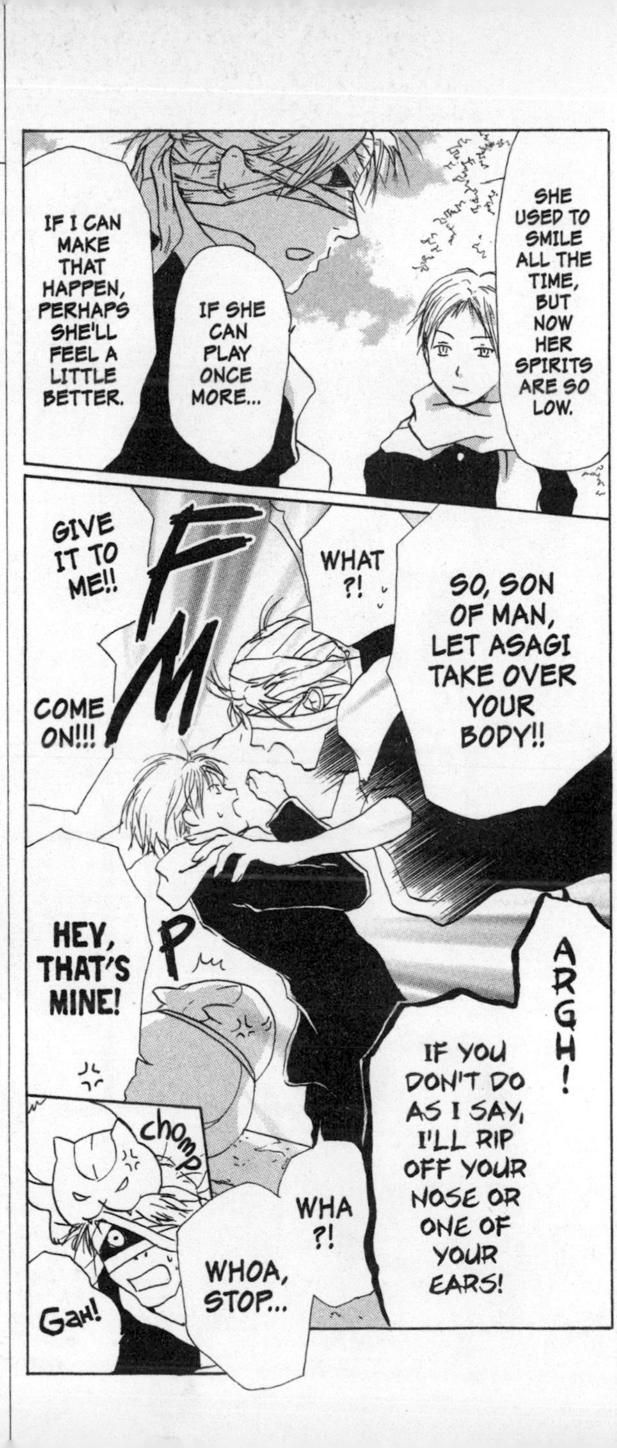
SHE USED TO SMILE ALL THE TIME, BUT NOW HER SPIRITS ARE SO LOW.
IF SHE CAN PLAY ONCE MORE...
IF I CAN MAKE THAT HAPPEN, PERHAPS SHE'LL FEEL A LITTLE BETTER.
SO, SON OF MAN, LET ASAGI TAKE OVER YOUR BODY!!
WHAT ?!
GIVE IT TO ME!!
FM
COME ON!!!
ARGH!
IF YOU DON'T DO AS I SAY, I'LL RIP OFF YOUR NOSE OR ONE OF YOUR EARS!
HEY, THAT'S MINE!
P
WHA ?!
WHOA, STOP...
chomp
GAH!

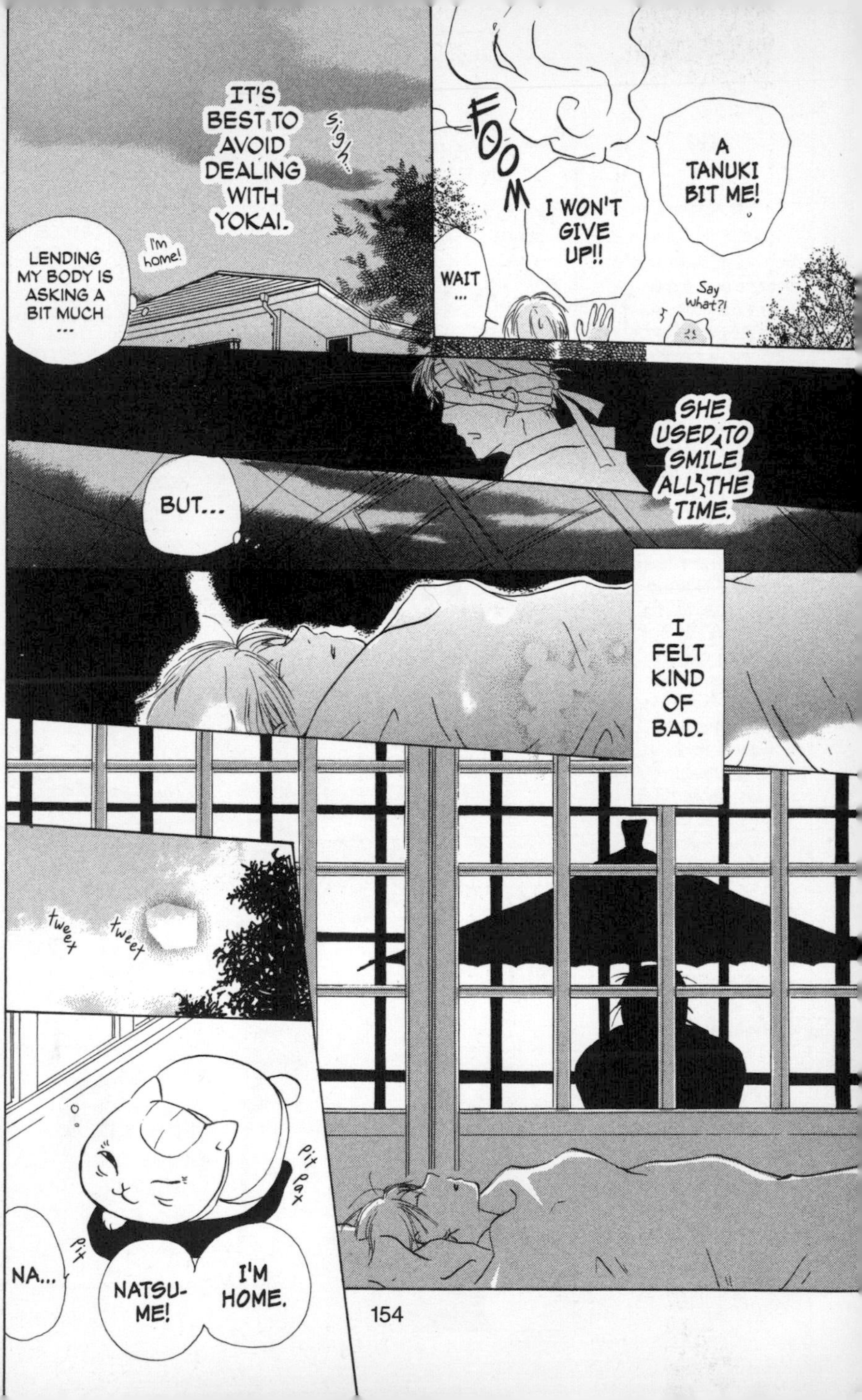
FOOM
A TANUKI BIT ME!
I WON'T GIVE UP!!
WAIT...
Say what?!
IT'S BEST TO AVOID DEALING WITH YOKAI.
sigh...
I'm home!
LENDING MY BODY IS ASKING A BIT MUCH...
SHE USED TO SMILE ALL THE TIME.
BUT...
I FELT KIND OF BAD.
tweet
tweet
pit pat
I'M HOME.
NATSU-ME!
pit
NA...

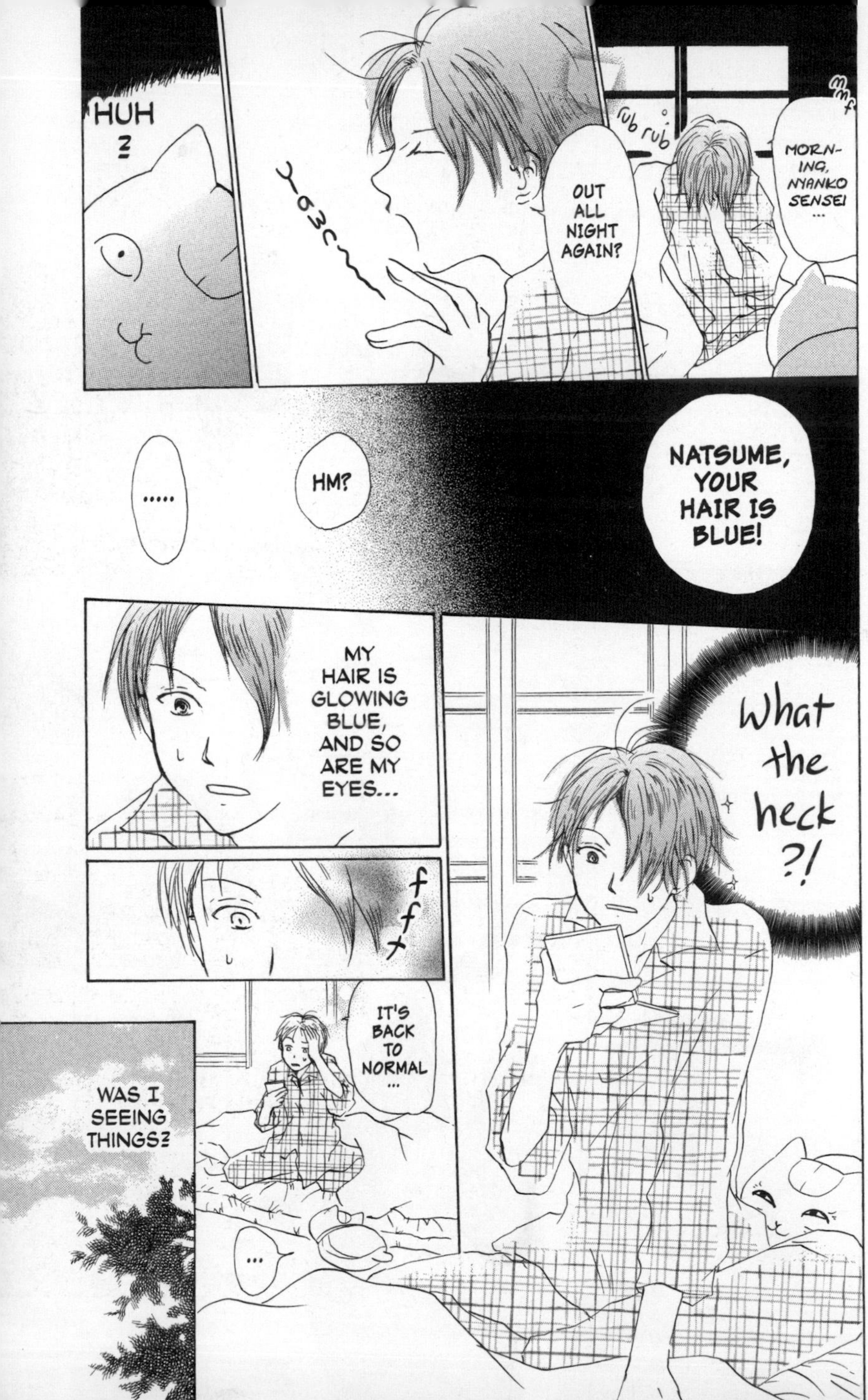
mmf
MORNING, NYANKO SENSEI...
rub rub
OUT ALL NIGHT AGAIN?
yawn~
HUH?
NATSUME, YOUR HAIR IS BLUE!
HM?
.....
What the heck?!
MY HAIR IS GLOWING BLUE, AND SO ARE MY EYES...
IT'S BACK TO NORMAL...
...
WAS I SEEING THINGS?

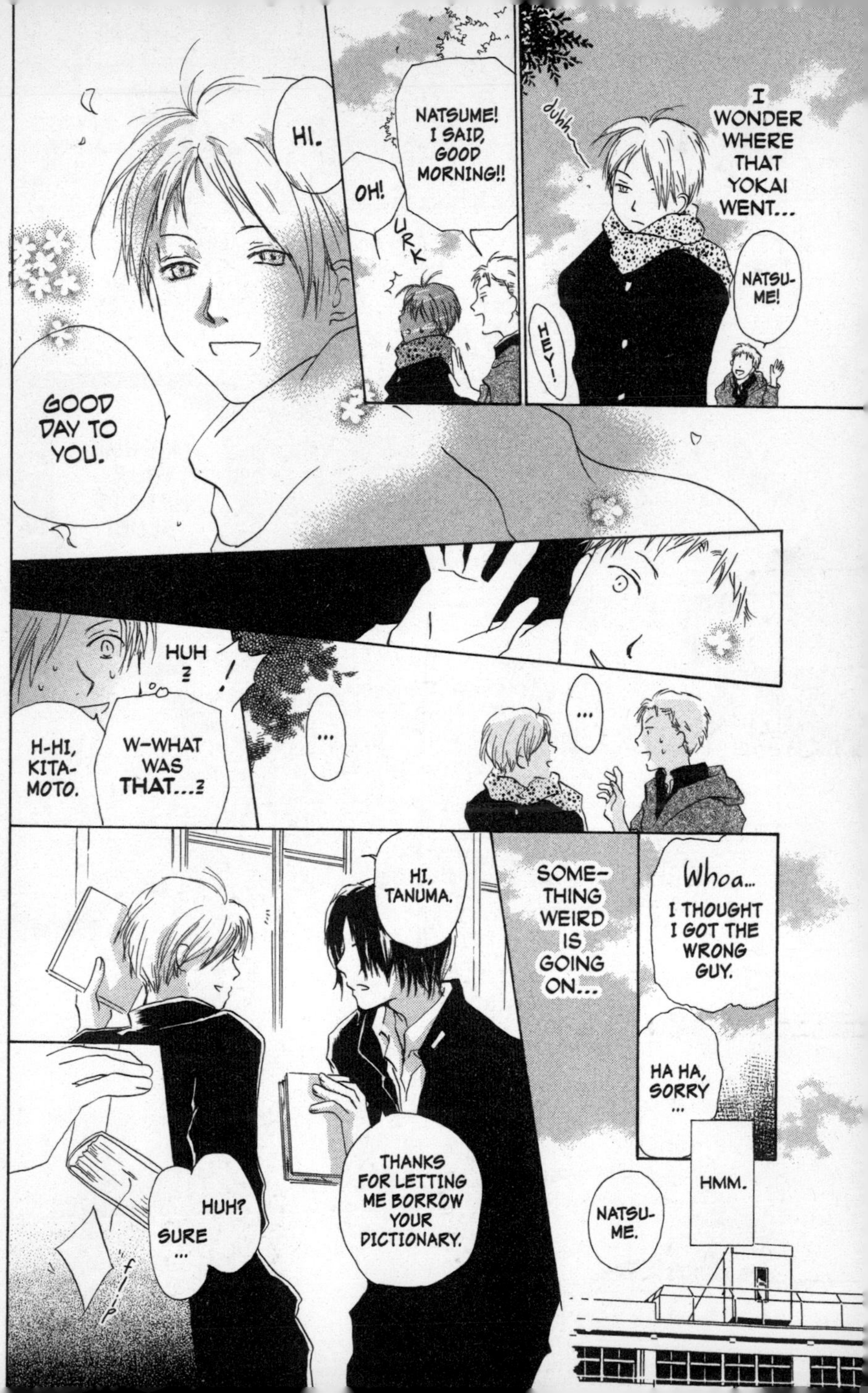
I WONDER WHERE THAT YOKAI WENT...
duhh
NATSU-ME!
HEY!
NATSUME! I SAID, GOOD MORNING!!
OH!
URK
HI.
GOOD DAY TO YOU.
...
...
HUH?
W-WHAT WAS THAT...?
H-HI, KITA-MOTO.
Whoa...
I THOUGHT I GOT THE WRONG GUY.
HA HA, SORRY ...
HMM.
NATSU-ME.
SOME-THING WEIRD IS GOING ON...
HI, TANUMA.
THANKS FOR LETTING ME BORROW YOUR DICTIONARY.
HUH? SURE ...
flip

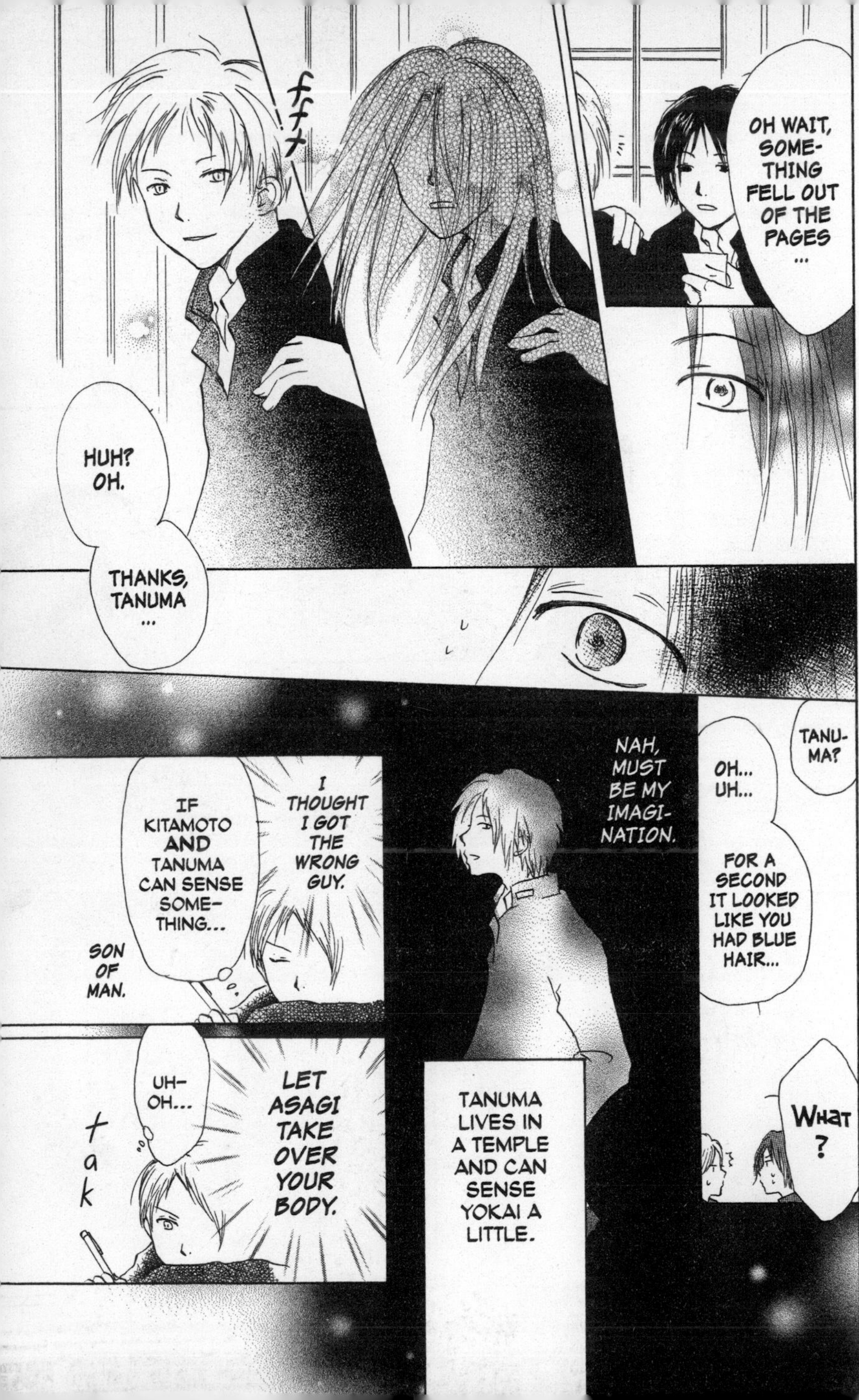
OH WAIT, SOMETHING FELL OUT OF THE PAGES ...
HUH? OH.
THANKS, TANUMA ...
TANUMA?
OH... UH...
FOR A SECOND IT LOOKED LIKE YOU HAD BLUE HAIR...
NAH, MUST BE MY IMAGINATION.
WHAT?
TANUMA LIVES IN A TEMPLE AND CAN SENSE YOKAI A LITTLE.
I THOUGHT I GOT THE WRONG GUY.
IF KITAMOTO AND TANUMA CAN SENSE SOMETHING...
SON OF MAN.
LET ASAGI TAKE OVER YOUR BODY.
UH-OH...
tak

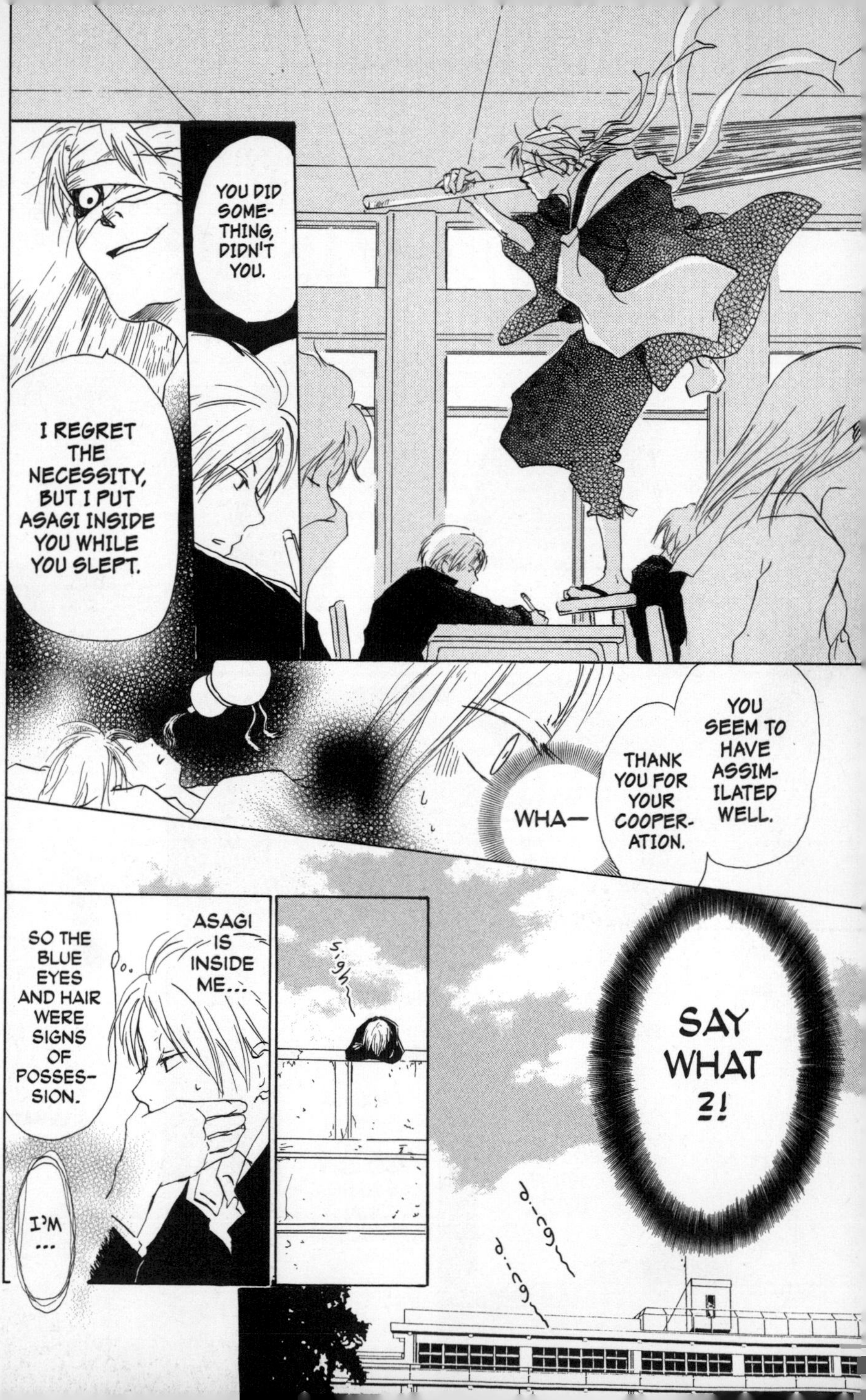
YOU DID SOMETHING, DIDN'T YOU.
I REGRET THE NECESSITY, BUT I PUT ASAGI INSIDE YOU WHILE YOU SLEPT.
YOU SEEM TO HAVE ASSIMILATED WELL.
THANK YOU FOR YOUR COOPERATION.
WHA—
SAY WHAT ?!
sigh~
ASAGI IS INSIDE ME...
SO THE BLUE EYES AND HAIR WERE SIGNS OF POSSESSION.
I'M ...

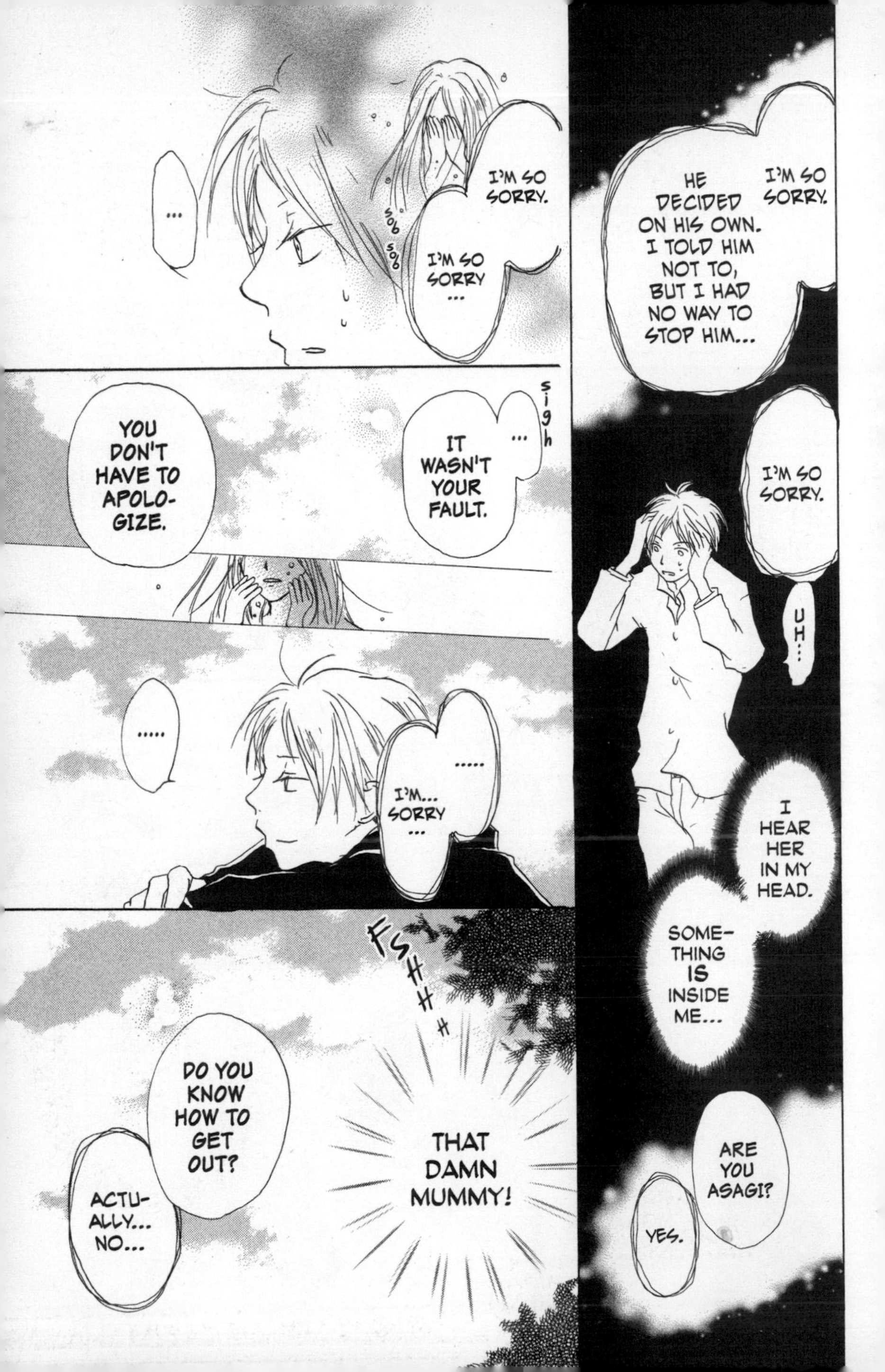
I'M SO SORRY.
HE DECIDED ON HIS OWN. I TOLD HIM NOT TO, BUT I HAD NO WAY TO STOP HIM...
I'M SO SORRY.
UH...
I HEAR HER IN MY HEAD.
SOMETHING IS INSIDE ME...
ARE YOU ASAGI?
YES.
I'M SO SORRY.
I'M SO SORRY...
sob sob
...
sigh
... IT WASN'T YOUR FAULT.
YOU DON'T HAVE TO APOLOGIZE.
...... I'M... SORRY...
.....
FSHHH
THAT DAMN MUMMY!
DO YOU KNOW HOW TO GET OUT?
ACTUALLY... NO...

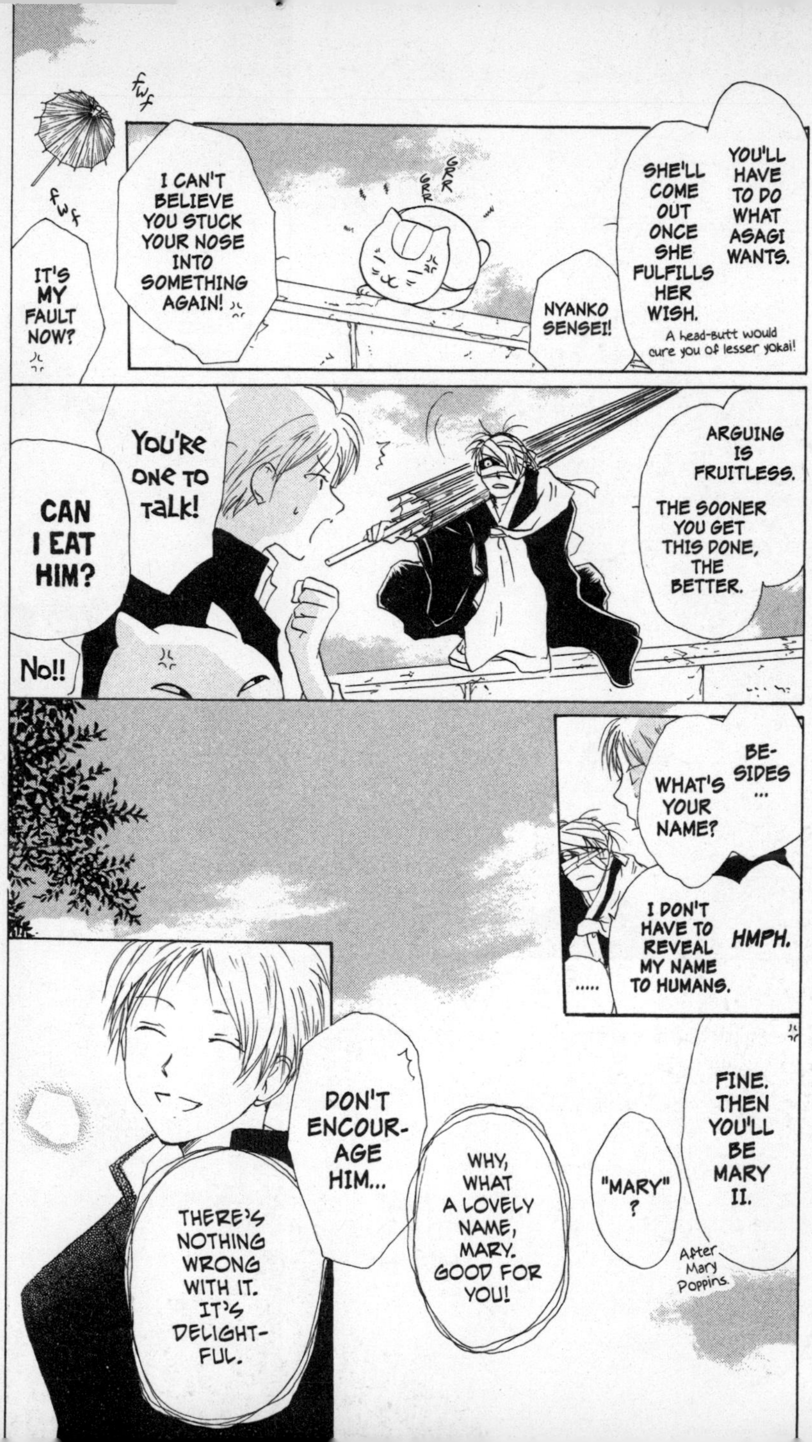
fwf fwf
YOU'LL HAVE TO DO WHAT ASAGI WANTS.
SHE'LL COME OUT ONCE SHE FULFILLS HER WISH.
A head-butt would cure you of lesser yokai!
NYANKO SENSEI!
GRR GRR
I CAN'T BELIEVE YOU STUCK YOUR NOSE INTO SOMETHING AGAIN!
IT'S MY FAULT NOW?
ARGUING IS FRUITLESS.
THE SOONER YOU GET THIS DONE, THE BETTER.
You're one to talk!
CAN I EAT HIM?
No!!
BESIDES...
WHAT'S YOUR NAME?
HMPH.
I DON'T HAVE TO REVEAL MY NAME TO HUMANS.
.....
FINE. THEN YOU'LL BE MARY II.
After Mary Poppins.
"MARY"?
WHY, WHAT A LOVELY NAME, MARY. GOOD FOR YOU!
DON'T ENCOURAGE HIM...
THERE'S NOTHING WRONG WITH IT. IT'S DELIGHTFUL.

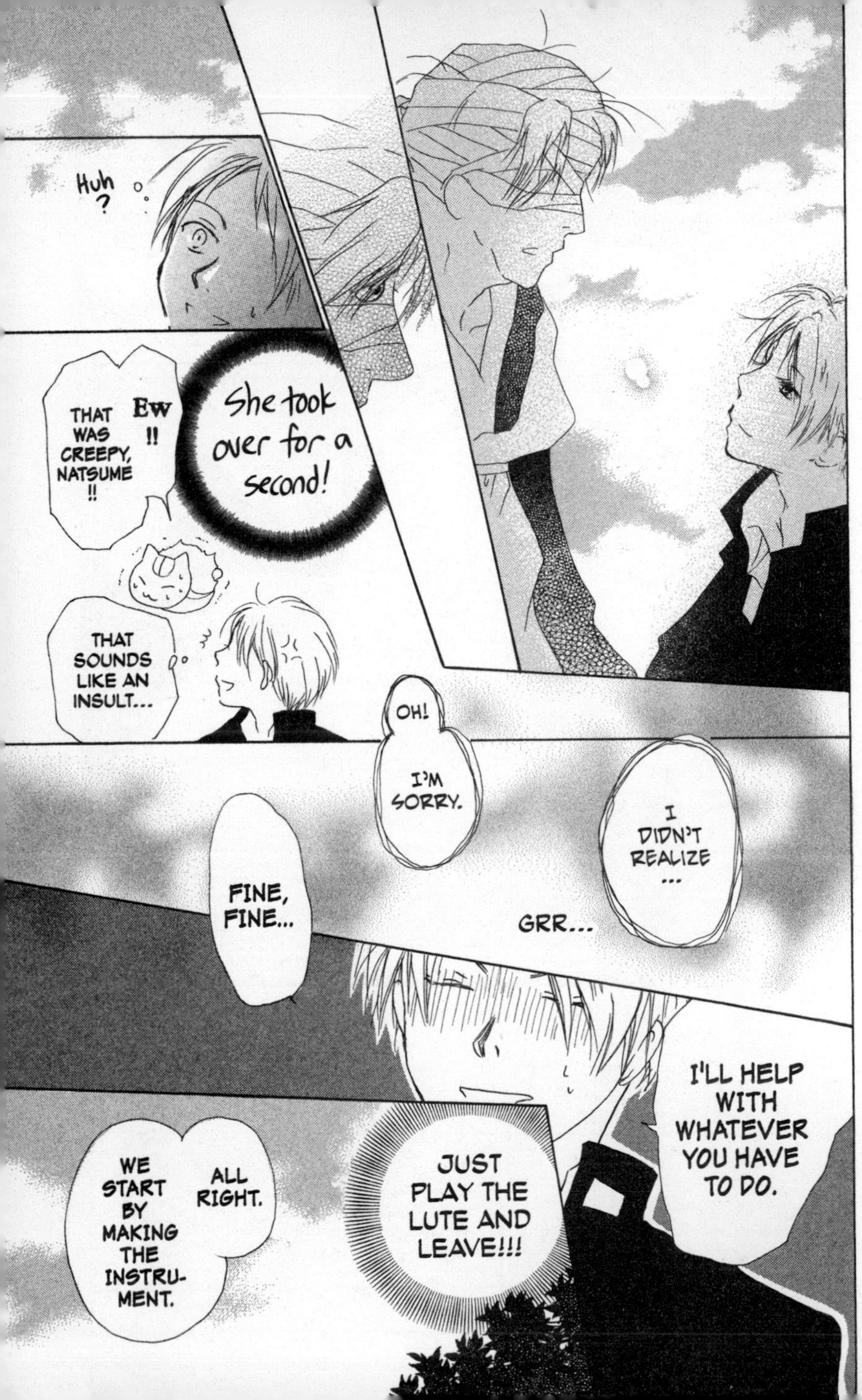
Huh?
She took over for a second!
Ew!!
THAT WAS CREEPY, NATSUME!!
THAT SOUNDS LIKE AN INSULT...
OH!
I'M SORRY.
I DIDN'T REALIZE...
GRR...
FINE, FINE...
I'LL HELP WITH WHATEVER YOU HAVE TO DO.
JUST PLAY THE LUTE AND LEAVE!!!
ALL RIGHT.
WE START BY MAKING THE INSTRUMENT.

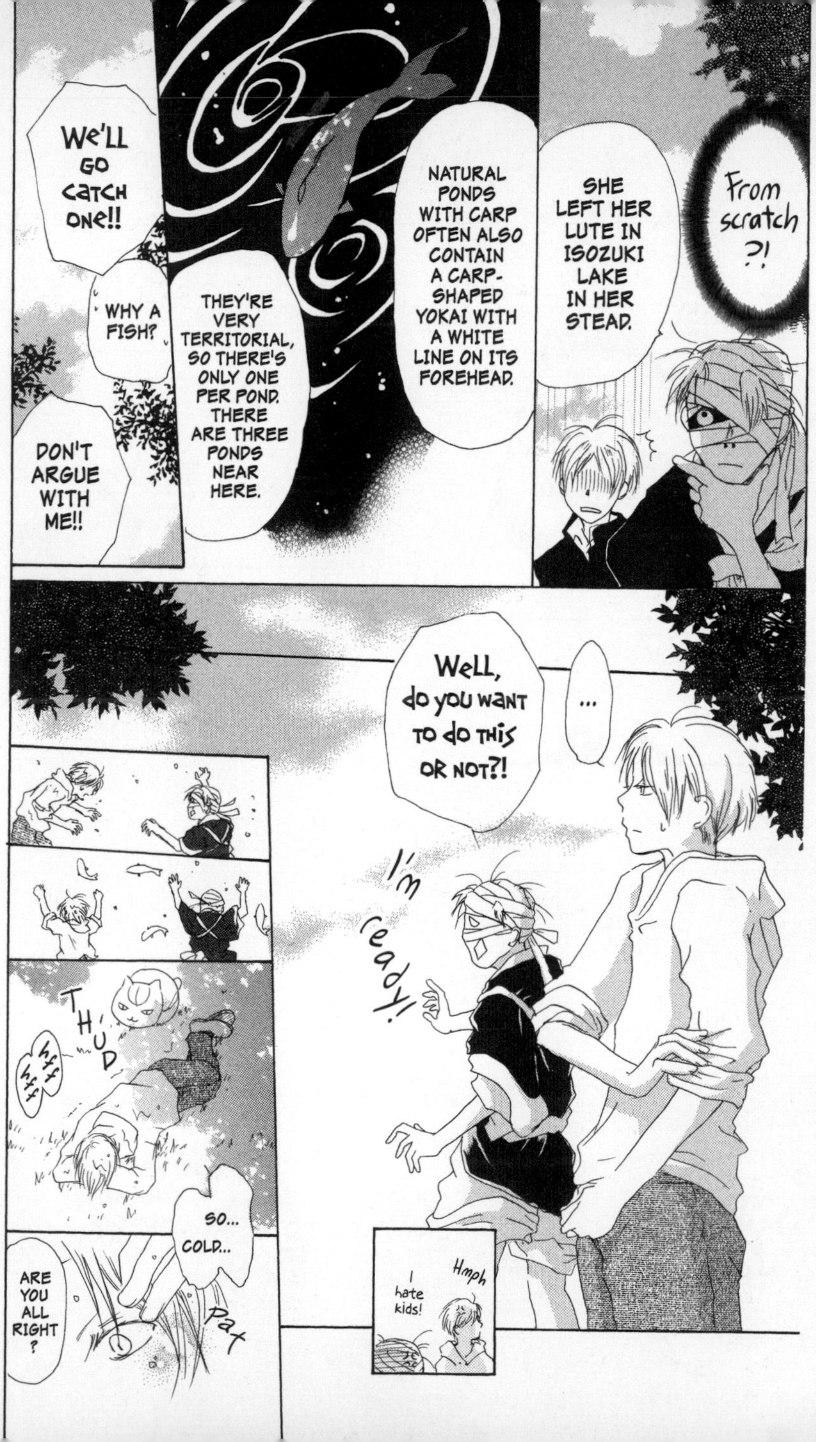
From scratch?!
She left her lute in Isozuki Lake in her stead.
Natural ponds with carp often also contain a carp-shaped yokai with a white line on its forehead.
They're very territorial, so there's only one per pond. There are three ponds near here.
We'll go catch one!!
Why a fish?
Don't argue with me!!
...
Well, do you want to do this or not?!
I'm ready!
Hmph
I hate kids!
THUD
hff hff
so... cold...
Pat
Are you all right?

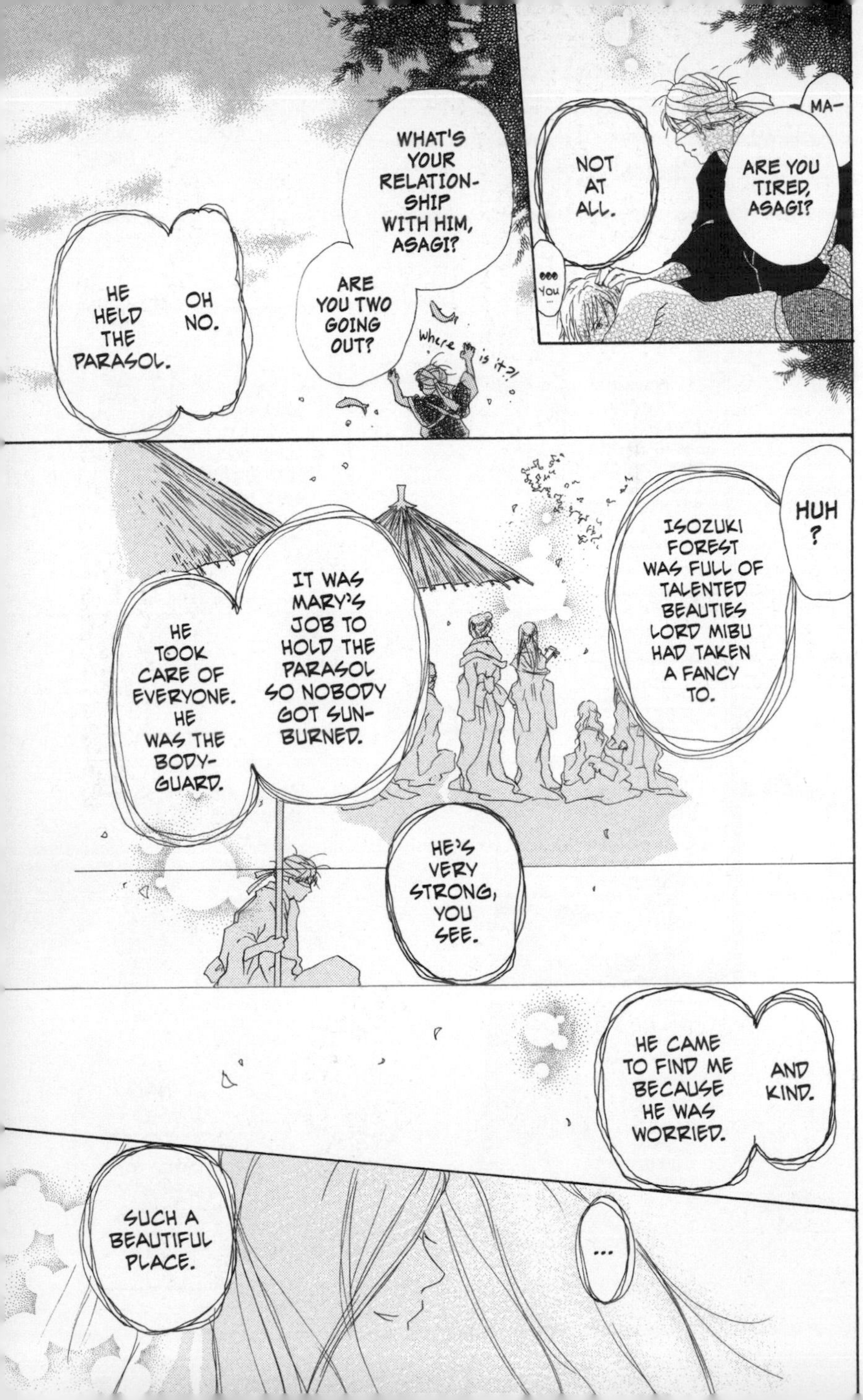
MA—
ARE YOU TIRED, ASAGI?
NOT AT ALL.
...You...
WHAT'S YOUR RELATIONSHIP WITH HIM, ASAGI?
ARE YOU TWO GOING OUT?
Where is it?!
HE HELD THE PARASOL. OH NO.
HUH?
ISOZUKI FOREST WAS FULL OF TALENTED BEAUTIES LORD MIBU HAD TAKEN A FANCY TO.
IT WAS MARY'S JOB TO HOLD THE PARASOL SO NOBODY GOT SUNBURNED.
HE TOOK CARE OF EVERYONE. HE WAS THE BODYGUARD.
HE'S VERY STRONG, YOU SEE.
HE CAME TO FIND ME BECAUSE HE WAS WORRIED. AND KIND.
...
SUCH A BEAUTIFUL PLACE.

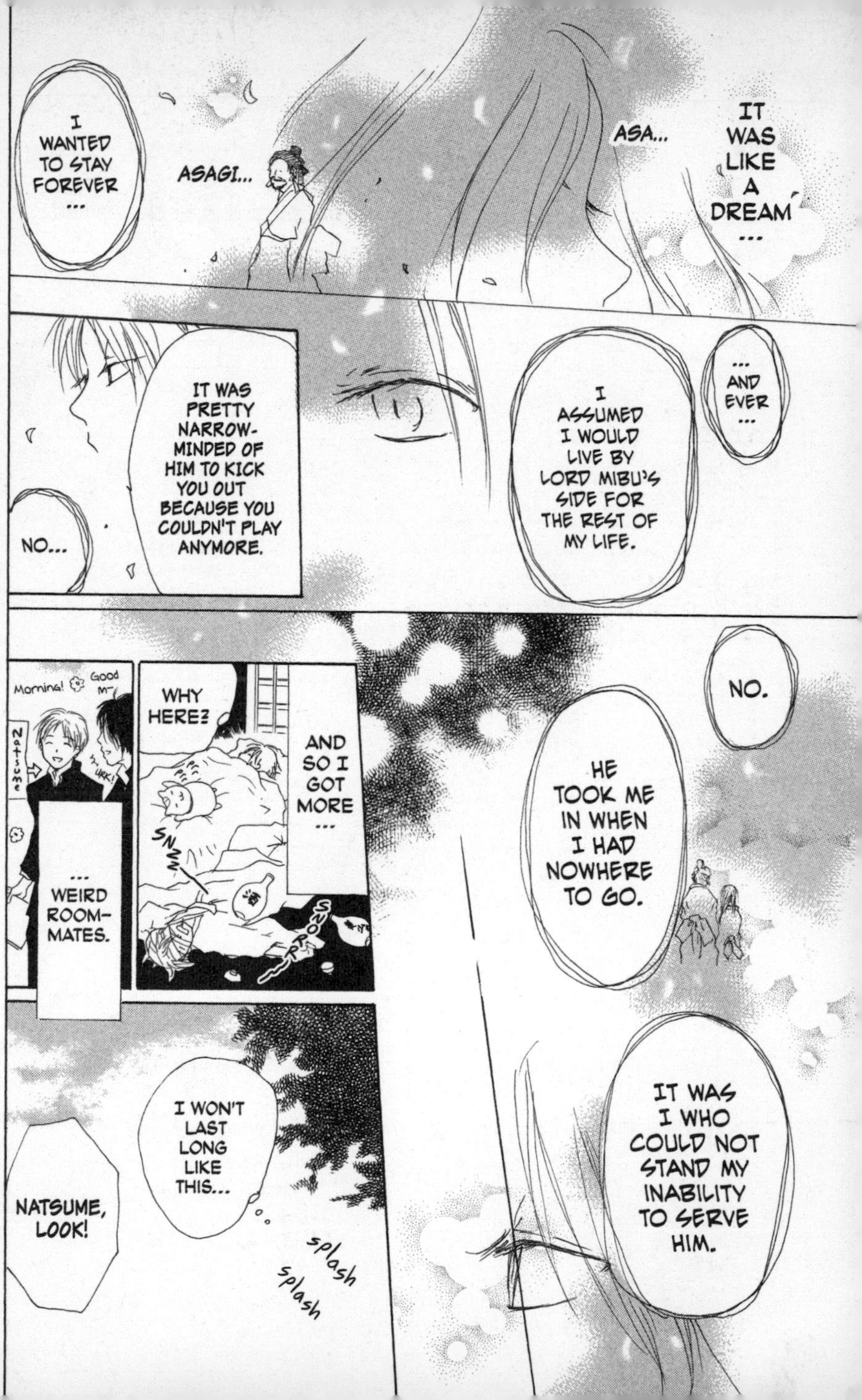
IT WAS LIKE A DREAM...
ASA...
ASAGI...
I WANTED TO STAY FOREVER...
...AND EVER...
I ASSUMED I WOULD LIVE BY LORD MIBU'S SIDE FOR THE REST OF MY LIFE.
IT WAS PRETTY NARROW-MINDED OF HIM TO KICK YOU OUT BECAUSE YOU COULDN'T PLAY ANYMORE.
NO...
NO.
HE TOOK ME IN WHEN I HAD NOWHERE TO GO.
IT WAS I WHO COULD NOT STAND MY INABILITY TO SERVE HIM.
WHY HERE?
AND SO I GOT MORE...
SNZZ
SNORRR
Good M–
Morning!
Natsume
URK!
...WEIRD ROOMMATES.
I WON'T LAST LONG LIKE THIS...
NATSUME, LOOK!
splash
splash

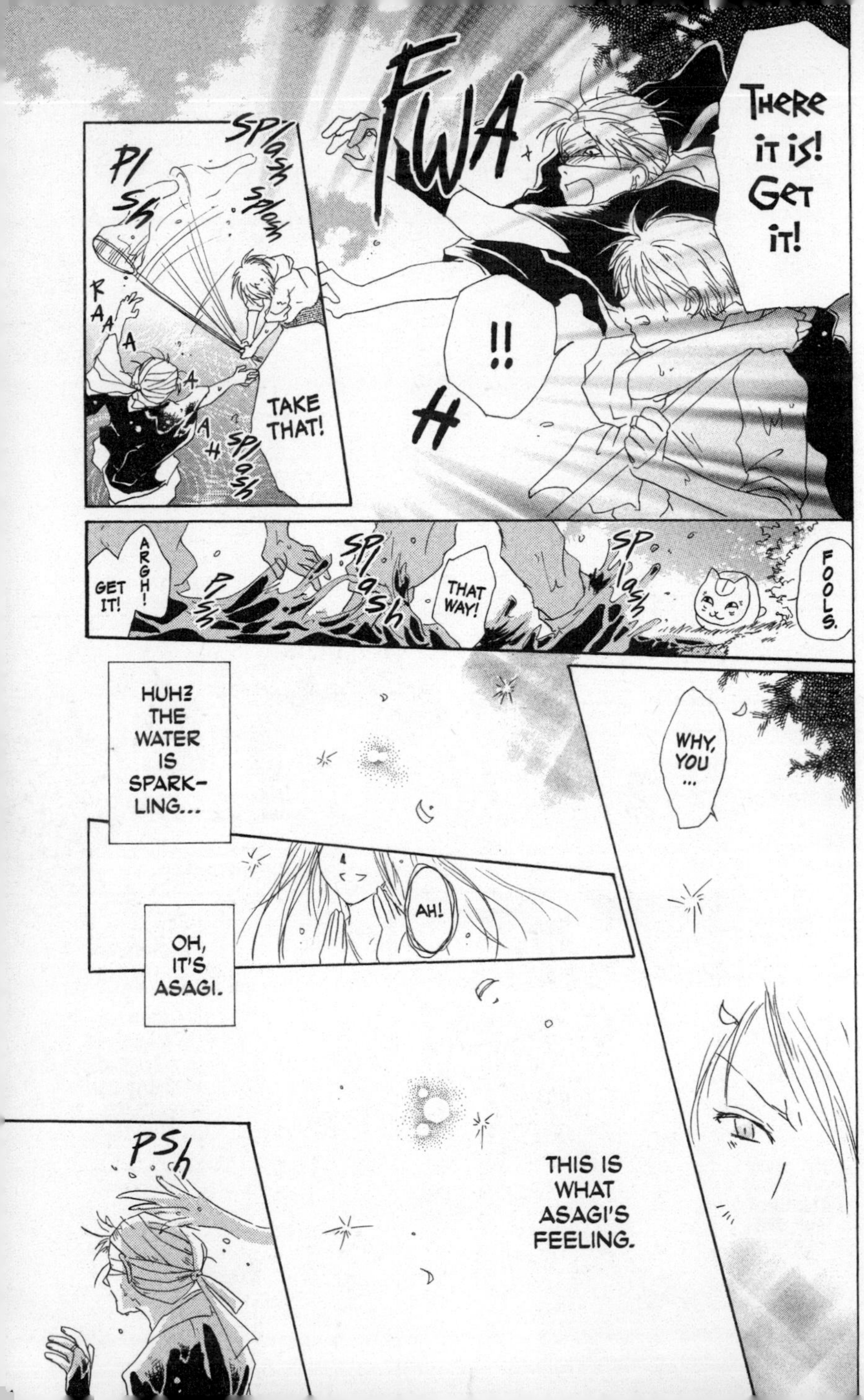
There it is! Get it!
FWA
!!
H
SPlash
PlSh
splash splash
RAAAAAH
TAKE THAT!
SPlash
FOOLS.
SPlash
THAT WAY!
SPlash
PlSh
ARGH!
GET IT!
WHY, YOU ...
THIS IS WHAT ASAGI'S FEELING.
HUH? THE WATER IS SPARKLING...
AH!
OH, IT'S ASAGI.
PSh

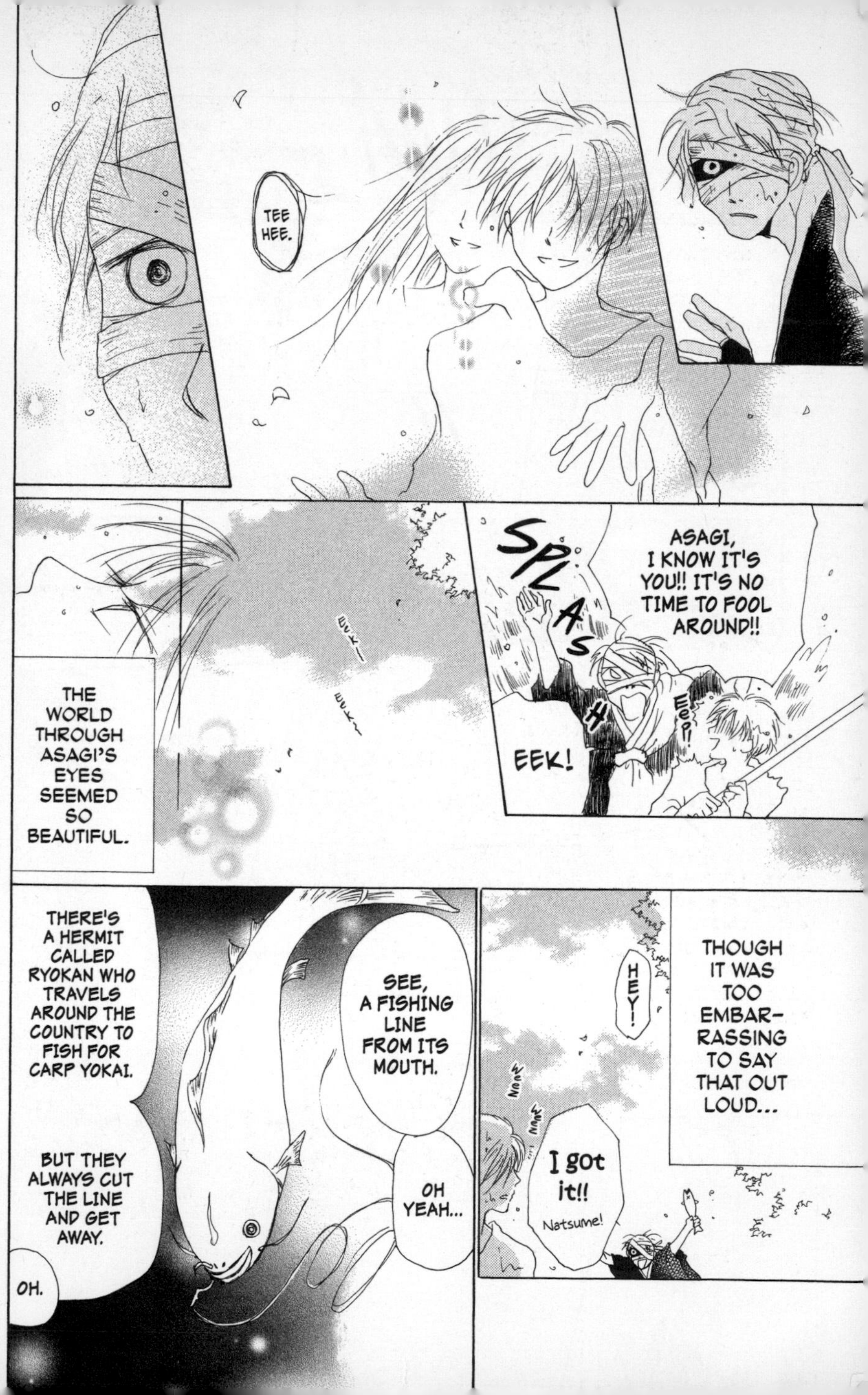
TEE HEE.
SPLASH
ASAGI, I KNOW IT'S YOU!! IT'S NO TIME TO FOOL AROUND!!
EEP!
EEK!
THE WORLD THROUGH ASAGI'S EYES SEEMED SO BEAUTIFUL.
THOUGH IT WAS TOO EMBARRASSING TO SAY THAT OUT LOUD...
HEY!
I got it!!
Natsume!
THERE'S A HERMIT CALLED RYOKAN WHO TRAVELS AROUND THE COUNTRY TO FISH FOR CARP YOKAI.
SEE, A FISHING LINE FROM ITS MOUTH.
OH YEAH...
BUT THEY ALWAYS CUT THE LINE AND GET AWAY.
OH.

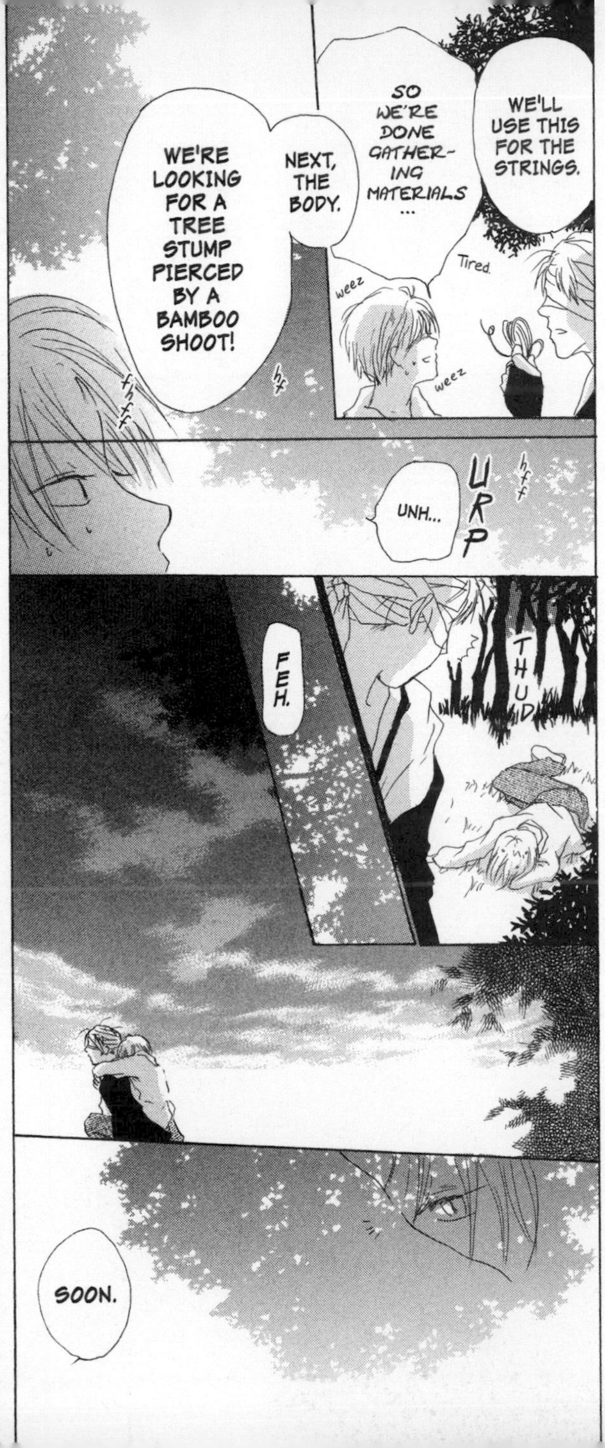
WE'LL USE THIS FOR THE STRINGS.
SO WE'RE DONE GATHERING MATERIALS...
Tired.
weez
weez
NEXT, THE BODY.
WE'RE LOOKING FOR A TREE STUMP PIERCED BY A BAMBOO SHOOT!
hff
hff
URP
hff
UNH...
THUD
FEH.
SOON.

10

❋When things don't work

When my rough draft isn't working out, I change things like names or the length and shape of people's hair right away. This is very effective for me personally. I feel it must be because the name and the visuals weren't the best fit for the character. This process of creation is so fun.

❋Letters

There are so many people who pour their hearts out in their letters that sometimes I get so excited I can't sleep at night. I read each and every single letter. At times like these, I feel honored and privileged to be a manga artist. I'm sorry I can't send replies. But I'll always treasure them.

End of $\frac{1}{4}$ columns.

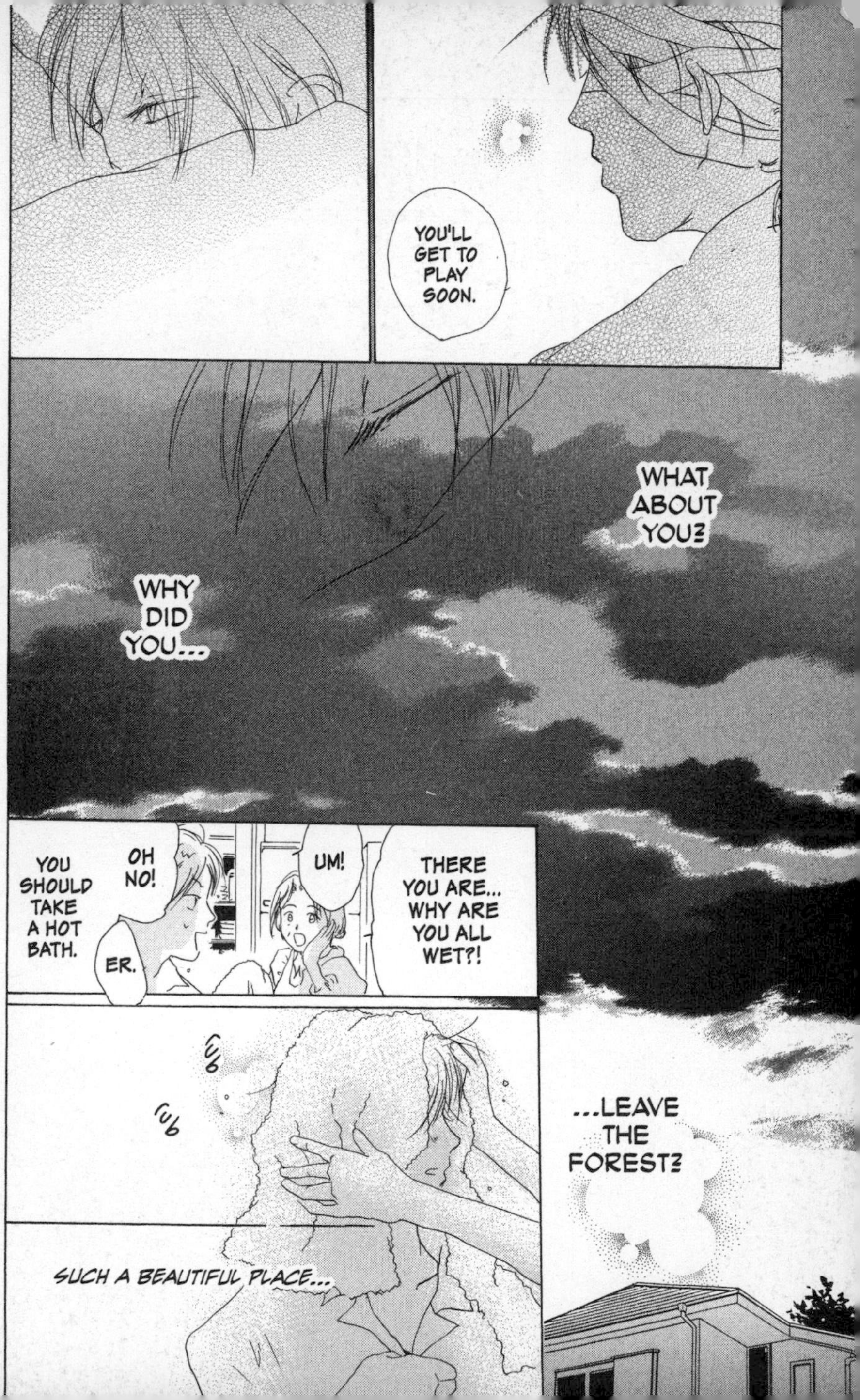
YOU'LL GET TO PLAY SOON.
WHAT ABOUT YOU?
WHY DID YOU...
...LEAVE THE FOREST?
THERE YOU ARE... WHY ARE YOU ALL WET?!
UM!
OH NO!
ER.
YOU SHOULD TAKE A HOT BATH.
rub
rub
SUCH A BEAUTIFUL PLACE...

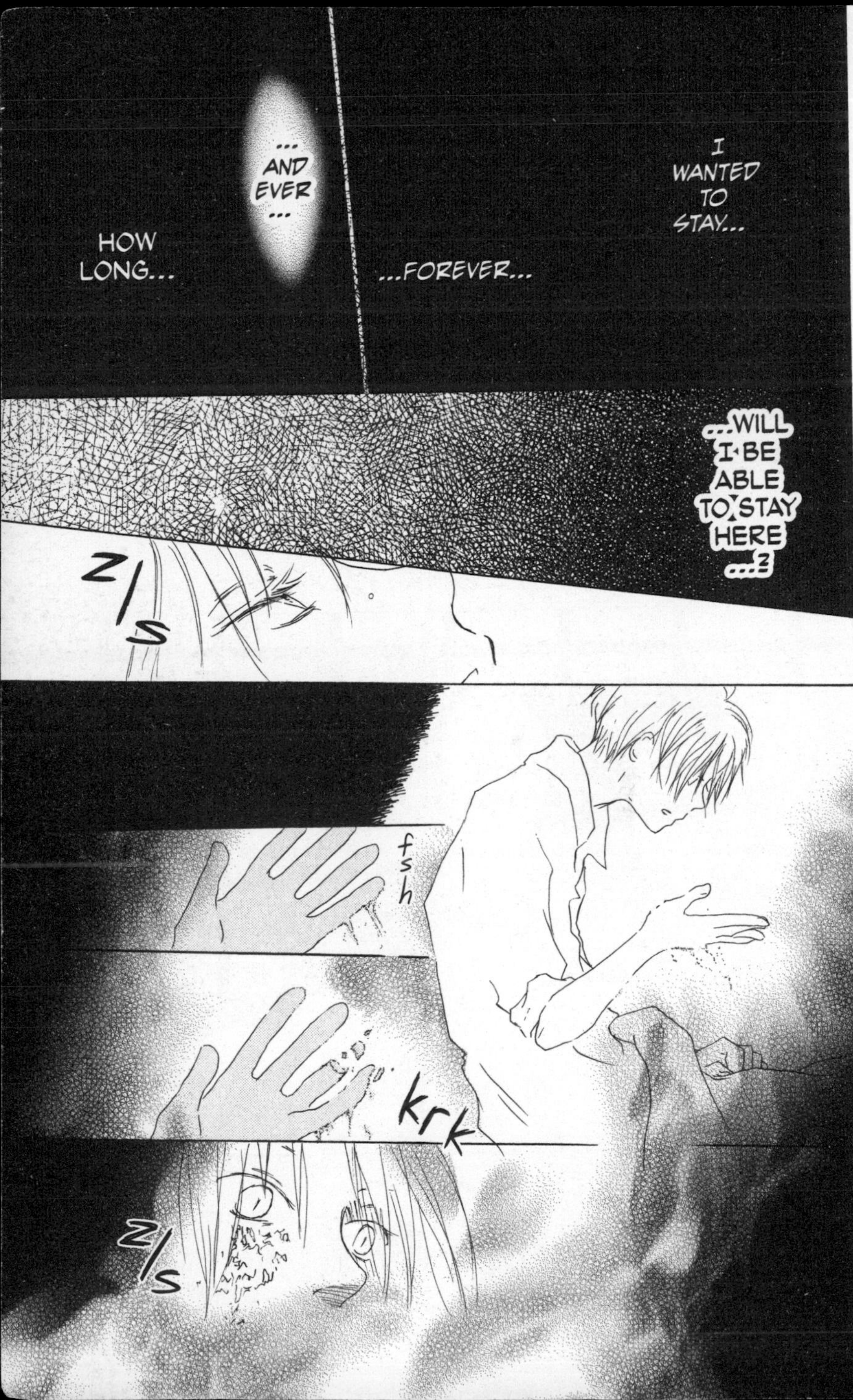
I WANTED TO STAY...
...FOREVER...
...AND EVER...
HOW LONG...
...WILL I BE ABLE TO STAY HERE...?
Z/S
fsh
krk
Z/S

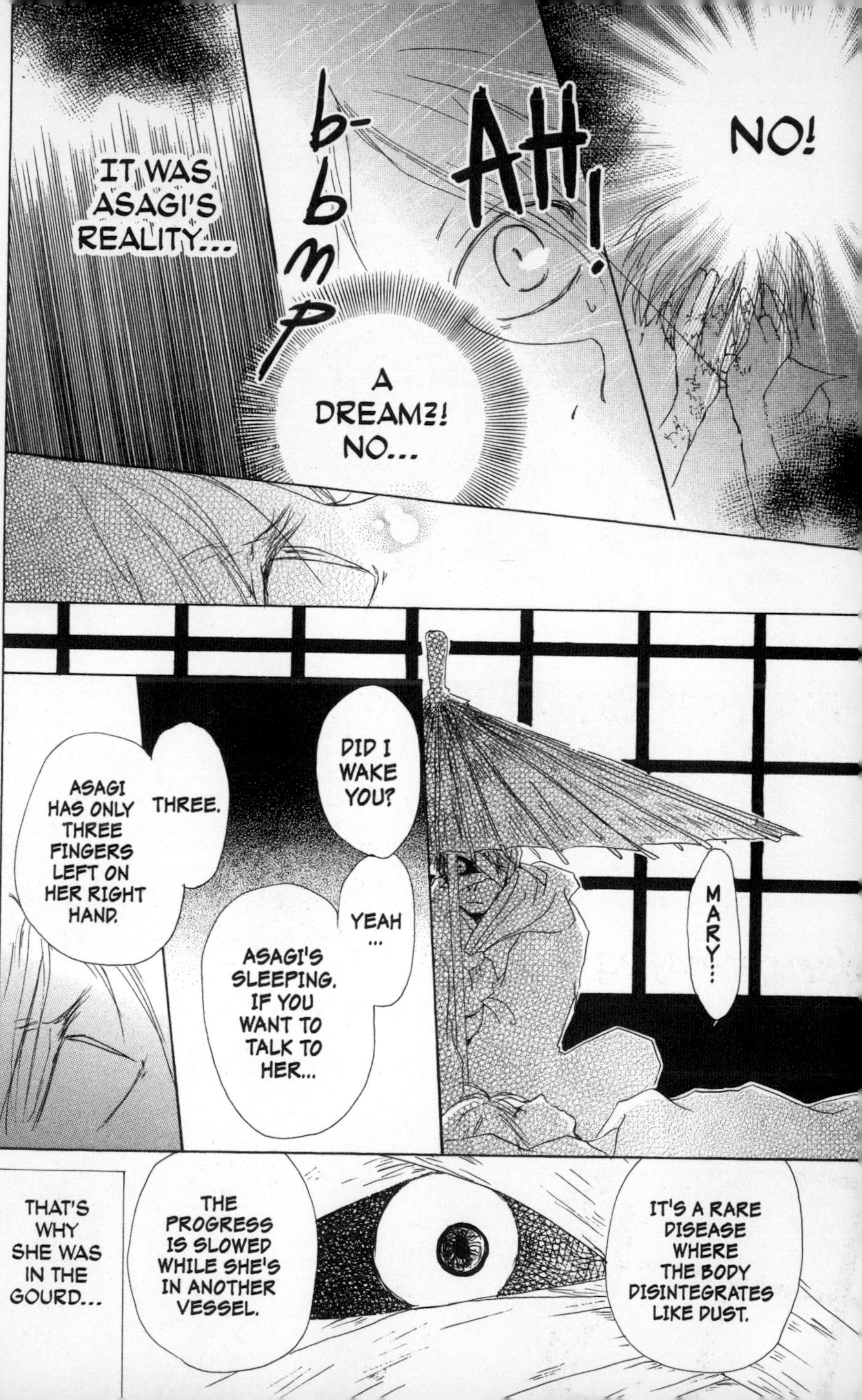
NO!
AH!
b-bmp
A DREAM?! NO...
IT WAS ASAGI'S REALITY...
MARY...
DID I WAKE YOU?
YEAH...
ASAGI'S SLEEPING. IF YOU WANT TO TALK TO HER...
THREE.
ASAGI HAS ONLY THREE FINGERS LEFT ON HER RIGHT HAND.
IT'S A RARE DISEASE WHERE THE BODY DISINTEGRATES LIKE DUST.
THE PROGRESS IS SLOWED WHILE SHE'S IN ANOTHER VESSEL.
THAT'S WHY SHE WAS IN THE GOURD...

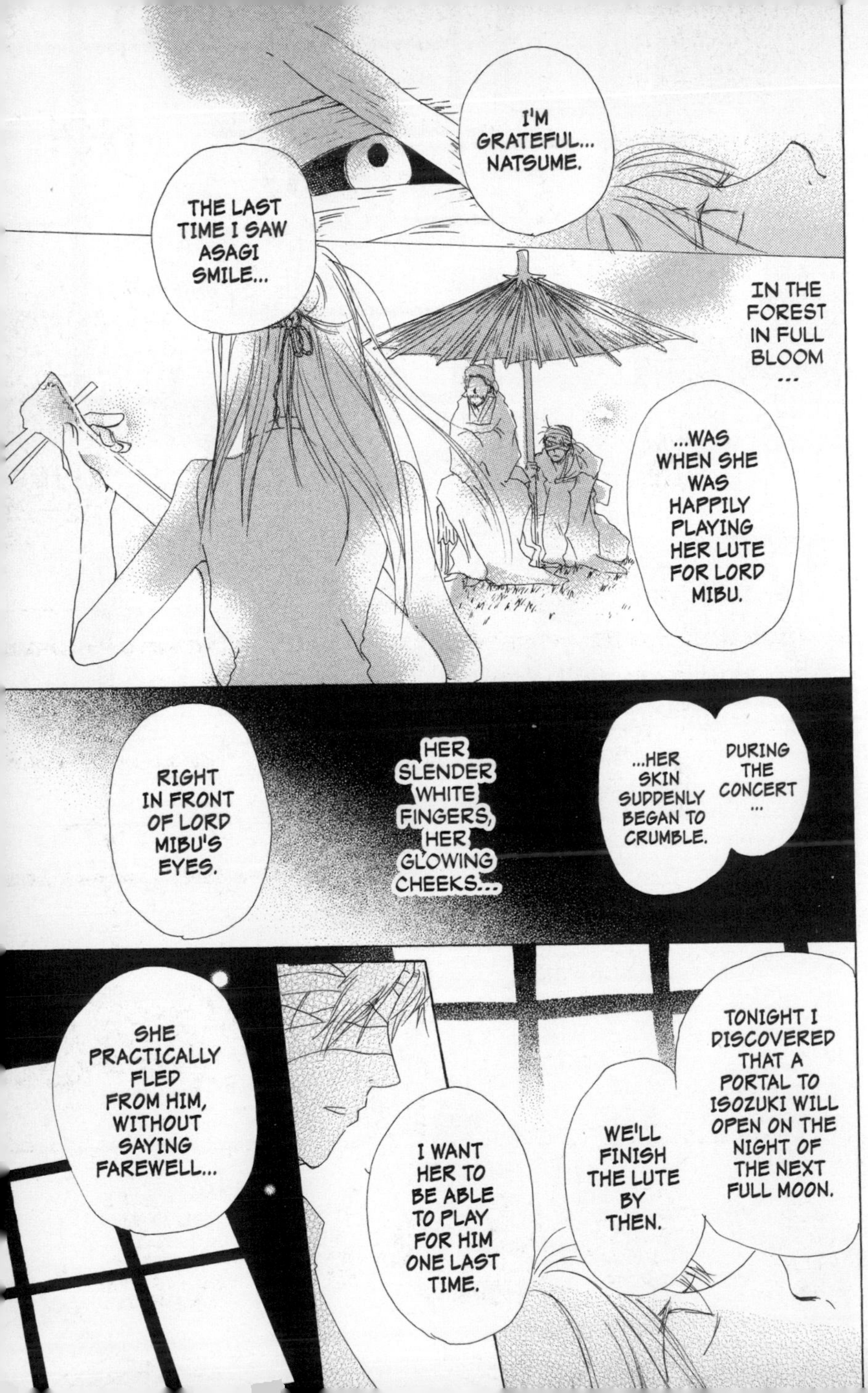

I'M GRATEFUL... NATSUME.
THE LAST TIME I SAW ASAGI SMILE...
IN THE FOREST IN FULL BLOOM ...
...WAS WHEN SHE WAS HAPPILY PLAYING HER LUTE FOR LORD MIBU.
DURING THE CONCERT ...
...HER SKIN SUDDENLY BEGAN TO CRUMBLE.
HER SLENDER WHITE FINGERS, HER GLOWING CHEEKS...
RIGHT IN FRONT OF LORD MIBU'S EYES.
TONIGHT I DISCOVERED THAT A PORTAL TO ISOZUKI WILL OPEN ON THE NIGHT OF THE NEXT FULL MOON.
WE'LL FINISH THE LUTE BY THEN.
I WANT HER TO BE ABLE TO PLAY FOR HIM ONE LAST TIME.
SHE PRACTICALLY FLED FROM HIM, WITHOUT SAYING FAREWELL...

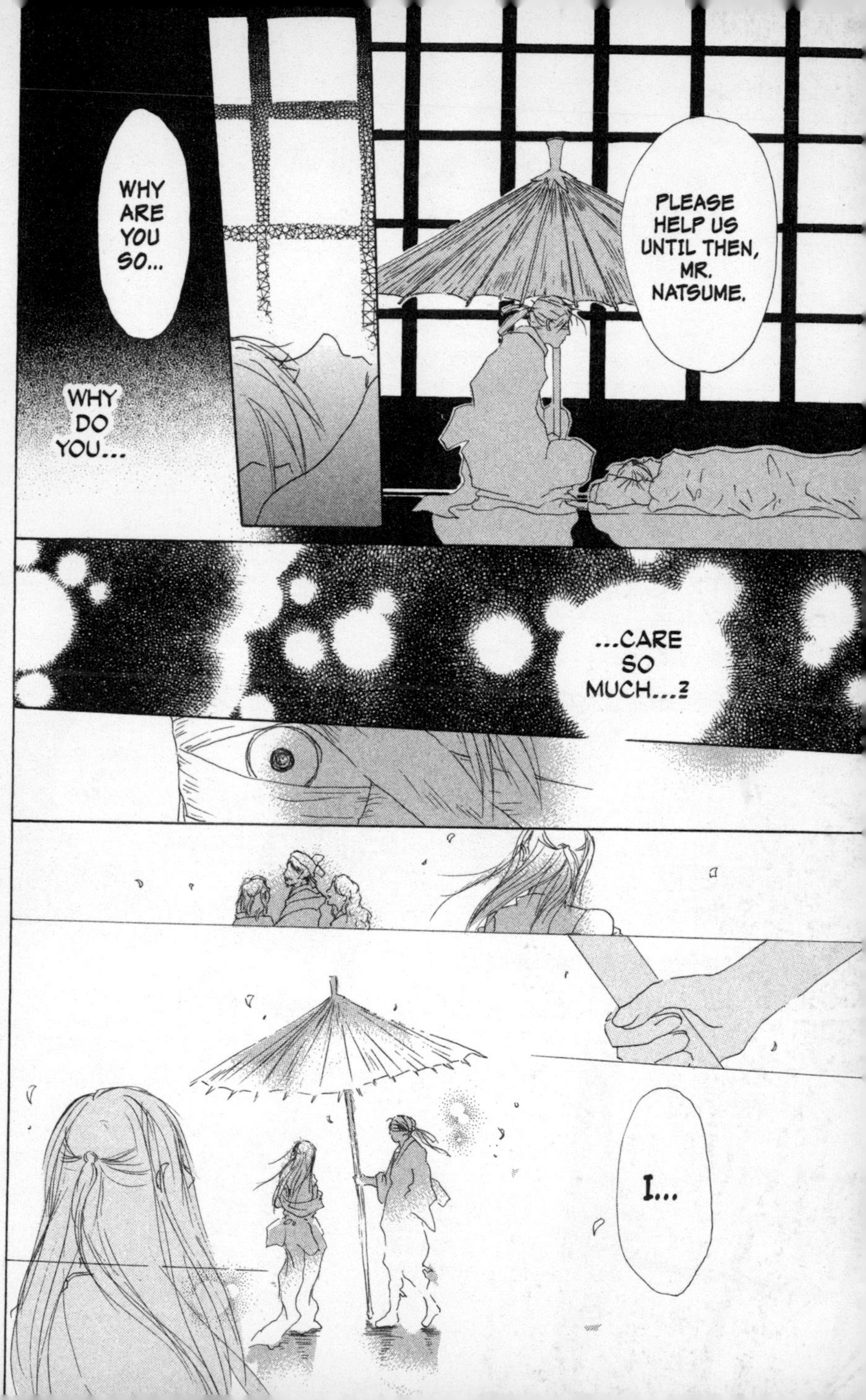
PLEASE HELP US UNTIL THEN, MR. NATSUME.
WHY ARE YOU SO...
WHY DO YOU...
...CARE SO MUCH...?
I...

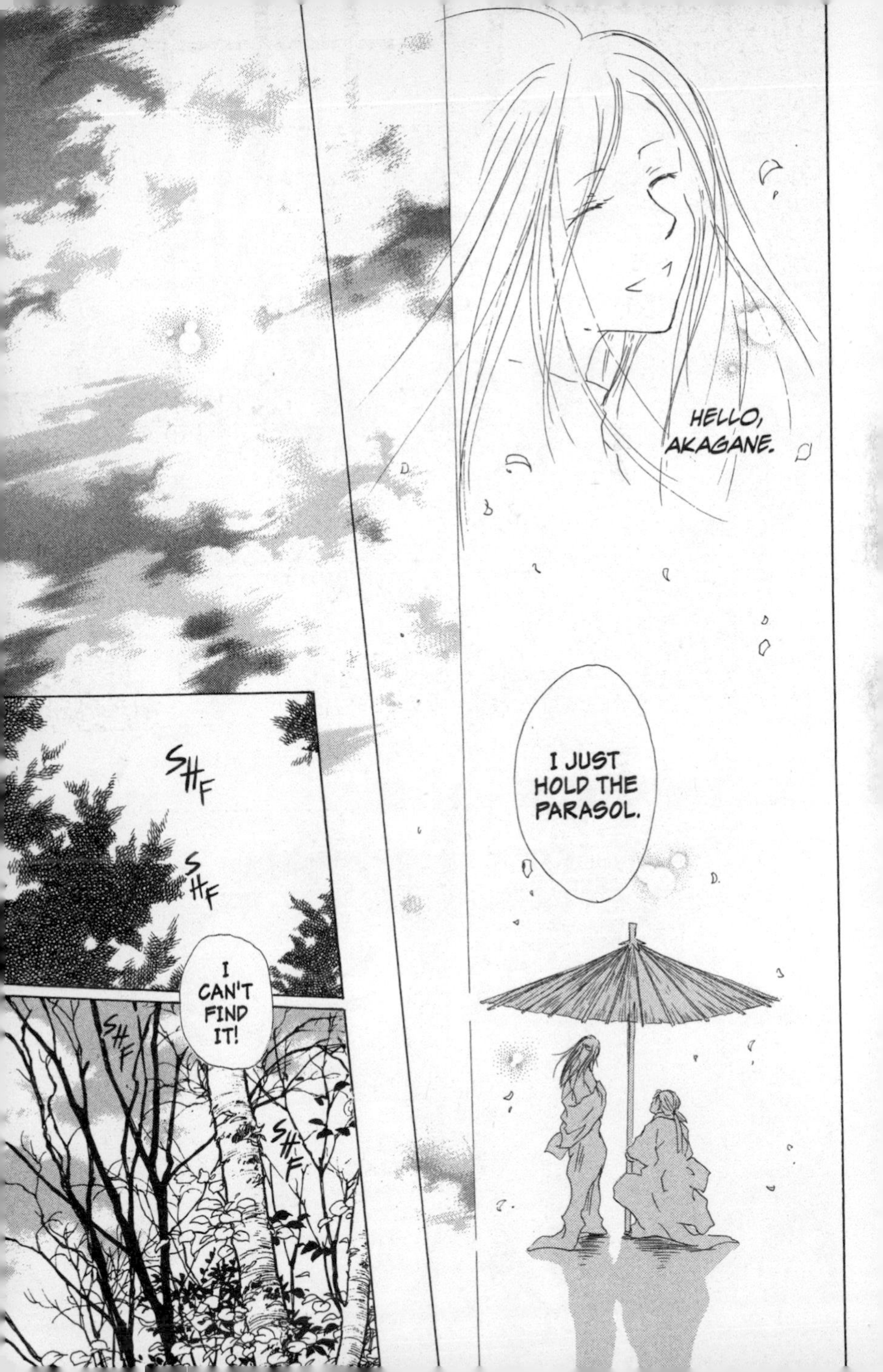
HELLO, AKAGANE.
I JUST HOLD THE PARASOL.
SHF
SHF
I CAN'T FIND IT!
SHF
SHF

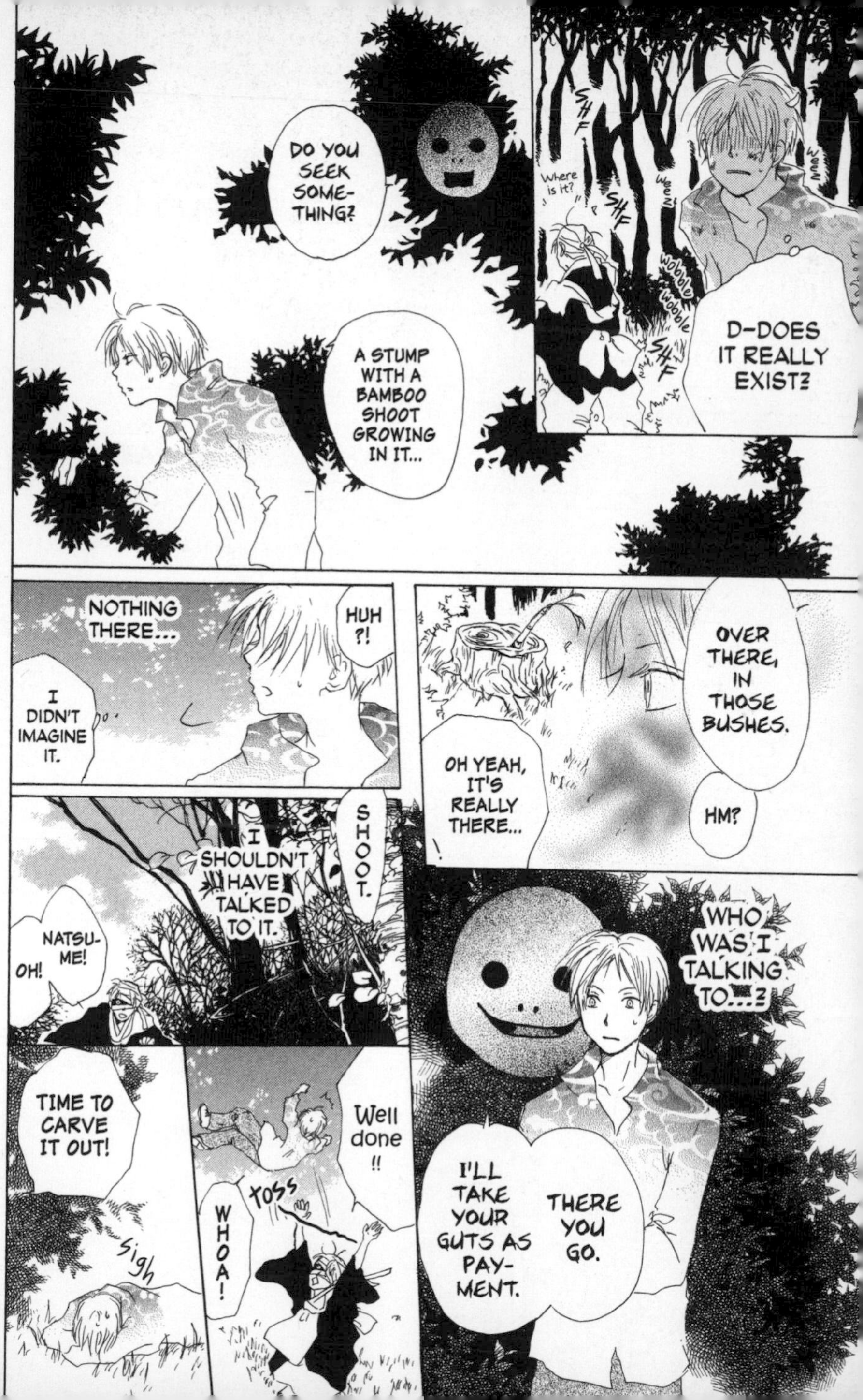
SHF
Where is it?
SHF
Ween
Ween
wobble wobble
SHF
D-DOES IT REALLY EXIST?
DO YOU SEEK SOME-THING?
A STUMP WITH A BAMBOO SHOOT GROWING IN IT...
OVER THERE, IN THOSE BUSHES.
HM?
OH YEAH, IT'S REALLY THERE...
!
HUH ?!
NOTHING THERE...
I DIDN'T IMAGINE IT.
WHO WAS I TALKING TO...?
THERE YOU GO.
I'LL TAKE YOUR GUTS AS PAY-MENT.
SHOOT.
I SHOULDN'T HAVE TALKED TO IT.
NATSU-ME!
OH!
Well done !!
TOSS
WHOA!
TIME TO CARVE IT OUT!
Sigh

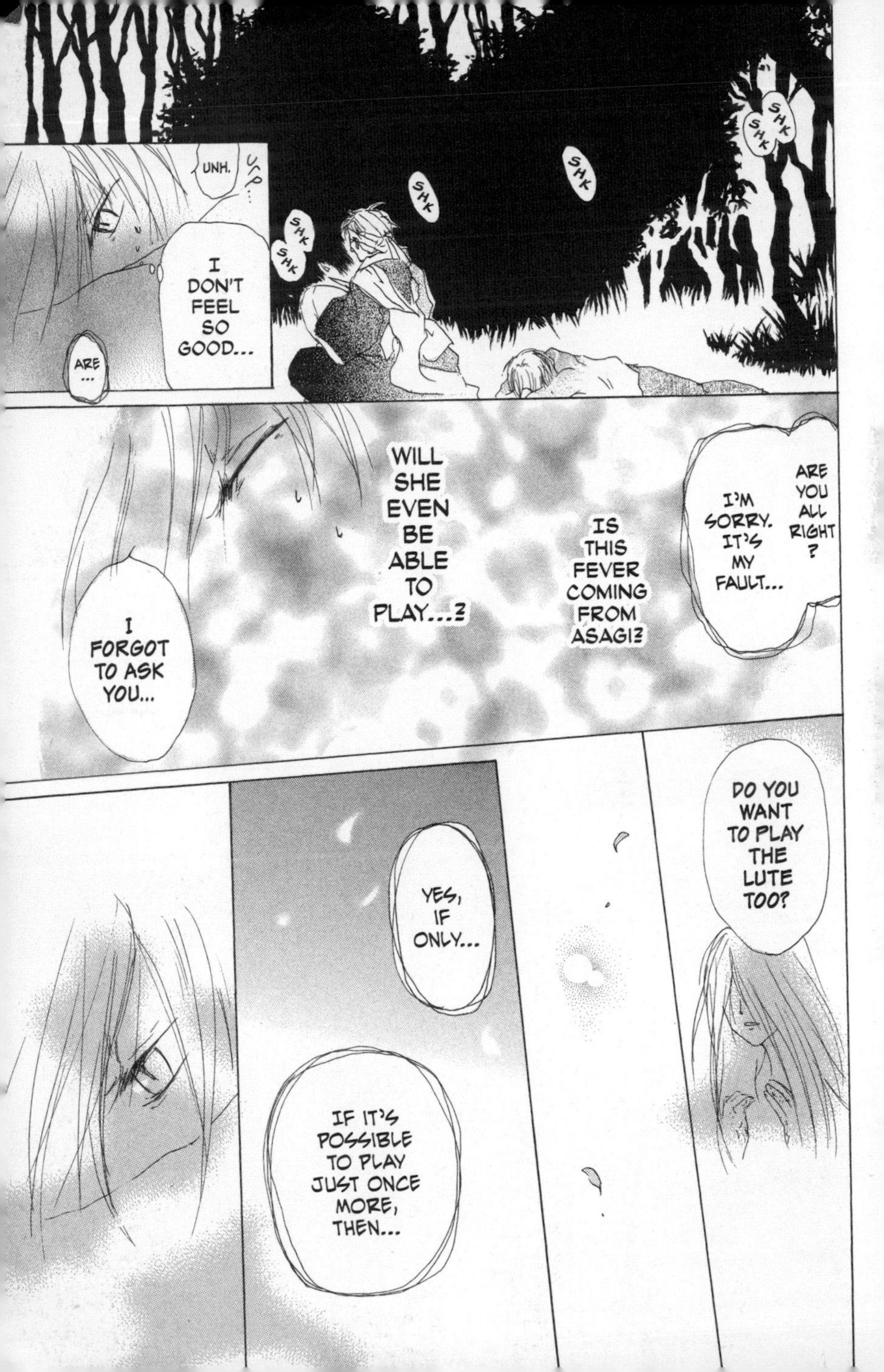
SHK SHK
SHK
SHK
SHK SHK
URP...
UNH.
I DON'T FEEL SO GOOD...
ARE ...
ARE YOU ALL RIGHT?
I'M SORRY. IT'S MY FAULT...
IS THIS FEVER COMING FROM ASAGI?
WILL SHE EVEN BE ABLE TO PLAY...?
I FORGOT TO ASK YOU...
DO YOU WANT TO PLAY THE LUTE TOO?
YES, IF ONLY...
IF IT'S POSSIBLE TO PLAY JUST ONCE MORE, THEN...

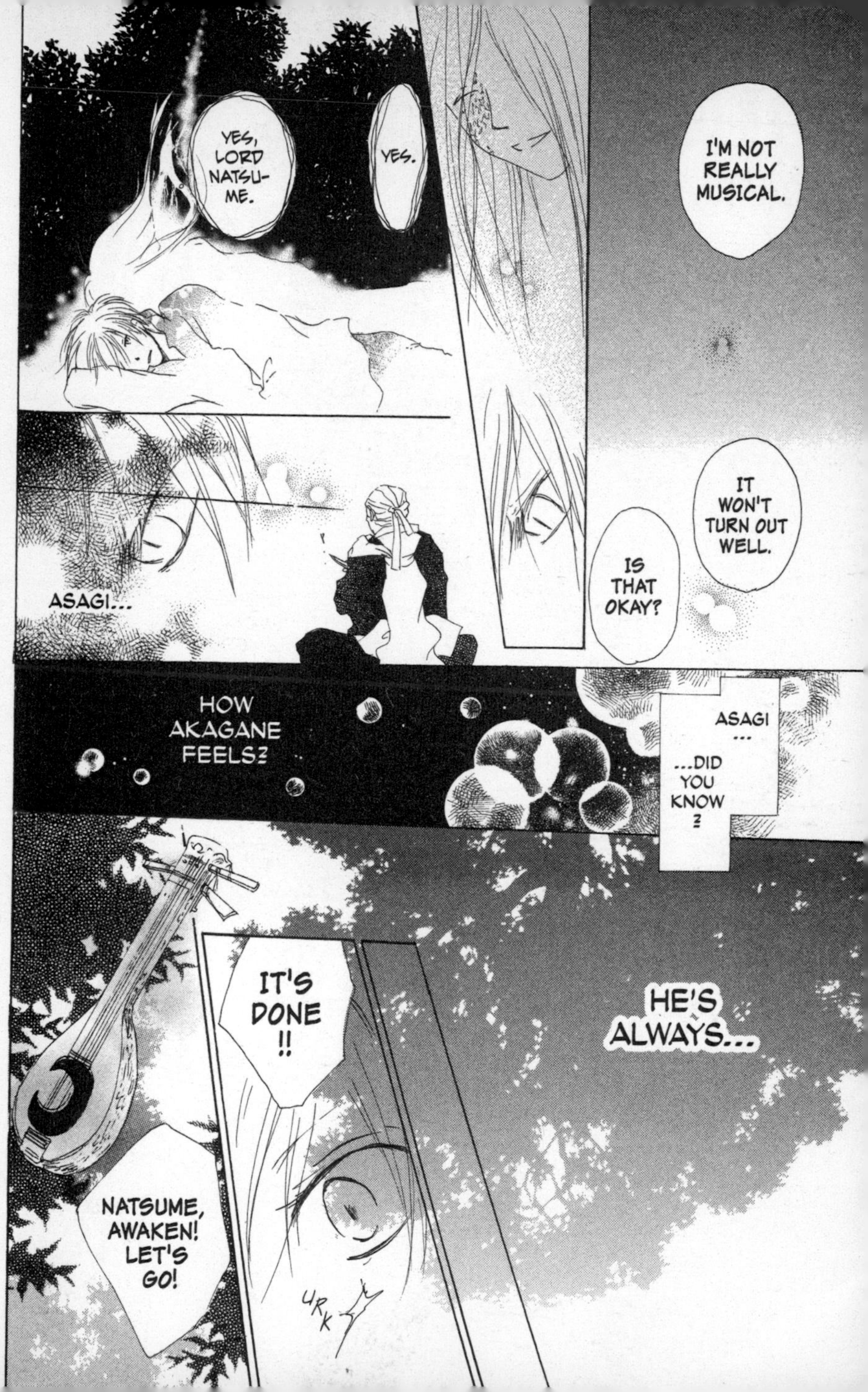
I'M NOT REALLY MUSICAL.
IT WON'T TURN OUT WELL.
IS THAT OKAY?
YES.
YES, LORD NATSU-ME.
ASAGI...
ASAGI ... ...DID YOU KNOW?
HOW AKAGANE FEELS?
HE'S ALWAYS...
IT'S DONE !!
NATSUME, AWAKEN! LET'S GO!
URK

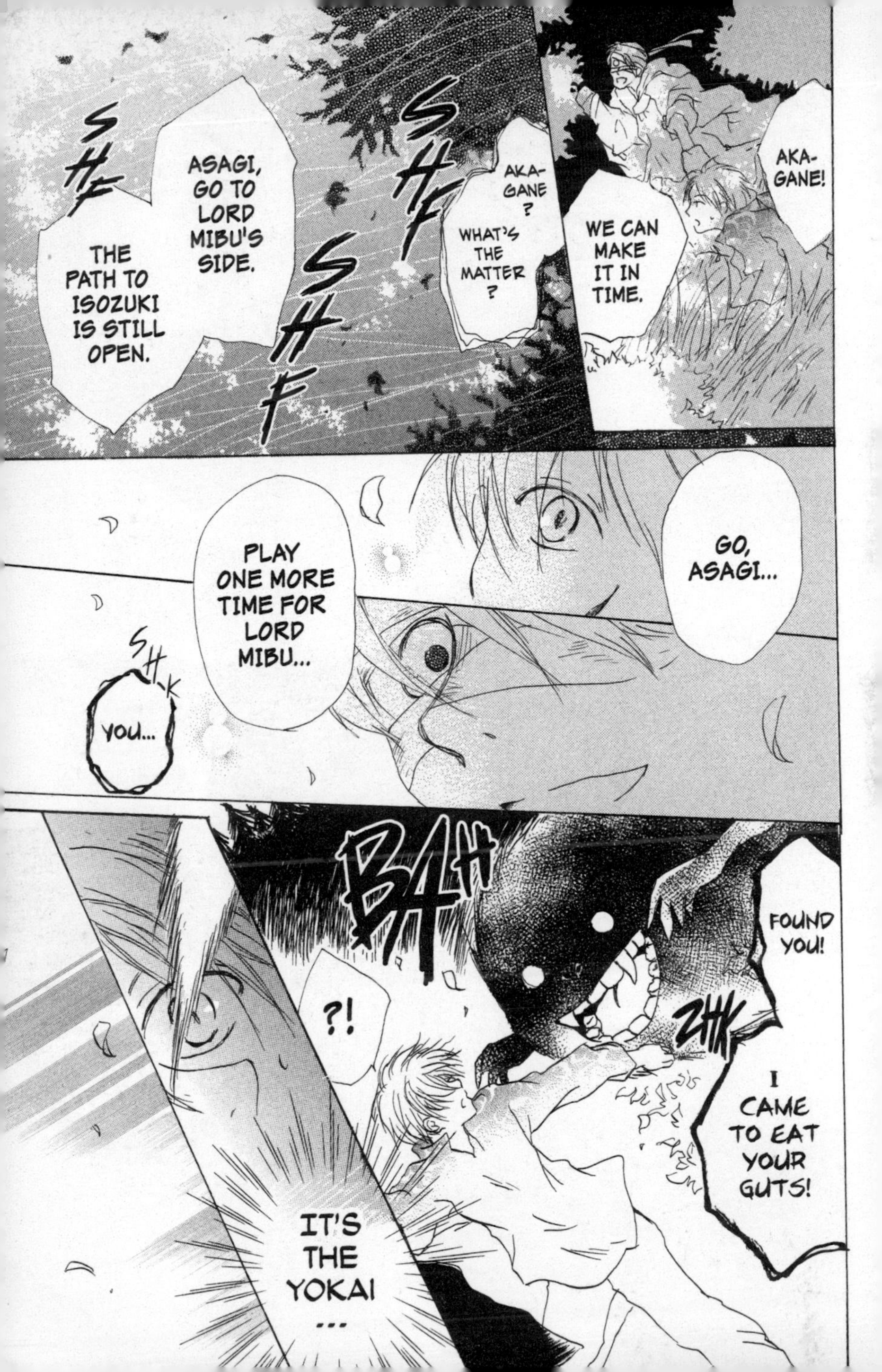
AKA-GANE!
WE CAN MAKE IT IN TIME.
SHF
AKA-GANE? WHAT'S THE MATTER?
SHF
SHF
ASAGI, GO TO LORD MIBU'S SIDE.
THE PATH TO ISOZUKI IS STILL OPEN.
SHF
GO, ASAGI...
PLAY ONE MORE TIME FOR LORD MIBU...
SHK
YOU...
BAH
FOUND YOU!
ZHK
I CAME TO EAT YOUR GUTS!
?!
IT'S THE YOKAI...

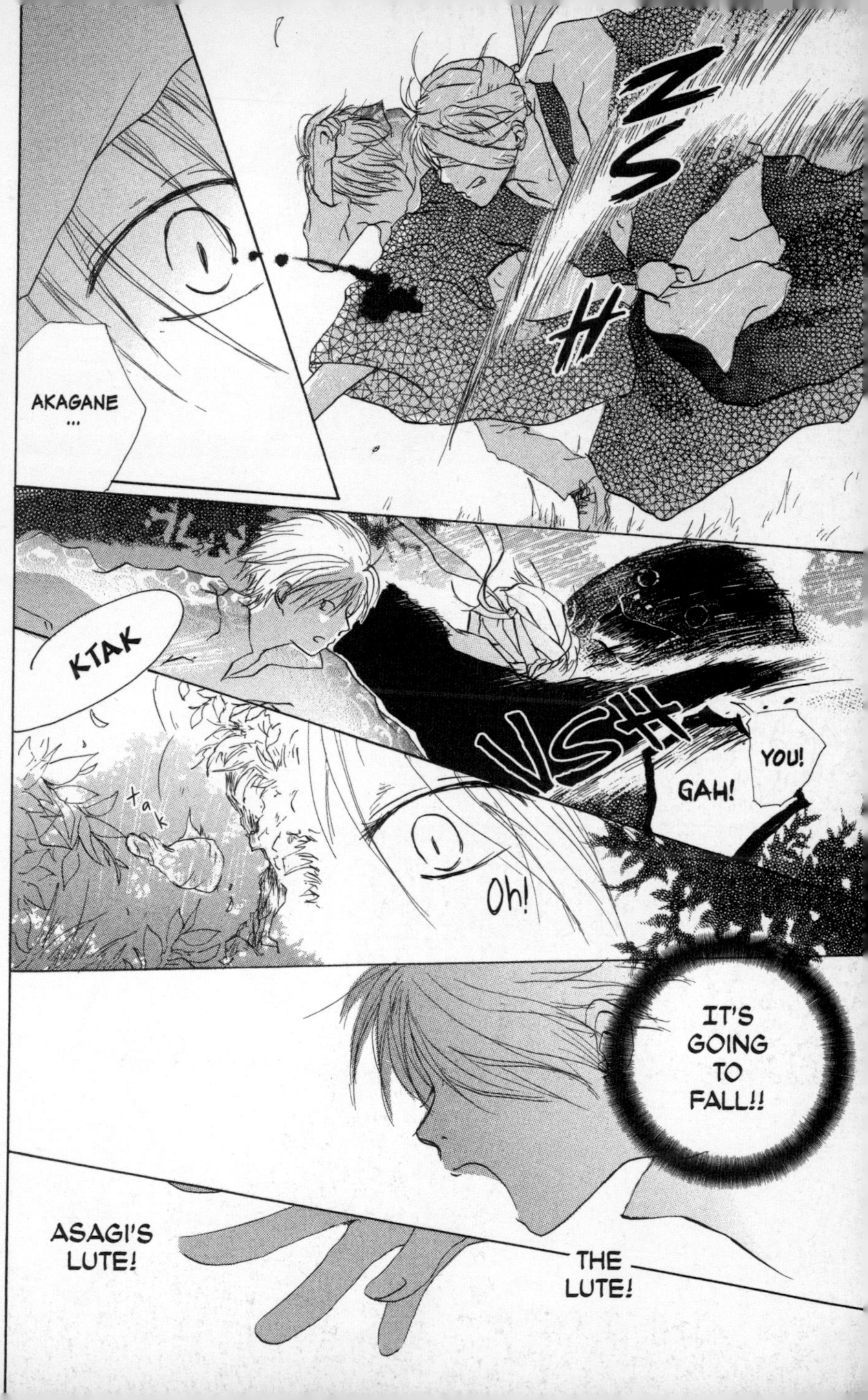

ZSH
AKAGANE ...
YOU!
GAH!
VSH!
KTAK
Oh!
tak
IT'S GOING TO FALL!!
THE LUTE!
ASAGI'S LUTE!

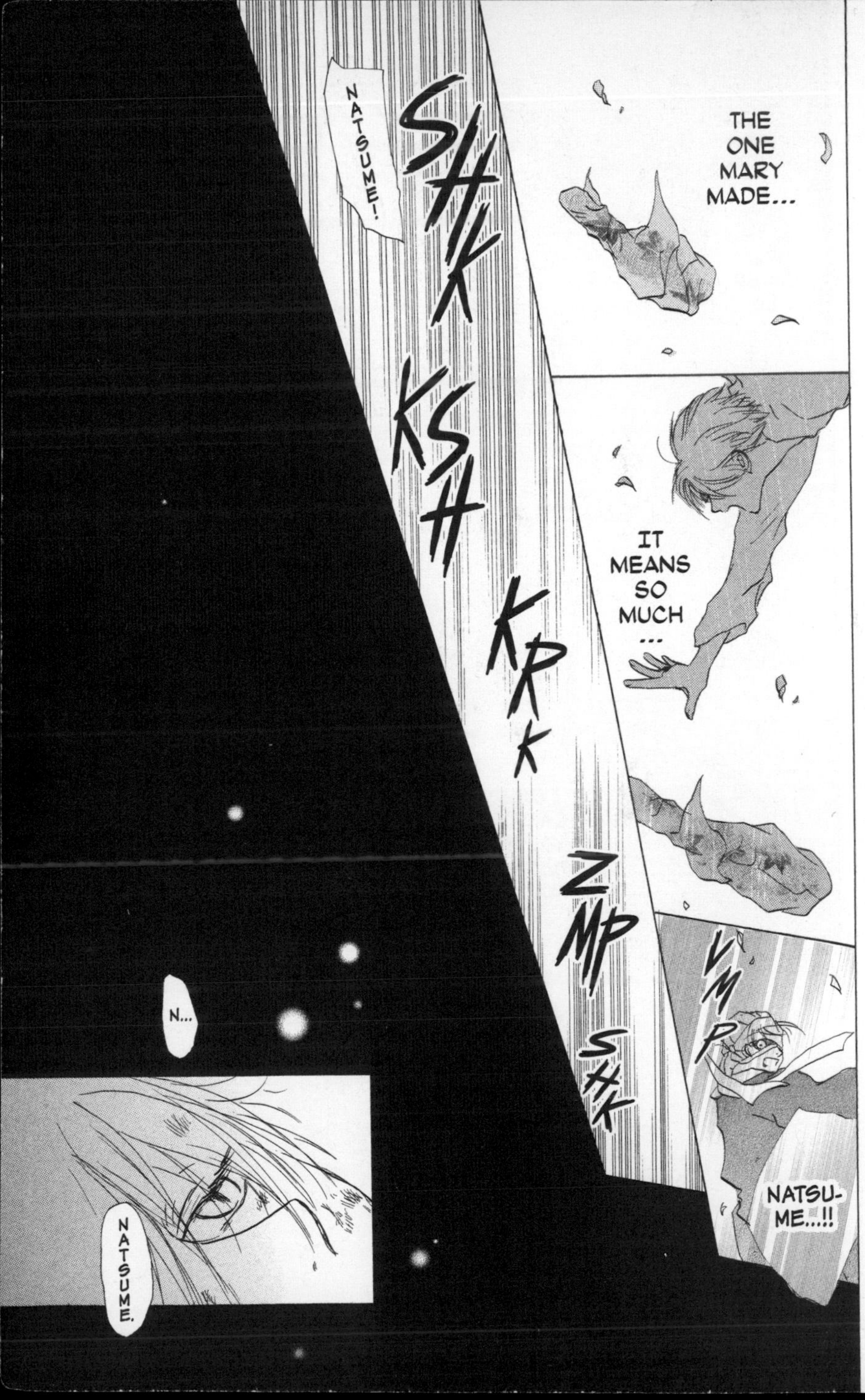
THE ONE MARY MADE...
IT MEANS SO MUCH ...
VMP
NATSUME...!!
NATSUME!
SHKK
KSHH
KRKK
ZMP
SKK
N...
NATSUME.

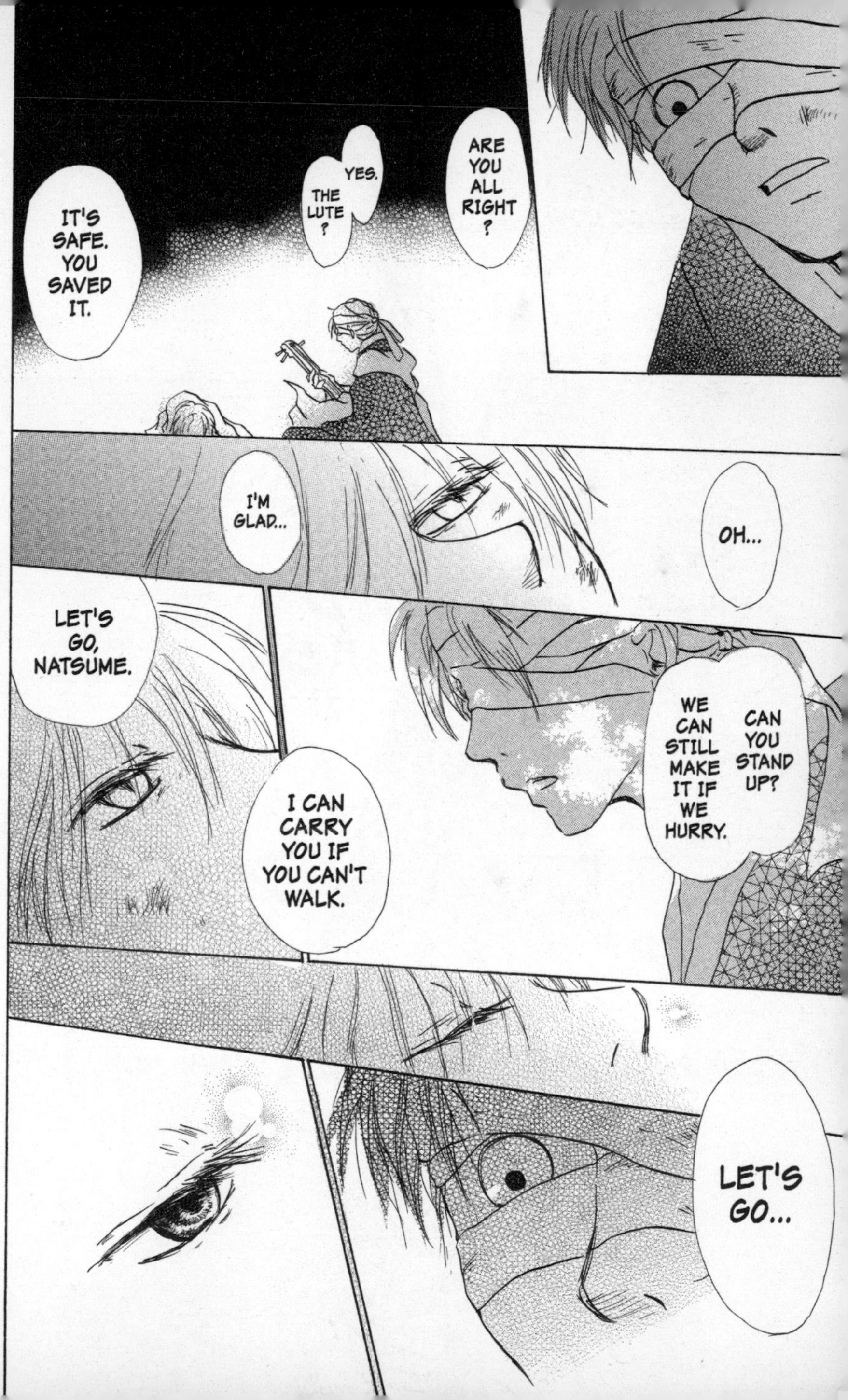
ARE YOU ALL RIGHT?
YES. THE LUTE?
IT'S SAFE. YOU SAVED IT.
OH...
I'M GLAD...
CAN YOU STAND UP?
WE CAN STILL MAKE IT IF WE HURRY.
I CAN CARRY YOU IF YOU CAN'T WALK.
LET'S GO, NATSUME.
LET'S GO...

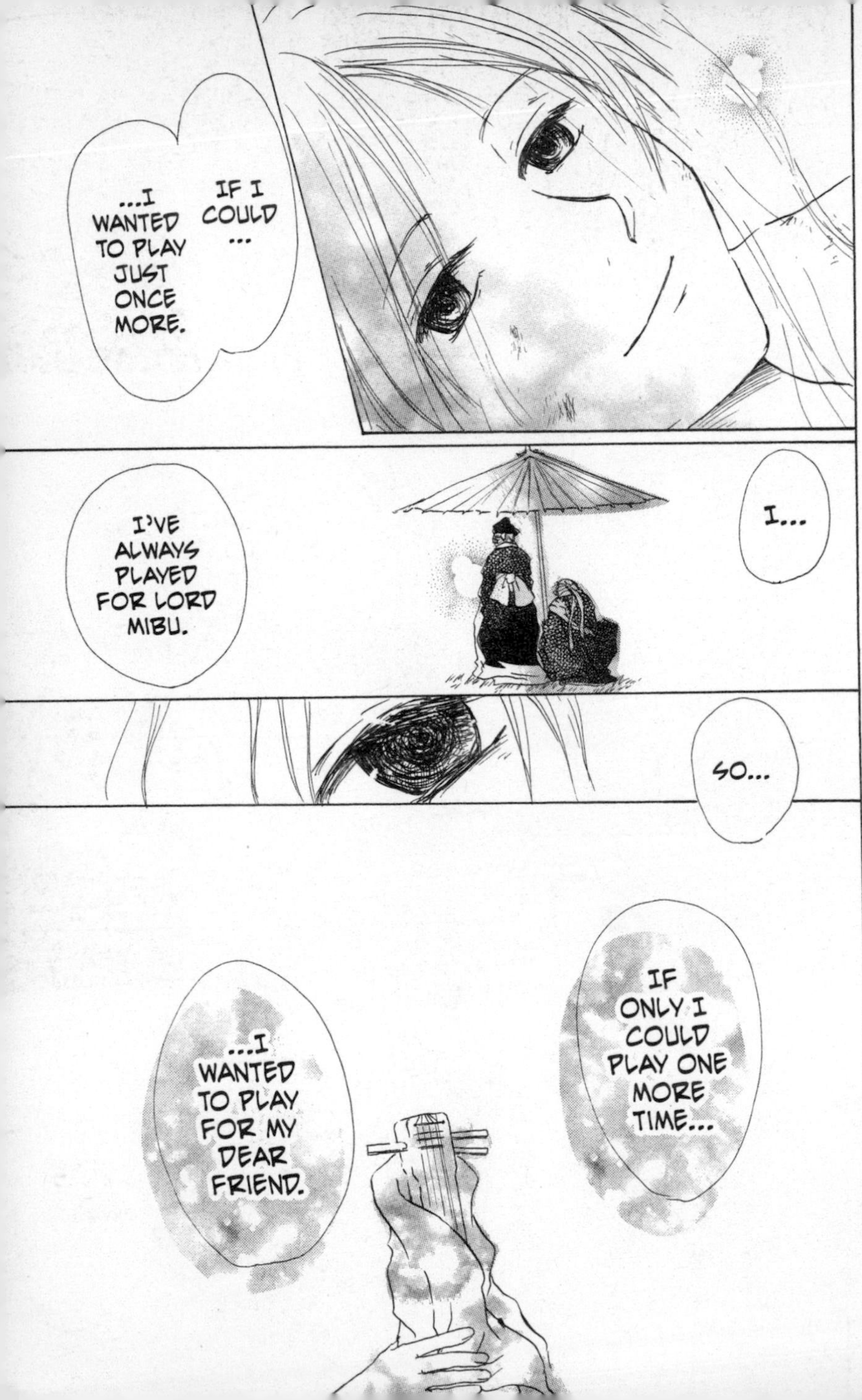
IF I COULD ...
...I WANTED TO PLAY JUST ONCE MORE.
I...
I'VE ALWAYS PLAYED FOR LORD MIBU.
SO...
IF ONLY I COULD PLAY ONE MORE TIME...
...I WANTED TO PLAY FOR MY DEAR FRIEND.

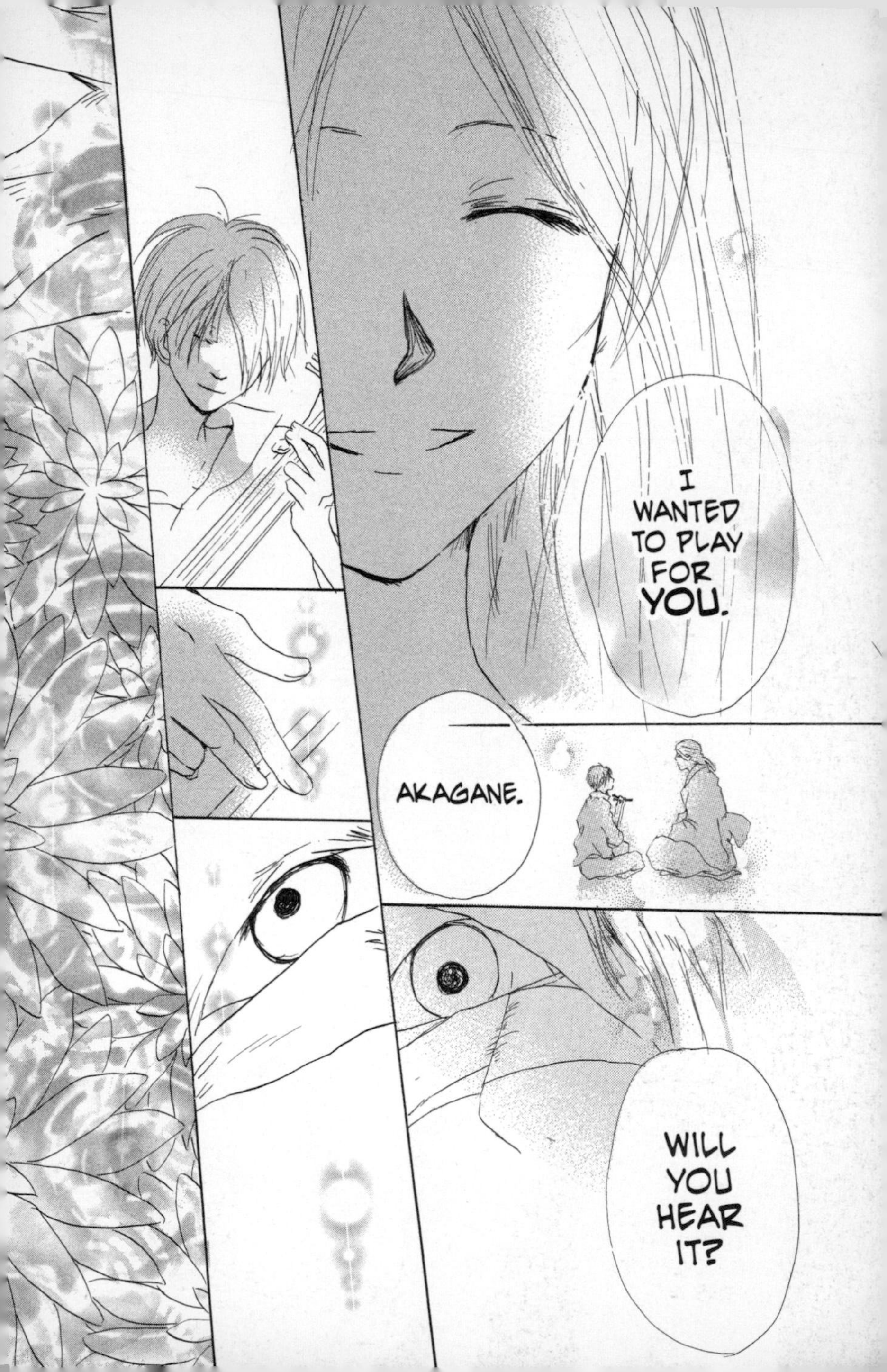
I WANTED TO PLAY FOR YOU.
AKAGANE.
WILL YOU HEAR IT?

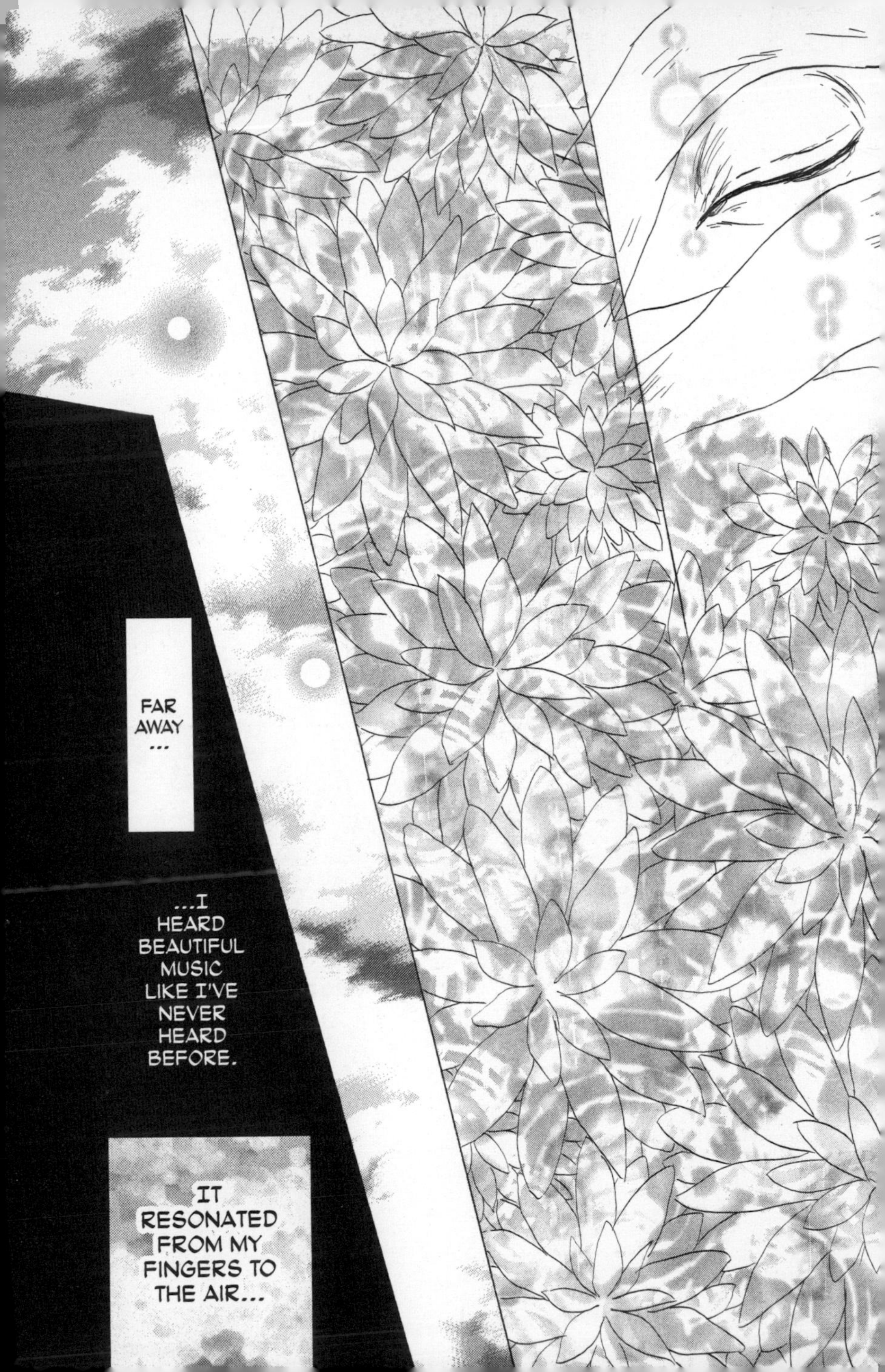
FAR AWAY...
...I HEARD BEAUTIFUL MUSIC LIKE I'VE NEVER HEARD BEFORE.
IT RESONATED FROM MY FINGERS TO THE AIR...

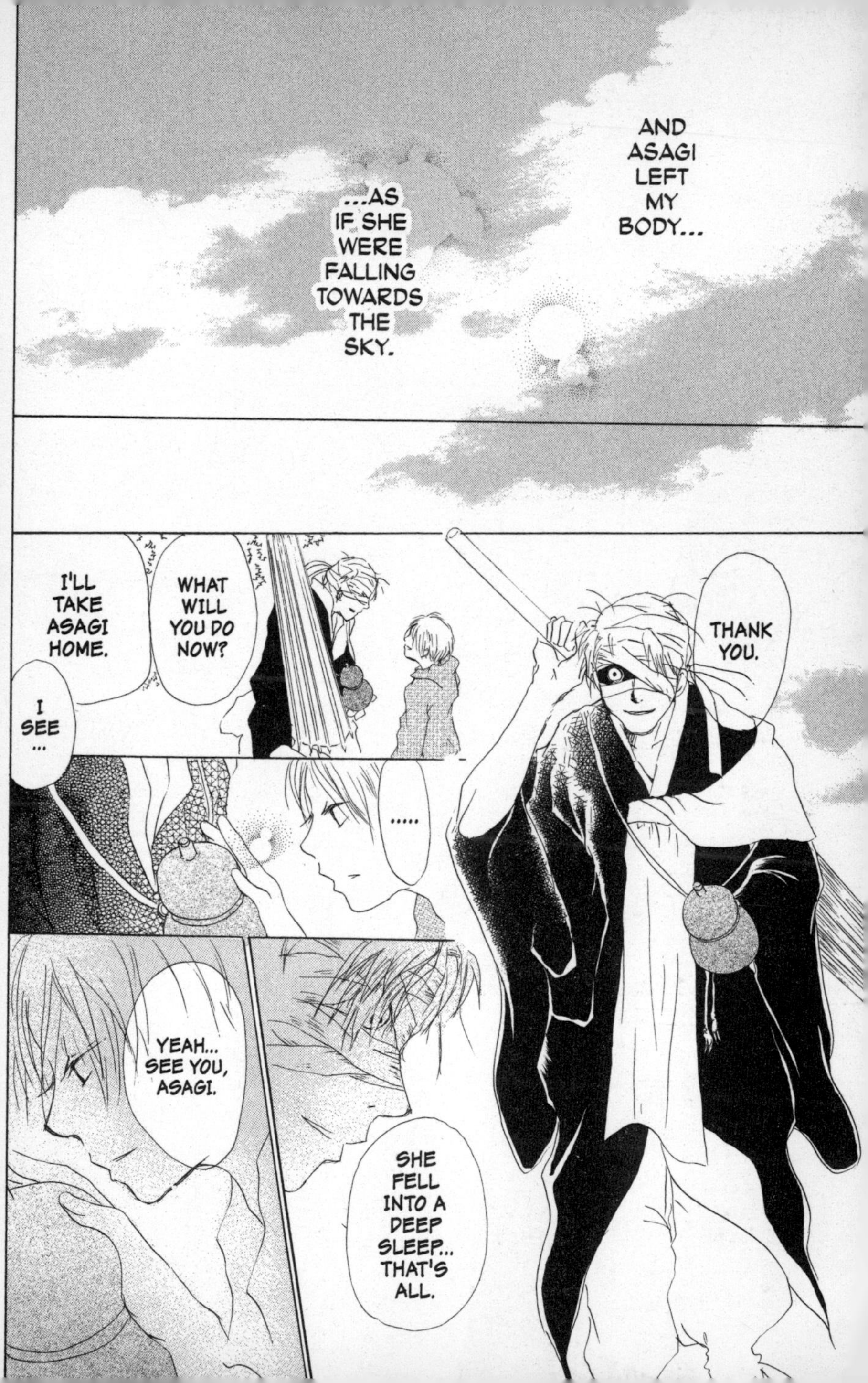
AND ASAGI LEFT MY BODY...
...AS IF SHE WERE FALLING TOWARDS THE SKY.
THANK YOU.
WHAT WILL YOU DO NOW?
I'LL TAKE ASAGI HOME.
I SEE...
.....
SHE FELL INTO A DEEP SLEEP... THAT'S ALL.
YEAH... SEE YOU, ASAGI.

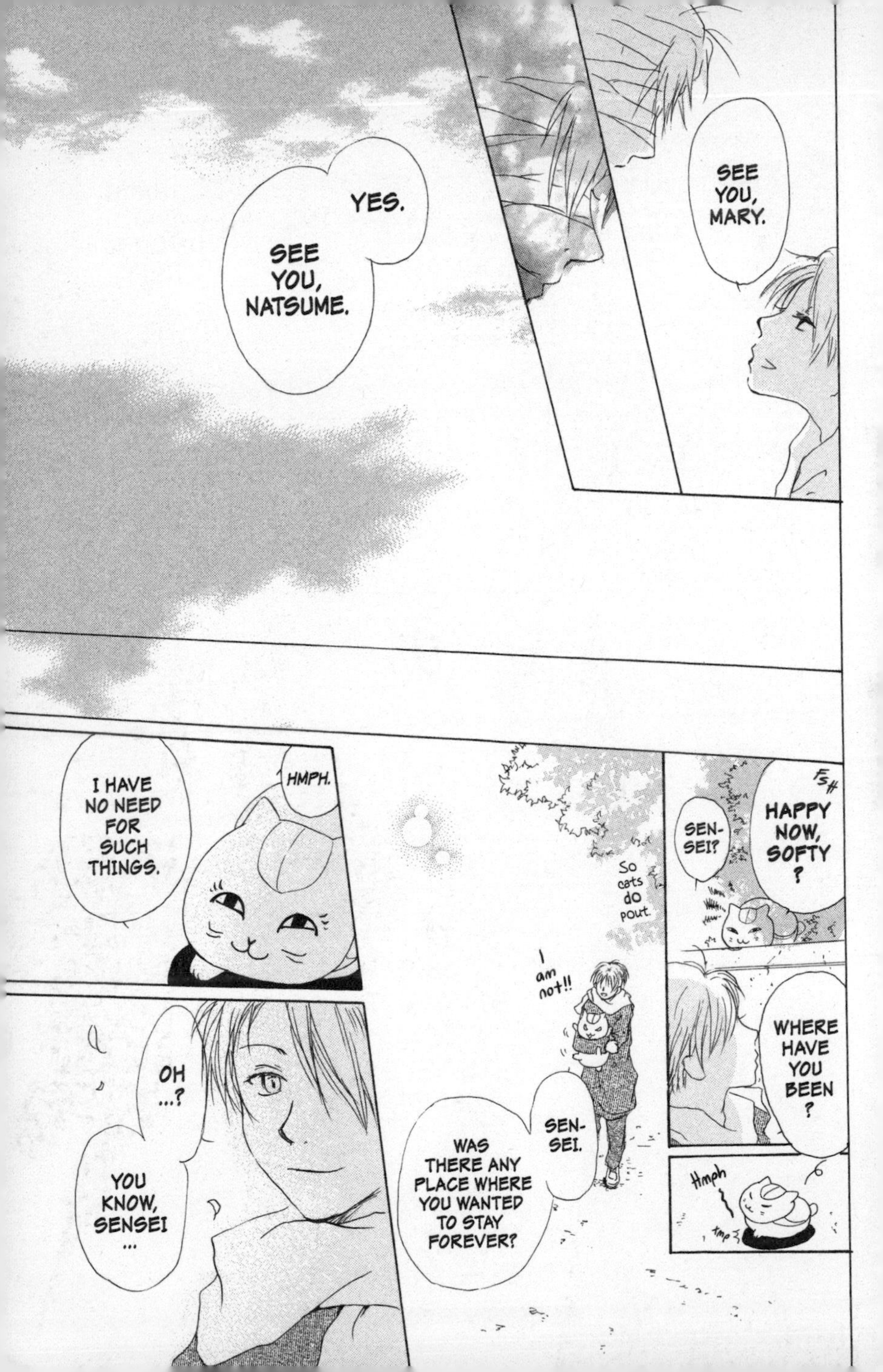
SEE YOU, MARY.
YES.
SEE YOU, NATSUME.
FSH
HAPPY NOW, SOFTY?
SEN-SEI?
WHERE HAVE YOU BEEN?
Hmph
tmp
So cats do pout.
I am not!!
SEN-SEI.
WAS THERE ANY PLACE WHERE YOU WANTED TO STAY FOREVER?
HMPH.
I HAVE NO NEED FOR SUCH THINGS.
OH ...?
YOU KNOW, SENSEI ...

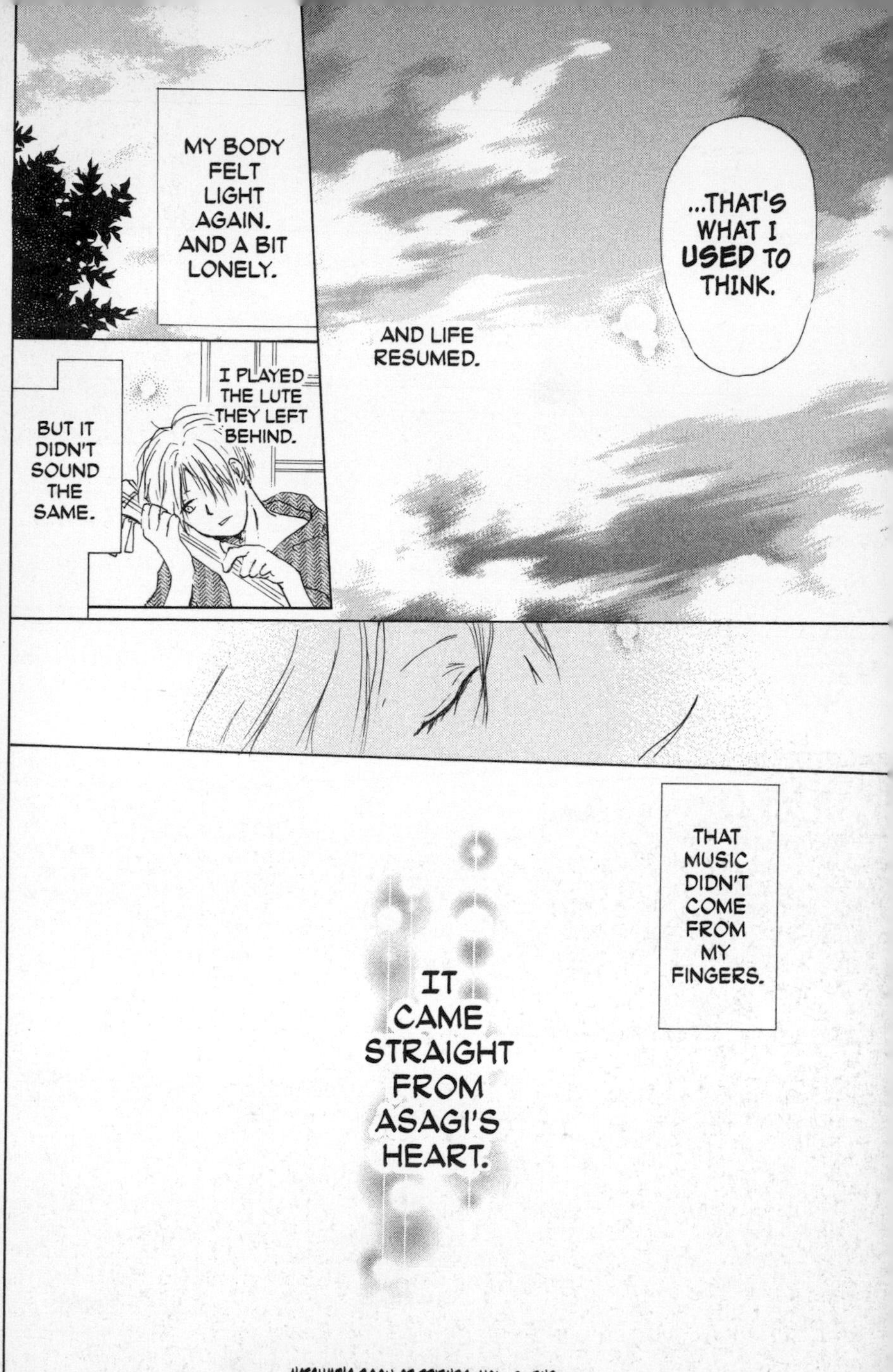
...THAT'S WHAT I USED TO THINK.
AND LIFE RESUMED.
MY BODY FELT LIGHT AGAIN. AND A BIT LONELY.
I PLAYED THE LUTE THEY LEFT BEHIND.
BUT IT DIDN'T SOUND THE SAME.
THAT MUSIC DIDN'T COME FROM MY FINGERS.
IT CAME STRAIGHT FROM ASAGI'S HEART.

NATSUME'S BOOK OF FRIENDS, VOL. 2: END

AFTER-WORD

Thank you for reading. How did you like it? This is my first series working with a main character who's the one with a special ability, so I wrestle with all sorts of difficult issues I've never dealt with before. Natsume is so dull that I keep wondering if I should've made him a girl like I usually do. But then when he deals with yokai, I'm glad he's a boy after all. It's a roller coaster ride.

I've got a couple of extra pages here at the end, so I'd like to write a bit about each of the episodes. There will be spoilers, so please read this only after you've

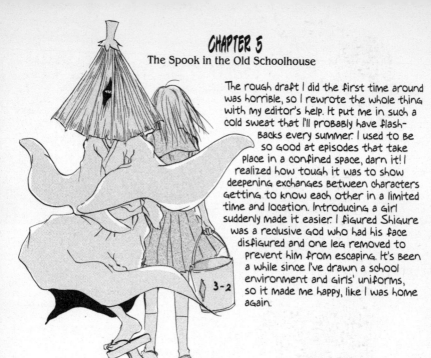

CHAPTER 5

The Spook in the Old Schoolhouse

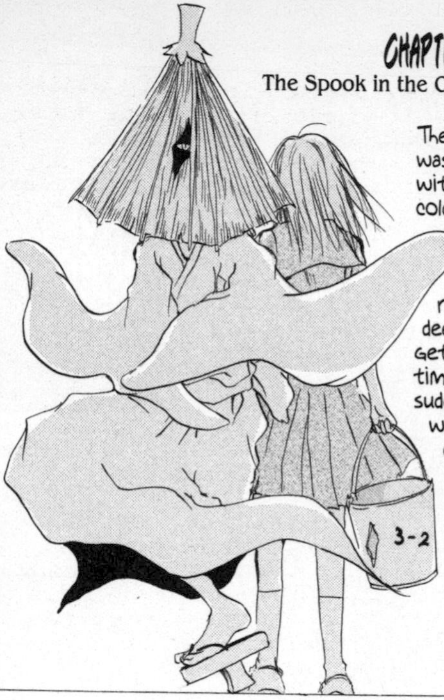
3-2

The rough draft I did the first time around was horrible, so I rewrote the whole thing with my editor's help. It put me in such a cold sweat that I'll probably have flash-backs every summer. I used to be so good at episodes that take place in a confined space, darn it! I realized how tough it was to show deepening exchanges between characters getting to know each other in a limited time and location. Introducing a girl suddenly made it easier. I figured Shigure was a reclusive god who had his face disfigured and one leg removed to prevent him from escaping. It's been a while since I've drawn a school environment and girls' uniforms, so it made me happy, like I was home again.

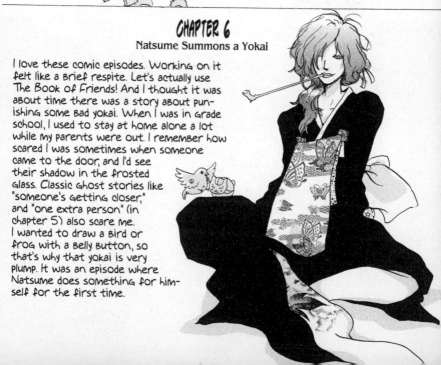

CHAPTER 6

Natsume Summons a Yokai

I love these comic episodes. Working on it felt like a brief respite. Let's actually use The Book of Friends! And I thought it was about time there was a story about pun-ishing some bad yokai. When I was in grade school, I used to stay at home alone a lot while my parents were out. I remember how scared I was sometimes when someone came to the door, and I'd see their shadow in the frosted glass. Classic ghost stories like "someone's getting closer," and "one extra person" (in chapter 5) also scare me. I wanted to draw a bird or frog with a belly button, so that's why that yokai is very plump. It was an episode where Natsume does something for him-self for the first time.

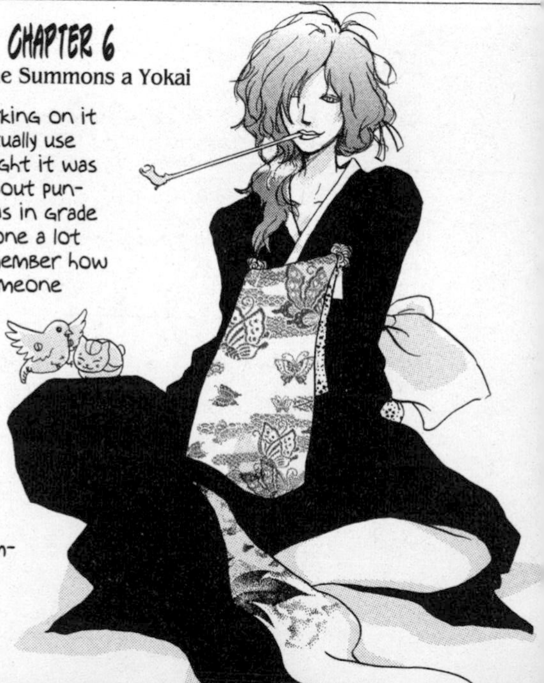

CHAPTER 7
He Can See

For the first time, Natsume meets someone else who can see yokai too. I was pretty nervous because I was breaking the established rule that only Reiko and Takashi Natsume were different. Natsume kept running away from yokai, but I made Natori into an expert who kept proactively learning about yokai. I wanted to draw someone who indentured yokai even though he doesn't like them.

I wanted his mark to look a little like a human figure upon closer inspection. Natori doesn't like Natsume's hypocrisy, and Natsume doesn't like how Natori doesn't bother to explain his actions and makes himself out to be worse than he really is. I feel like Natsume finally realized how difficult it is for people to understand each other, no matter how similar or different they are.

I wanted an episode about Natsume lending his body to a yokai. The stories up to here were about Natsume positioned in between humans and yokai. But totally immersing Natsume among yokai was more difficult than I thought. It felt oddly lonesome. The world of the yokai is always close by but a step removed. This time, Natsume was the one stepping into it. But Asagi and Akagane were fun characters to draw. Akagane has to be strong and skilled. But he basically works at a harem, so he shouldn't be very good-looking. And that's how he was created. I thought I should've been a little more meticulous since I had 50 pages to work with.

CHAPTER 8
Asagi's Lute

I used to rush headlong into my work. But in Natsume, I feel like I'm taking more care connecting the story one episode at a time. It feels a little odd. I'll do my best to make careful progress.

The most fun I have working on this title is when I'm imagining what the yokai look like. I hope they look scary or creepy at a quick glance, but a little goofy. I imagine powerful yokai as a blend of Western and Japanese styles, or Japanese with a bit of the Western demonic influence.

The people who gave me the ceramic cat that became the model for Nyanko Sensei had a decorative monkey mask above the door of their house. When I was little, I thought it looked like a large moth with eyespots on its wings. I was scared of it and couldn't go through that door. But it was gone one day. They must've put it away out of consideration for me. I'm sure it wouldn't be scary if I looked at it now, but that's the kind of creepiness I hope to express.

Please continue with your support!

• Special thanks to: •
Tamao Ohki
Chika
Mr. Sato
My sister   Thank you so much.

Let me know what you thought, if possible.

Yuki Midorikawa
c/o Shojo Beat
P.O. Boz 77010
San Francicso, CA 94107

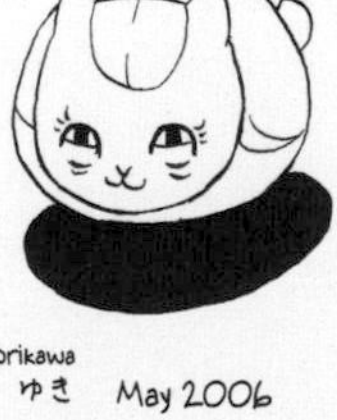

Thanks for reading. I'll work hard so that you'll want to read my manga again.

Yuki Midorikawa
緑川 ゆき   May 2006

Natsume's
BOOK of FRIENDS

VOLUME 2 END NOTES

PAGE 11, PANEL 3: *Kappa*
Child-sized water goblins that are usually green with webbed hands and feet, a turtle-like shell, and a platelike water reservoir in the top of their heads. If their reservoir runs dry, kappa become weak and may even die, so the water level must be maintained. They are also fond of cucumbers, which is why cucumber sushi rolls are called *kappa-maki*.

PAGE 12, PANEL 1: *The Haunted Challenge*
The Japanese is *kimodameshi*, which literally means "a test of one's guts." These courage trials usually take the form of a dark path, a graveyard or another supposedly haunted place. Ghost stories and haunted challenges are usually associated with summer in Japan.

PAGE 27, PANEL 1: *Kekkai*
A protective ward or barrier.

PAGE 61, PANEL 1: *Deep-fried shrimp*
The Japanese is *ebi fry*, and this deep-fried shrimp is dipped in flour, then egg, then panko bread crumbs—and finally it is deep-fried. It is usually eaten with *tonkatsu* sauce (a type of thick Worcestershire sauce) or tartar sauce.

PAGE 61, PANEL 2: *Bad for cats*
It's an old wives' tale in Japan that shrimp and squid are bad for cats. While large amounts might give a kitty an upset stomach, the reality is that occasional seafood treats won't harm them.

Yuki Midorikawa
is the creator of *Natsume's Book of Friends*, which was nominated for the Manga Taisho (Cartoon Grand Prize). Her other titles published in Japan include *Hotarubi no Mori e* (Into the Forest of Fireflies), *Hiiro no Isu* (The Scarlet Chair) and *Akaku Saku Koe* (The Voice That Blooms Red).

NATSUME'S BOOK OF FRIENDS

Vol. 2
Shojo Beat Edition

STORY AND ART BY Yuki Midorikawa

Translation & Adaptation Lillian Olsen
Touch-up Art & Lettering Sabrina Heep
Design Fawn Lau
Editor Pancha Diaz

Natsume Yujincho by Yuki Midorikawa
© Yuki Midorikawa 2006
All rights reserved.
First published in Japan in 2006 by HAKUSENSHA, Inc., Tokyo.
English language translation rights arranged with HAKUSENSHA, Inc., Tokyo.

The rights of the author(s) of the work(s) in this publication to be so identified
have been asserted in accordance with the Copyright, Designs and Patents Act 1988.
A CIP catalogue record for this book is available from the British Library.

The stories, characters and incidents mentioned in this publication are entirely fictional.

Printed in the U.S.A.

Published by VIZ Media, LLC
P.O. Box 77010
San Francisco, CA 94107

10 9 8 7 6 5 4 3 2
First printing, April 2010
Second printing, March 2012

PARENTAL ADVISORY
NATSUME'S BOOK OF FRIENDS is rated T for Teen
and is recommended for ages 16 and up.
This volume contains fantasy violence.
ratings.viz.com

www.viz.com

www.shojobeat.com

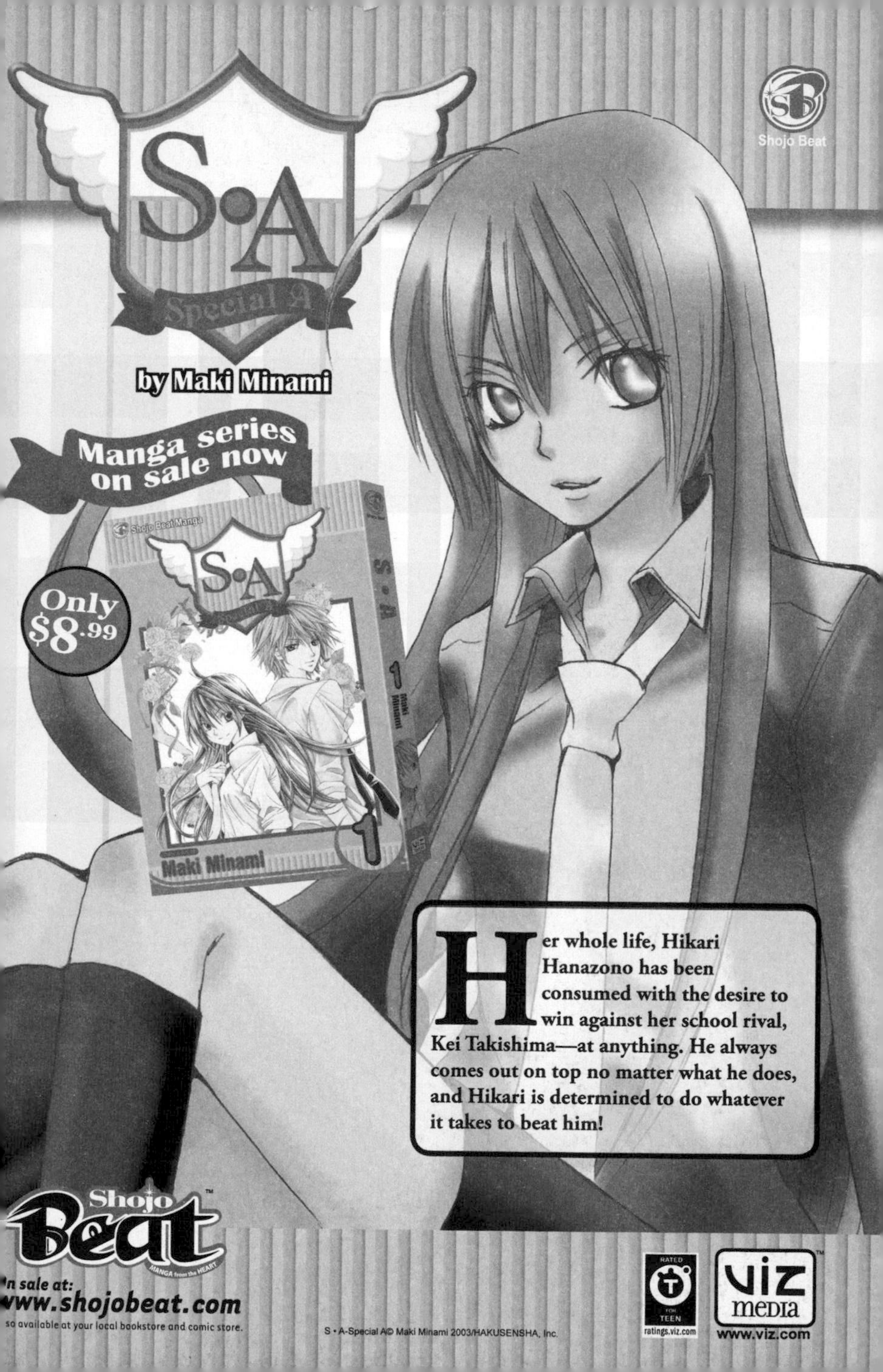

Shojo Beat
S•A
Special A
by Maki Minami
Manga series on sale now
Only $8.99
Shojo Beat Manga
S•A
1
Maki Minami
Her whole life, Hikari Hanazono has been consumed with the desire to win against her school rival, Kei Takishima—at anything. He always comes out on top no matter what he does, and Hikari is determined to do whatever it takes to beat him!
Shojo Beat
MANGA from the HEART
n sale at:
www.shojobeat.com
so available at your local bookstore and comic store.
S • A-Special A© Maki Minami 2003/HAKUSENSHA, Inc.
RATED
T
TEEN
ratings.viz.com
VIZ media
www.viz.com

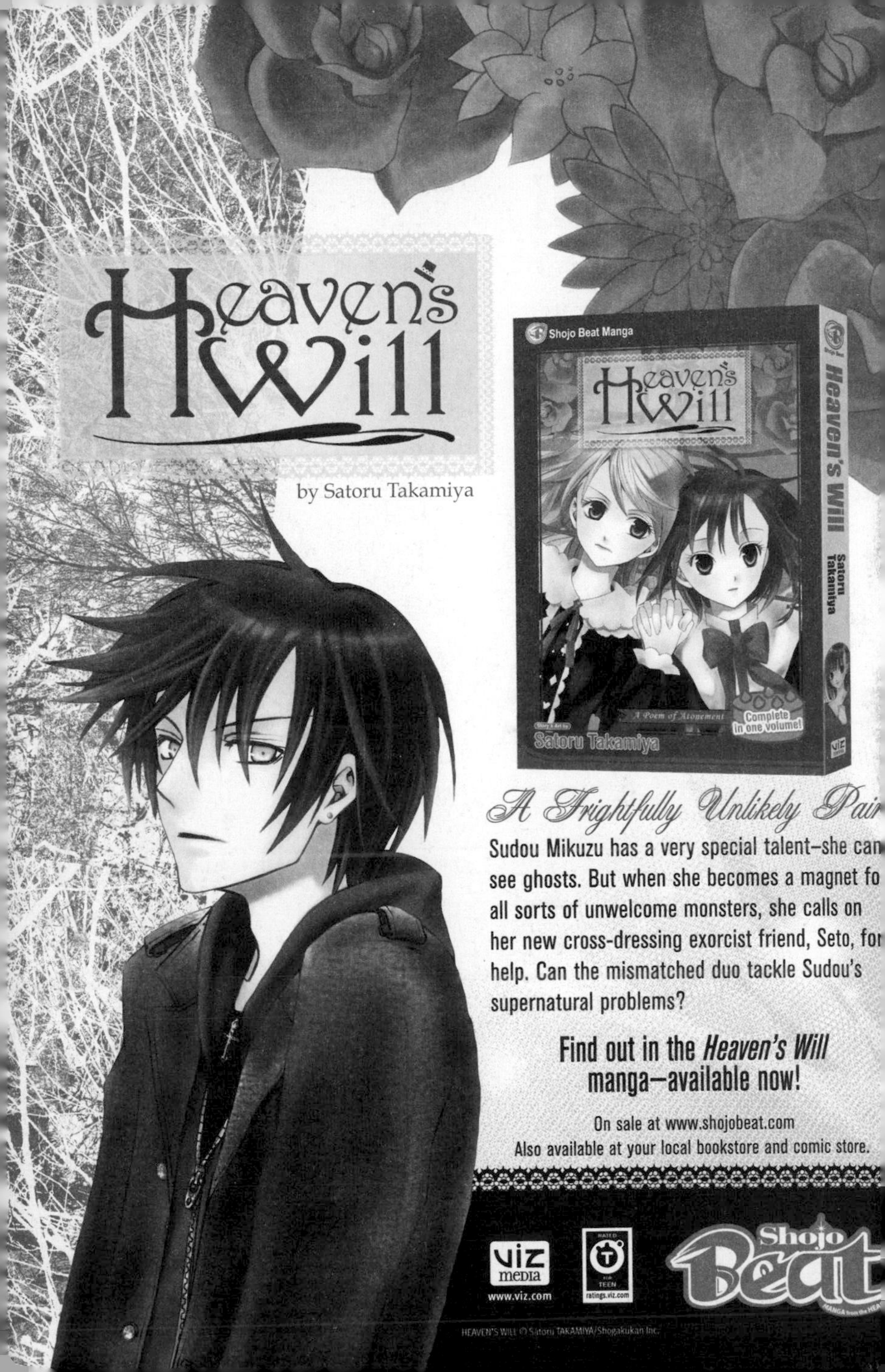
Heaven's Will
by Satoru Takamiya
Shojo Beat Manga
Heaven's Will
Satoru Takamiya
A Poem of Atonement
Complete in one volume!
A Frightfully Unlikely Pai
Sudou Mikuzu has a very special talent–she can see ghosts. But when she becomes a magnet fo all sorts of unwelcome monsters, she calls on her new cross-dressing exorcist friend, Seto, fo help. Can the mismatched duo tackle Sudou's supernatural problems?
Find out in the Heaven's Will manga—available now!
On sale at www.shojobeat.com
Also available at your local bookstore and comic store.
VIZ media
www.viz.com
RATED T TEEN
ratings.viz.com
Shojo Beat
HEAVEN'S WILL © Satoru TAKAMIYA/Shogakukan Inc.

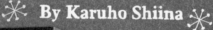

SURPRISE!

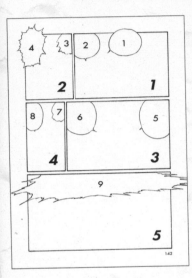

You may be reading the wrong way!

It's true: In keeping with the original Japanese comic format, this book reads from right to left—so action, sound effects, and word balloons are completely reversed. This preserves the orientation of the original artwork—plus, it's fun! Check out the diagram shown here to get the hang of things, and then turn to the other side of the book to get started!

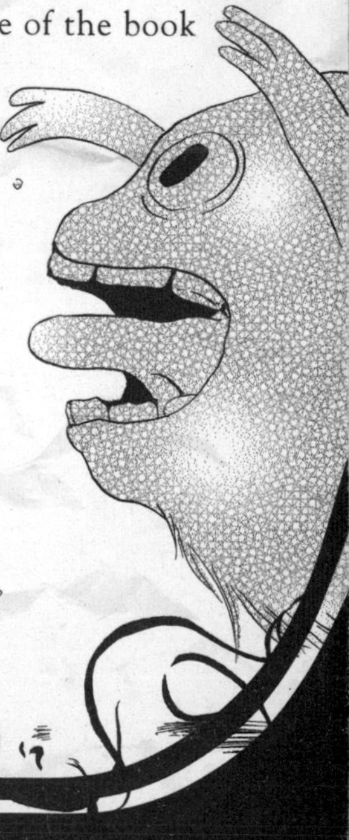